ESSAY'D

ESSAY'D // 30 DETROIT ARTISTS

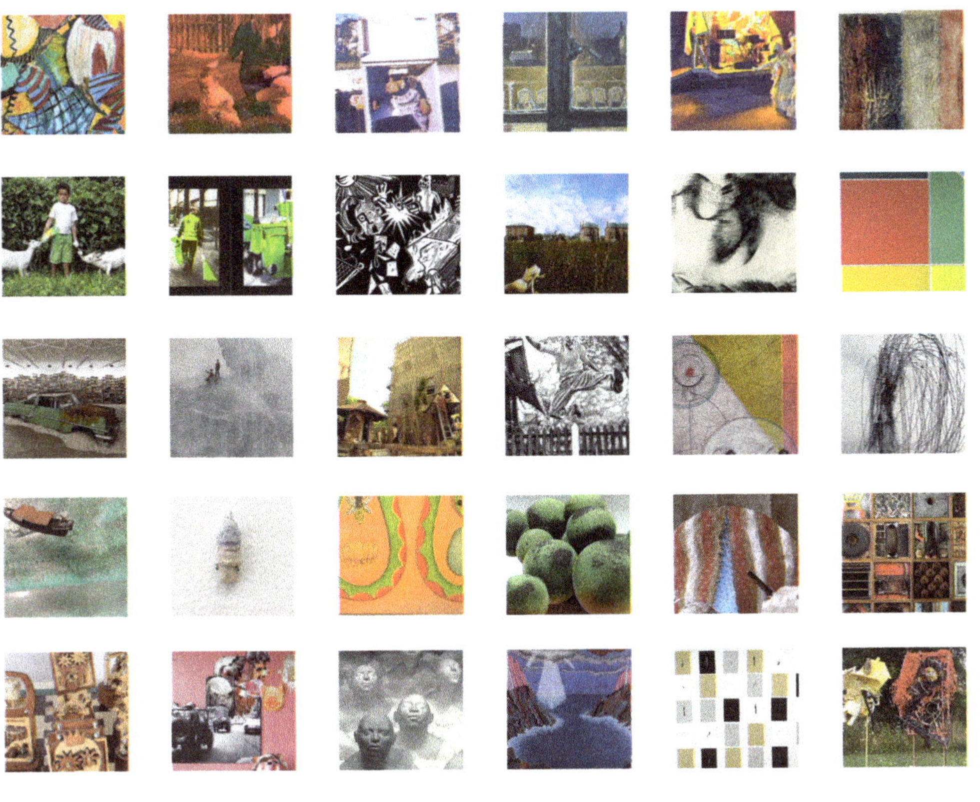

Written, Edited, and Compiled by
Dennis Alan Nawrocki,
Steve Panton, Matthew Piper,
and Sarah Rose Sharp

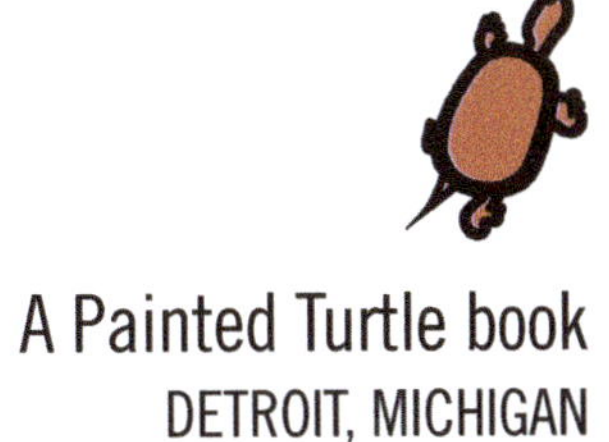

A Painted Turtle book
DETROIT, MICHIGAN

Saffell Gardner
Corrie Baldauf
Melanie Manos
Kathleen Rashid
Tzarinas of the Plane
Kathryn Brackett Luchs
Corine Vermeulen
Rose E DeSloover
Carl Wilson
Nicole Macdonald
Lynne Avadenka
David Rubello
Scott Hocking
Susan Goethel Campbell
Frank Pahl
Andrew Krieger
Megan Parry
Elizabeth Youngblood
Michael McGillis
Dylan Spaysky
Mary Fortuna
Marie Woo
Sandra Cardew
Clinton Snider
Andy Malone
Shanna Merola
Chido Johnson
Jon Strand
Toby Millman
Matt Corbin

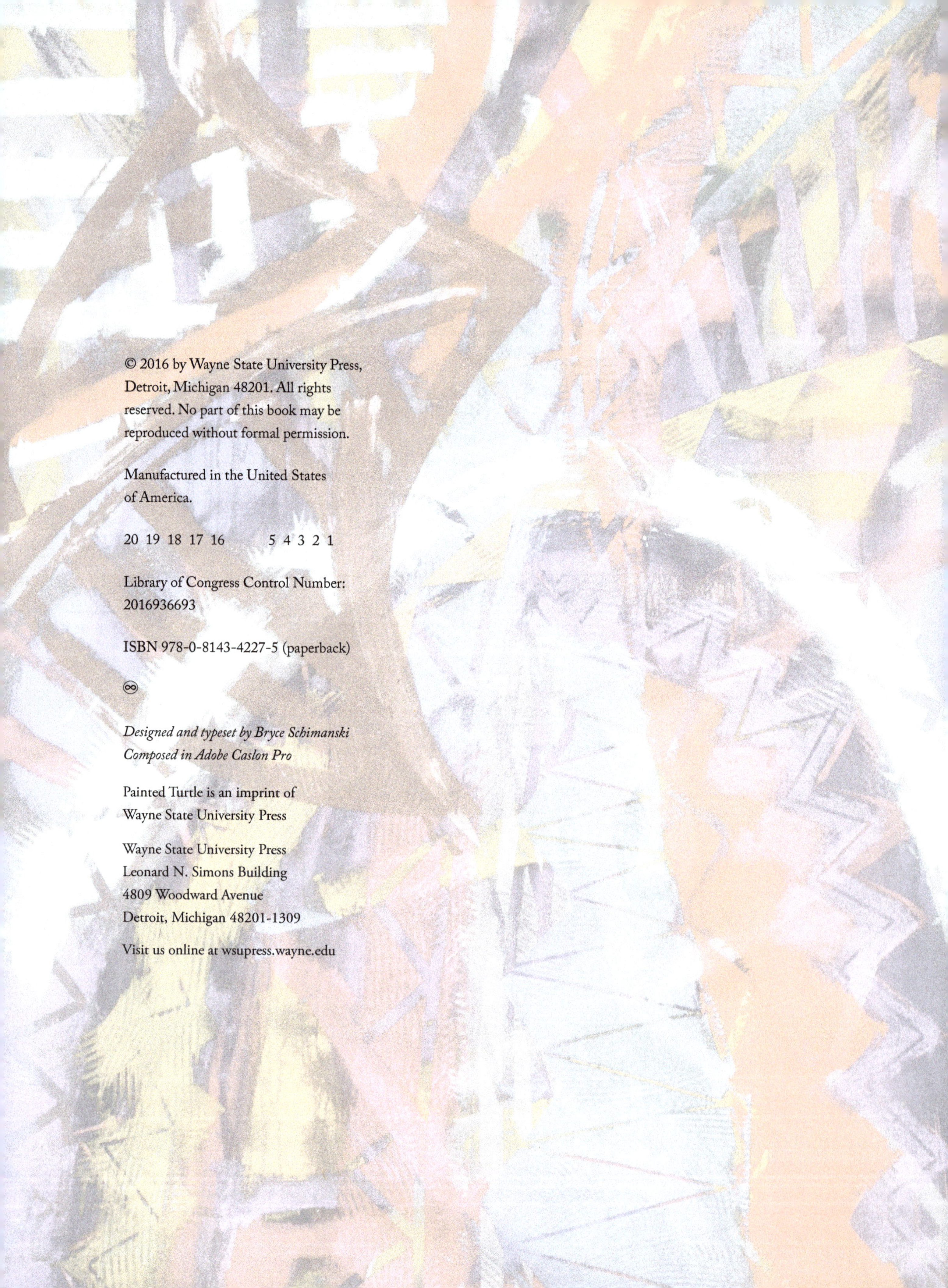

Manufactured in the United States of America.

20 19 18 17 16 5 4 3 2 1

Library of Congress Control Number: 2016936693

ISBN 978-0-8143-4227-5 (paperback)

∞

Designed and typeset by Bryce Schimanski
Composed in Adobe Caslon Pro

Painted Turtle is an imprint of Wayne State University Press

Wayne State University Press
Leonard N. Simons Building
4809 Woodward Avenue
Detroit, Michigan 48201-1309

Visit us online at wsupress.wayne.edu

CONTENTS

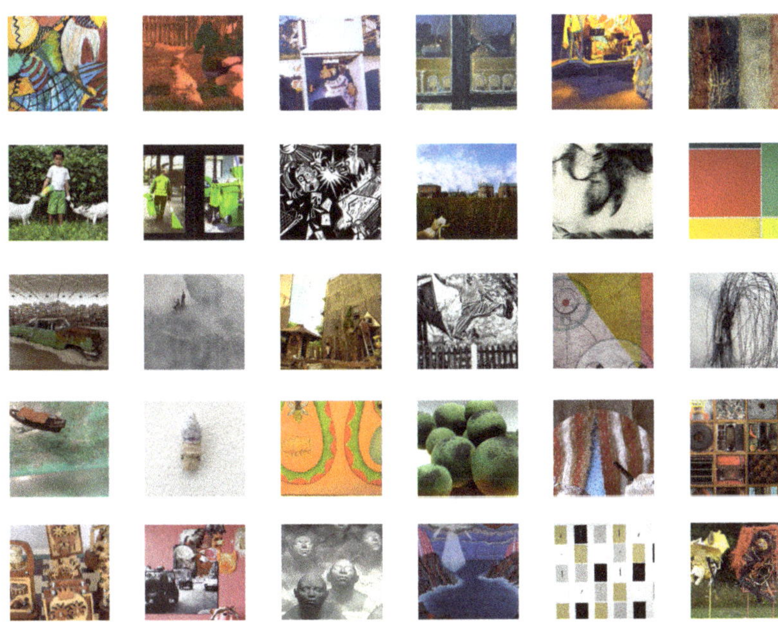

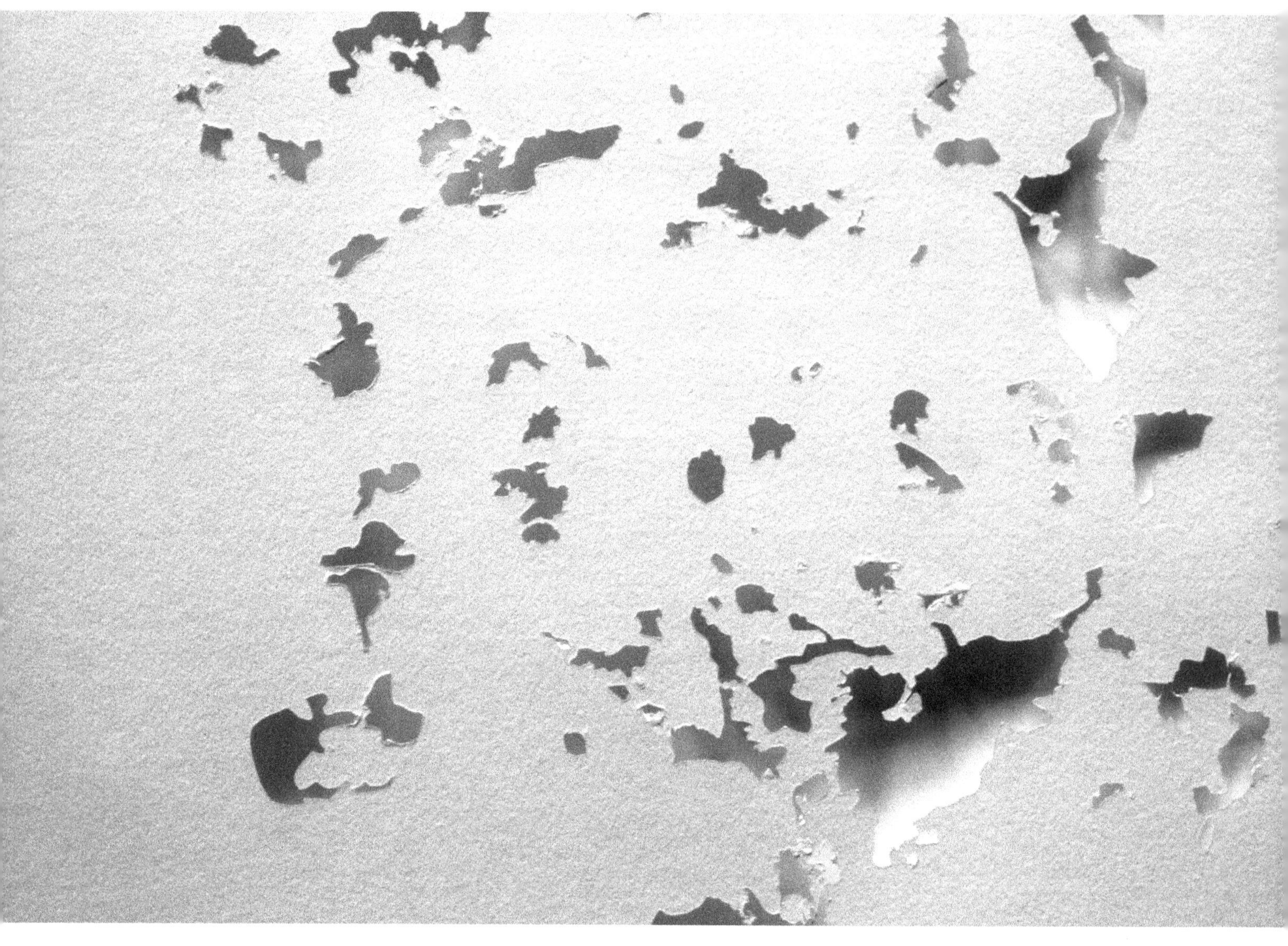

ACKNOWLEDGMENTS

First and foremost, we wish to warmly thank all the artists with whom we worked to produce the essays herein. They touched and inspired us as we moved along month by month, kept us on our toes and honest as we visited, conversed, wrote, revised, and bantered back and forth. Heartfelt appreciation as well to Noel French, our expeditious guide/agent/lawyer, who kept us focused on our goal of publication, and to Lawyers for the Creative Economy for connecting us to him in such a thoughtful and timely manner.

At the press, we are grateful to director Jane Hoehner, enthusiastic supporter of the arts, whose broad, canvassing gaze has focused on multiple Michigan projects, including our own. Kudos as well to Rebecca Emanuelsen, savvy copyeditor, who regularized the irregularities in our prose—no mean feat, that. And gratitude to Bryce Schimanski, designer of the elegant cover and oh-so-readable pages you hold in your hands.

We are obliged as well to Clara DeGalen for her guest essay. And to our many readers for their perusals of our paragraphs and trenchant, sometimes unsparing comments upon them.

Finally, we commend one another—who have spurred each other on, sharpened each other's prose, and, best of all, snatched friendship from the jaws of creative collaboration.

DAN, MP, SP, SRS

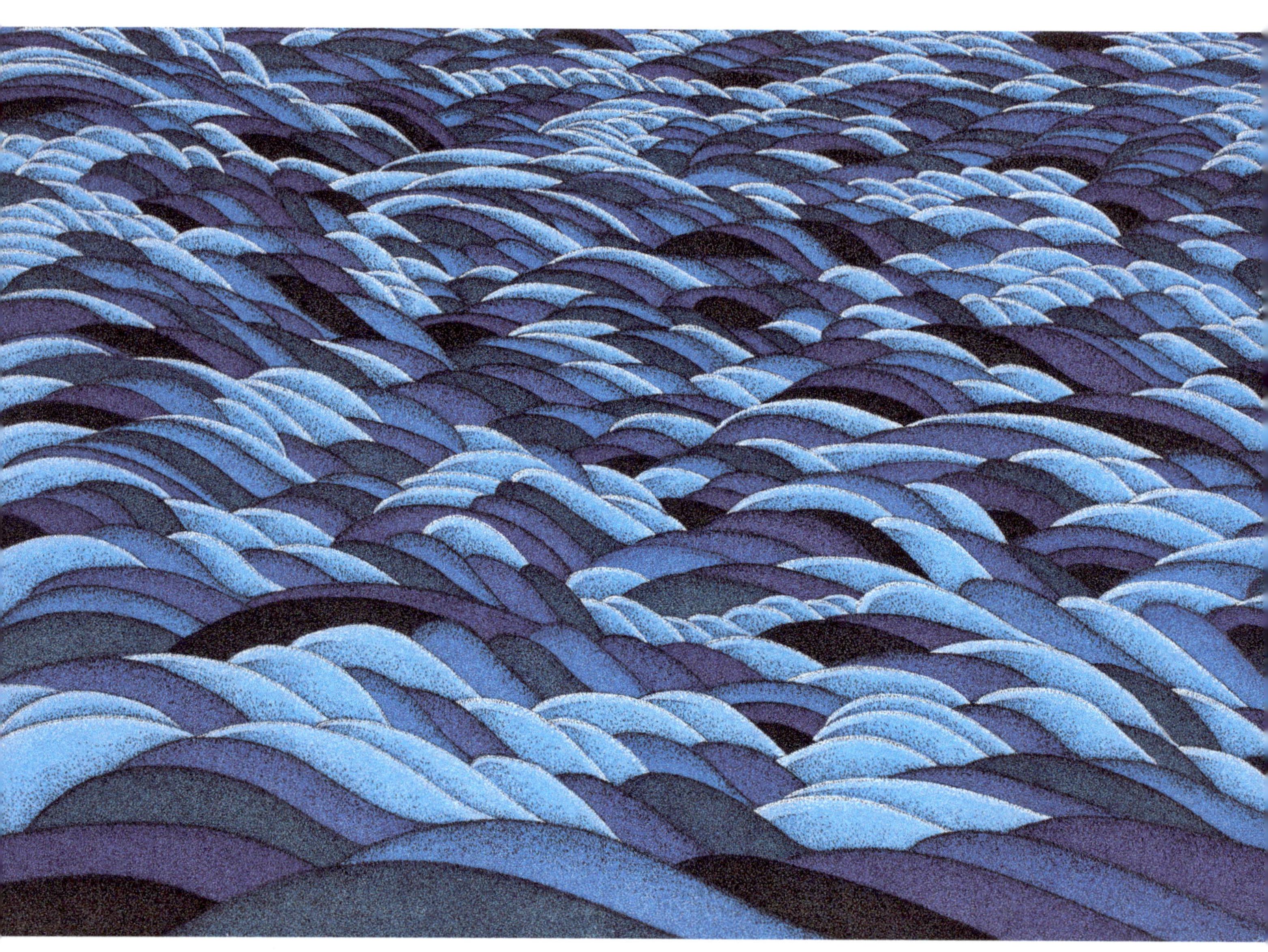

INTRODUCTION

Essay'd is a writing project which publishes short essays about Detroit artists on a monthly basis. The essays are intended for a general reader, and aim to broaden the audience for Detroit art. The writers choose the artists they write about. There is no suggestion that this is a systematic attempt to identify the "best" or "most important" Detroit artists, or even to define what those terms mean. With time, though, we expect a fairly comprehensive survey to emerge. The position the essays take to their subject is not critical, but neither is it reverential. The objective is to create a platform for Detroit artists, not a pedestal.

This short, declarative mission statement, conceived and penned by Steve Panton in the fall of 2014, launched Essay'd just two years ago. Since then, we have been guided by this modest, low-key preamble and bespoke prose as, entry by entry, we continue to wend our way through the populous aesthetic playing field of metro Detroit's art community. "We," besides Panton, includes Dennis Nawrocki, Matthew Piper, and Sarah Rose Sharp, who joined up with him to essay the artistic practice of our environs. All in all, we are four different writers, with divergent backgrounds, prose styles, and, perhaps most importantly, our own idiosyncratic interest in an eclectic selection of artists. We knew that a remarkably diverse cohort of noteworthy art purveyors abounded in the city's precincts, but some had gone missing—lost, it seemed, in the black hole of

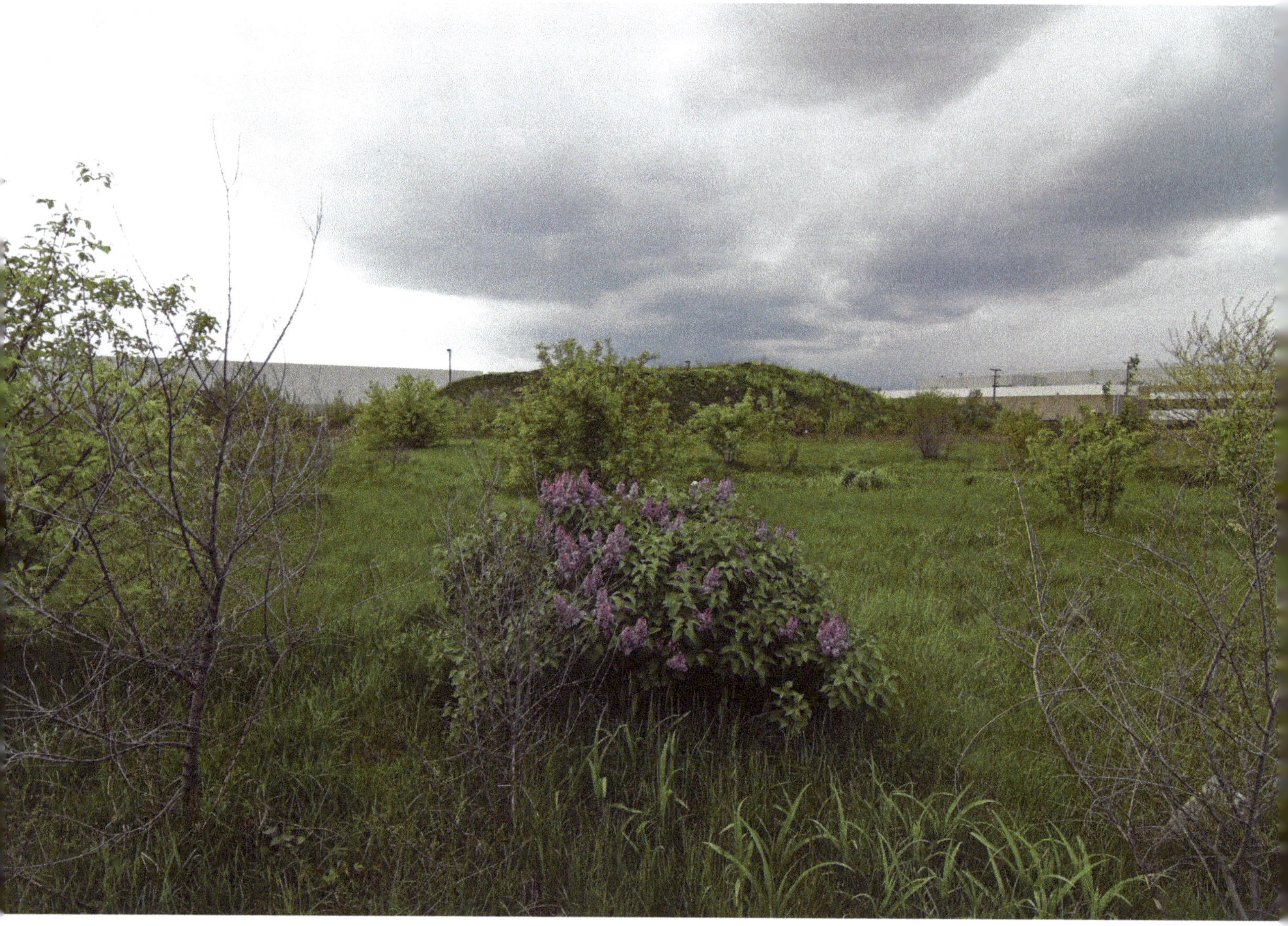

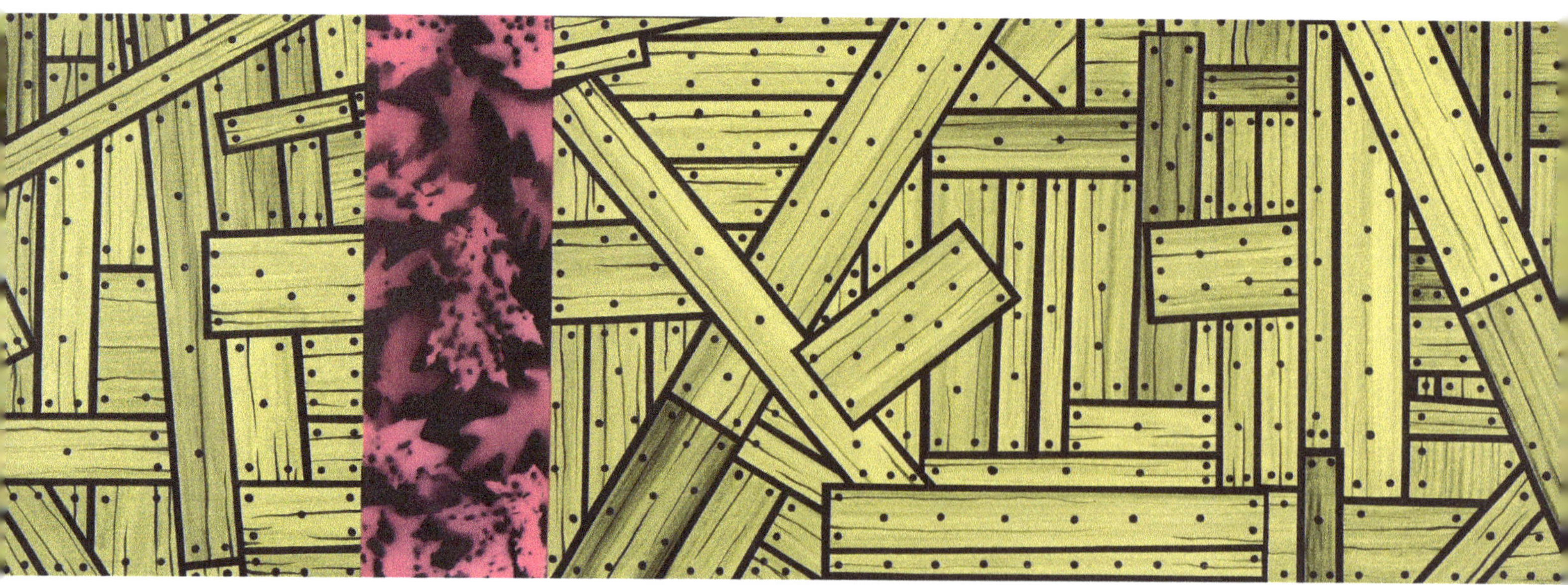

absent explication and documentation of their exhibiting activities and evolving oeuvres. Reviews of their exhibitions were not our goal—other work is being done sowing in that field—but we believed that overviews or profiles of their art and careers might add a salutary, steadying balance to other art coverage, and perhaps even create an engaging and enduring record of a stretch of their careers to date.

A website seemed the most expansive and accessible way to proceed at the outset. This format, in a media-rich era, would reach a comparatively large audience quickly, efficiently, and succinctly with a single, full-to-brimming page of text accompanied by multiple illustrations. Perhaps we could be seen as the twenty-first-century equivalent of the late twentieth-century text *Artists in Michigan: 1900–1976*, a compendium of artistic achievement drafted by a corps of compilers under the leadership of Dennis Barrie and published by the Archives of American Art and WSU Press in 1989. Somewhat akin to but also in contrast to that groundbreaking tome, we would be less formal and academic, less beholden to exhibition lists and bibliography than to evaluating, considering, and shaping the narratives of careers that are currently unfolding. The breadth of our entries is borne out, at least anecdotally, by the fact that not all the artists essayed, when initially proposed, were familiar to all the writers of Essay'd, which attests to the density of the local art scene as well as to the independent nature of the four main authors' points of view.

It is also part of our DNA that when an essay on a given artist is submitted, it undergoes peer review by the other three writers. In this way, clarity of prose, solidity of argument, coherence of organization, points of grammar, and niceties of language are considered and scrutinized. The same procedure holds true for the submissions of occasional guest writers. Yet another component of the Essay'd regimen are the intermittent exhibitions at the 9338 Campau gallery of actual artworks by the artists profiled on the website. This ongoing feature periodically provides readers and gallery goers with examples, in the flesh, of the art introduced online since the previous exhibition of featured artists.

Thus, in this best of all possible worlds, Essay'd proffers visitors encounters both intellectual and sensory, documents the art and artists of our own fair city, and broadens the audience for the same—on the web, in the gallery, and now (trumpet fanfare please) in hard-copy, book-length form!

DAN, SP, MP, SRS

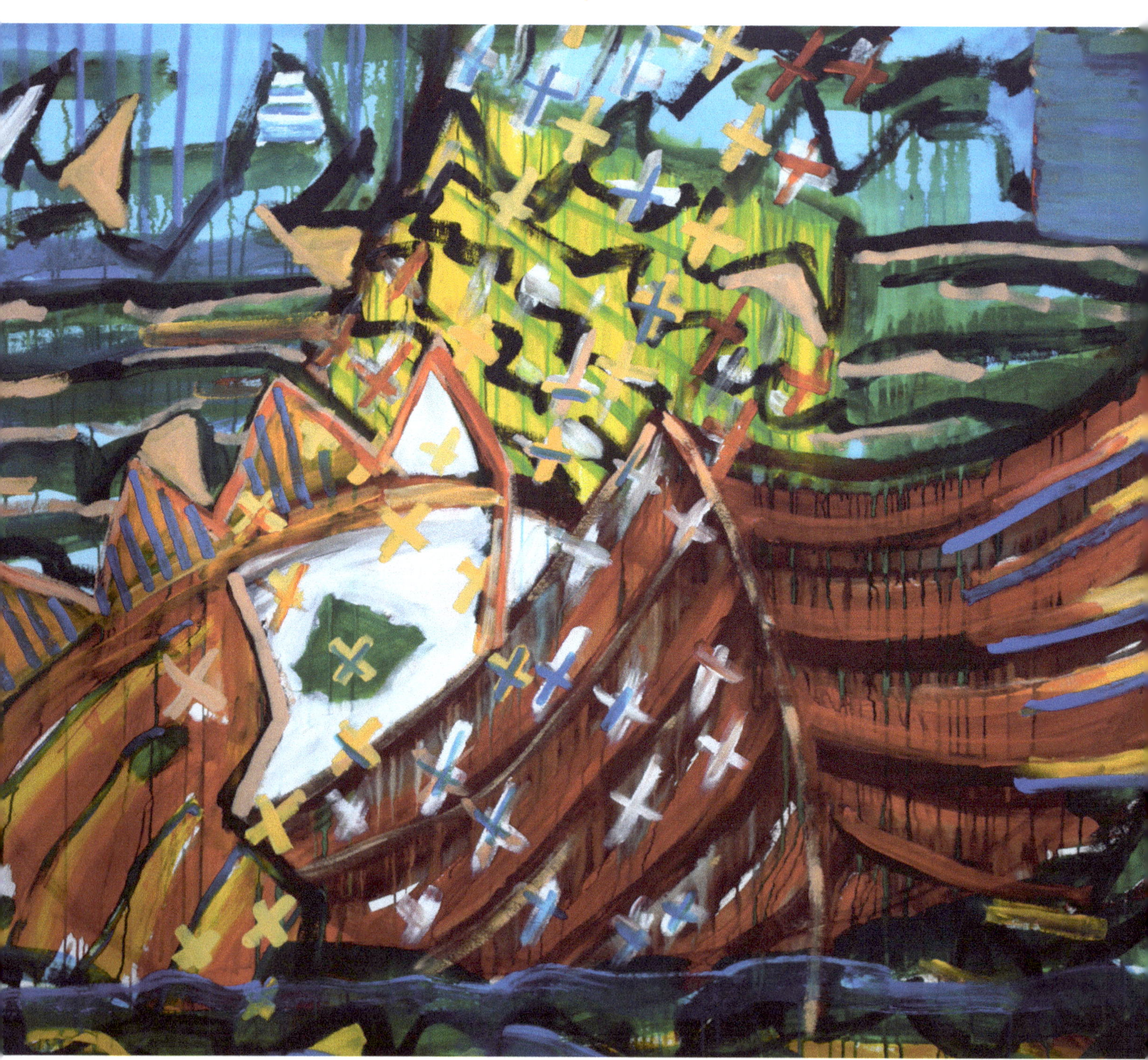

Lost Kings. 1987. Acrylic on paper, 60 x 72 in.

1 // SAFFELL GARDNER

Born Detroit, 1954
BFA, MFA, Wayne State University
Lives in Highland Park, Michigan

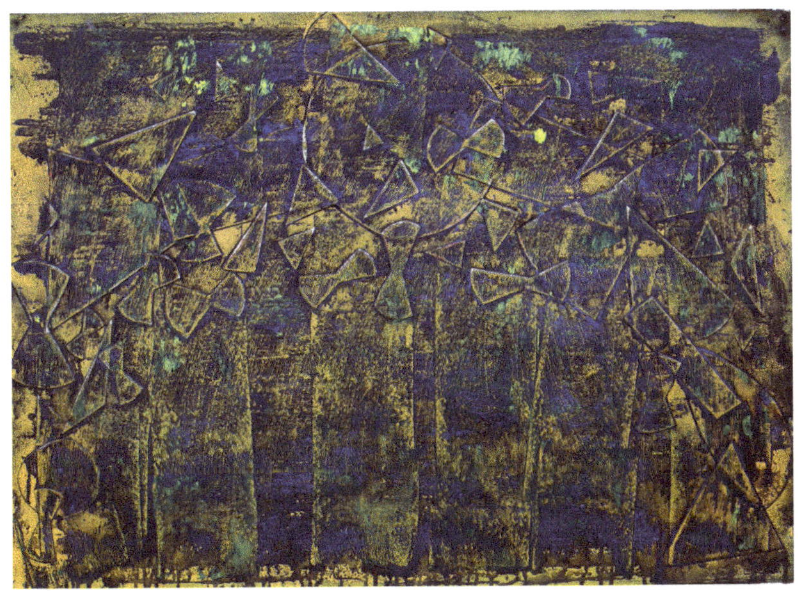

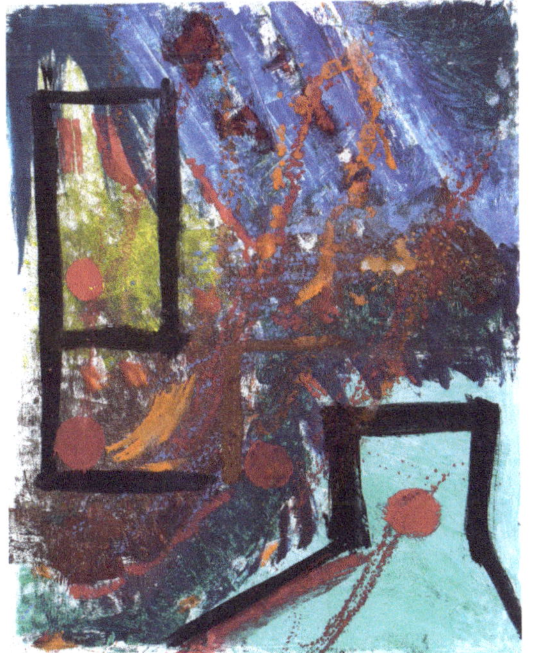

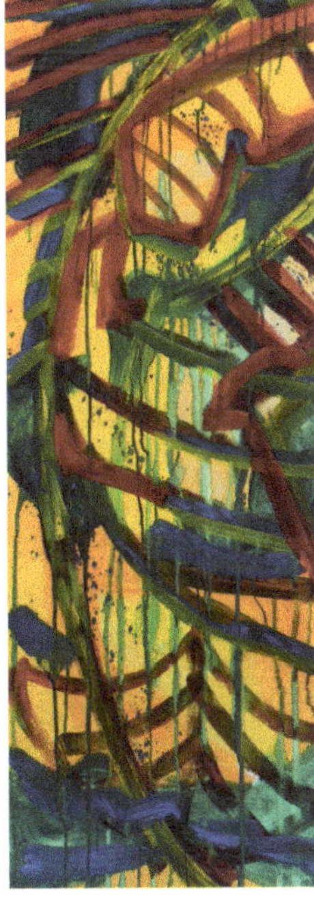

Over a career spanning five decades, painter Saffell Gardner has created a large body of work that combines a consistent, and highly personal, artistic vocabulary with a relentless desire to experiment through new materials and techniques. Working at the edge of the tradition belatedly recognized as Afro-Futurism and inhabiting a creative state that allows him to move easily between abstraction and symbolism, Gardner has used his practice to extensively explore, and creatively reimagine, the past, present, and future of the African diaspora in America.

In Gardner's work, abstract composition is both an end in itself and the "armature" on which

(*Top*) *Cosmic Xhango.* 1978. Mixed-media collage, 22 x 30 in.
(*Bottom, left*) *Spanish Red.* 1980. Acrylic on paper, 46 x 36 in.
(*Bottom, right*) *Thunder Skies.* 1992. Acrylic on paper, 60 x 21 in.

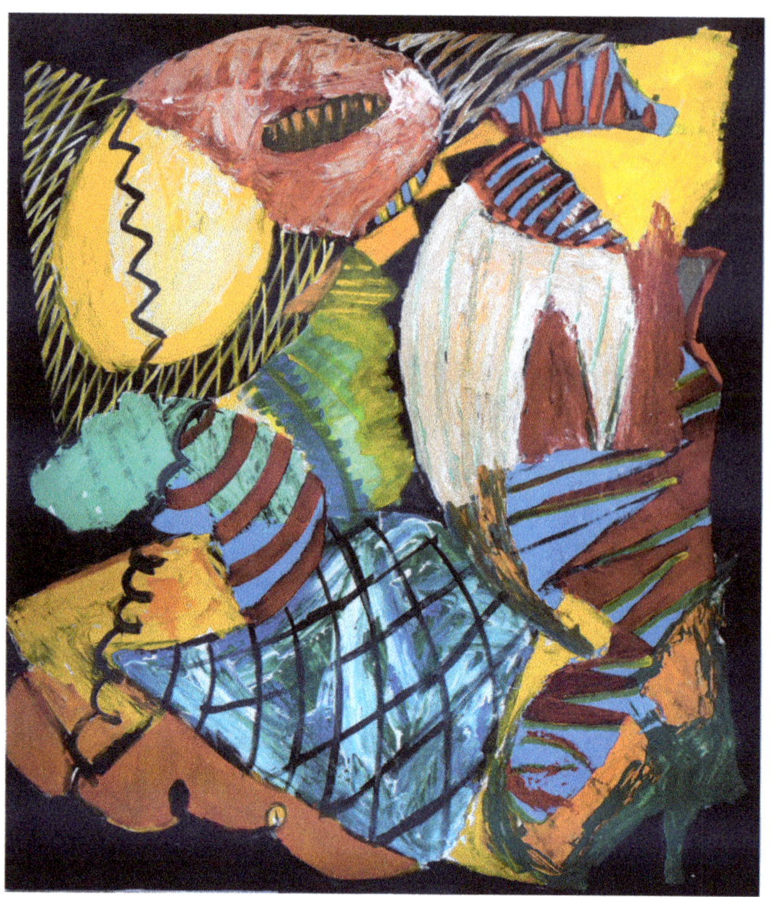

Astro Black. 1992. Acrylic on paper, 72 x 60 in.

further meaning can emerge from the synchronicity between unconsciously recurring forms and corresponding elements in the experience of the African diaspora. For example, sometime in the 1970s a distinctive "bow tie" like form started to repeatedly appear in Gardner's work, as in ***Cosmic Xhango*** (1978). Eventually, he had the epiphany that this was the double-sided thunder ax of Xhango, the Yoruba orisha of thunder and lightning, an eternal moral presence dispensing justice from the skies. An important reference point for Gardner, and others of his generation, is Robert Farris Thompson's 1984 book *Flash of the Spirit*, with its major thesis that more African visual culture and philosophy crossed the Atlantic to the Americas than is generally recognized.

In 1985 Gardner traveled to Senegal, a short but powerful trip during which he visited Gorée Island—a memorial to the embarkation point where slaves were loaded, through the "door of no return," onto ships for the Middle Passage across the Atlantic. Sometime earlier, he had produced an intense series of work with repeated visual and named references to the door—for example, *Starry Door* and ***Spanish Red*** (1980). As a result of the visit, he started to use the image of the door as a more specific vehicle for reimagining the mental state of someone leaving their home continent and heading for a life of slavery in an unknown place. This experience of the Middle Passage has been a consistent concern of Gardner's and is often reflected in his work through references to ships, sails, the elements, and the ocean. The unsettling sense of a small boat at the mercy of the elements, heading to an unknown destination, is captured particularly effectively in 1992's ***Thunder Skies***, which is part of an extended series of "totems," identified by their elongated aspect ratio. Often accompanying the boat and the ocean is a characteristic "sawtooth" motif that can alternatively imply sharks' teeth and/or the vicissitudes of life's ups and downs. The sharks' teeth reference the legend that embarking slave ships were surrounded by sharks and that Africans would rather jump into the ocean than face a life of slavery. Visually quite similar to the sharks' teeth is the image of the crown, as seen, for instance, in ***Lost Kings*** (1987). The crown speaks to the loss of personal identity that was inherent in the nature of slavery and the Middle Passage, and hence the corresponding possibility that any African American might be descended from nobility. What is clear overall is that in the years following the trip to Senegal, Gardner's works became more ambitious in terms of scale, and they show him becoming increasingly confident in his personal symbolic vocabulary.

Another consistent influence on Gardner's work has been music from the outer limits of the American jazz tradition. In the early 1980s he attended a performance by the legendary Art Ensemble of Chicago, and their ability to combine ritual, visual spectacle, and multi-instrumental avant-garde jazz into a transcendental experience had a powerful impact. Sun Ra, the bandleader from Saturn whom Gardner met briefly met in the 1970s, and whose music he listens to on a regular basis, is another important figure. Paintings with names like *Things Are Orange on Saturn*, ***Astro Black*** (1992) (named for a Sun Ra tune), and ***Mystical Afronaut*** (2005) imply a similar extraterrestrial dimension to the time-space continuum that Gardner is focused on. This is reflected visually through the inclusion of large, sweeping arcs and spheres, creating an expansive feeling that starts to imply planetary orbits and the exploration of a larger and boundless cosmology.

STEVE PANTON,
AUGUST 2014/OCTOBER 2015

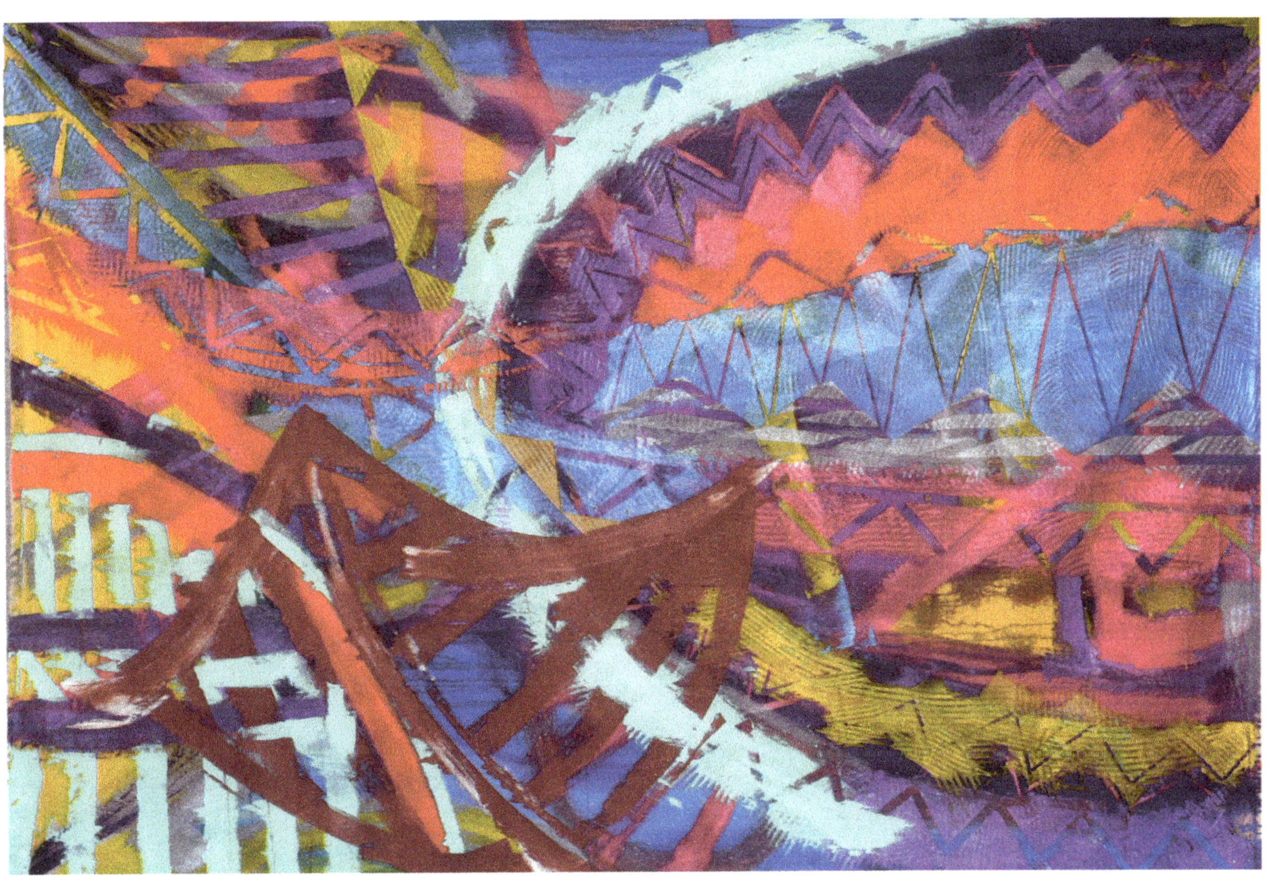

Mystical Afronaut. 2005. Acrylic on canvas, 72 x 84 in.

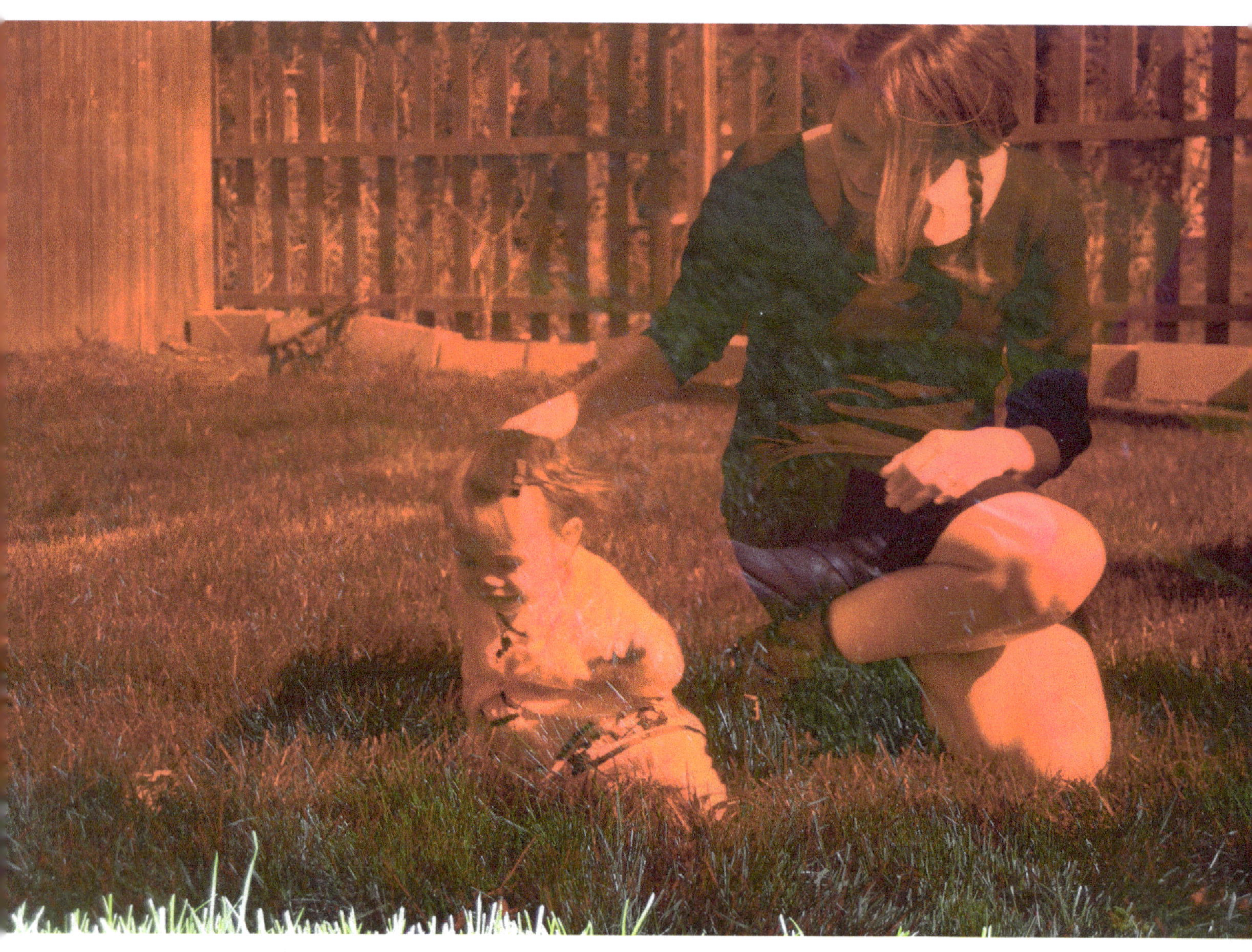

Ruby Filter (Improvisation with the Lees). 2014. Filter and light.
Photography by Chris Lee.

2 // CORRIE BALDAUF

Born Chicago, Illinois, 1981
BFA, Kansas City Art Institute
MFA, Cranbrook Academy of Art
Lives in Detroit

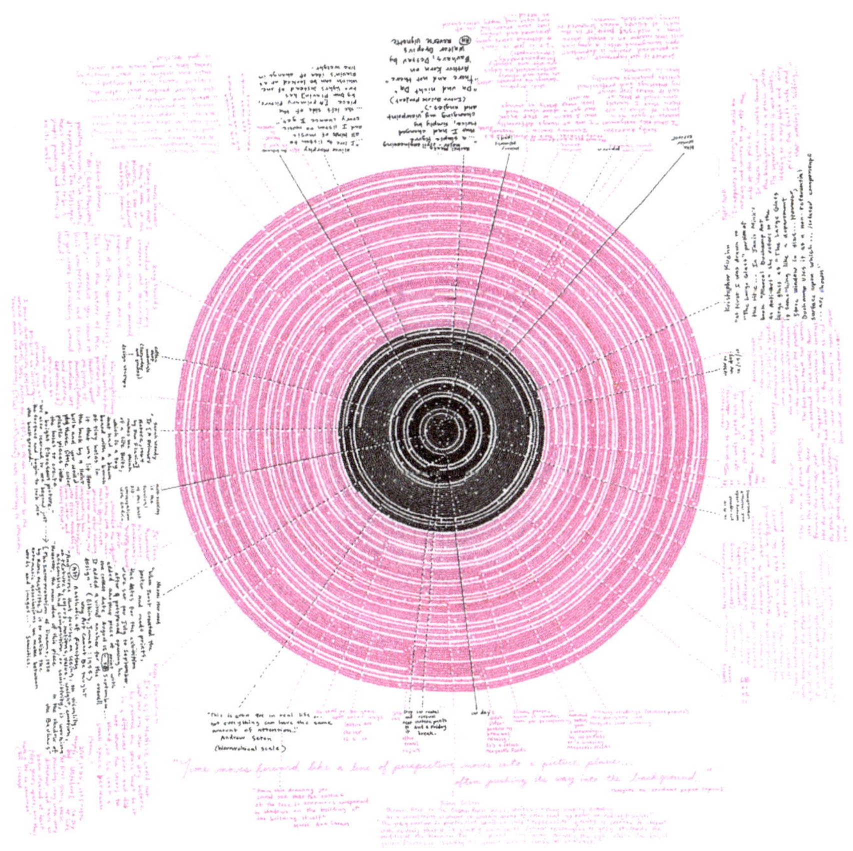

Time moves forward like a line of perspective moves into a picture plane . . . often pushing its way into the background. 2010. Ink and graphite on wood panel, 16 x 16 in.

It is hard to talk about Corrie Baldauf's work without talking about Corrie Baldauf. Fine art culture, by design or default, tends to take on an air of exclusivity and the artist persona can be steeped in irony and detachment. In this respect, Baldauf's personality is a breath of fresh sincerity, and her work reflects the power of optimism, a practice that Baldauf has honed for decades, though never to the point of reflexivity. "Optimism is hard work," Baldauf will tell you.

Baldauf's projects are deeply intertwined with the world and those human interactions taking place around her, and seek in many ways to interact with that world without altering it physically. One mechanism for this is her series ***Circle Drawings*** (2005–present)—at a glance present as mandalas of tight, concentric rings, but further investigation will reveal them to

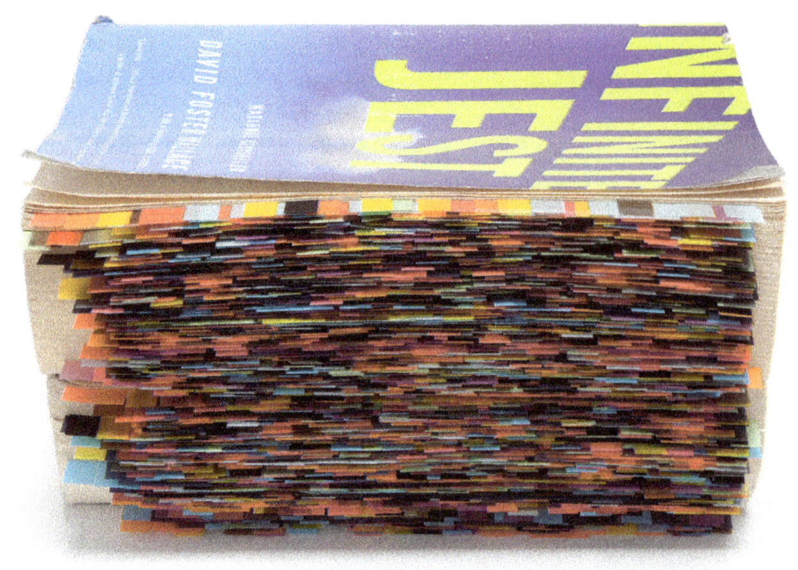

All the Colors in Infinite Jest. 2014. Book, Semikolon color flags, 2.5 x 9.25 x 6 in. Photography by P. D. Rearick.

be meticulous registers for snippets of overheard conversations, obsessively charted and detailed in word clusters bordering the circle. Another is her series ***Optimism Filters*** (2008–present), slabs of colorful plexiglass that Baldauf uses in conjunction with cameras to create filtered views of life encounters, sometimes having her subjects hold the filters themselves so the device is evident in the picture, sometimes shooting to create entirely tinted or altered images through the filters. Finally, there is the collaborative series produced with father-and-son sign painters Craig Signs, which Baldauf has been working on since 2007. While the notations in the circle drawings are cumulative and subtle, the ***vinyl signs*** are bold and definitive, recording the accumulation of messages that reflect the economic state of cities that she is a part of. She views advertisement as far more than a reflection of the specific services being offered; rather, it marks the decline or growth in the places we live and work.

These efforts to color reality or look at the world with new eyes become more significant when taken as part of the critical relationship Baldauf has with color. As the majority of art deals in color to a certain extent, the impact of this choice is not readily apparent, but the more Baldauf's work is taken as a whole, the more it becomes clear that *color* is her medium of choice, played out across a number of different expressive media, including photography, film, works in ink on paper, and even her own daily style of dress. More recently, it has cropped up in her 2014 ***"Infinite Jest" Project (Phase 1)***, a work in which Baldauf marked out every instance of color appearing in David Foster Wallace's masterwork, *Infinite Jest*, with a page flag of corresponding color. The resulting edition, bristling with more than 2,700 flags, serves as an effective case in point for the kind of compulsive, addiction-driving mentality that is the work's major theme, but it is also evidence of the impressive extent to which color appears in Wallace's work—an intentional choice, Baldauf thinks, to help keep readers engaged in what is collectively regarded as a highly challenging literary milestone, equally brilliant and alienating.

But none of this serves to capture the true uniqueness of Baldauf's viewpoint. While it may be generally said of artists that they bring value to society by utilizing their art to showcase a worldview outside the mainstream, Baldauf's perspective is singular above all. Her attention

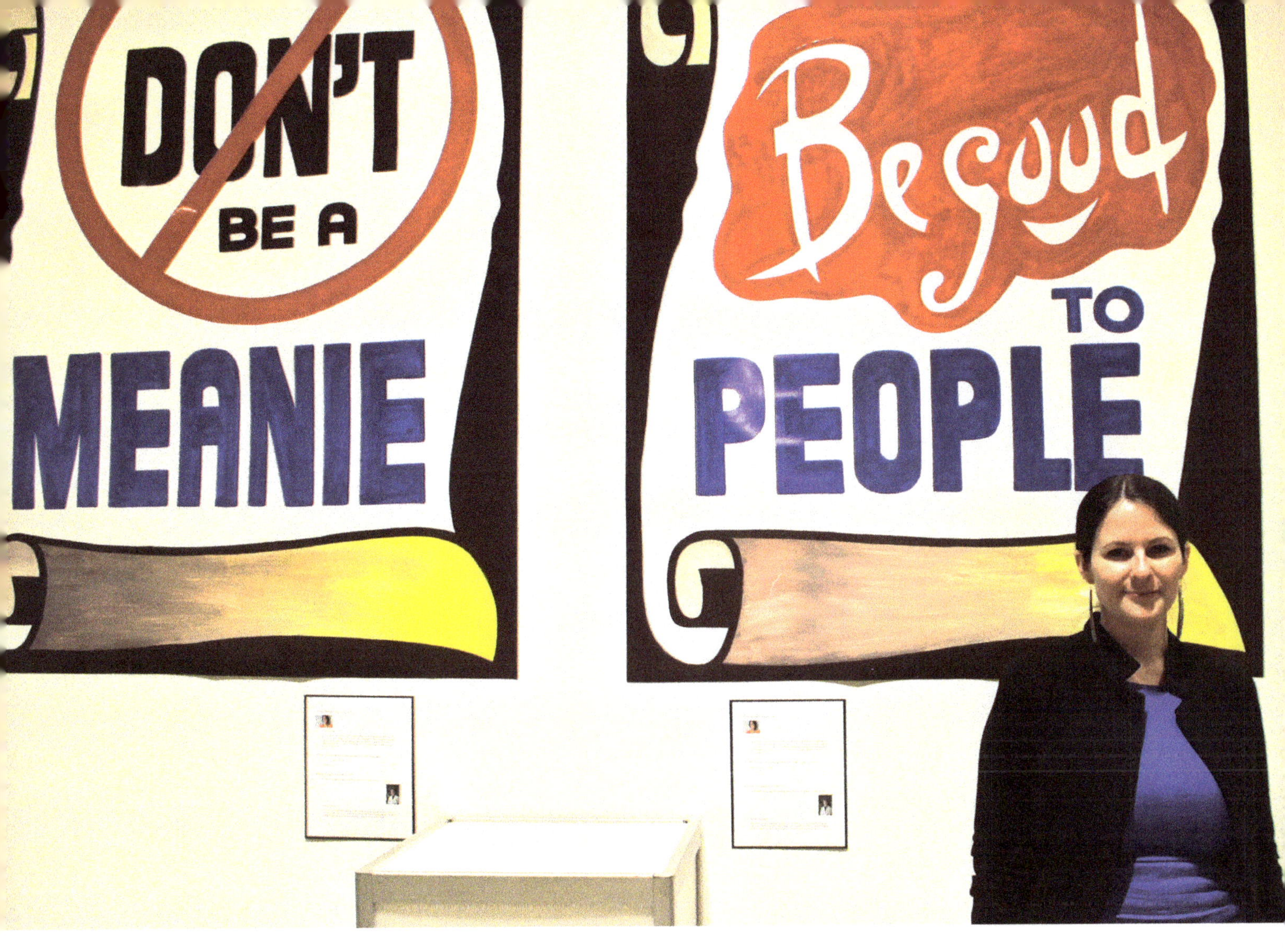

is constantly tuned in to things that are ubiquitous to the point of invisibility. Spend some time with her and you will find that Baldauf possesses little of the common lexicon, often questioning the meaning or exact wording of everyday aphorisms in the manner of a nonnative speaker, deeply curious about subtext that most people have long learned to take for granted. Much like a child still learning the world, Baldauf takes nothing for granted, and the act of engaging with her over the meaning of common things gives them fresh light and newness. However, there is deep intentionality to this perspective, and it would be a grave mistake to take this 2011 Kresge Grant recipient and professor of fine arts at several metro Detroit universities for a child.

With roots in Kansas City and an art-and-teaching practice based in Detroit for nearly a decade, Baldauf represents the intersection of Midwestern sincerity, an honest love of engagement with people, and a rare humility in seeing the world as it is and as it could be.

Don't Be a Meanie, Be Good to People (Improvisation with Dr. Johann Gudjonsson and Craig Signs). 2014. Car paint on vinyl, photography, dimensions variable. Photography by Sarah Rose Sharp.

It seems fitting that she reaches out using color, perhaps the most understandable and most available medium—and one of the first we are given access to as we come to know the world.

SARAH ROSE SHARP,
SEPTEMBER 2014

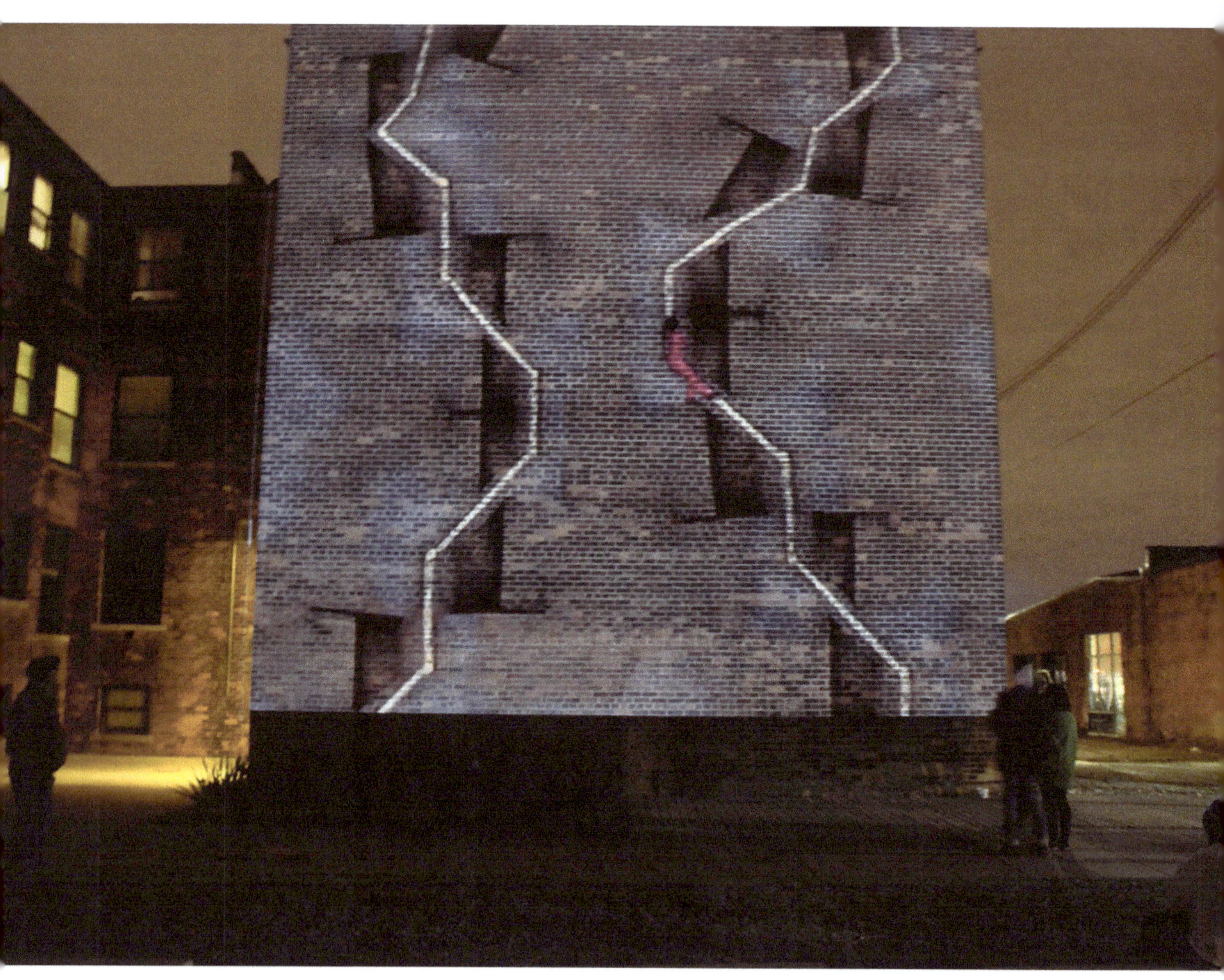

The Climb (71 Garfield). 2012. Video projection.

3 // MELANIE MANOS

Born Detroit, 1964
BA, University of California at Los Angeles
MFA, University of Michigan
Lives in Ann Arbor, Michigan

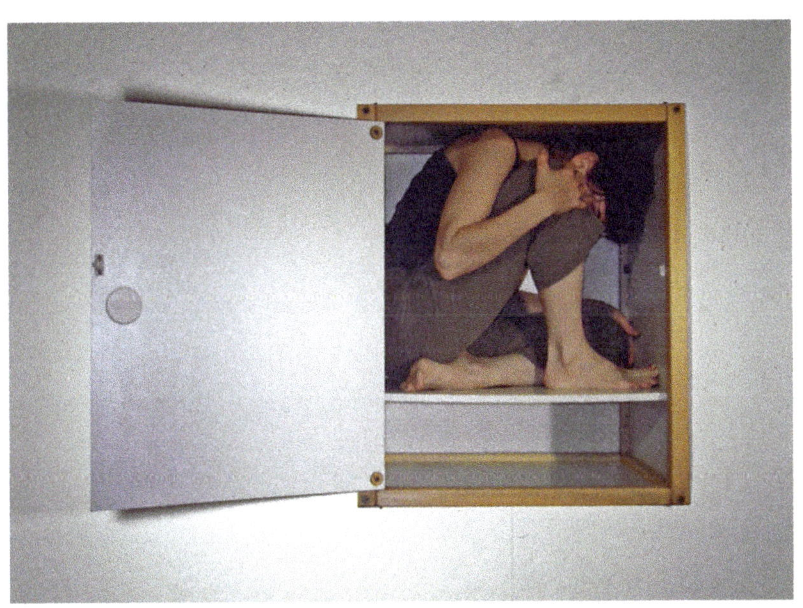

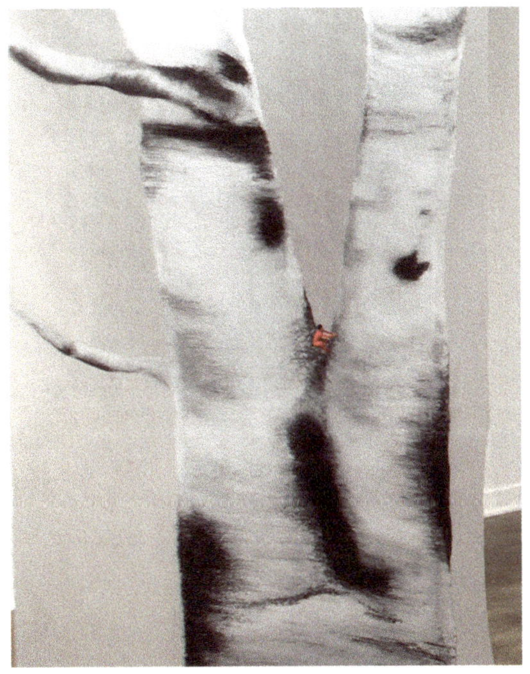

To date, Melanie Manos has scrunched into the upper shelves of walk-in closets; inserted her body between exposed wall studs; inhabited the interiors of defunct, doorless refrigerators; squeezed into rolling metal utility cabinets; ducked into niches and crevasses of attics; walked the rafters; clambered up, over, and down interior walls; climbed the exteriors of multistoried buildings; and, most recently, shinnied into the upper reaches of gigundo, sequoia-sized tree trunks. A number of Manos's intrepid feats have been achieved digitally or on video and, surprisingly perhaps, beget as potent a reflexive audience reaction—fear, unease, release—as her literal, physical performances. She is indeed the consummate

(*Top*) *Cabinet Thinker*. 2006. C-print, 28 x 48 in.
(*Bottom*) *A Heightened State* (detail). 2014. Mixed-media installation.

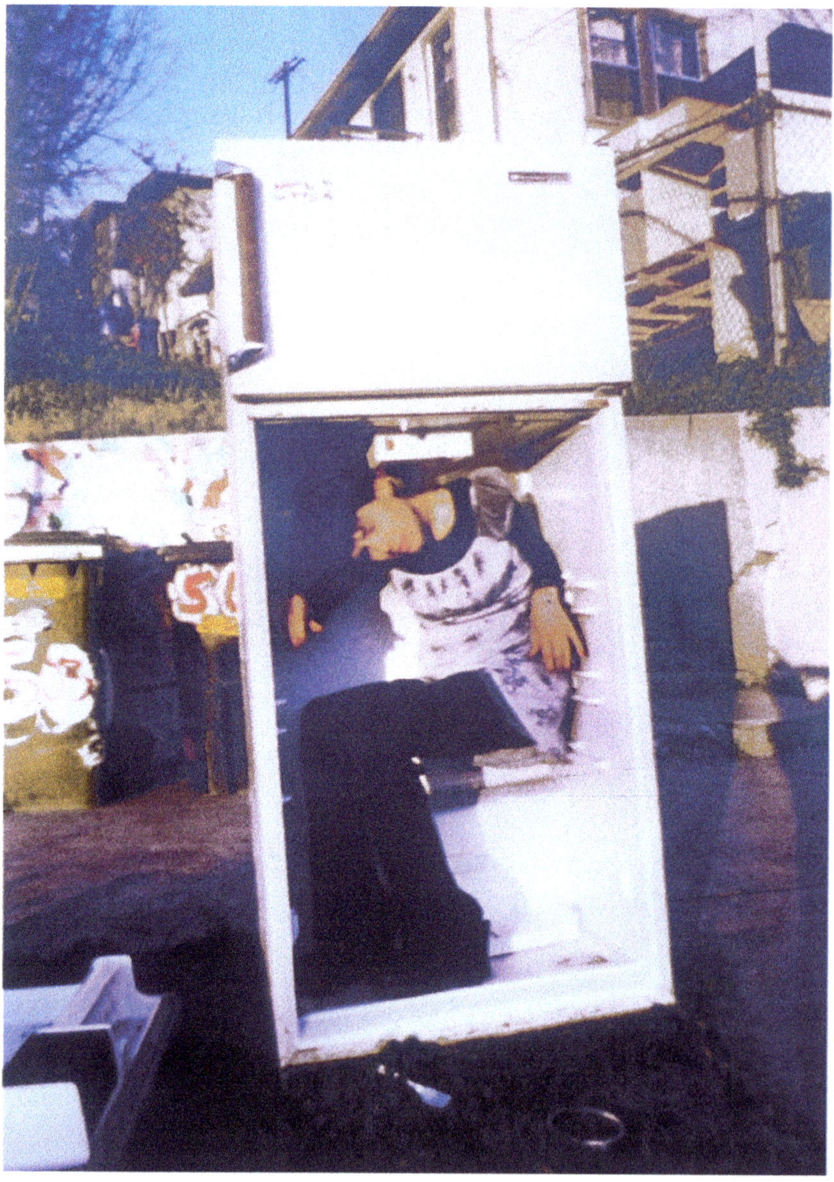

Fridge (Seated). 2002. C-print, 60 x 40 in.

interdisciplinary artist who works in performance, digital media, and installation, exhibiting not only nationally but internationally.

Her most recent climbs, documented at Re:View Contemporary Gallery in Detroit in July–August 2014, represent an apex of a sort—perhaps her Mount Everest—and are indicative of her practice of scaling higher and taller edifices. Titled ***A Heightened State*** (2014), her installation of several huge drawings of tree trunks on narrow lengths of vellum suspended from the ceiling stretched fifteen feet to the floor below. Collaged here and there among the branching limbs were miniature images of Manos (several per tree) stretching and straining higher and higher among the birches and maples of her imaginary forest.

This turn to a natural setting comes as something of a surprise in her oeuvre. Manos's riveting live performances fifteen years ago at the beginning of her career were quite different in kind, albeit not in theme or intention, which has always been physical and social. Notably, in her art, the body struggles against the built—or lately the organic—environment. Beginning in 2002, she garnered attention for her determined efforts to squeeze herself into restrictive containers, primarily of a domestic sort. The challenge of contorting herself into small spaces certainly addresses the constraints women perennially face—as well as the concomitant urge to liberate themselves. Her ***Fridge (Seated)*** (2002) and ***Cabinet Thinker*** (2006) are indicative of this group of actions.

In the ambitious body of work that followed, Manos inaugurated her "climbs" as, lured beyond quotidian, household furnishings, she "climbed" the outside walls of buildings via the magic of video projection. In ***The Climb (71 Garfield)*** (2012) and ***The Climb***

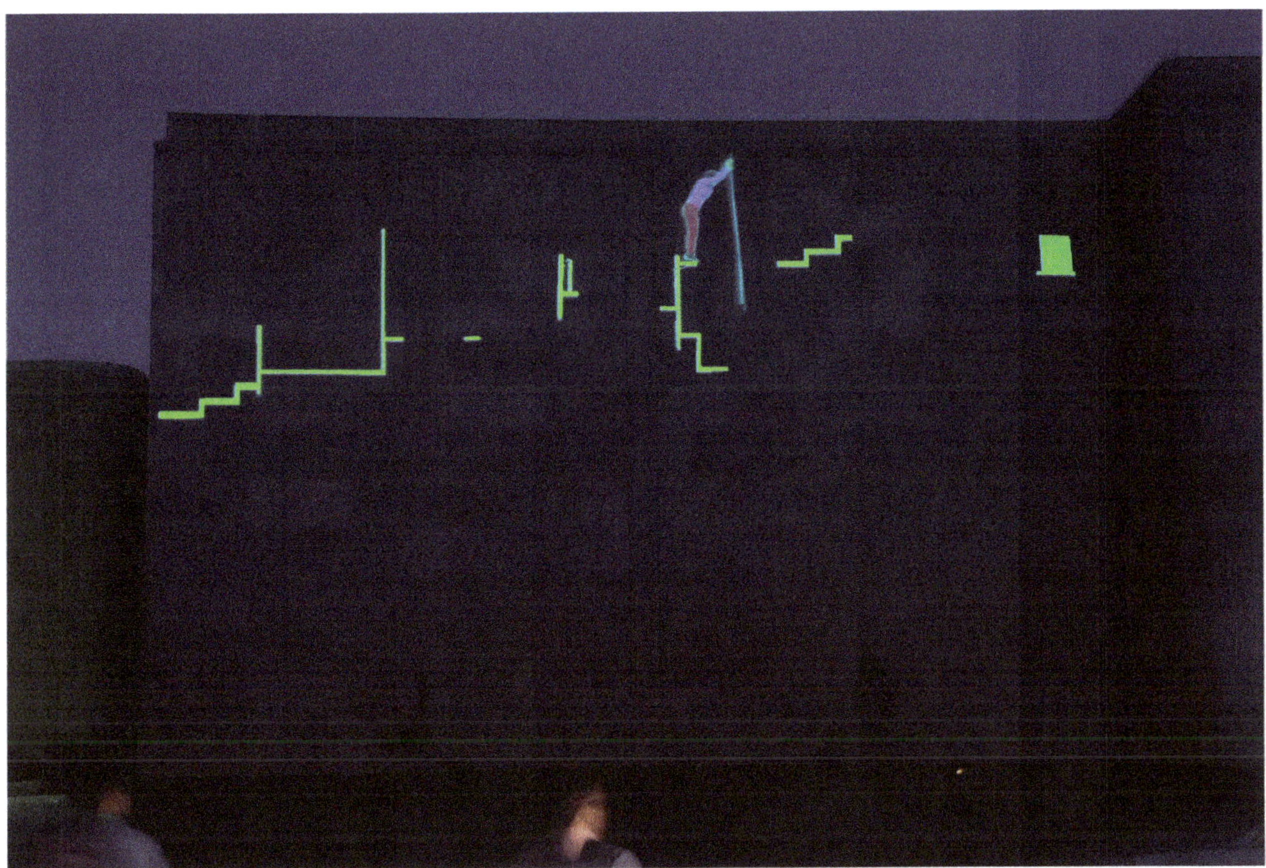

(54 Jefferson) (2013) she scaled the multistoried facades of a loft building and museum, respectively. The first, located in Detroit, and the second, an exhibition venue in Grand Rapids, Michigan, depict Manos soundlessly mounting the urban cliffs of these two structures in "existential loops of human effort, moving along a tightrope between absurdity and solemnity," as described by the artist. The projections, meticulously planned and produced at the University of Michigan Duderstadt Video Studio (where Manos teaches in the Stamps School of Art and Design), engage a spectator in the fiction of the climb as if it were real. One viscerally responds to the halting moves and faux falters of the person "climbing" the wall. And, charged up by the artist's quixotic quest, we realize that the impetus to strive and reach further is as much everyone's goal as it is the artist's. Hence, for Manos the challenging vertical allure of the forest in 2014's *A Heightened State* (an encounter due in part to Manos's recent artist residencies in rural settings, plus the massive concrete columns of the gallery)

The Climb (54 Jefferson). 2013. Video projection. Photography by Diane Carroll Burdick.

might seem to have been a predestined incentive for her vision to expand outward and upward. Truly, Mount Everest might loom somewhere in the future.

DENNIS ALAN NAWROCKI,
SEPTEMBER 2014

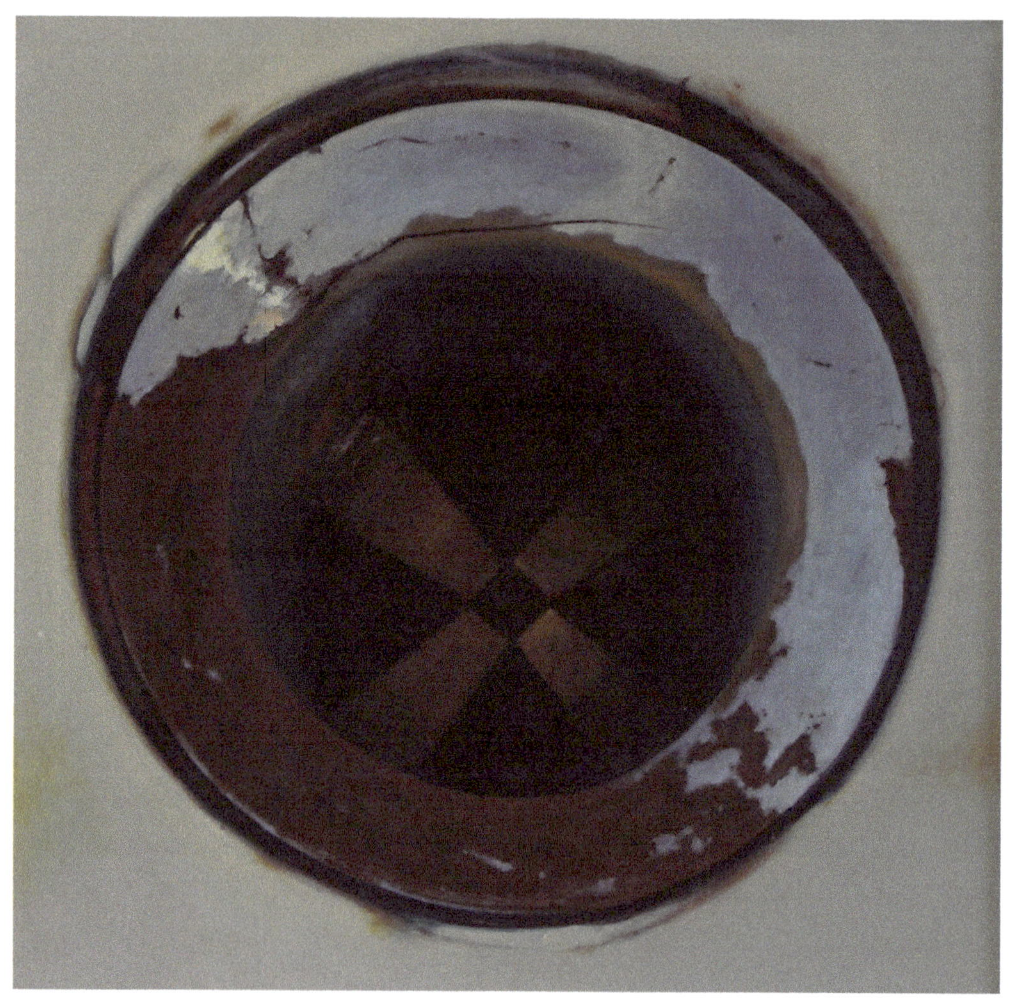

Drain. 2004. Oil on canvas, 34 x 34 in.

4 // KATHLEEN RASHID

Born Detroit, 1956
BFA, BA, Wayne State University
Lives in Detroit

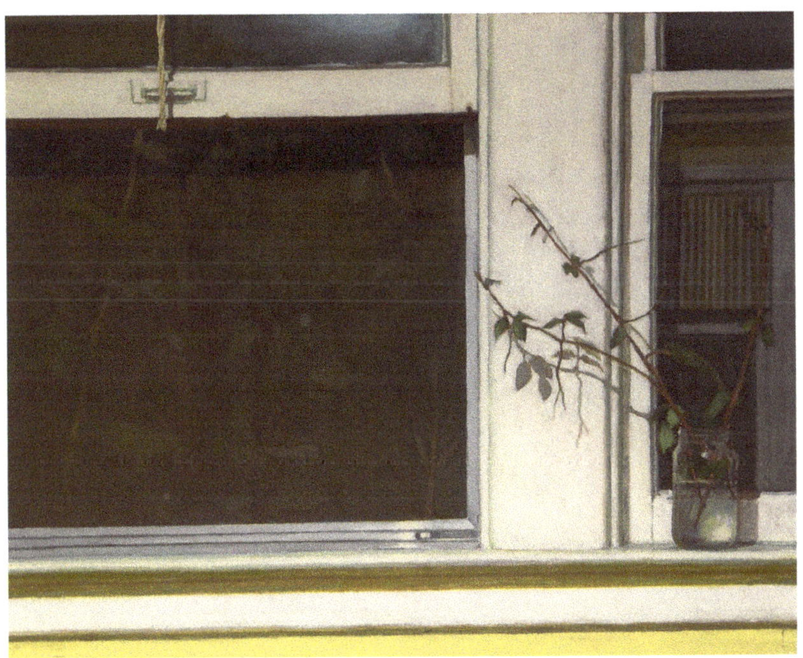

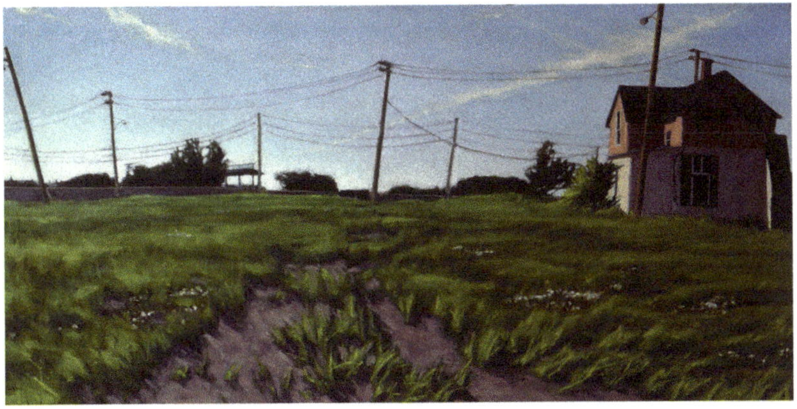

(*Top*) *Screen.* 1979. Oil on canvas, 32 x 38 in.
(*Bottom*) *Denton.* 1982. Oil on canvas, 24 x 48 in.

Alongside contemporaries such as Ed Fraga and Carl Demeulenaere, Kathleen Rashid is one of a prodigiously talented group of artists who emerged from Wayne State University's art department in the mid to late 1970s. By all accounts she arrived on the earth with a fully formed ability to draw, and at Wayne entered a school still basking in the glow of the "Cass Corridor" era and awash with experienced and talented teachers such as Robert Wilbert and Pat Quinlan. She emerged ready to paint whatever she saw.

Rashid's early work after graduation shows a delight in close observation, the ability to render subtle visual effects (for example, the view through a wire mesh in 1979's ***Screen***, or, somewhat later, the view through the dirty window in 1990's ***Busy Bee Hardware at Night***), and an interest in the often overlooked—themes that would reoccur continually through her

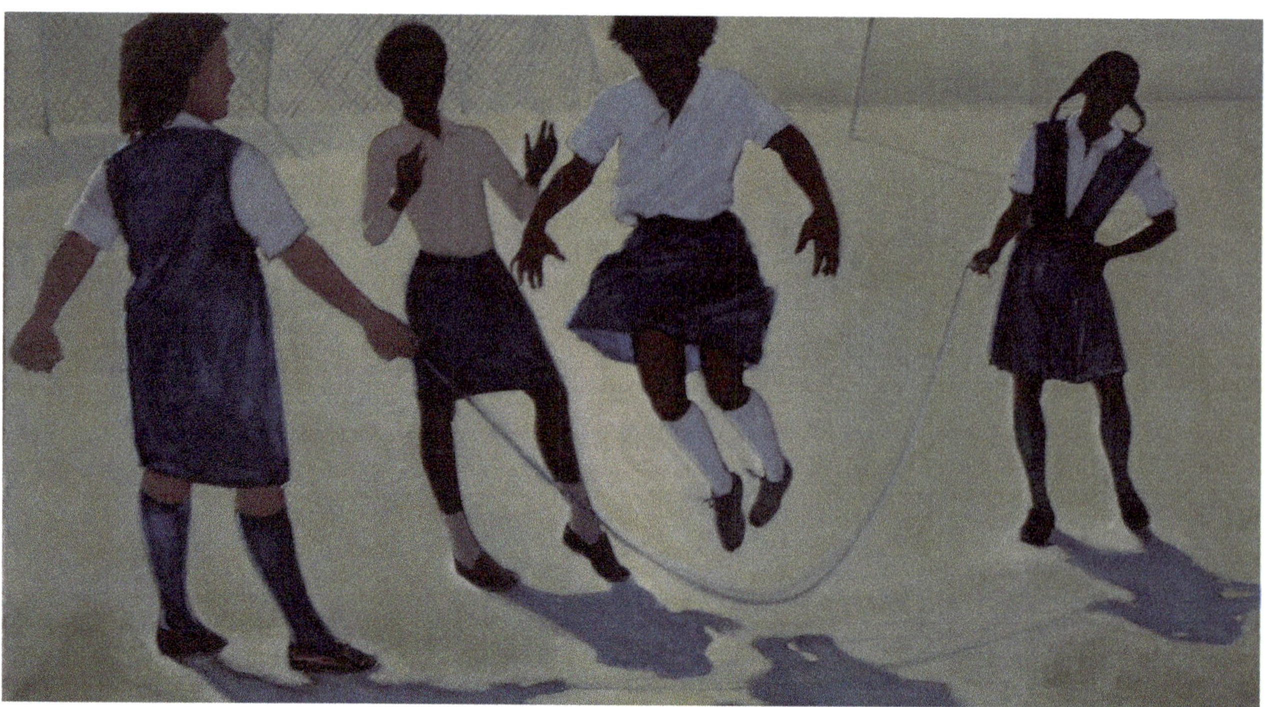

Jump Rope. 1985. Oil on canvas, 33 x 60 in.

career. Also evident is a fascination with inside and outside light, which draws obvious comparison with Edward Hopper. In 1984 Rashid had a landmark solo show at the Willis Gallery, which at the time was probably the most influential gallery in the city.

Through the 1980s and into the early 1990s the subject matter of Rashid's paintings ranged from urban landscapes and domestic interiors to memory scenes and portraits. One evening, though, in her loft/studio in Detroit's Atlas Building, as she picked at a bowl of popcorn, she stared at the endless visual complexity of the manufacturing marks and reflections in the metal bowl and had the epiphany that all the subject matter she needed was right at hand. The following will consider two examples from the early period, ***Denton*** (1982) and ***Jump Rope*** (1985), and three examples from the later period, ***Frying Pan*** (1994), ***Left Wrist*** (1995), and ***Drain*** (2004).

Denton is a view of the last house remaining in an area cleared in the early 1980s for urban renewal. It is noteworthy both for Rashid's early interest in Detroit's urban landscape and also for her commitment to painting on site rather than from photographs. In

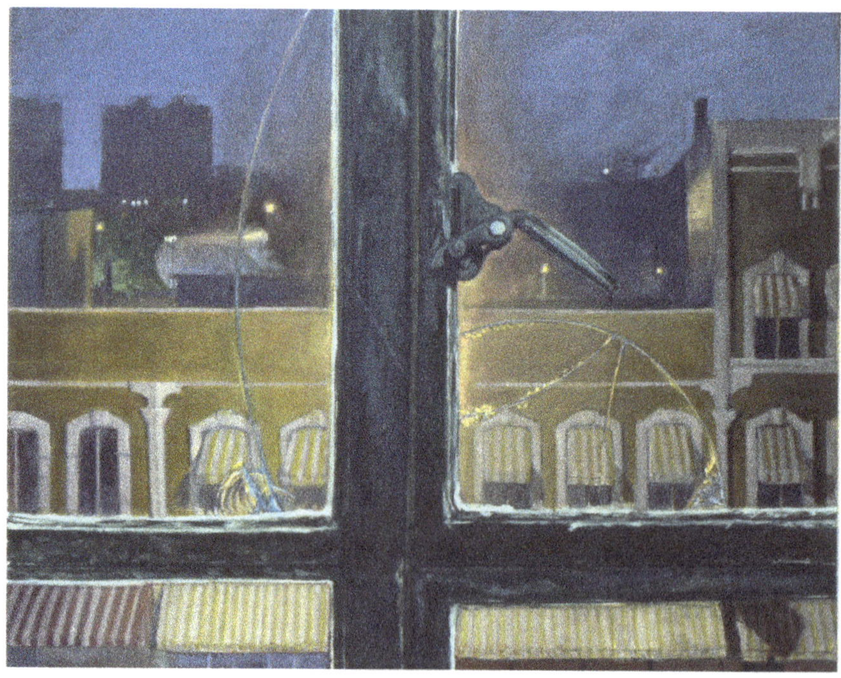

Busy Bee Hardware at Night. 1990. Oil on canvas, 40 x 44 in.

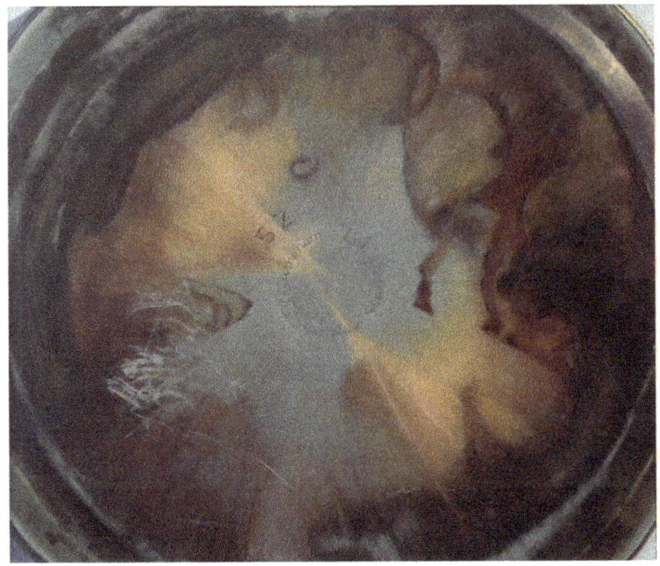

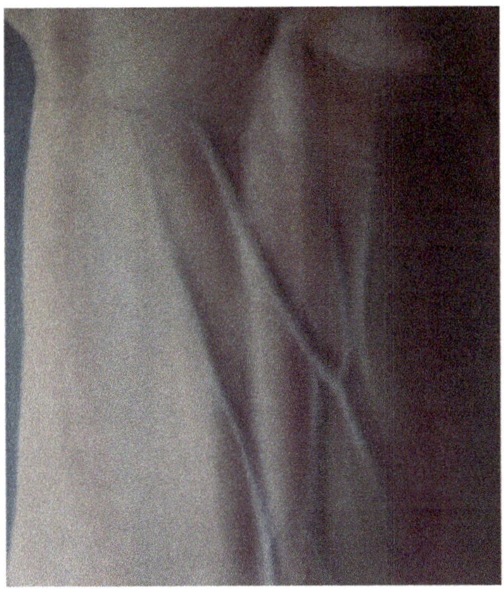

(Left) Frying Pan. 1994. Oil on canvas, 40 x 46 in. *(Right) Left Wrist.* 1995. Oil on canvas, 24 x 20 in.

recent years Rashid has returned to repaint several sites she originally studied in the late seventies/early eighties. What interests her most is not the change in the landscape (which is obvious) but the rather more subtle subject of the change in Detroiters' attitudes to representation.

Jump Rope is a rare example of a painting done from memory rather than direct observation. The painting is of the schoolyard at St. Agnes on Rosa Parks and the figure on the left is the artist, while the other figures are childhood friends. Rashid's father was a Lebanese store owner and her family was one of the few to stay in the area during the emotionally charged period when it transitioned into an almost totally Black neighborhood.

Frying Pan and *Drain* are two examples from the latter period. They feature everyday objects and consciously remove questions of composition to address questions of perception—when do you really see something? Although undoubtedly technical tours de force, it would be a mistake to see such paintings as technical exercises; rather, Rashid's objective is to get the viewer to look beyond the obvious, and as such it is totally consistent with her long-term personal commitment to promoting peace and tolerance. Detroit's recent history casts a long shadow, but, tellingly, Rashid has declined to use her unique experience and artistic relationship with the city to directly further her practice, rather using it to inform her objectives in a more general sense. If there is one quality that pulls together work from both periods it is a celebration of the human level and a refusal to accept the mercenary and alienating qualities of contemporary life. It has been paralleled by an attitude to art that has been described by one reviewer as "quixotic," with Rashid refusing to compromise her principles for the sake of self-promotion. For example, *Left Wrist* was one of a series of beautiful paintings created for a group show on the subject of light that Rashid withdrew to protest the show's sponsorship by an energy company, instead displaying a statement explaining her decision. Despite this highly principled approach, Rashid's paintings have managed to reach a wide range of admirers, and hence she quietly continues to be an inspiration to many—both artists and nonartists alike.

STEVE PANTON,
SEPTEMBER 2014

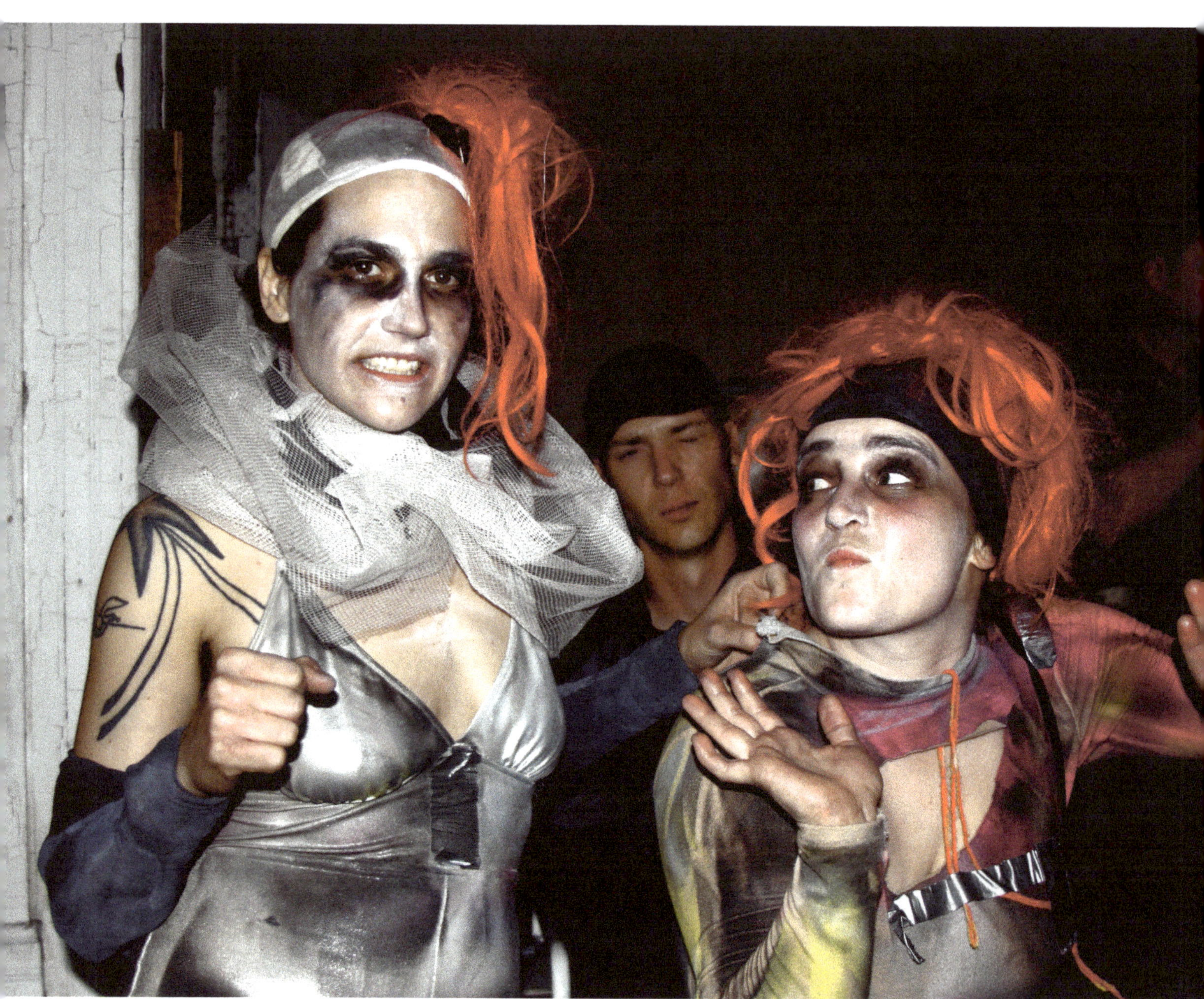

Performance at The Yes Farm. 2009. Photography by Sarah Rose Sharp.

5 // TZARINAS OF THE PLANE

Faina Lerman, born Riga, Latvia, 1975
BFA, College for Creative Studies
Lives in Hamtramck, Michigan

Bridget Michael, born Detroit, 1977
Certified Massage Therapist, Irene's Myomassology Institute
Lives in Hamtramck, Michigan

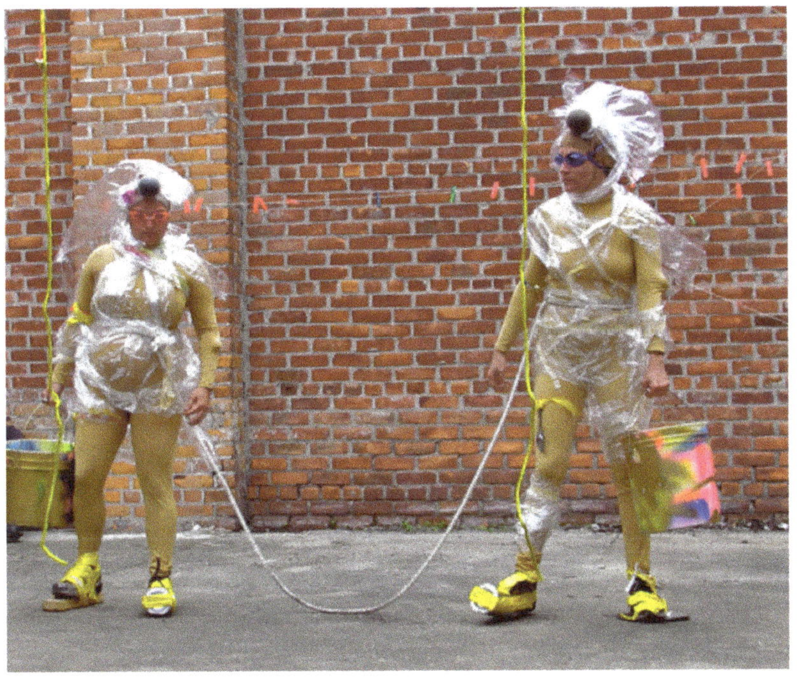

Performance at Ocelot Print Shop. 2013. Photography by Sarah Rose Sharp.

Is it possible to be deadly serious and exceptionally playful at the same time? The work of the two-woman performance art duo Tzarinas of the Plane demonstrates the compelling outcome of total commitment to impulse and fun. Their body of work is a tour de force in performance art, managing to eschew all hint of pretension with their joyful energy and inclusive, open-ended narratives. Viewing one of their performances, the audience is imbued with a feeling of wonderment in the truest sense: the potential of untold outcomes, the complete inability to predict what will happen next, and the realization that anything is truly possible when the Tzarinas are writing the rules.

Individually, the Tzarinas are Faina Lerman, artist and

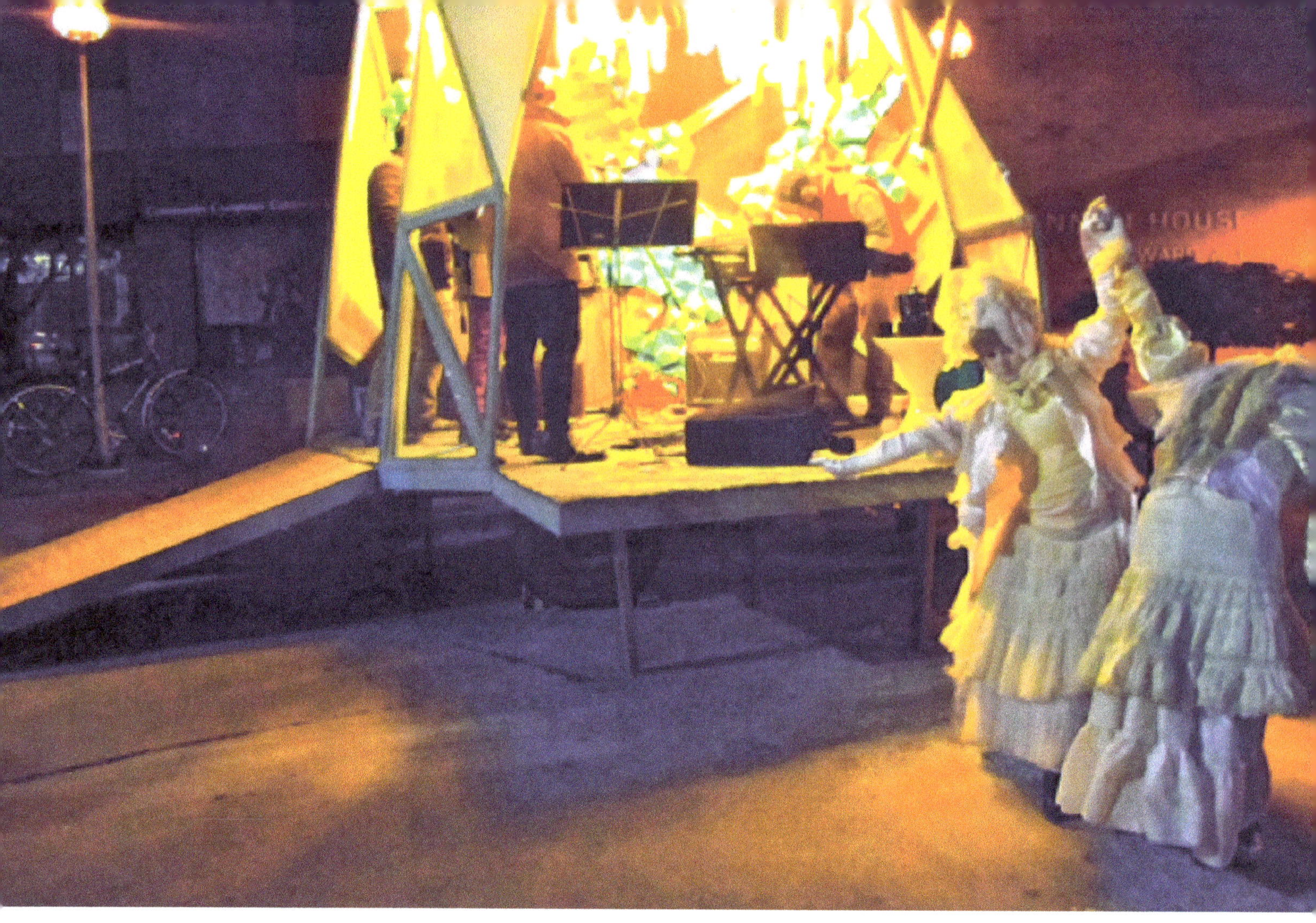

Performance at DLECTRICITY Festival. 2012. Photography by Sarah Rose Sharp.

cofounder of Popps Packing, an art space and residency in Hamtramck, and Bridget Michael, singular spirit and accomplished solo performer in her own right. Michael has the true actor's gift of being able to slip entirely into a repertoire of characters, which includes Fanny Toupee, a washed-up lounge singer, Raylin Hatcher, a young art student, hostess with the mostest Linda Linda Linda, DoDo the Clown, and even a tassel-bedecked dancer named Cookie, allowing a range of personas to occupy her body, sometimes with alarmingly quick turnover. Lerman has been primarily a visual artist, and curating is a family affair over at Popps, which she comanages with her husband, artist Graem Whyte.

But there is a level accessed by Lerman and Michael as the Tzarinas of the Plane that transcends the sum of their parts as individual artists. Their performance pieces crop up in small venues, like Public Pool, 2739 Edwin, and The Yes Farm, as often as they play big venues, such as the ***2012 DLECTRICITY Festival*** or their performance at ArtPrize 2014 in Grand Rapids. The Tzarinas have been working at play together since 2008, and in that time have developed a repertoire that ties together disparate themes with the common elements of wild DIY costuming, minimal dialogue augmented by found or specifically recorded audio elements, physical movement that ranges from spastic to graceful, and a perfectly stoic execution of unmitigated silliness. Indeed, audiences often seem to hesitate to laugh at the Tzarinas' comedic efforts, such is the fierce energy of dedication they bring to their performances.

Take, for example, their *2013 performance at the opening of Ocelot Print Shop*, where they executed a special piece that transformed the two artists into connected parts of a machine, joined at the waist by a rope, clad in plastic wrap and resonant chunks of metal. This last provided an active soundtrack to the action, which was chiefly comprised of the washing and hanging of sheets of paper along clotheslines that skewed radically through the open-air performance space. Even as the Tzarinas reached a fever pitch, rebounding between the clotheslines, adjusting to accommodate the line between them and audience members interspersed within their performance space, the rhythm remained unbroken.

This audial detail is an important indicator of the intensive preparation and practice that goes into work that seems, at first exposure, to be highly spontaneous and loosely choreographed, but upon closer reading or reflection reveals deep sophistication and process-intensive building of planned performances that still allow for spontaneity and unexpected twists, a structure that Lerman describes as, "Agenda items in a meeting, but whatever happens between them is what's happening." While the movements may not be exhaustively planned, as such, every new work by the Tzarinas represents an exhaustive discovery and development process, borne of being "hard at play."

SARAH ROSE SHARP,
OCTOBER 2014

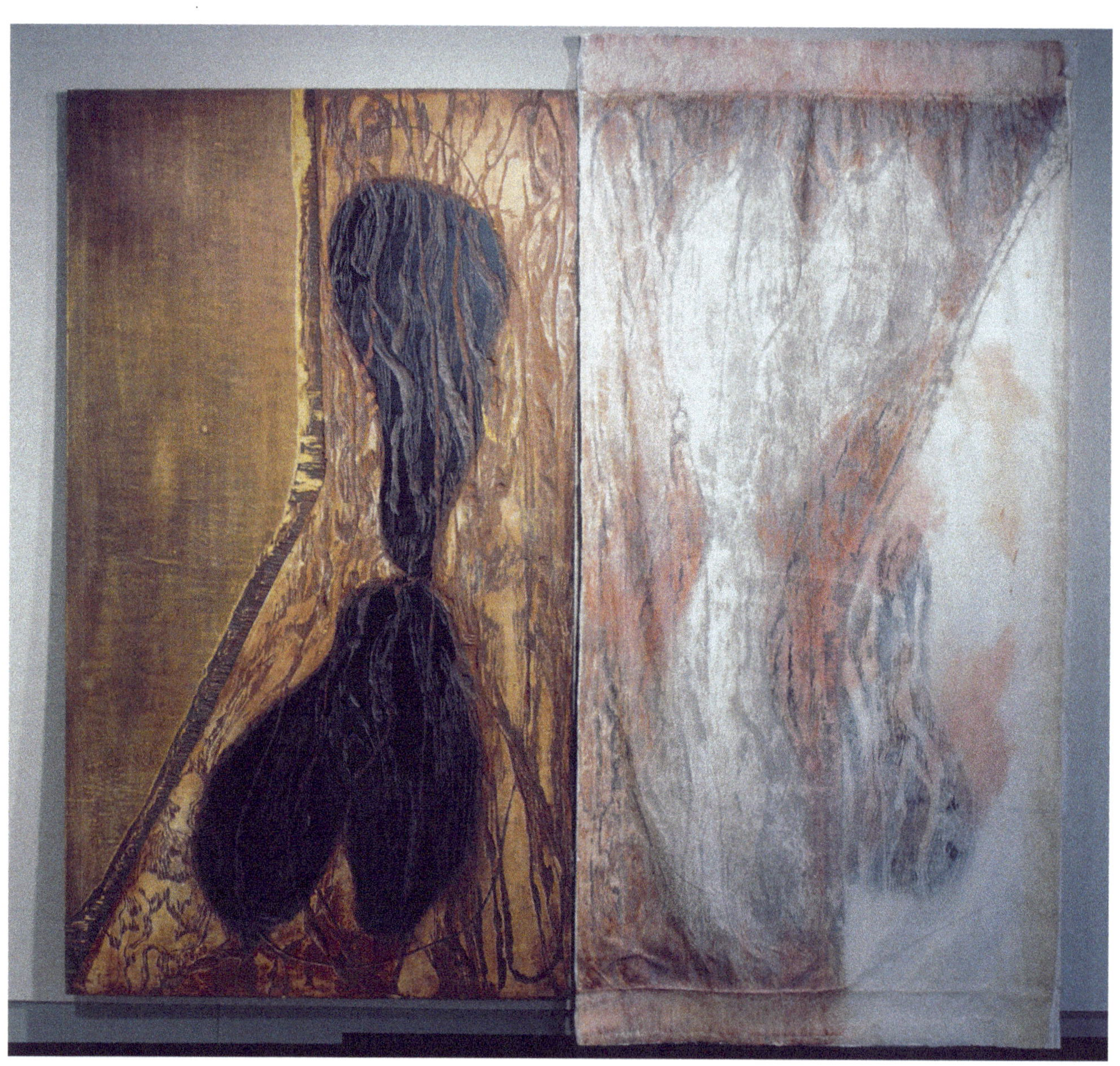

Feeder. 1997. Inks, stain, on carved birch plywood printed on layered glassine papers. 96 x 96 in.

6 // KATHRYN BRACKETT LUCHS

Born Detroit, 1950
BFA, MFA, University of Michigan
Lives in Lewiston, Michigan

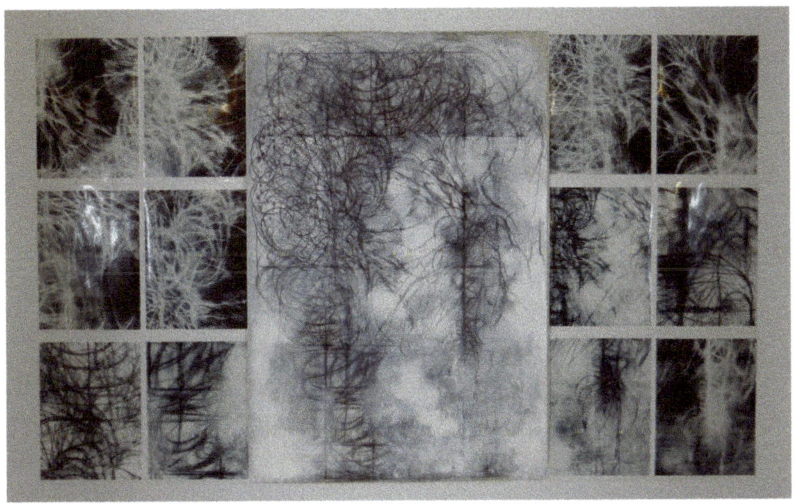

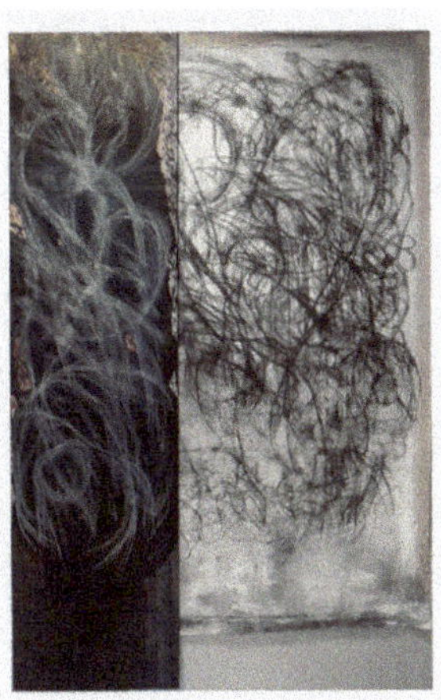

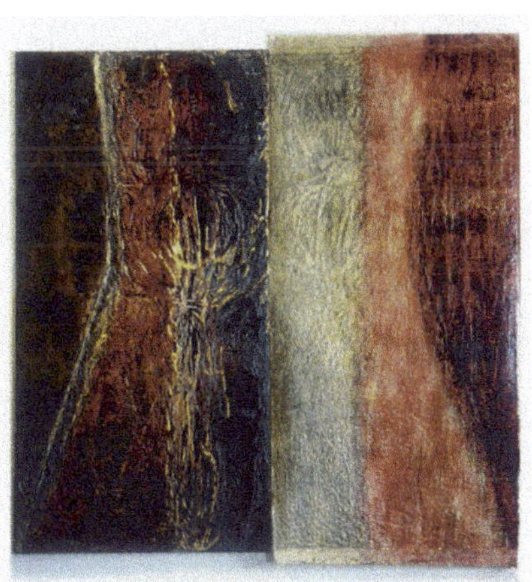

(*Top*) *Birdy*. 2013. Charcoal pencil on gesso on canvas / photographic details on graphic films, 88 x 144 in.
(*Bottom, left*) *Jazzpur's Wing*. 2011–12. Sumi ink, conté, varnish on carved birch plywood / charcoal pencil on gesso on canvas, 96 x 60 in.
(*Bottom, right*) *China Bird*. 2003. Inks on carved birch plywood / inks and graphite rubbings on layered glassine papers, 96 x 96 in.

I grew up in the Detroit vicinity [and later] moved to what is now called Detroit's Cass Corridor, where I would for the next years paint and also film many of the experimental artists who were there between 1973 and 1988. These early influences were essential experiences—gutsy, primal, personal, "hands-on stuff." Ever since, I have experimented with works that mix material approaches and personal thought.

Kathryn Brackett Luchs has been making *big*, odd-couple "hybrids" (her preferred term) since the late eighties, often pairing plywood and glassine, canvas and photographs, hard and soft, sturdy and fragile as her signature practice. As such, her work challenges the conventions of modest scale, tautness, framing, and single sheets of paper associated with the print medium (which she in fact teaches at the University of Michigan Stamps

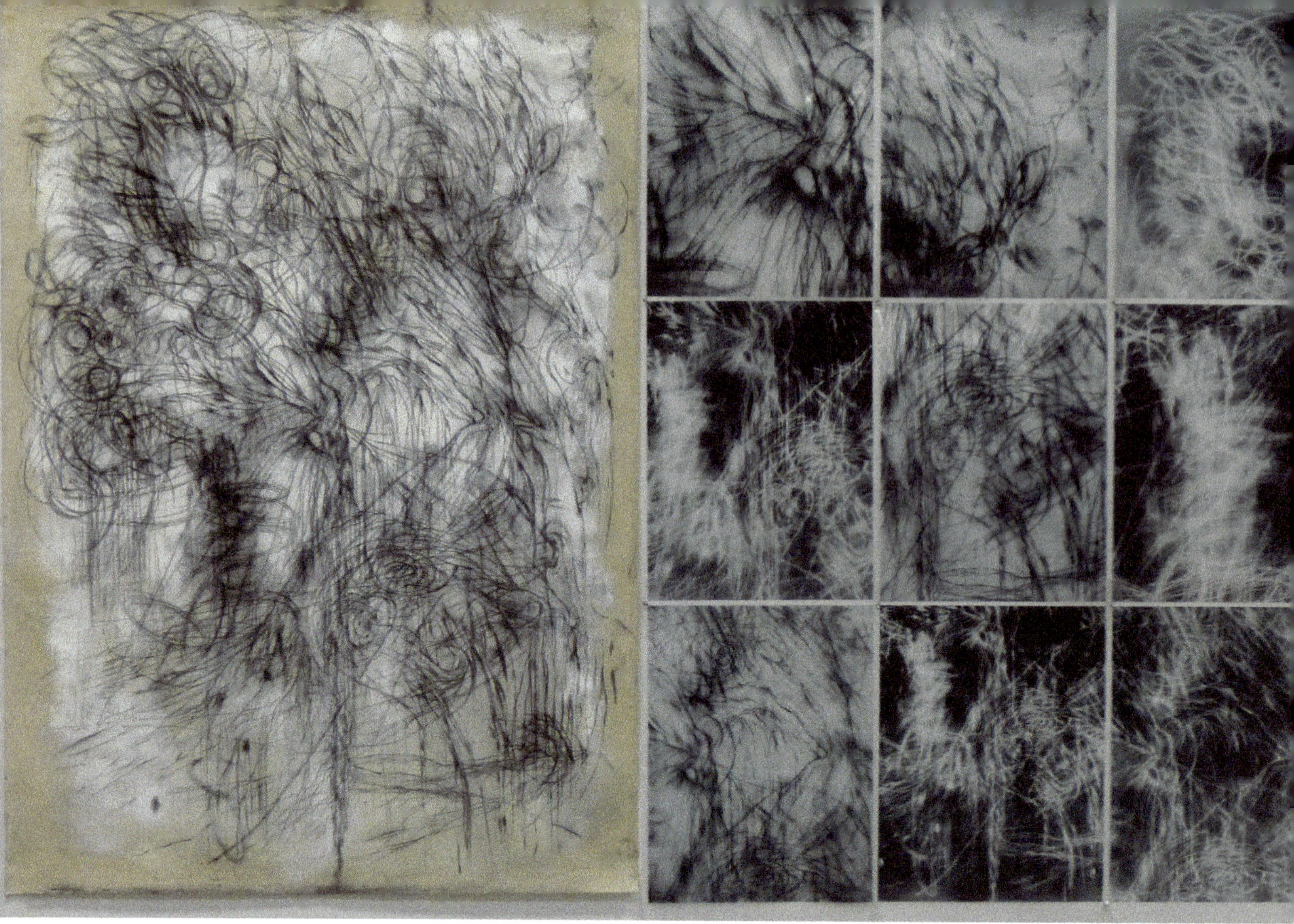

Allegory. 2013. Charcoal pencil on gesso on canvas / photographic details on graphic films, 84 x 122 in.

School of Art and Design). Her combinations have instead been conspicuously expansive and enveloping, imposingly large, and relentlessly experimental in execution and appearance. In her studio multiple compositions are usually underway simultaneously.

That Brackett Luchs has lived in semirural environs post-Detroit (Holly, Ann Arbor, South Lyon, Lewiston) accounts in part for the flora and fauna that predominate in her imagery since the eighties: moths, wings, birds, bark, nests. Even in her recent abstract compositions of the last several years, words such as chrysalis, cocoon, birdy, and fossil (along with allegory, Buddha, and hybrid) persist in her titles.

Notable too is her commitment to a compositional format that joins at the hip a matrix (or "the parent block," per the artist) and an abutting image derived from it (the "offspring")—or lately, a cluster of "details" appropriated from the matrix. This elemental structure is apparent in both ***Feeder*** of 1997 and ***Birdy*** of 2013: in the former, the gouged, carved, and inked plywood panel on the left yields the pale, rosy, evanescent woodcut on layers of glassine on the right; in the latter, the kinetic whorls of charcoal on gessoed canvas beget the flanking grids of photographs right and left, reminiscent of a triptych with central image and paired wings.

In both series, early and recent, as well as in transitional examples, such as ***Jazzpur's Wing*** (2011–12), Brackett Luchs's basic

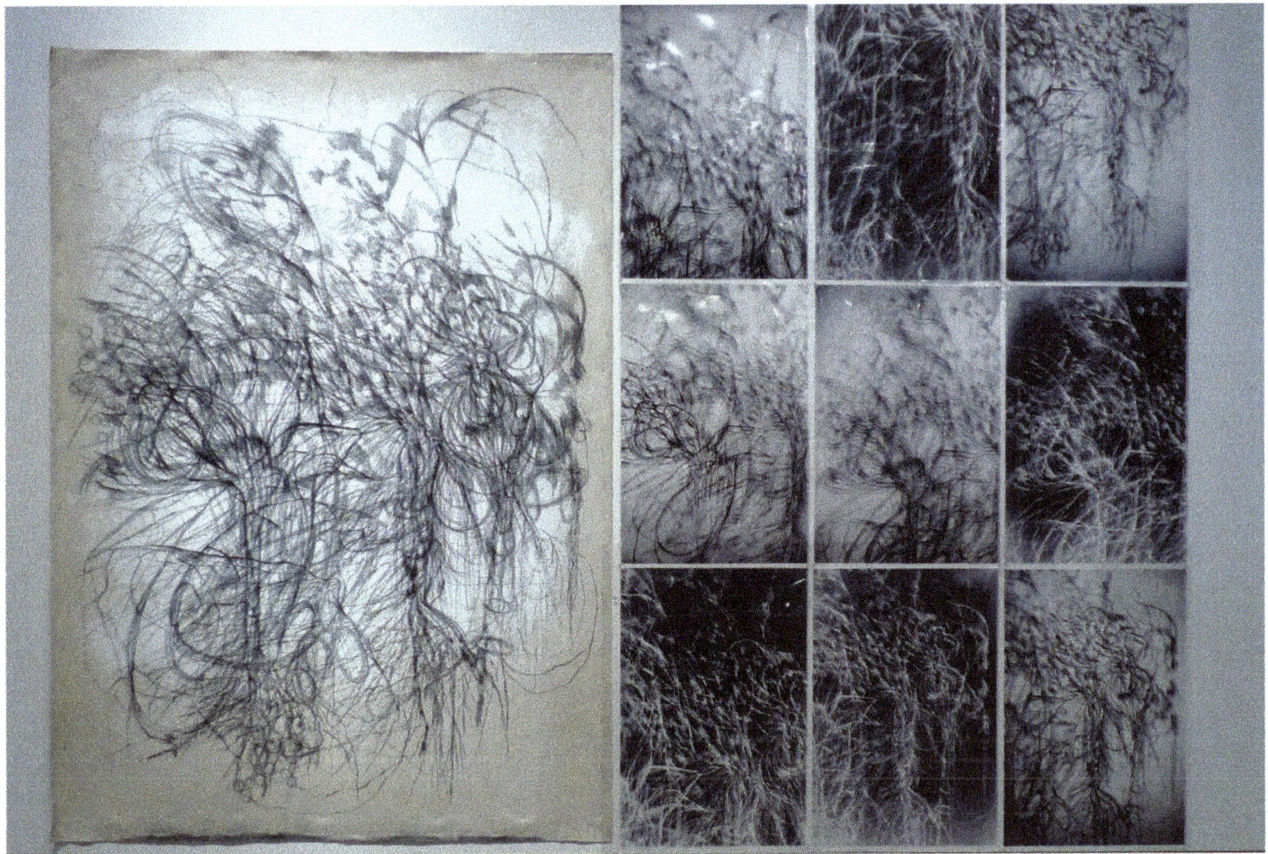

Fossil & 9 Films. 2013. Charcoal pencil on gesso on canvas / photographic details on graphic films, 88 x 123 in.

configuration is maintained as her profound intentions are broadened and deepened. Almost from the outset, the core concepts of matrix as pivotal element, coupled with the embrace of part and whole, persist as the overriding thematic thrust of her art. Just as neither one technique nor process is sufficient to conjure up a totality—hence Brackett Luchs's mixed-media process in ***China Bird*** (2003) and ***Fossil & 9 Films*** (2013)—neither a singular print on glassine or drawing on canvas, nor variations of images or clusters of photographs on their own, can adequately convey a comprehensive vision. Instead, burrowing in, building incrementally, adding facets, layers, and nuances via diverse graphic techniques, reveals more than a single scan or first impression. Both multiplicity and the application of Duchampian "brain fact" (i.e., fusing it all together in the mind's eye) breed clarity and understanding.

In her latest images, such as *Birdy* (the largest so far at seven by twelve feet), ***Allegory***, and *Fossil & 9 Films* (all 2013), Brackett Luchs does just that. Devoid of color and divested of imagery, they embody a rarefied realm, cool and purified but fraught with waves of energy. Whether structured as diptych, triptych, or polyptych, a surrender to the sweeping, caroming curves, spirals, and coils of charcoal on canvas is irresistible. The eye darts back and forth across a swarm of enlarged photographic details spawned by the dance on the canvas, disposed symmetrically or asymmetrically, reveling, as the artist avers, in perpetual "states of changing or becoming."

DENNIS ALAN NAWROCKI,
OCTOBER 2014

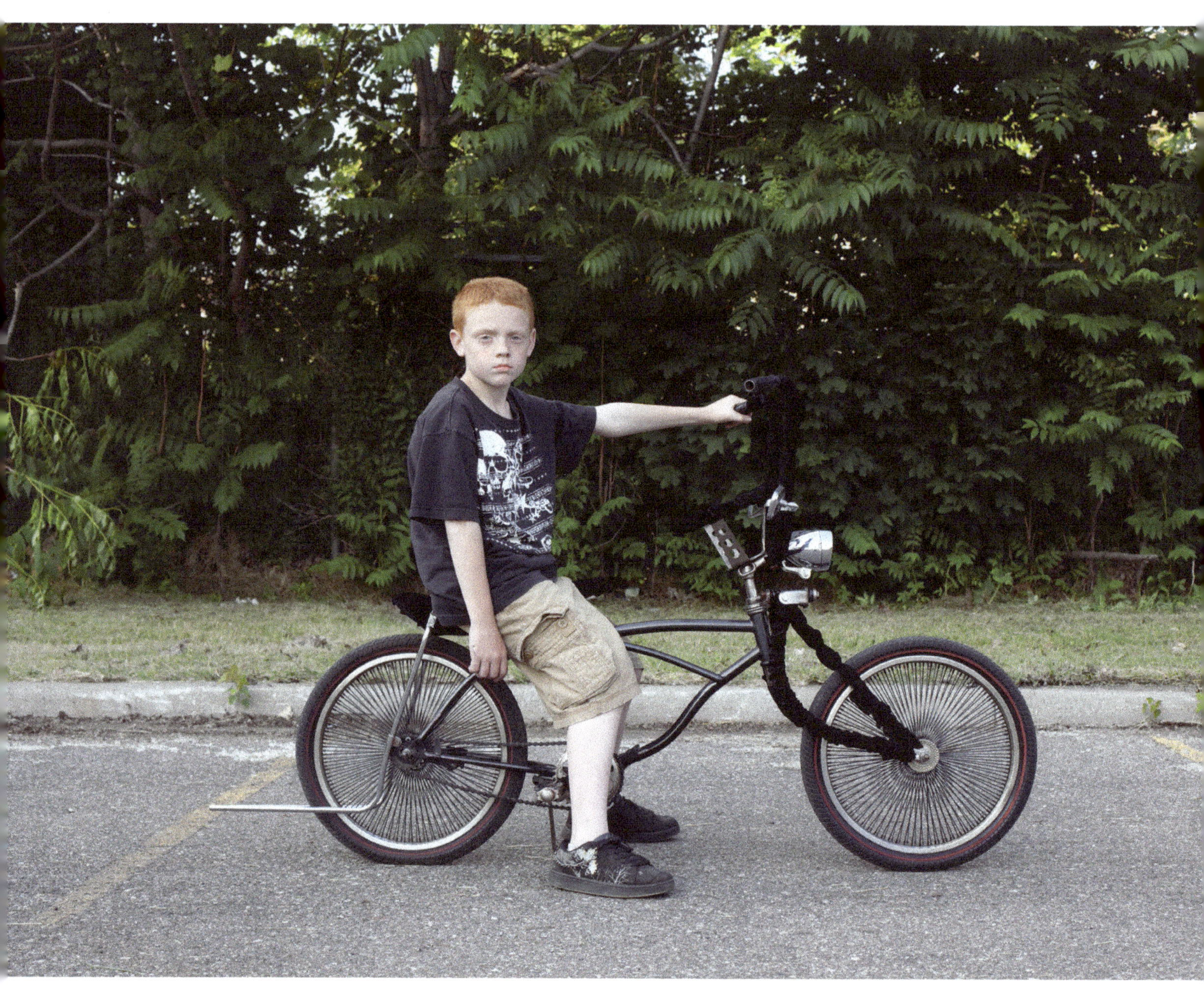

Boy with Lowrider Bicycle, from *Your Town Tomorrow*. 2009. Pigment print.

7 // CORINE VERMEULEN

Born Gouda, the Netherlands, 1977
BFA, The Design Academy, Eindhoven
MFA, Cranbrook Academy of Art
Lives in Detroit

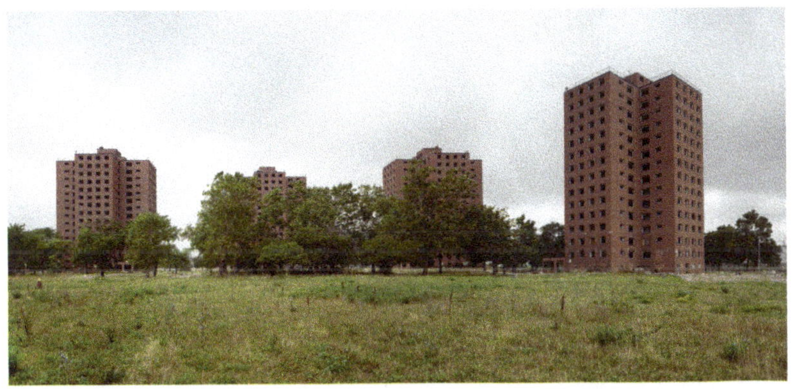

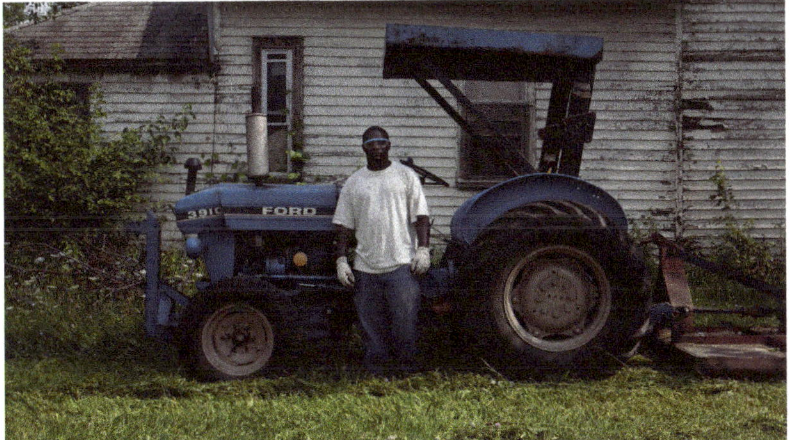

(*Top*) *Brewster-Douglass Housing Projects*, from *Your Town Tomorrow*. 2009. Pigment print.
(*Bottom*) *Rick*, from *Your Town Tomorrow*. 2008. Pigment print.

Photographer Corine Vermeulen's meticulously constructed projects, such as ***Your Town Tomorrow*** (Detroit, 2007–12), ***The Walk-in Portrait Studio*** (Detroit, 2009–14), and *Obscura Primavera* (Medelin, Colombia, 2009–14), reflect an artist willing to devote significant periods of time to, and seriously immerse herself in, her subject. Her works display an exemplary combination of empathy for their subjects and a very European sense of distance. The resulting images are instantly recognizable while remaining constantly surprising in their freshness.

After graduating from Cranbrook Academy of Art in 2004, Vermeulen relocated in 2006 to the city of Detroit—whose condition she saw as occupying a "unique place in our current socioeconomic system"—to begin the project *Your Town Tomorrow*. The work was envisioned not as

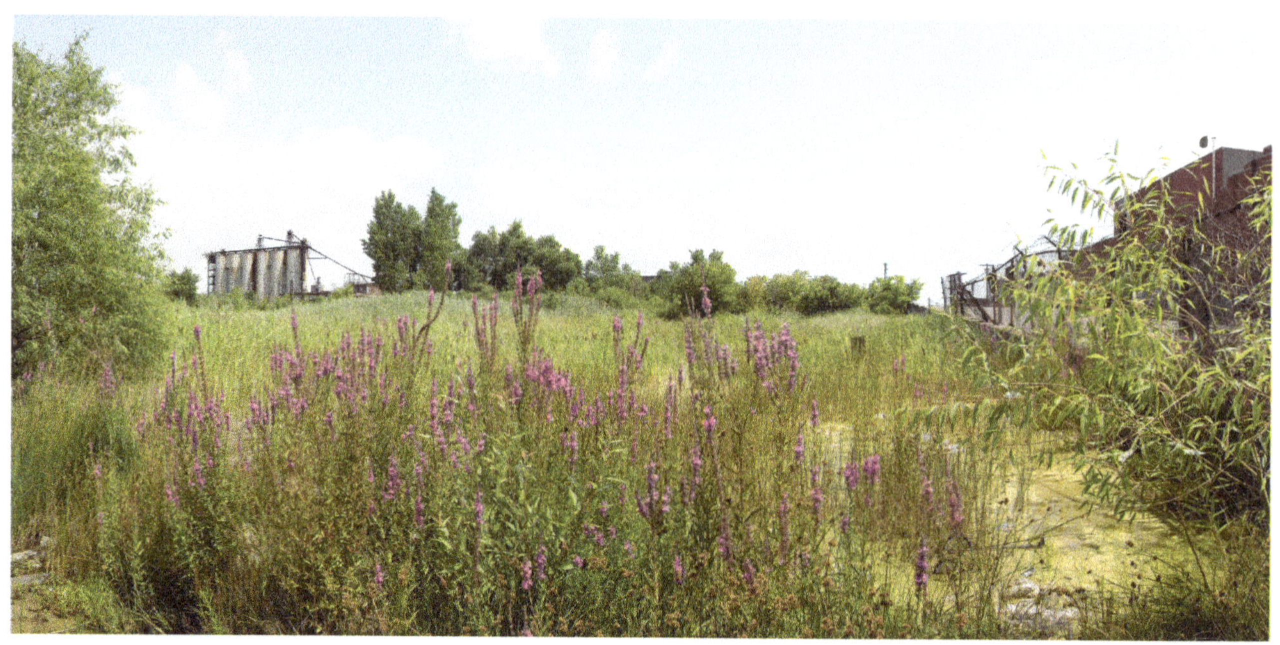

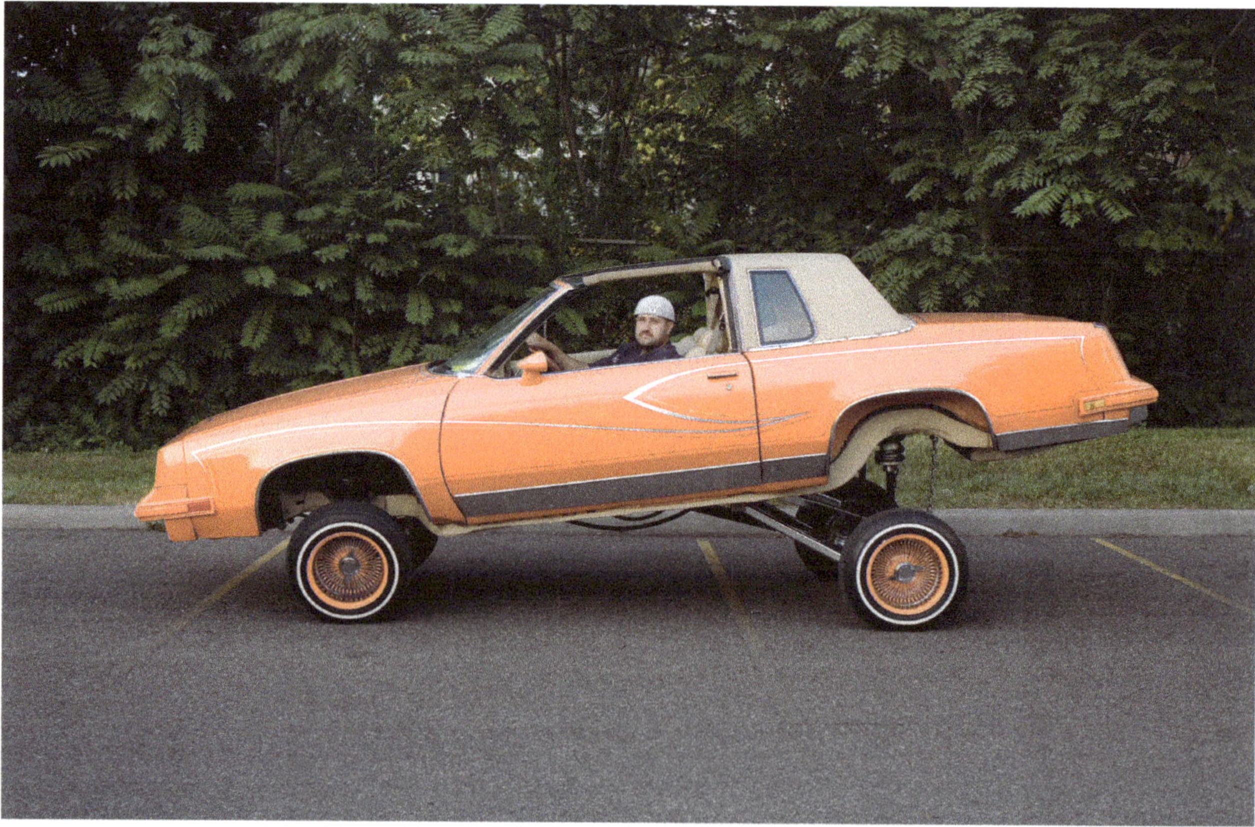

(*Top*) *Prairie and the Former Koenig Coal Yard Silos*, from *Your Town Tomorrow*. 2007. Pigment print.
(*Bottom*) *Salvador "Chavo" and His Radical Hopper, an '83 Cutlass Supreme*, from *Your Town Tomorrow*. 2008. Pigment print.

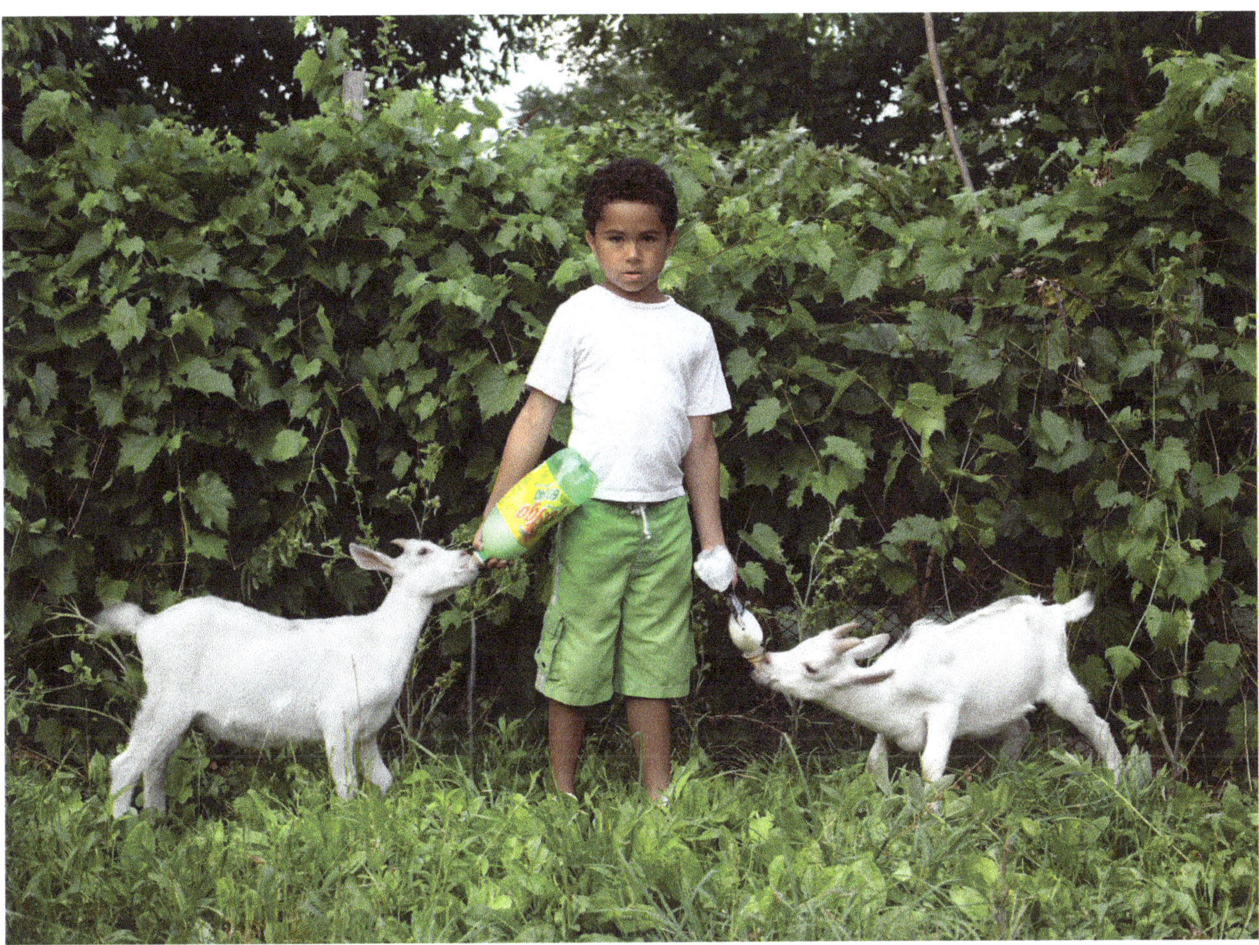

PJ and Goats, from *Your Town Tomorrow*. 2011. Pigment print.

a survey of Detroit "as is," but rather as a "glimpse into an alternate reality, where everyday life stands at a crossroads: between hope and despair, vulnerability and strength, the past and the future." Although huge in scope, Vermeulen kept the project visually and conceptually coherent by using a variety of devices such as a distinct palette (green, white, black, and earth colors dominate with other colors used sparingly, and rarely in combination), a restricted subject matter (portraits and landscape dominate), an emphasis on nature (both directly in terms of landscape, but also indirectly through the location of portraits), an exclusion of contemporary technology and focus on agriculture, a repeated use of flat lighting conditions, a consistent relationship to the gaze of the portrait subject (typically expressionless and looking beyond the camera), and a recurring presence of vernacular creativity (through painted signs, tricked-out bikes, and heavily accessorized cars).

Vermeulen is clearly sensitive to the critical position race plays in how an image will be received by an American audience, and one feels she is consistently attempting to transcend this by forcing the viewer to focus on the humanity of her subjects; only the young, white, urban pioneers who were often the focus of the early stages

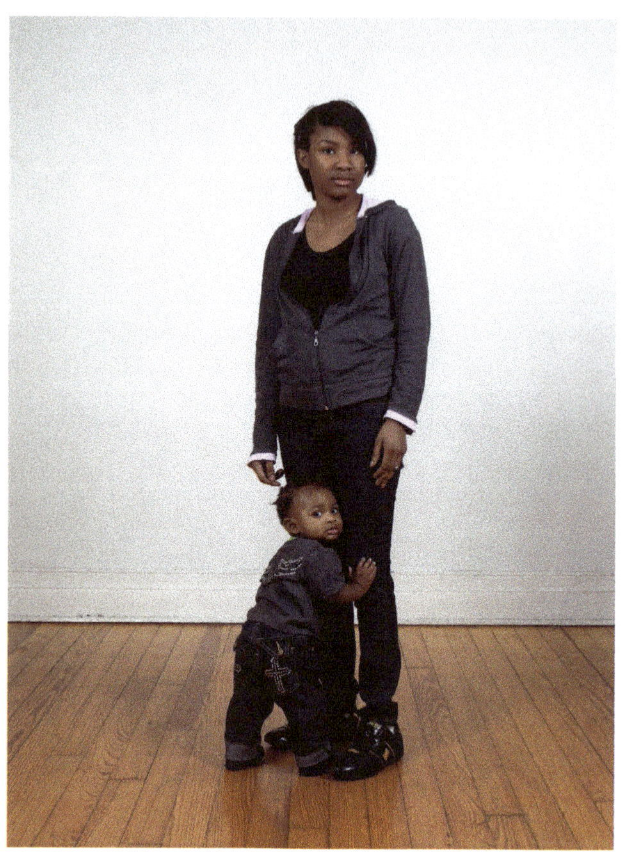

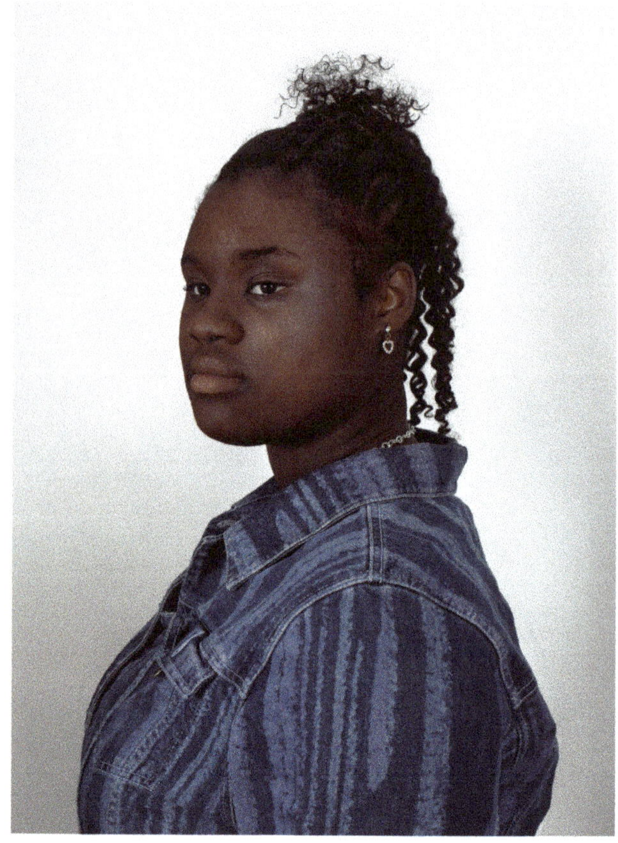

(*Left*) *Breanna and Her Son Perrion (Catherine Ferguson Academy)*, from *Walk-in Portrait Studio.* 2011. Pigment print. (*Right*) *Zana*, from *Walk-in Portrait Studio.* 2009. Pigment print.

of the project might, in retrospect, be seen as stereotypes. Overall, the series can be seen as a document of an exceptionally talented photographer in a unique time and place, but there is an alternative interpretation that starts from the centrality of themes such as self-sufficiency, sustainability, and racial diversity, and sees the project as an extended utopian tableau—utopian in the sense that, as Ernest Bloch wrote, "We need the most powerful telescope, that of polished utopian consciousness, in order to penetrate precisely the nearest nearness."

Vermeulen's next project, *The Walk-in Portrait Studio*, focused directly on the citizens of Detroit. Inspired by Walker Evans's License Photo Studio in New York, she set up a portrait studio in a formerly foreclosed home in a hard-knocks part of the city. Neighbors were encouraged by fliers, posters, and direct invitation to visit the studio and have their portraits taken. Over a five-day period, eighty-five people took part, trading a story about the neighborhood in return for a print of their portrait. Despite the informality and chance-driven nature of the walk-in studio, Vermeulen was characteristically systematic in identifying and controlling all of the parameters that could affect the image. Some of the resulting images (e.g., ***Zana***, 2009) were displayed in a local art gallery, giving a quietly dignified public

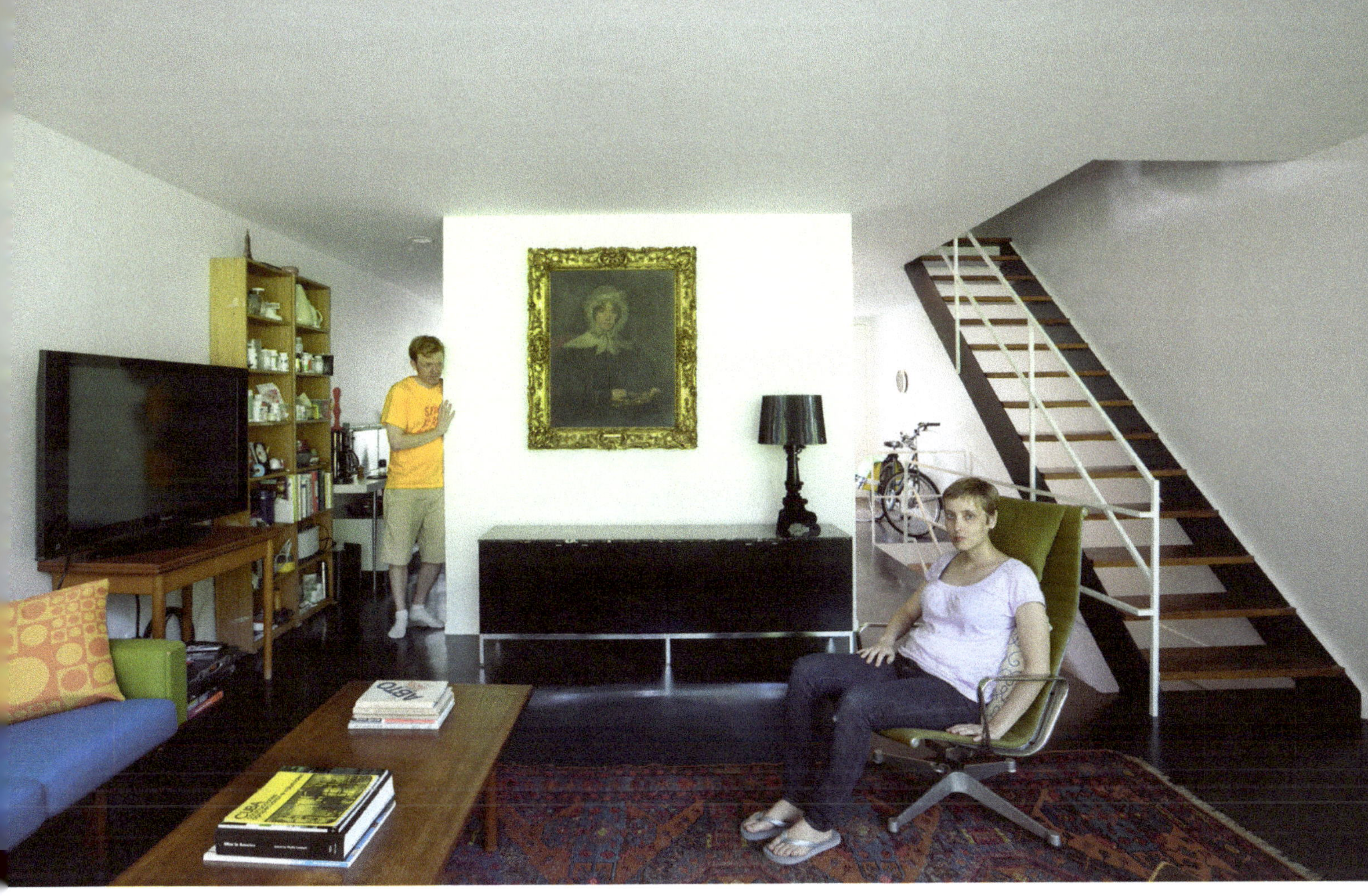

Danielle and Jonathan, from *Thanks for the View, Mr. Mies.* 2009. Pigment print.

face to city residents who are often treated as invisible. After this first iteration, Vermeulen took the walk-in studio to various schools in Detroit and surrounding areas, including the Catherine Ferguson Academy, a school for young single mothers (see ***Breanna and Her Son Perrion***, 2011). An interesting counterpoint to these portraits is a parallel project in which she photographed residents of Mies van der Rohe's Lafayette Park in their homes, a series featured in the *New York Times* (see ***Danielle and Jonathan***, 2009). More recently she has taken the concept to other community organizations and social groups in the city, displaying the completed project at an exhibition at the Detroit Institute of the Arts in November 2014, a fitting climax to a substantial body of work.

STEVE PANTON,
OCTOBER 2014/DECEMBER 2015

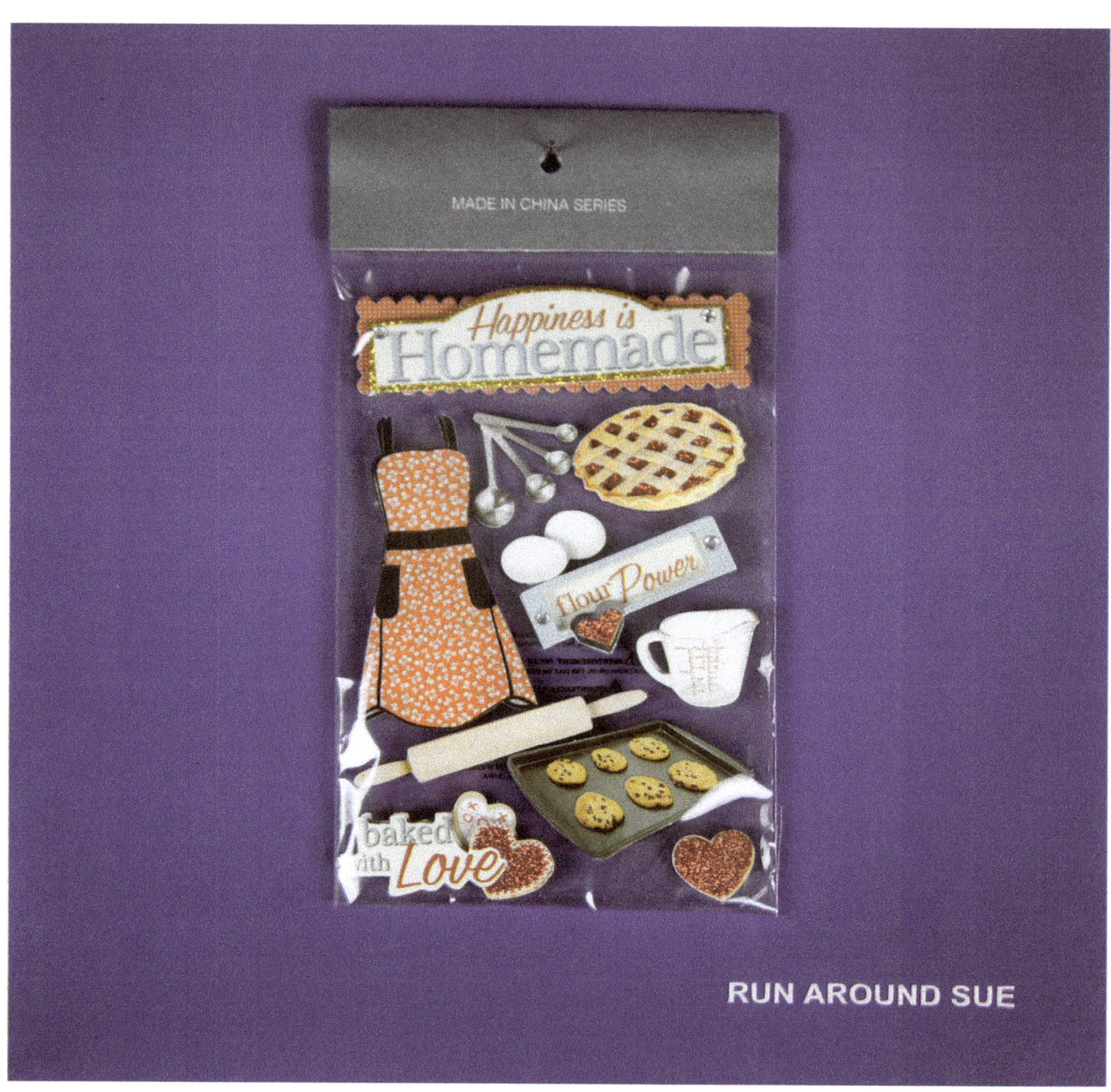

Run Around Sue. 2005. Found objects, house paint, 12 x 12 in.
Photography by Robert Stewart.

8 // ROSE E. DESLOOVER

Born Monroe, Michigan, 1944
BA, Alverno College, Milwaukee, Wisconsin
MFA, Claremont Graduate School, Claremont, California
Lives in Farmington Hills, Michigan

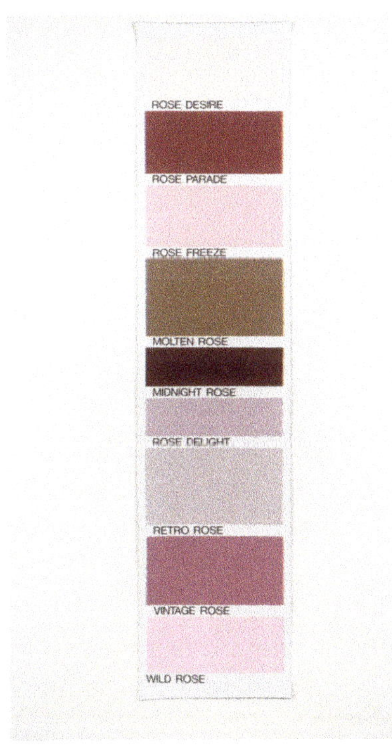

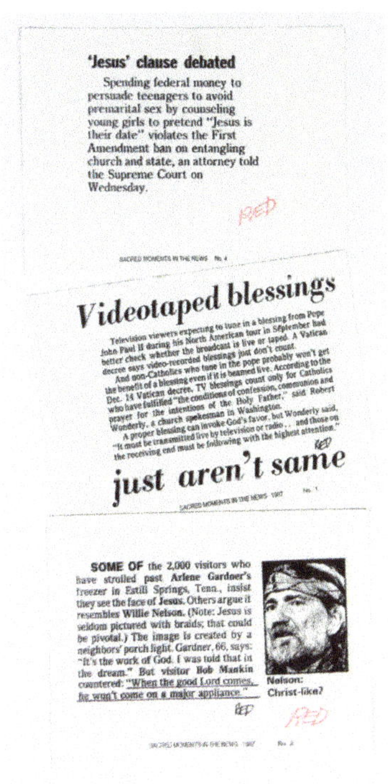

'Jesus' clause debated

Spending federal money to persuade teenagers to avoid premarital sex by counseling young girls to pretend "Jesus is their date" violates the First Amendment ban on entangling church and state, an attorney told the Supreme Court on Wednesday.

Videotaped blessings just aren't same

A proper blessing can invoke God's favor ... and those on "It must be transmitted live by television or radio ... the receiving end must be following with the highest attention."

SACRED MOMENTS IN THE NEWS 1987

SOME OF the 2,000 visitors who have strolled past **Arlene Gardner's** freezer in Estill Springs, Tenn., insist they see the face of **Jesus**. Others argue it resembles **Willie Nelson**. (Note: Jesus is seldom pictured with braids; that could be pivotal.) The image is created by a neighbors' porch light. Gardner, 66, says: "It's the work of God. I was told that in the dream." But visitor **Bob Mankin** countered: "When the good Lord comes, he won't come on a major appliance."

Nelson: Christ-like?

SACRED MOMENTS IN THE NEWS 1987

(*Left*) *Self-Portrait.* 1999. Paint color charts, 87 ½ x 20 in. Photography by Robert Stewart.

(*Right*) *Items*, from the series *Sacred Moments in the News.* 1987–2001. Found media printed on cardstock. 4 x 6 in. Photography by Sarah Nesbitt.

Though the vows taken by Rose E. DeSloover when she became a nun were dissolved when she left the convent fourteen years later to more freely pursue the art practice that had become her higher calling, there remains a thread of both religion and faith that runs throughout a number of her signature bodies of work.

Most literally dealing with religion is DeSloover's mail art series, ***Sacred Moments in the News*** (1987–2001), a process comprised of found news items—specifically related to religion in some way—converted to postcards and sent out in signed editions to a mailing list that grew to a couple of hundred recipients, both acquaintances and strangers. Another work, ***Cinderella's Shoes / Rapture*** (1997/2008) utilizes three pairs of satin liturgical shoes bought by DeSloover from a white-elephant sale at the Verona Fathers'

Mission in Monroe, Michigan. DeSloover notes the "most significant" fact that these shoes, which had belonged to the bishop who confirmed her, fit her feet. With its religious subject matter and careful denotation of synchronicity, this marks a transition toward a kind of universal faith or belief in a larger picture, away from a specific religious order such as the one that DeSloover worked within for so many years.

This display also employs two of the most prevalent mechanisms within DeSloover's work: strict use of found objects (the determination to create no new pieces was made by DeSloover during her church-subsidized stint in graduate school) and a fascination with what she terms the "domestication of color." DeSloover's obsession with house paint as a medium contains both an aesthetic and a literary interest. Fostered early by her own name, Rosemary, amplified by red cheeks and red hair, and reinforced by her initials, RED (synchronicity everywhere!), DeSloover began to experiment in grad school with portraiture and composition that utilized the kind of paint-color charts that are readily available at any hardware store. As is obvious in her *Self-Portrait* (1999), DeSloover is drawn to identify with colors and their names, extrapolating layers of meaning from her ready-made palette—the choice to limit herself to preexisting colors was

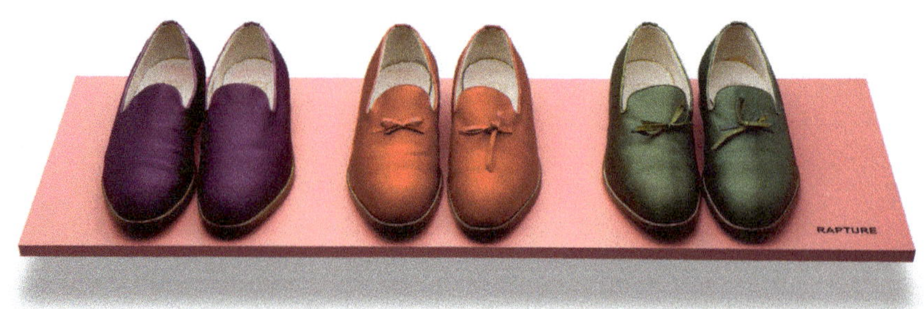

Cinderella's Shoes

Sometime in the seventies, I bought three pair of satin, liturgical shoes---green, red and purple--- in a white elephant sale at the Verona Fathers' Mission in Monroe, Michigan. They were Florsheim shoes, size 10, with very little wear.

The shoes had belonged to Bishop H. C. Donnelly of Toledo, the Bishop who confirmed me with a slap on the cheek in 1957.

Most significant --- the shoes fit me.

Art In Fact #3, 1997

In 2008 I updated the piece by painting the shelf "Rapture"— a deep rose color.
RED

Cinderella's Shoes / Rapture. 1997/2008. Found objects, house paint, 14 x 36 in. Photography by Robert Stewart.

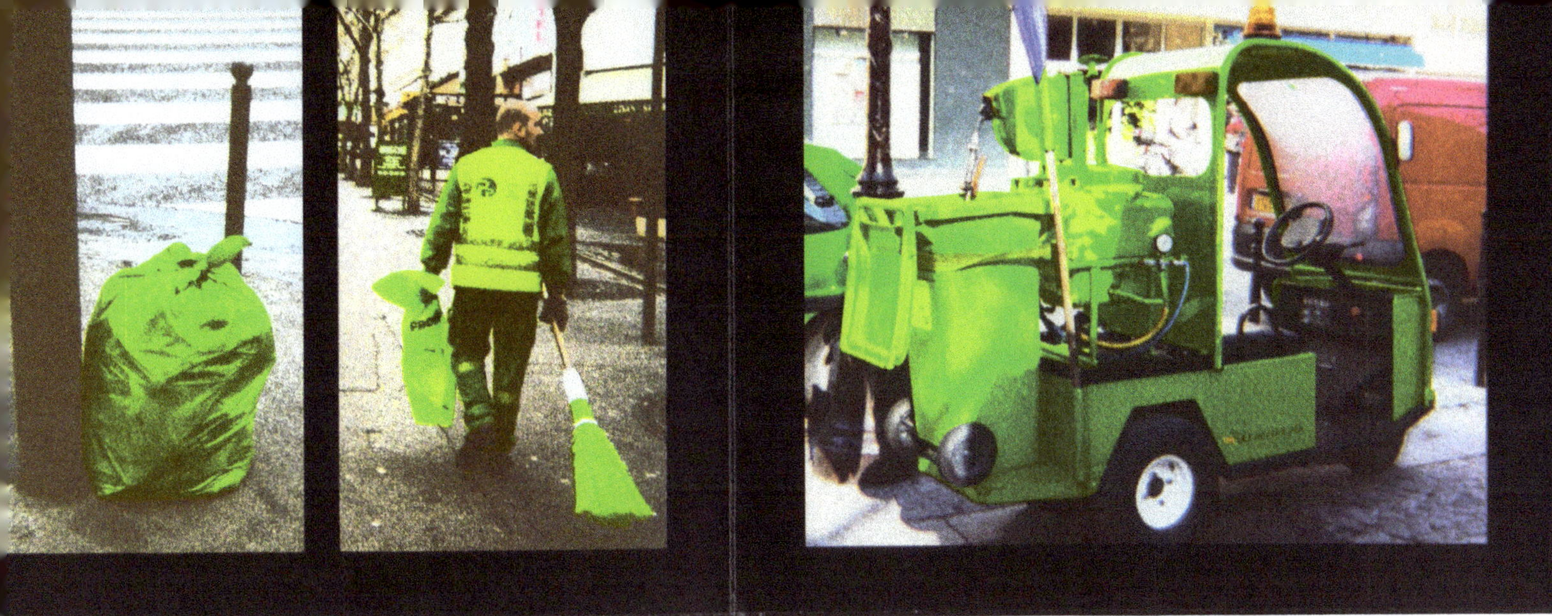

Interior spread from *Protecting Paris.* 2012. Artist's book, 5.25 x 12.5 in. Photography by Sarah Nesbitt.

an important subset of DeSloover's discipline around found objects. This practice has further evolved to include found objects paired with colors/names as a form of portraiture, as in her work ***Run Around Sue*** (2005), a portrait of friend and performance artist Sue Carman Vian.

From here, colors and their attendant meanings have generated several significant arcs in DeSloover's work. "Kryptonite"—a neon green that was first adopted in her portrait of her teacher and major influence, light artist James Turrell—has become a signifier of protective energy, which DeSloover employed in her piece ***Protecting Paris*** (2012), a collaboration with poet Darcy Brandel, and even in her daily wardrobe, depending on her need for protection against influential or threatening forces. Kryptonite, in DeSloover's world, is the single weakness of Superman (a persona that she had lovingly attached to Turrell due to his charisma and force of personality), but she is quick to mention that she really thinks of the "Superman" more in the Nietzschean sense. This is only one of DeSloover's interactions with canonical philosophers; in 2002 she participated in an intensive six-week seminar on the unfinished *Arcades Project (Passagenwerk)* by Walter Benjamin, which DeSloover describes as opening a cracked door to find an entire warehouse of kinship and an inspirational wellspring that continues to inform her practice today.

Indeed, much like the *Arcades Project*, DeSloover's decades of work—both as a conceptual artist and as an educator/administrator for forty-four years at Marygrove College in Detroit—defy easy analysis, and perhaps benefit more from a process not unlike one that DeSloover herself might employ: a careful collecting of artifacts and evidence, a conscious noting of seeming synchronicity, and an overwhelming sense that these elements coalesce into a bigger picture, perhaps slightly beyond our vantage point.

SARAH ROSE SHARP,
NOVEMBER 2014

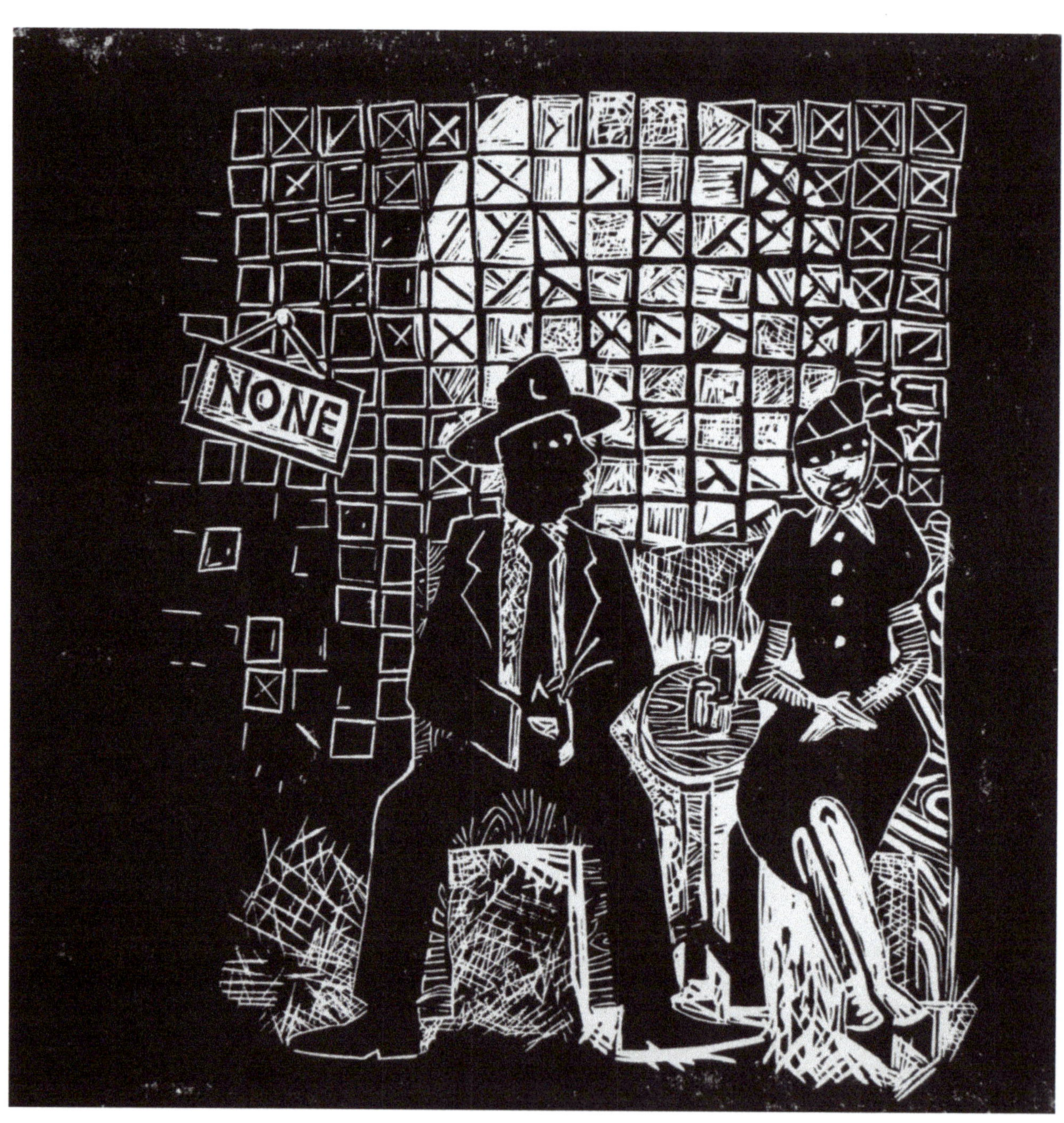

Waiting for My Change to Come. 2008. Linoleum block print, 12 x 12 in.

9 // CARL WILSON

Born Detroit, 1956
Lives in Hamtramck, Michigan

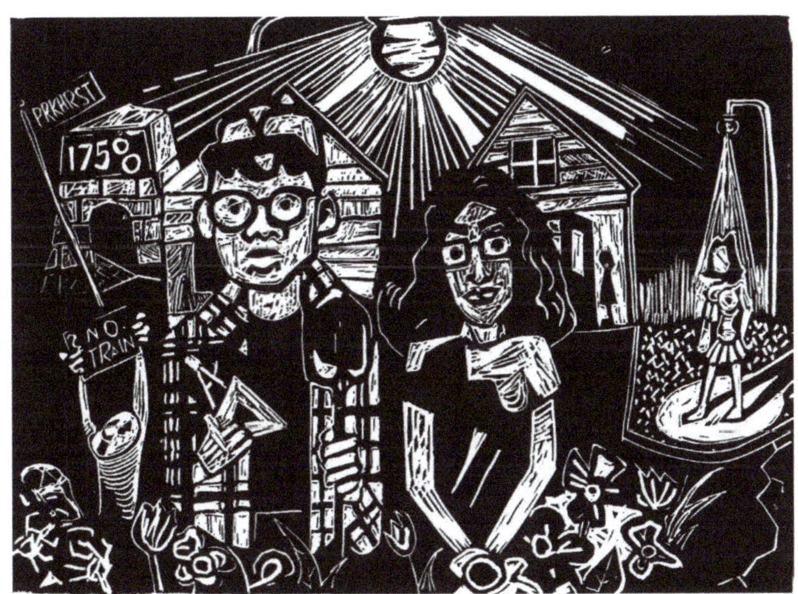

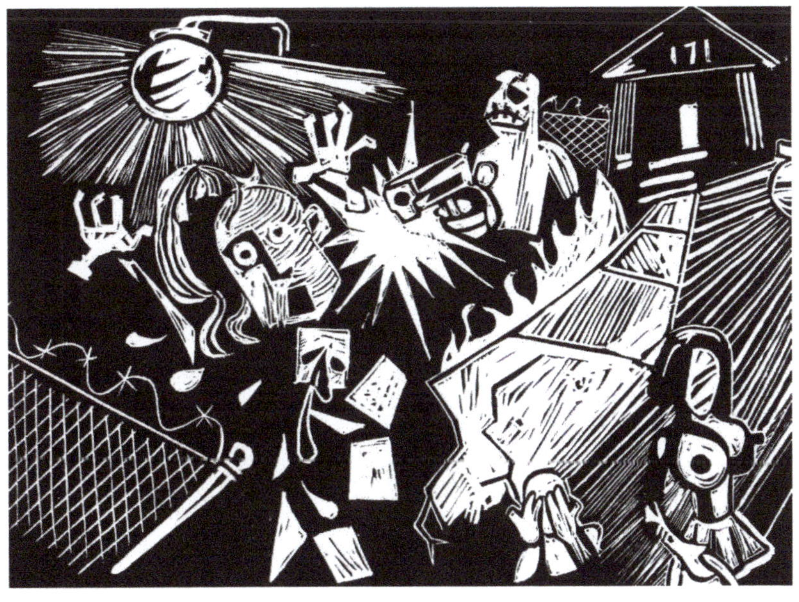

Carl Wilson's autobiographical print projects are clever, heartfelt, and often filled with self-deprecating humor, but most of all they show an artist with an exceptionally refined capacity to reflect unflinchingly on life, its pleasures and demons. To be sure, Wilson has seen more than his fair share of the latter: raised in humble and difficult circumstances on Detroit's east side, falling prey early in his life to a manipulative religious organization he calls "the cult," spending years breaking his health in automotive assembly plants, and then finally, after emerging from all these tribulations into a new phase of his life, suffering cancer and two years of total deafness. All this

(*Top*) *O Pioneers!* 2012. Relief print, 9 x 12 in.
(*Bottom*) *Coco Popped.* 2012. Linoleum block print, 9 x 12 in.

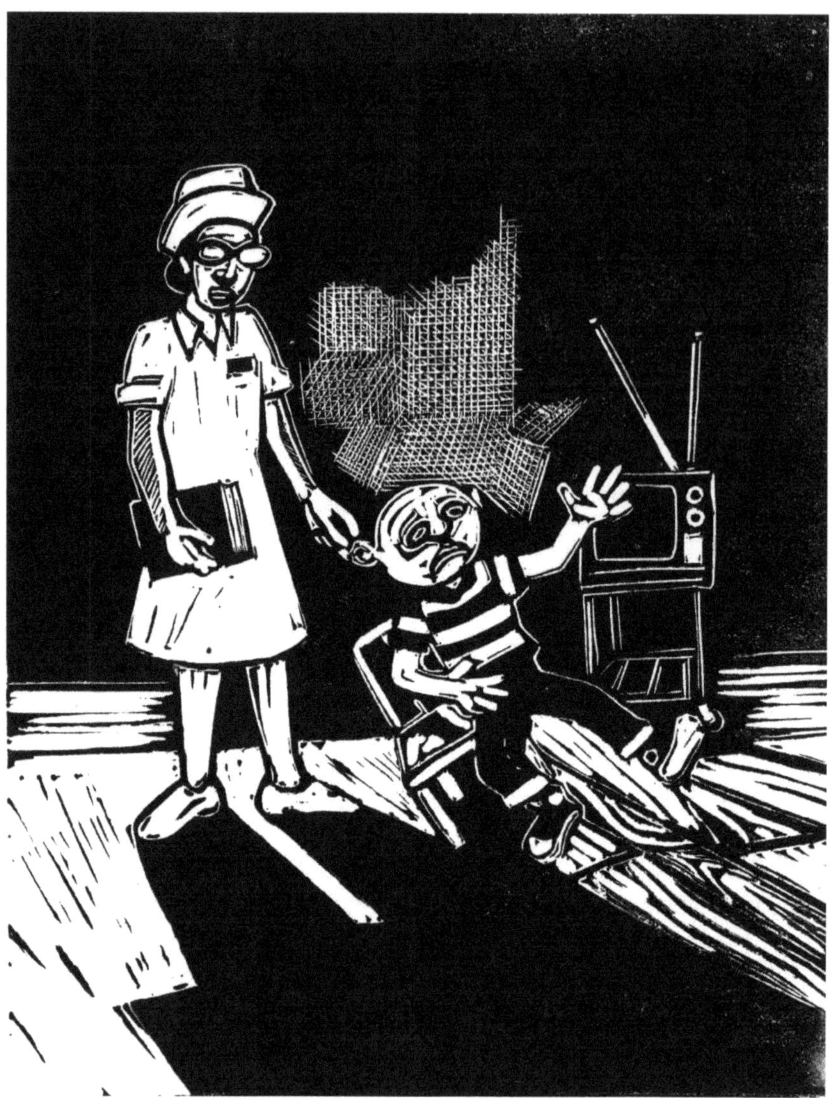

Boy, You Need Jesus. 2014. Linoleum block print, 12 x 9 in.

informs the story of a natural artist who, thanks in part to a timely buyout from Ford Motor Company, but more importantly the loving support of his new wife and emergence from the constraints of a stifling religion, decided late in life to devote himself full-time to his work. It also explains the apparently fearless way in which he opens himself up through his work—for after all these experiences, what more is there to worry about?

For an artist committed to working from a position of total emotional honesty, and without self-imposed boundaries, there is a fitting balance in choosing the medium of linocut, the inherent limitations of which force the artist to focus on the essence of the subject matter. That Wilson had a natural feel for this style of printing was obvious from the start, as an early work, ***Waiting for My Change to Come*** (2008), demonstrates. The woman in the print is Wilson's mother and the context is her being "let go" from a waitress job during the Depression because "good white women" needed the work. The body language speaks of a quiet dignity and Wilson's belief in his mother's commitment to "combating ignorance with excellence."

Wilson's first complete series of work in this medium was *The Parkhurst Papers*, based on the varied experience of living in the John R/Parkhurst neighborhood, an area that is home to much crime, especially prostitution, and a small community of artists and pioneering creative types. Wilson's prints look in a characteristically nonjudgmental way at both sides of the neighborhood. For example, ***Coco Popped*** (2012) is about the tragic murder of a transgender prostitute known to Wilson and his wife, and ***O Pioneers!*** (2012) is a humorous, but essentially generous, portrait

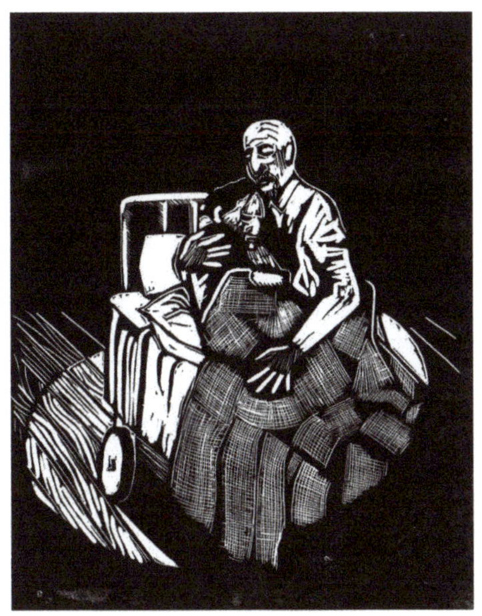

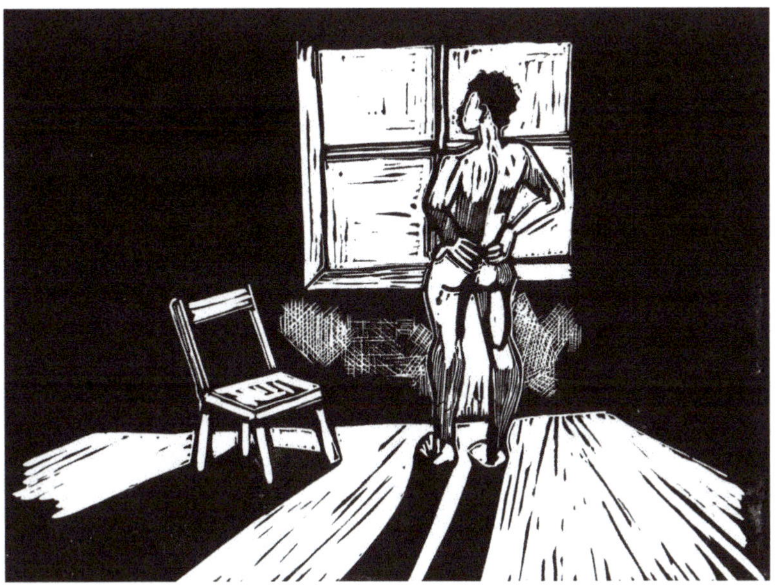

(*Left*) *Goodbye.* 2014. Linoleum block print, 12 x 9 in. (*Right*) *Burn.* 2014. Linoleum block print, 9 x 12 in.

of two prominent new residents. The series formed much of the basis on which Wilson was chosen as a 2013 Kresge Fellow, a significant achievement for a largely self-taught artist.

In the later series *Her Purse Smelled Like Juicy Fruit*, Wilson created a collection of prints based on the life of his mother, Louise Wilson. The prints (e.g., ***Boy, You Need Jesus*** and ***Goodbye***, both 2014) tell the story of a stoic and enigmatic woman working to raise a family with very little money and a husband diagnosed with paranoid schizophrenia. As a group, they tell the more universal story of a mature man looking back with love on his childhood relationship with his mother.

A current project, *The Killing Floor*, presents a more somber tone, befitting its examination of issues relating to cult-like religions and the destructive influence they exert on their followers. The print ***Burn*** (2014), with its naked female figure staring out at the world through the window of a sparse room, addresses Wilson's reflection on the relationship between the cult's repression of the sexual imagination of its members and corresponding feelings of low self-worth. In refining this emotionally complex subject into a printable composition, Wilson follows a sequence of experience, reflection, and conceptualization that is very similar to the experiential learning cycle many educationalists recognize as the foundation of deep learning. Ultimately this may be the core of Wilson's project: first to learn from his own experiences, then to encourage us to learn from ours.

STEVE PANTON, NOVEMBER 2014

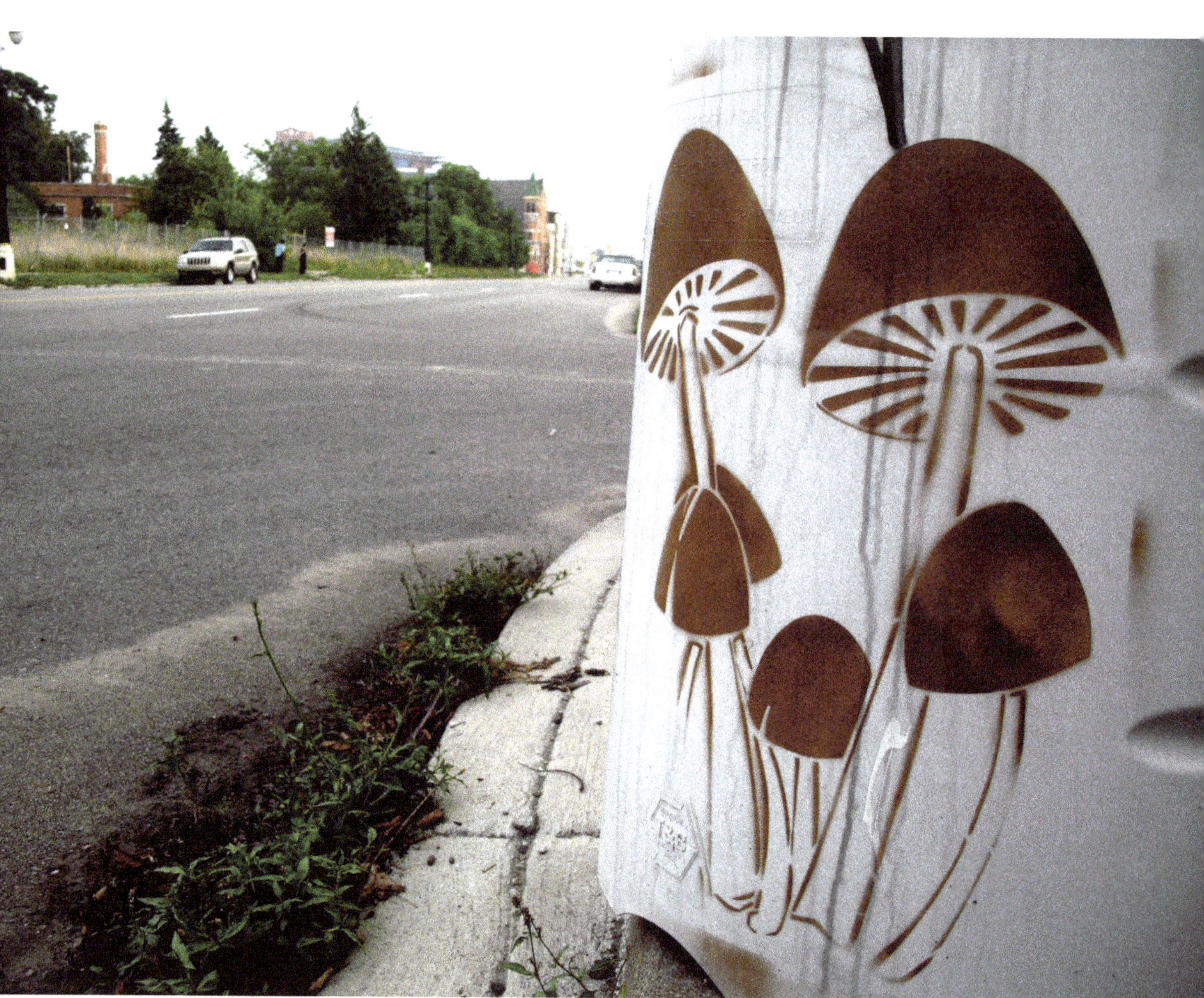

Brown Mushrooms. c. 2006. Spray paint.

10 // NICOLE MACDONALD

Born Detroit, 1978
BA, University of Michigan
Lives in Detroit

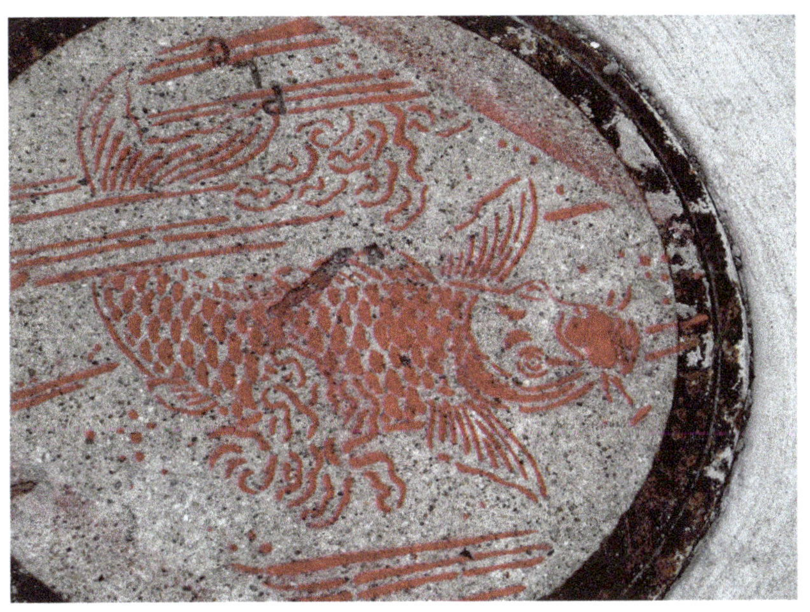

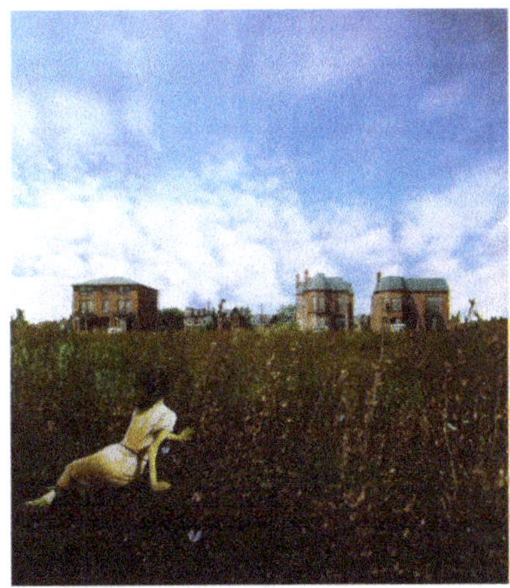

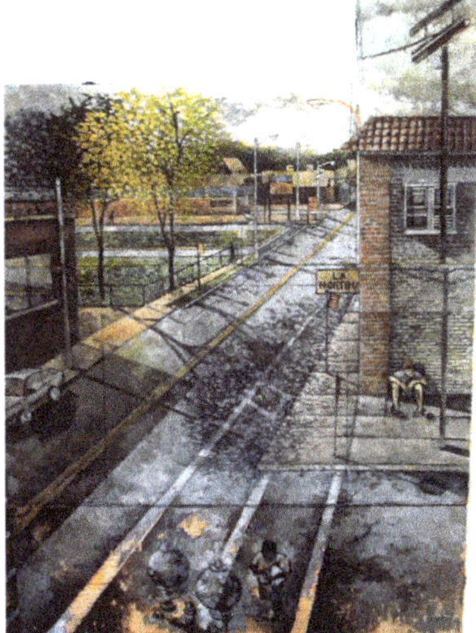

Detroit and its environs have been at the forefront of Nicole Macdonald's art since her natal street art forays in the late 1990s right up to her current, now seasoned pursuit of Motor City subjects. As filmmaker, tagger, collagist, painter, and muralist, her practice has segued from anonymous to public interventions, from local to national topics, and from inner to outward direction in subject, format, and ambition. Early on, for instance, to intrigue viewers, she described the imagery of her collages as "the best places you'll never see," whereas an expansive 2014 declaration professed: "The whole point is to reach people.

(*Top*) *Fish on Canfield*. c. 2006. Spray paint.
(*Bottom, left*) *Christina in Brush Park*. 2009. Paper collage, board, wood, 20 x 10 x 3 in.
(*Bottom, right*) *La Nortena*. c. 2003–4. Oil, cardboard, Masonite, wood, 48 x 30 in.

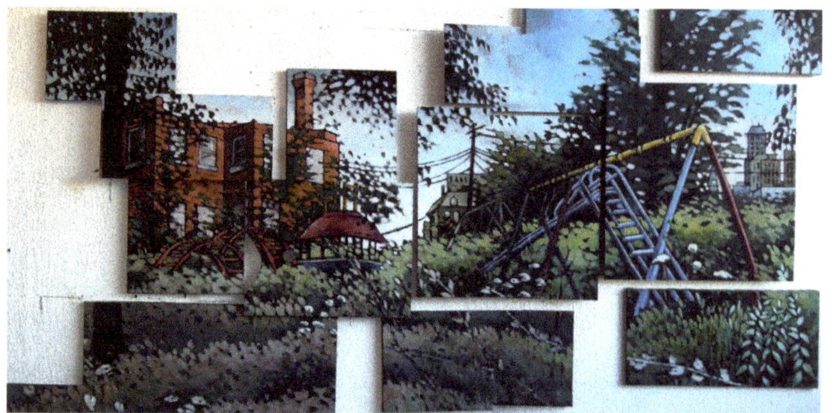

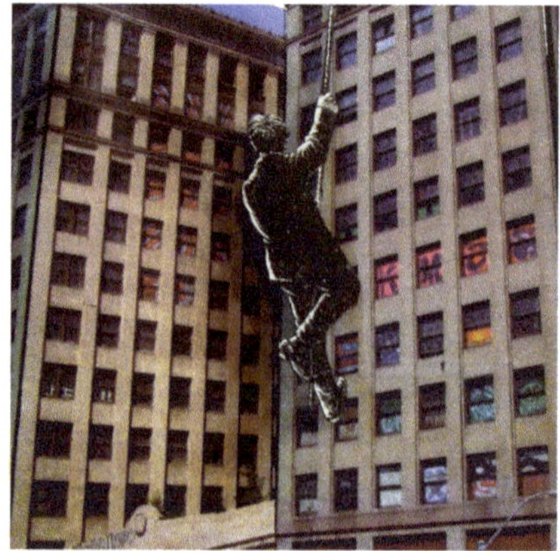

(*Left*) *Fourth Street Playground.* 2010. Oil, wood, canvas (fourteen panels), 5 x 8 ft. (*Right*) *Urban Explorer.* 2009. Paper collage, board, wood, 20 x 10 x 3 in.

I've done a lot of things where it's just for myself or a particular event. The intention [now] is I want all Detroiters to be interested and engaged."

Wherever one looks, then or now, one notes that Macdonald has always worked, as she says, from the "ground up," whether limning the streets, thoroughfares, streetscapes, neighborhoods, nature's rampant, omnivorous growth throughout the city, or—presently—Detroit's sung and unsung personalities. As such, she falls in with a determined corps of regional painters who have focused on the Motor City, each with a distinctive take on its environs: Taurus Burns, Darcel Deneau, Andy Krieger, Lisa Poszywak, Bryant Tillman, Clinton Snider.

For her part, Macdonald debuted her artistic and sociopolitical intentions via signature-free, hand-cut, spray-painted stencils in countless out-of-the-way locations across the D. Among her earliest images were clusters of mushrooms emerging from the bases of lampposts, red carp swimming across manhole covers, and cheery flowers eking out a life in crevices between sidewalk and concrete wall or moldy, battered lengths of plywood, all intended to ameliorate barren, blighted streetscapes (***Brown Mushrooms***, ***Fish on Canfield***, both 2006). Some of these "remedies to decay" remain in situ and visible, while many have been obscured, overpainted or effaced, and still others have faded or worn away.

Yet another clutch of Macdonald's pointed critiques draw upon the hoary tradition of collage, to which she applies a witty Detroit inflection. ***Christina in Brush Park*** (2009) cheekily appropriates and relocates Andrew Wyeth's iconic Christina to the Motor City, where she yearns longingly for a derelict, silhouetted-against-the-sky Brush Park mansion rather than her Maine farmhouse. In contrast, an intrepid, suited adventurer in ***Urban Explorer*** (2009) poises midrope as he stares admiringly at the Lafayette Building, one of the city's classic 1920s skyscrapers demolished in 2009. Concurrently, painted streetscapes, rendered in traditional oil on canvas or wood, also figure in Macdonald's oeuvre. Such examples as ***Fourth Street Playground*** (2010) and ***La Nortena*** (2003–4), whether executed on multiple or single canvases, are firmly and deftly brushed compositions. In the latter, the facile, fluent stroking counterpoints the emphatic diagonals that zoom the eye deep into the scene, while in the former

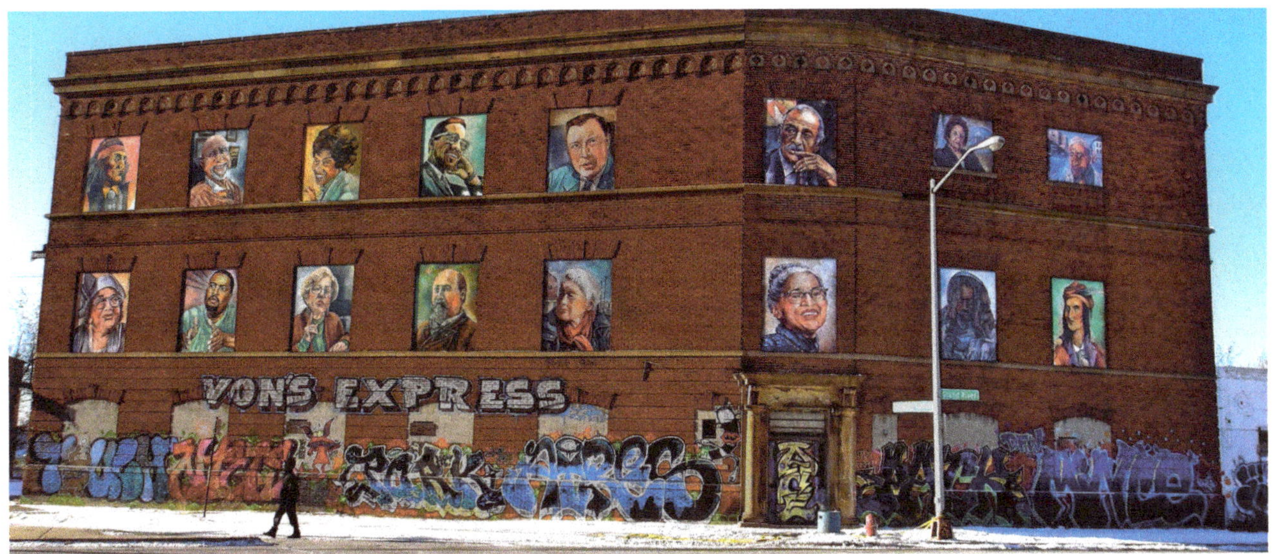

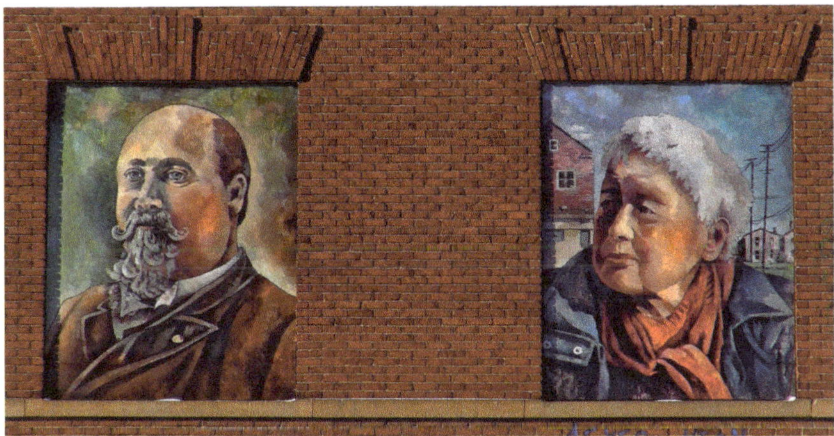

(Top) Detroit Portrait Series (sixteen portraits). 2014. Acrylic, wood, 10 x 7 ft. (7); 8 ½ x 10 ft. (7); 6 x 7 ft. (2). *(Left) Hazen Pingree, Grace Lee Boggs* (detail from *Detroit Portrait Series*). 2014. Acrylic, wood, 10 x 7 ft. (2).

the rhythmic dashes of pigment hurry the eye back and forth across the sprawl of stretchers.

But none of these multifarious directions quite prepare one for the Brobdingnagian portraits that Macdonald has unveiled of late. Titled the ***Detroit Portrait Series*** (2014–present), her tribe of sixteen heads takes on a totemic presence both in scale and persona. Each, rendered in acrylic on wood, stars an iconic Detroiter, a number internationally known, others not. Spurred by a reading of Howard Zinn's *A People's History of the United States*, she resolved to visualize her own people's "history." "Service, sacrifice, diversity, and struggle" were her core criteria for inclusion, personified by the vivid portrayals of ***Hazen Pingree***, Yusef Shakur, and ***Grace Lee Boggs*** standing beside the equally memorable John Conyers, Rosa Parks, and Malcolm X. Moreover, not content to simply portray these larger-than-life figures in isolation, Macdonald has taken her ever-expanding cast of characters on tour, having exhibited them thus far at Eastern Market, Cass Café, Central Methodist Church, and the "Big Painting at the Factory" show. Now—drumroll please—Macdonald's full complement of protagonists, one and all, are the new residents of the second and third floors of an unoccupied building on Grand River just north of I-94. Handsomely ensconced in sixteen windows along the facade of a solid, brick structure on the corner, their effigies gaze out at the passing parade, shining forth as salutary beacons for the citizenry of Detroit.

DENNIS ALAN NAWROCKI,
NOVEMBER 2014

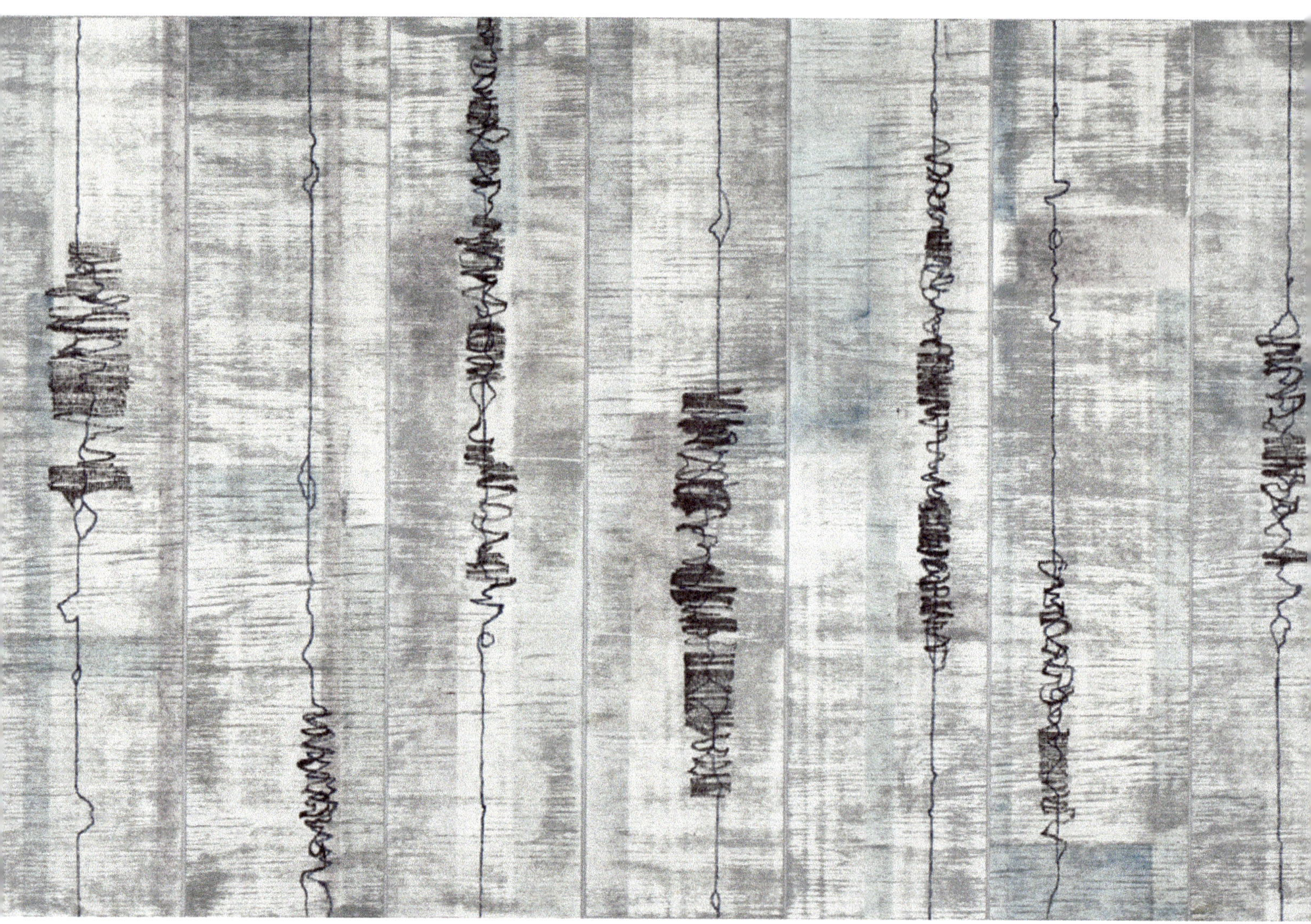

Winter. 2010. Relief printing, typing, pochoir, 36 x 54 in.
Photography by R. H. Hensleigh.

11 // LYNNE AVADENKA

Born Pontiac, Michigan, 1955
BFA, MFA, Wayne State University
Lives in Huntington Woods, Michigan

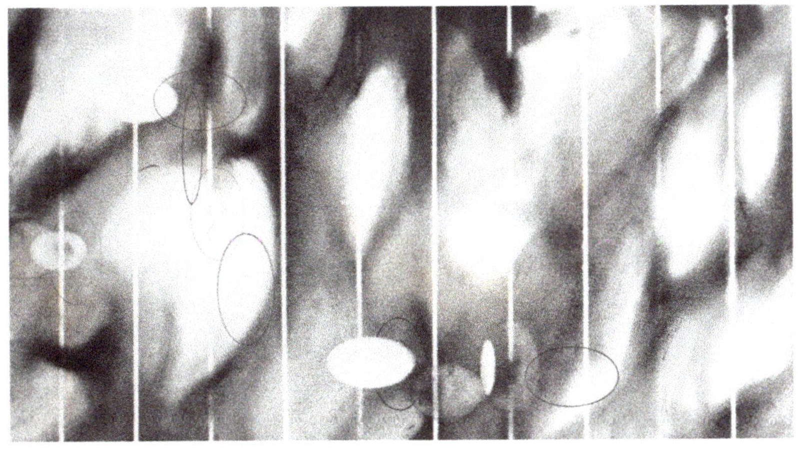

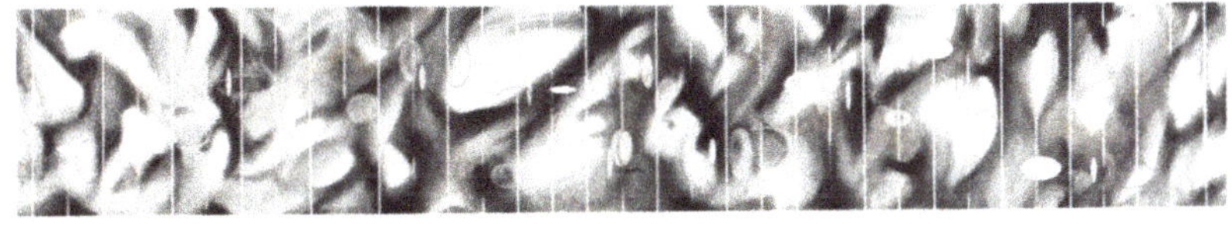

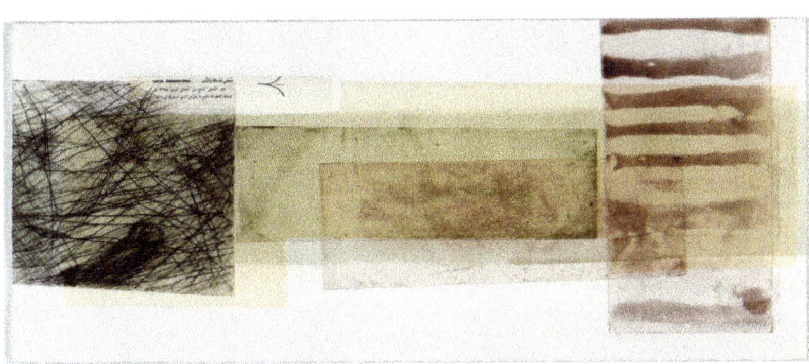

"Typography is what language looks like," says a letterpress sign hanging in Lynne Avadenka's expansive studio space, which houses the letterpress equipment, flat files, and giant cutting tables that facilitate her work of book arts and printmaking. The visualization of language is of course a key issue for an artist who deals in typesetting as an elemental force in her work, but not more so than content, Avadenka stresses, and neither more so than the exploration of the marks made available by relief printmaking. Indeed, any

(*Top*) *A Season* (detail). 2010. Powdered graphite, paint, paper, 21 x 80 in. Photography by R. H. Hensleigh.

(*Middle*) *A Season*. 2010. Powdered graphite, paint, paper, 21 x 80 in. Photography by R. H. Hensleigh.

(*Bottom*) *The Reunion of Broken Parts*. 2011. Intaglio monoprint with chine collé, 11 x 26 in. Photography by R. H. Hensleigh.

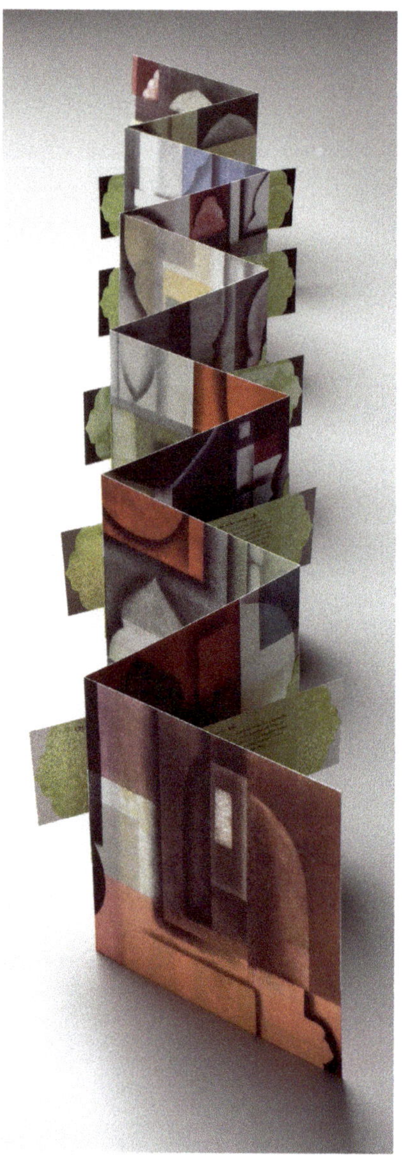

By a Thread. 2006. Offset lithography, die-cutting, 8 x 60 in. Photography by R. H. Hensleigh.

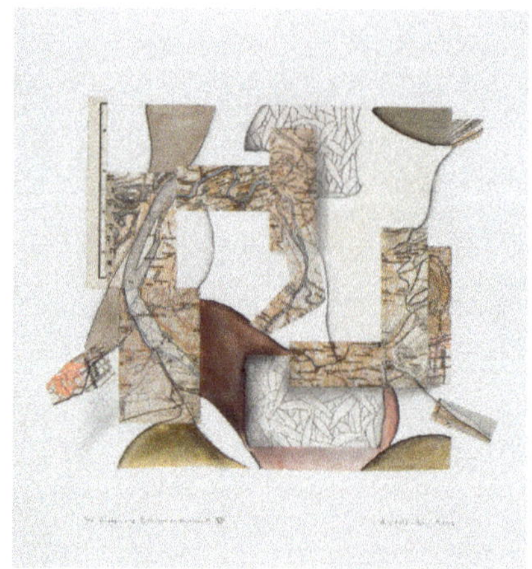

The Distance between Monuments. 2006. Drawing, collage, 11 ½ x 16 ½ in. Photography by R. H. Hensleigh.

given work by Avadenka may fall somewhere slightly different on a Venn diagram designating the intersection of language (content), design, and physical impact.

For her part, Avadenka is both meticulous and freewheeling in her exploration of these elements, emphasizing that her mastery of book- and printmaking as arts—which she has taught at WSU, CCS, Penland School of Crafts, Center for Book Arts in New York, and Dartmouth—in no way eliminates the possibility of surprises. Her interest in printmaking lies not in replication for its own sake, but as a mechanism to explore the specific graphic qualities that emerge through working into the metal or wood substrate.

If typography is what language looks like, then surely ***By a Thread*** (2006) is very much what a conversation would look like if you managed to translate it into a physical object. The conversation in this case is between Scheherazade, mythic Persian queen and storyteller of *One Thousand and One Nights*, and Esther, Jewish queen in the Old Testament's book of Esther. The exchange of the conversation is facilitated by the offset binding, which draws you through the conversation in one direction, then back through in reverse.

This points to one of Avadenka's major sources: an exploration of Jewish identity, through examination of the Old Testament text (language/content), employment of Hebrew type (design), and multiple visits and artist residencies in Europe and Israel, which have resulted in the incorporation of found artifacts in prints or collages (physical impact). A second theme that appears across a wide range of works is the use of ovals, deployed graphically, symbolically (to represent loss), or alphabetically. In the latter case, ***A Season*** (2010) lays out the text of the Old Testament's book of Ecclesiastes with ovals employed as the typeface, applied manually over an inchoate background of powdered graphite, another of Avadenka's dearest mediums.

Looking over a wide cross section of Avadenka's work, which includes dozens of original book editions, one-offs, and prints, one gets the sense of wonder at the tools in her arsenal. Nothing

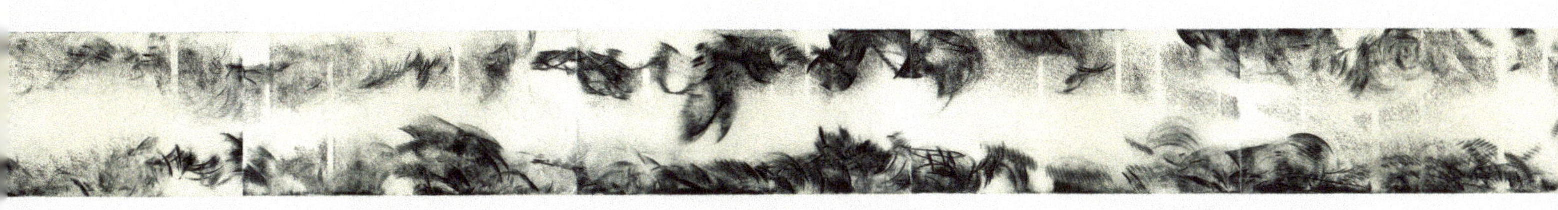

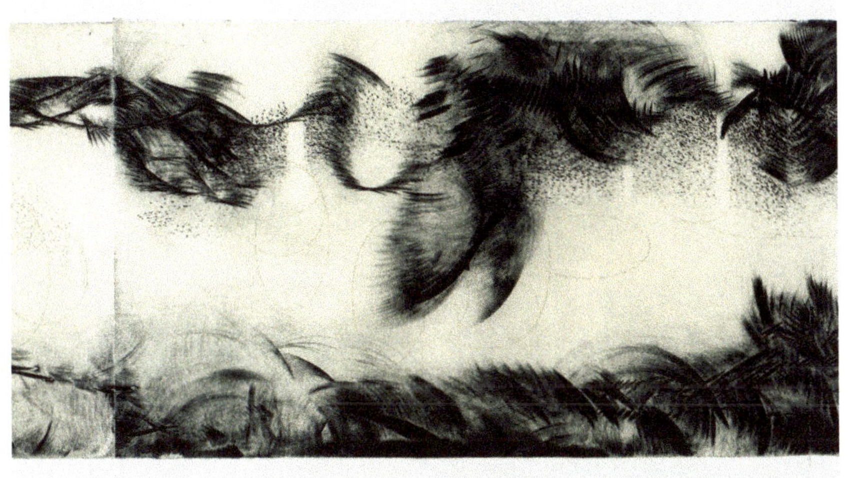

(*Top*) *After Jabès.* 2013. Intaglio monoprint with chine collé, letterpress, 19 x 120 in. Photography by R. H. Hensleigh.

(*Left*) *After Jabès* (detail). 2013. Intaglio monoprint with chine collé, letterpress, 19 x 120 in. Photography by R. H. Hensleigh.

is off limits in her practice. A series of collages, with a graphic nod to Russian constructivism, can be shuffled and deployed in an order both random and utterly interrelated, like a deck of cards. A stunning ***four-season series*** (2010) employs a Japanese rubbing technique (Japanese print and folding screens being a second cultural wellspring for Avadenka's sometimes quite minimalist aesthetic) to transfer the pattern of a piece of birch bark onto four sets of seven trees, each overlaid with color to reflect the four seasons and adorned with an abstracted run of text, again from Ecclesiastes. ***The Reunion of Broken Parts*** (2011), a series of monoprints that incorporate *chine collé*, found Avadenka dissecting an Arabic text on algebra, juxtaposing definitions of precise mathematical concepts with abstracted backgrounds. ***The Distance between Monuments*** (2006) is a drawing and collage made from slicing and recombining maps from a text that laid out monuments in Germany. The large-scale interconnected prints ***After Jabès*** (2013) utilize such a wide range of mark-making that they come to resemble the effect of twin blackbirds dissolving physically into the page through a feat of avian histrionics.

With such a diverse spread of interests, one suspects that Avadenka's professional position as artistic director of the community letterpress printshop Signal Return is merely a gambit to gain more access to additional printing techniques. But in reality, this position fits perfectly with Avadenka's clear mission to utilize multitudinous approaches in capturing not just what language looks like but the very boundaries of physical space and communication—especially between cultures—when captured on paper.

SARAH ROSE SHARP,
FEBRUARY 2015

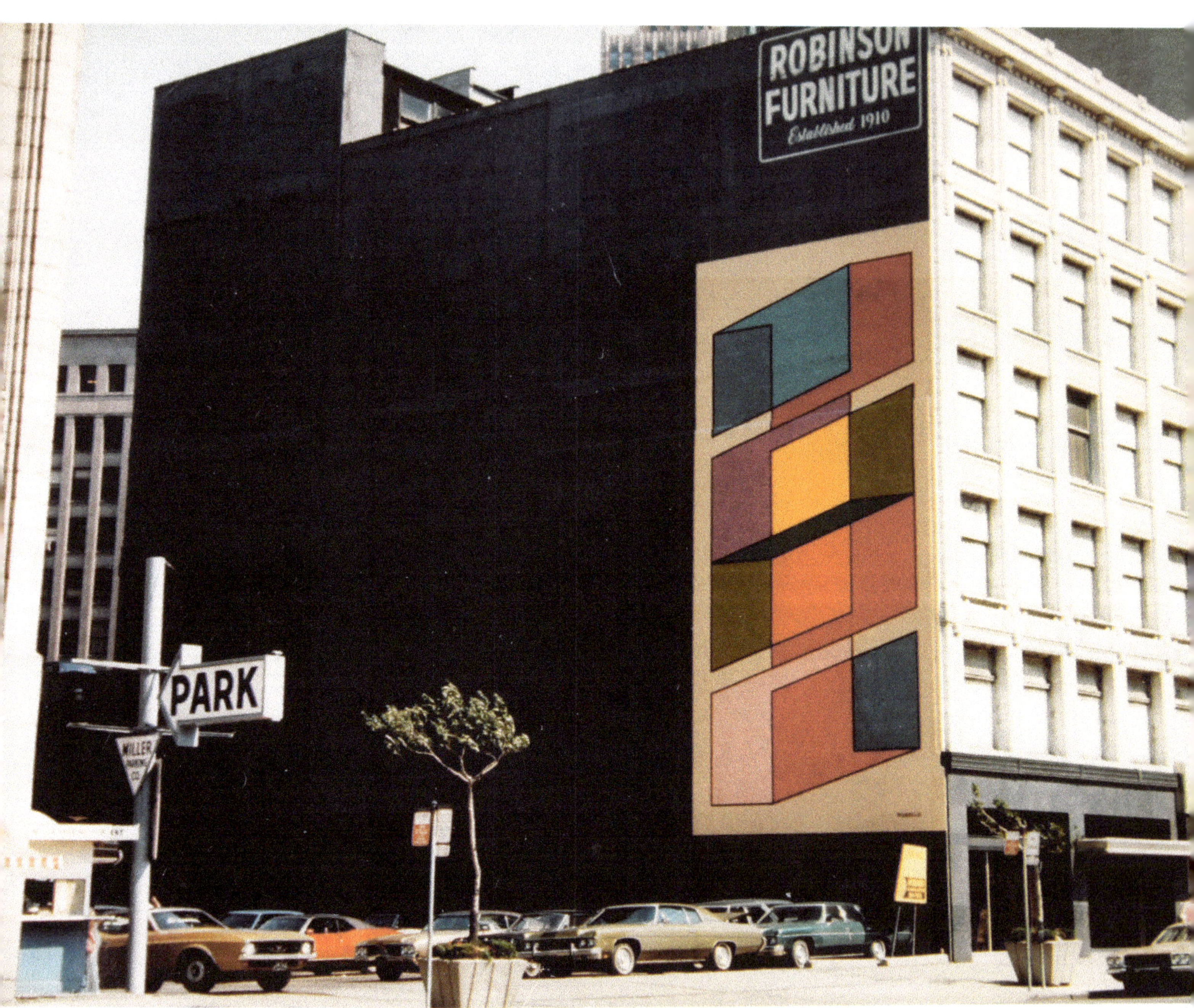

Color Cubes. 1973 (painted over 2014). Mural, 50 x 25 ft.

12 // DAVID RUBELLO

Born Detroit, 1935
BFA, Accademia di Belle Arti di Roma
MFA, University of Michigan
Lives in Ray, Michigan, and Palm Coast, Florida

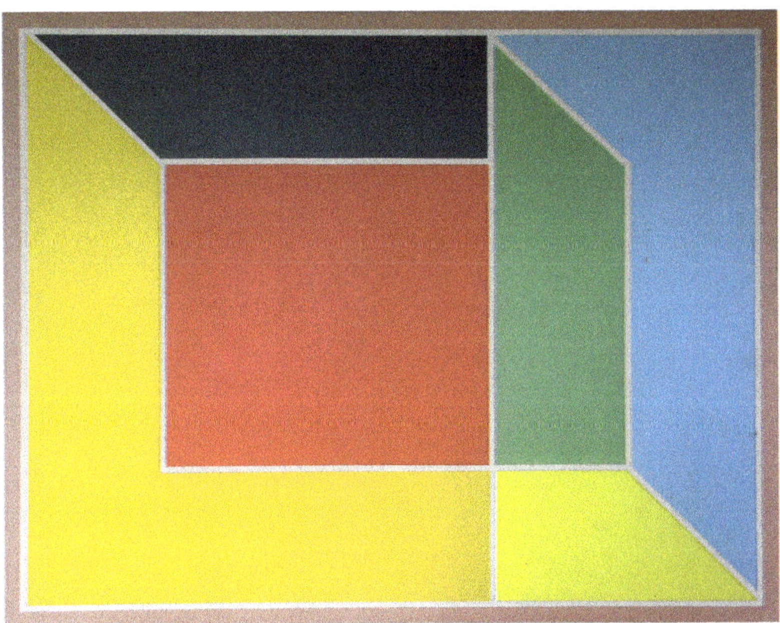

Room. 1970. Acrylic on canvas, 24 x 30 in. Photography by Matthew Piper.

If there are tendencies that unite what is categorically understood as "Detroit art" in the late twentieth and early twenty-first centuries, the two- and three-dimensional paintings of David Rubello stand outside of them. If Detroit art is messy, Rubello's is meticulous. If Detroit art tends toward representation, Rubello's insists on abstraction. If Detroit art is a reflexive interrogation of the postindustrial condition, Rubello's formalist paintings exist in an idealized, apolitical, and ageographic universe of pure visuality, where form is content and content simply form.

Yet Rubello is a Detroit artist, and by folding him into that category, the category itself becomes enlarged, becomes more clearly connected to aesthetic traditions, both classical and modern, that continue to

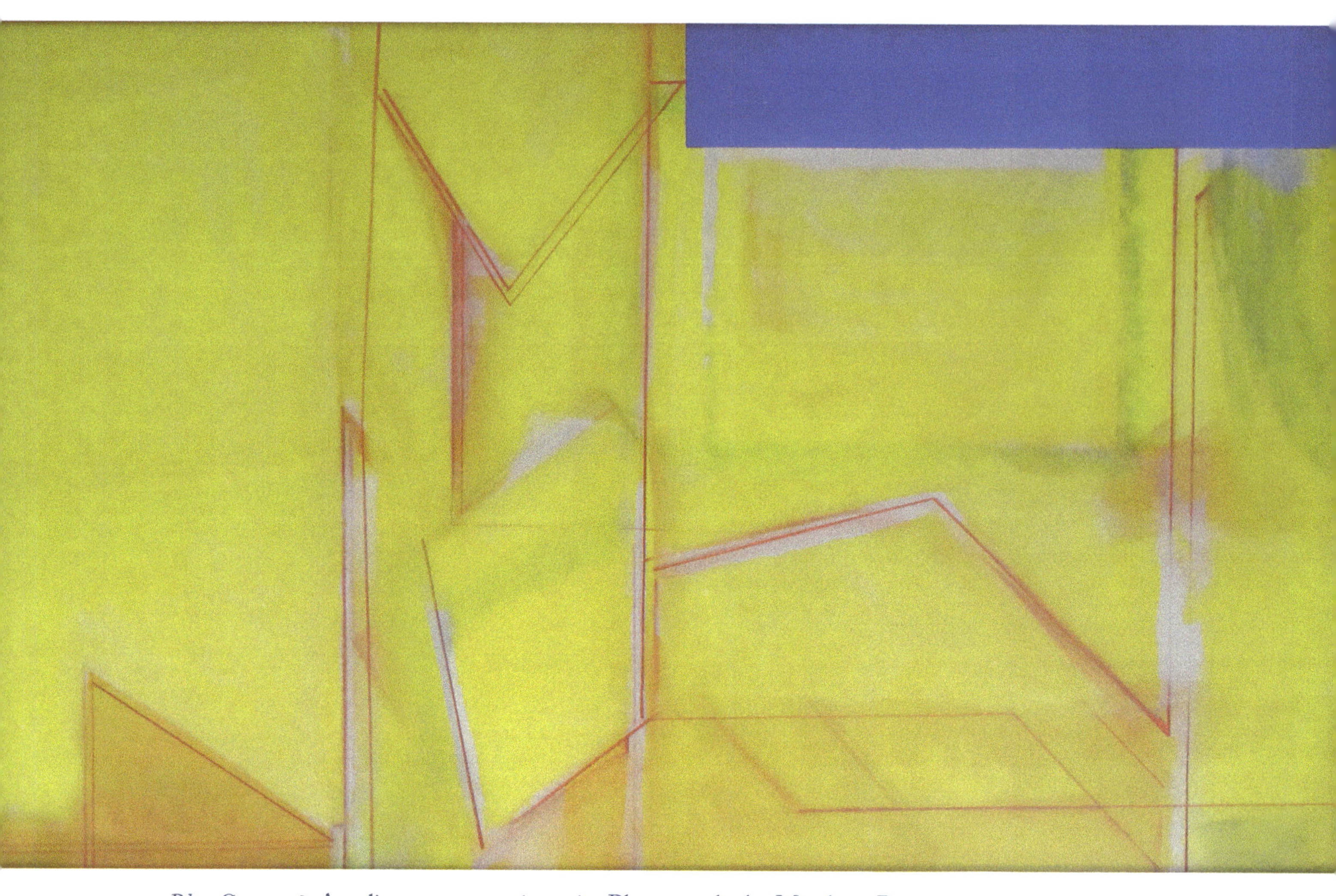

Blue Cut. 1978. Acrylic on canvas, 36 x 55 in. Photography by Matthew Piper.

inform art and design worldwide. Since the late 1960s, he has experimented with line, shape, color, and perspective in an expansive, evolving body of work that retains an essential precision and verve even as it charts new territory in geometric abstraction, dimensionality, and interactivity.

Rubello's formal art education began in Detroit in the 1950s at Cass Technical High School and at the Detroit Society of Arts and Crafts (now the College for Creative Studies), where he studied under local luminaries Guy Palazzola and Sarkis Sarkisian. His postsecondary studies in Europe, meanwhile, had a powerful and lasting influence on his vision. As a figurative painter at the Academy of Fine Art in Rome in the late fifties and early sixties, Rubello encountered ancient, illusionistic experiments with perception and Renaissance innovations in perspective that would significantly inform his later, abstract works. After academic dabbling in nascent genres like pop art and action painting, Rubello turned decisively toward geometric abstraction under the tutelage of Richard Mortensen at the Royal Academy of Fine Arts in Copenhagen in the midsixties.

Rubello's most well-known work, the iconic fifty-by-twenty-five-foot mural ***Color Cubes***, painted on a downtown Detroit high-rise in 1973 and painted over in 2014, was representative of the idiosyncratic approach to geometric abstraction that he refined at the University of Michigan in the early seventies. Like *Color Cubes*, his hard-edge acrylic paintings and screen prints of the time tend toward bold, saturated coloring and a deceptive, superficial clarity, but, upon closer examination, they engross the viewer in an illusionistic interplay between two- and three-dimensionality—see ***Room*** (1970). The result is a kind of pop "geometric surrealism," to borrow a phrase from art historian Werner Spies.

In the late seventies, after a return trip to Rome to continue his study of perspective, Rubello's art took another decisive turn: ***Blue Cut*** (1978) was the first work he made with the idea that his paintings should "come out from the wall." In that piece, he achieves this effect two-dimensionally, by juxtaposing two distinct, seemingly unrelated picture planes in the same work. It is perhaps inevitable that just a few years later, Rubello would begin a now decades-long exploration of abstract work in three dimensions, typified by more recent pieces like ***Foyel*** (1999), ***Flag*** (2007), and ***Intruder*** (2010), sculptural paintings that escape the confines of two-dimensionality in order to literally share space with the viewer.

Rubello never entirely gave up painting in two dimensions. (Nowadays, he tends to construct his three-dimensional paintings, made of wood and acrylic, in his

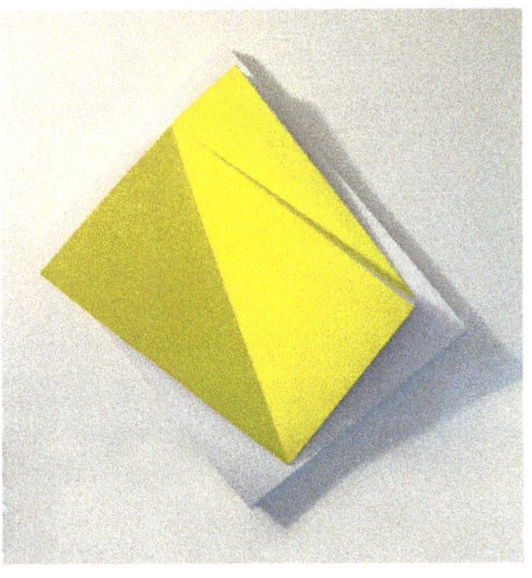

Foyel. 1999. Acrylic on wood, 23 x 23 x 4 in. Photography by Matthew Piper.

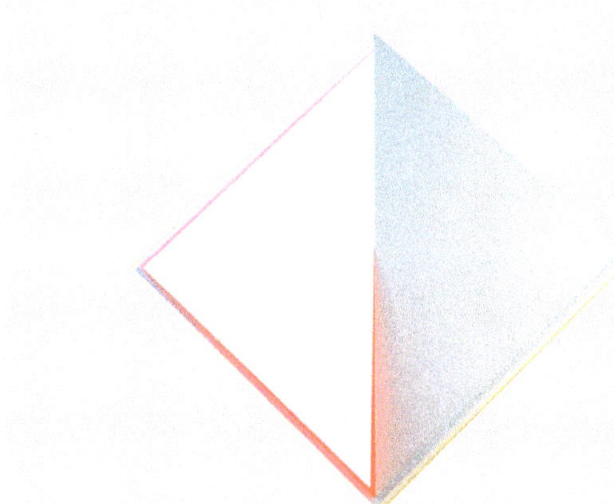

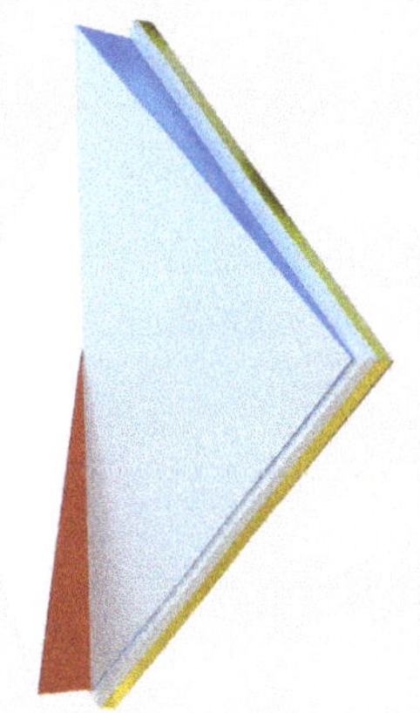

(Left and Right) Flag. 2007. Acrylic on wood, 34 x 34 x 3 in. Photography by Matthew Piper.

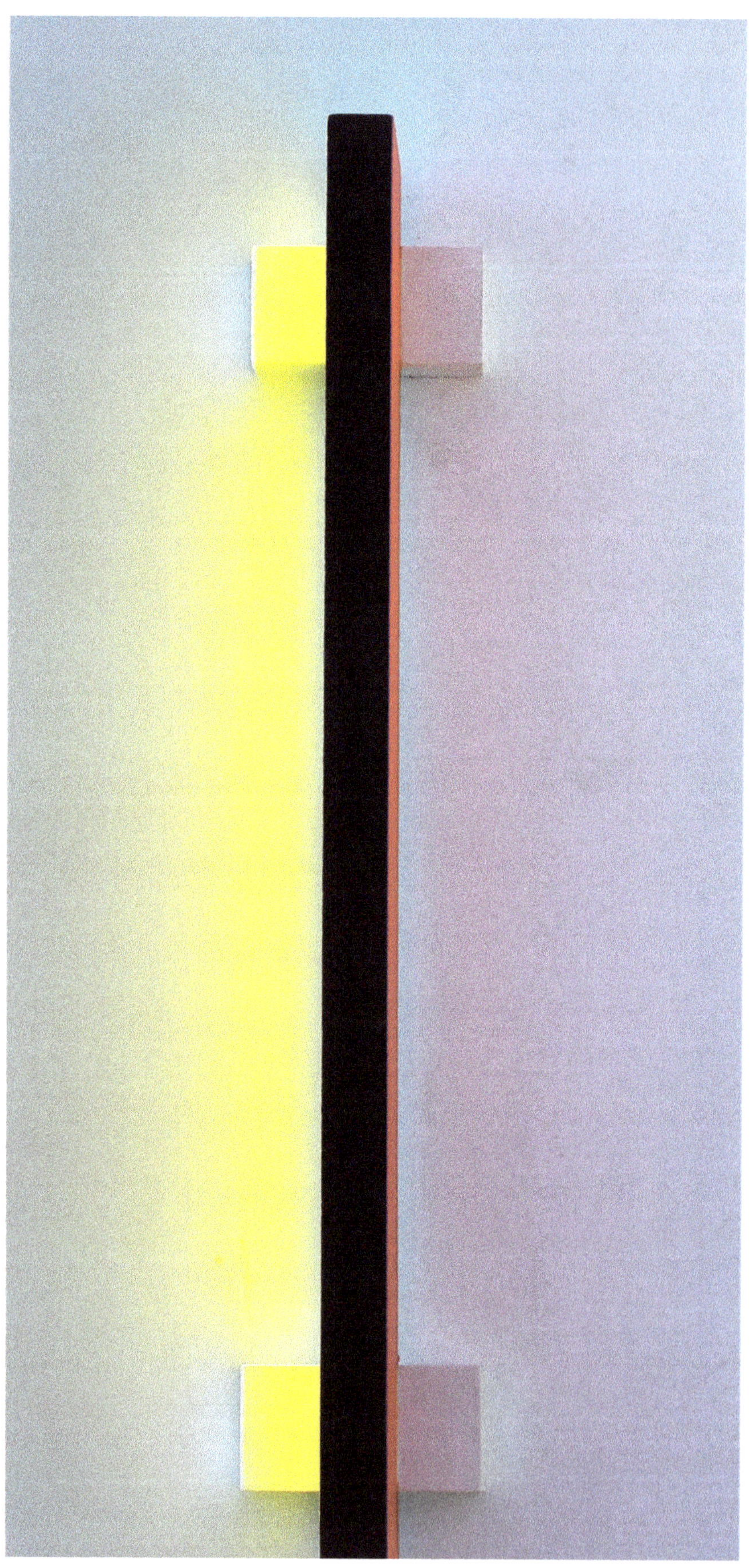

Michigan studio and paint on canvas while wintering in Florida.) But his three-dimensional work forever changed the direction of his art by opening up new opportunities for formal experimentation, perceptual play, and interactivity. It is as a result of working in three dimensions that he began to explore the idea of "reflected color," by which a richly colored surface, often imperceptible from certain vantage points, is oriented very near and at a right angle to a white surface, casting a subtle, colored shadow upon the latter. And it is through his three-dimensional explorations that Rubello came to his distinctive "movables," kinetic paintings that incorporate one or more movable parts, allowing for variable configurations. (See, for example, ***Yellow Ribbons***, 2012.) "My desire," Rubello says, "has always been to include the viewer, because painting as it stands is always something that you're just looking at. And I thought, wouldn't it be interesting if, instead of just looking at it, you became part of it?"

MATTHEW PIPER, FEBRUARY 2015

Intruder. 2007. Acrylic on wood, 24 x 16 in. Photography by Matthew Piper.

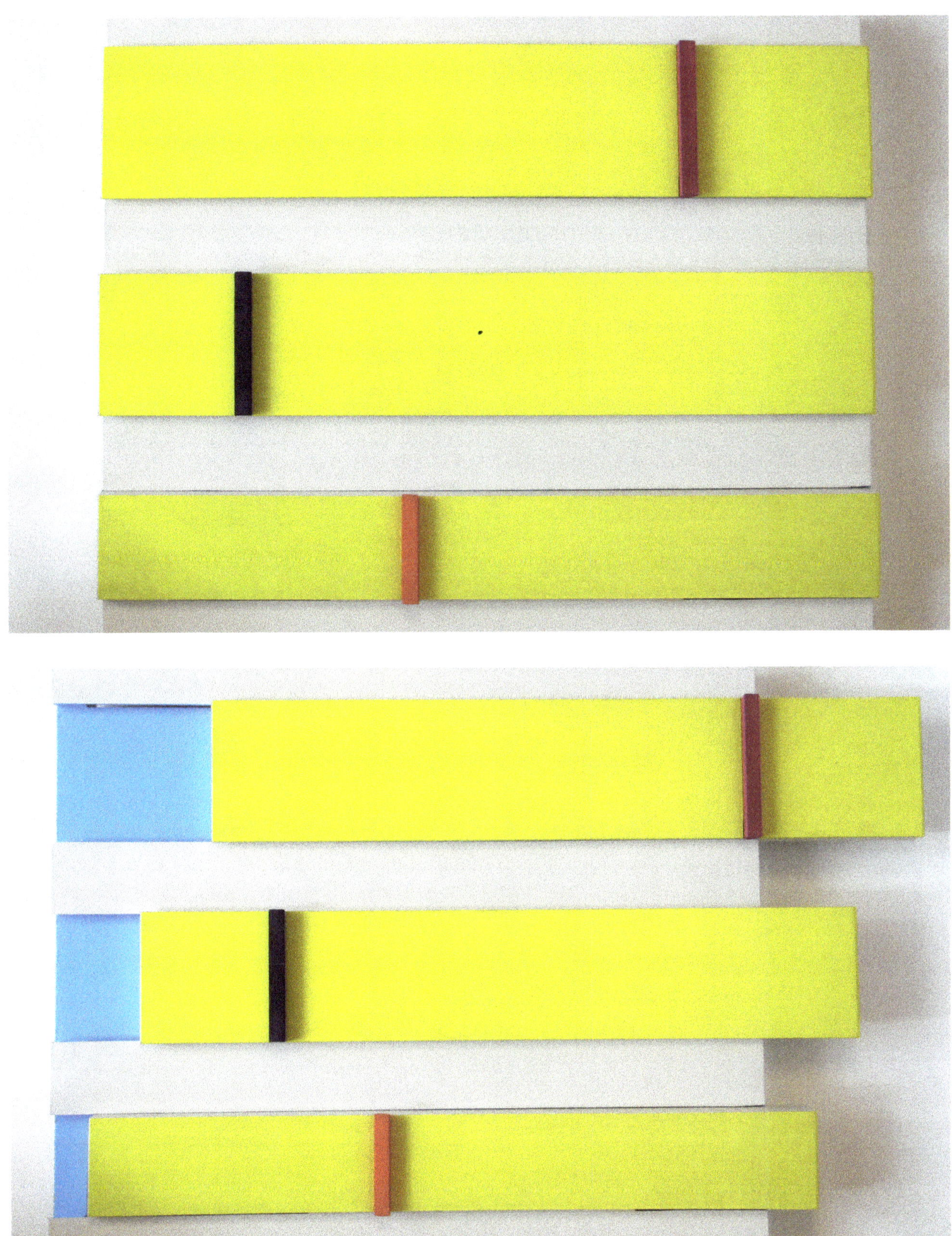

Yellow Ribbons. 2012. Acrylic on wood. Dimensions variable. Photography by Matthew Piper.

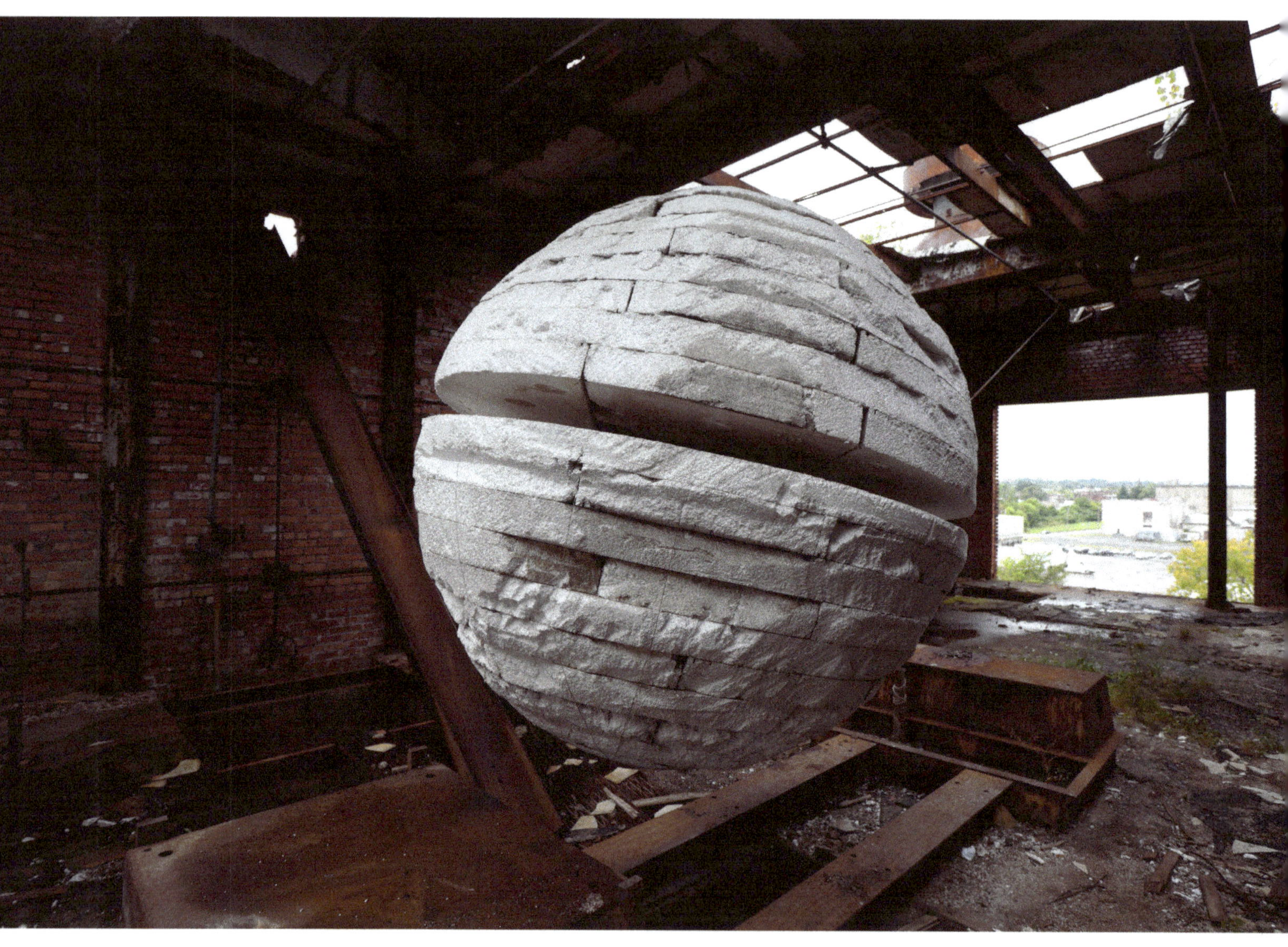

Sisyphus and the Voice of Space. 2010. Site-specific installation and photographs using discarded polystyrene / photographic documentation. Image courtesy of the artist and Susanne Hilberry Gallery.

13 // SCOTT HOCKING

Born Redford, Michigan, 1975
BFA, College for Creative Studies
Lives in Detroit

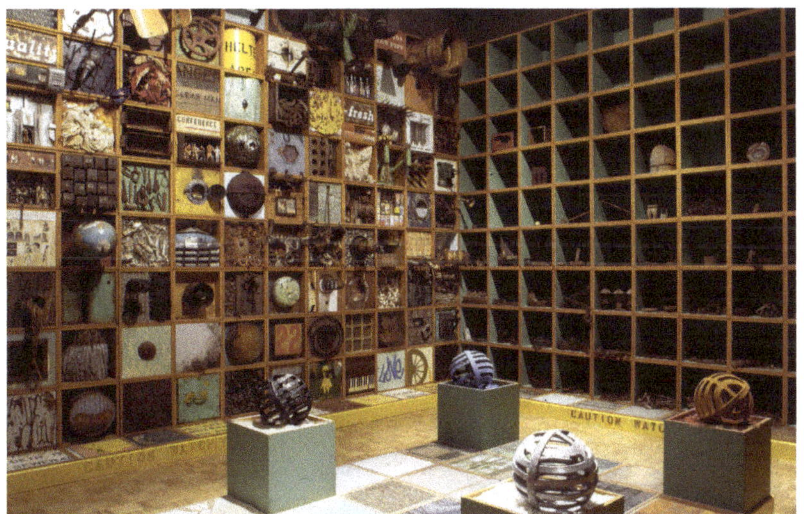

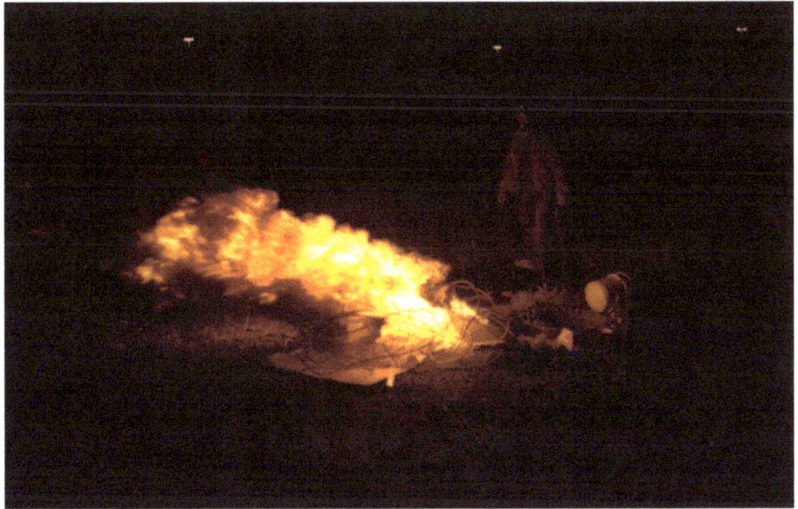

If James Brown was the hardest working man in show business, Scott Hocking is arguably the hardest working artist in Detroit. Even a virtual trip through the monumental site-specific installations, photographic studies, and gallery projects on his website is an exhausting business. But hard work can only get you so far, and doesn't by itself explain how Hocking, alongside contemporaries such as Clinton Snider and Mitch Cope, has managed to develop an international practice based in, and often quite literally on, the city of Detroit.

(*Top*) *Relics,* southeast view of installation, Detroit Institute of Arts. 2001. Mixed-media installation. Image courtesy of the artist and Susanne Hilberry Gallery.

(*Bottom*) *Country Boy's Fire,* from the project *Scrappers.* 2000–4. Image courtesy of the artist and Susanne Hilberry Gallery.

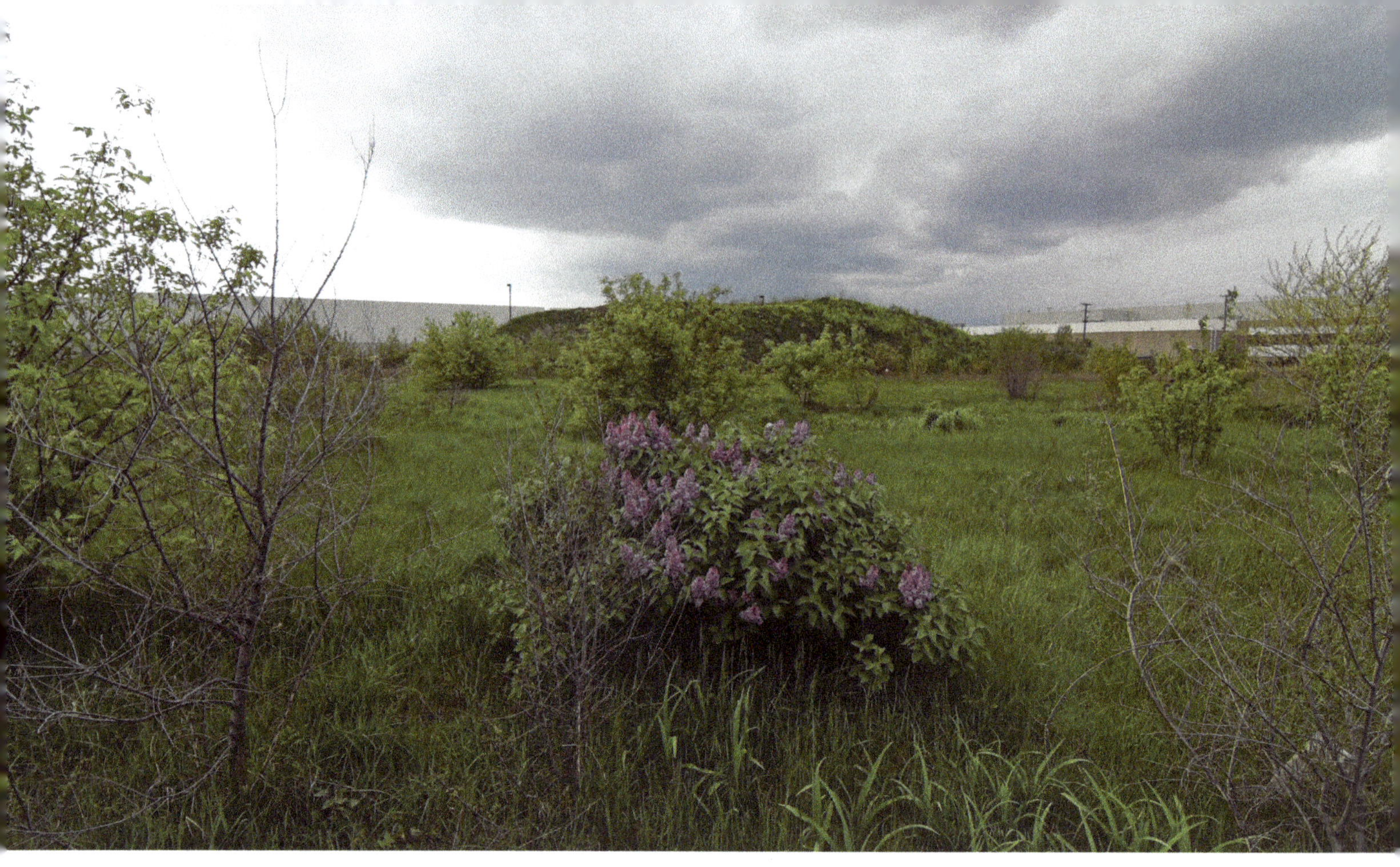

Lilac, from the photography series *The Zone*. 1999–2015. Image courtesy of the artist and Susanne Hilberry Gallery.

Hocking shot to prominence in 2001 with ***Relics***, a collaboration with Snider that was first shown in a prestigious exhibition to celebrate the city's tricentenary. Comprised of hundreds of purpose-built wooden boxes containing thousands of everyday objects recovered from the city, it established many of the recurring themes in Hocking's work. These include the tension between the symbolic qualities of the objects and their former functional properties, an exploration of the ambiguous relationship between permanence and transience, a rigorously experiential approach to history, and a pseudo-museum-like display that either epitomized, or parodied, an anthropological picking over of the city's bones. The installation included both industrial and personal artifacts, but was centered on the industrial. The dominant color was a factory green and the dominant surface finish was rust. Formulating the installation around identically sized boxes allowed it to be redisplayed and/or sold in different configurations, but also nodded to commodification and interchangeable manufacturing, two key concepts from the culture that generated the relics.

Scrappers (2000–4) and ***The Zone*** (1999–2015) are Hocking's most obviously documentary works. *Scrappers* is a photographic series on the reality of the scrap-metal industry and the lives of some homeless men who scrap to survive. *The Zone* is a long-term study of a former residential area that is being progressively cleared to make way for an industrial "Renaissance Zone." The term "cleared"

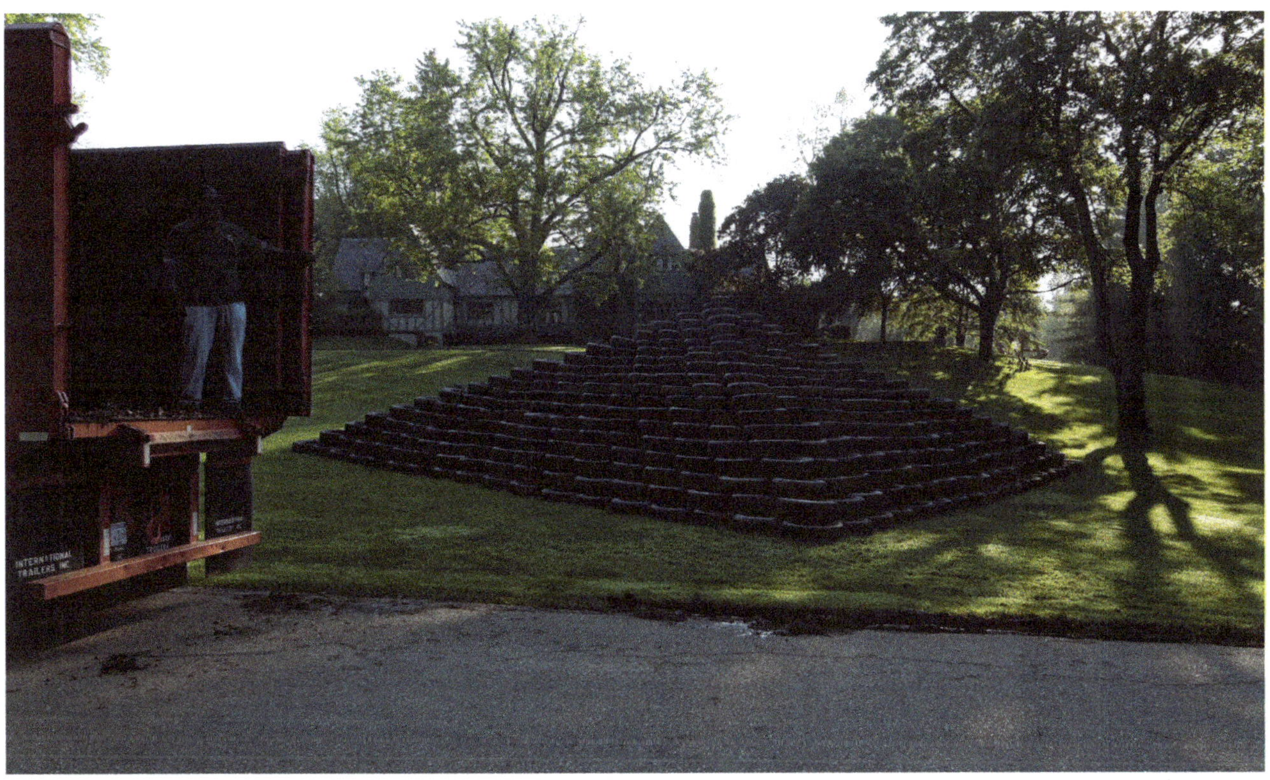

(Right) Tire Pyramid, Recycling Morning. 2006. Site-specific installation of illegally dumped tires. Image courtesy of the artist and Susanne Hilberry Gallery.

is important in comparison to "cleaned," a more expensive process necessary for a former industrial site. These two projects in conjunction with ***Tire Pyramid*** (2006)—which is simultaneously a temporary art piece on the lawn of a hyperwealthy Detroit art patron and an investigation of the economics of tire dumping/recycling—show Hocking's keen awareness of the interactions between micro-/macroeconomic forces, social structures, and the physical environment of the city.

Both *Tire Pyramid* and *The Zone* (a reference to Andrei Tarkovsky's eerie 1979 film *Stalker*) point to an interest in more universal themes. This is continued in site-specific works such as ***Garden of the Gods*** (2009–11), ***The Egg*** (2007–13), ***Sisyphus and the Voice of Space*** (2010), and especially ***Ziggurat and Fisher Body 21*** (2007–9). In these works Hocking strikingly juxtaposes classical forms and mythology with Detroit's surreal postindustrial landscape. The resulting images are ambiguous; are they mnemonic devices intended to tap into some collective unconscious, a commentary on the almost mythic scale of devastation in the city, or harbingers of some civilization yet to arrive? Hocking is reluctant to give the viewer easy answers, talking only of the richness of his personal experiences in executing the work and a desire to reintroduce a sense of mystery to the world.

Hocking's 2012 gallery installation ***Mercury Retrograde*** is comprised of a 1955 Mercury Monterey, around three hundred taxidermy animals in diorama cases, and various materials, most notably salt. It

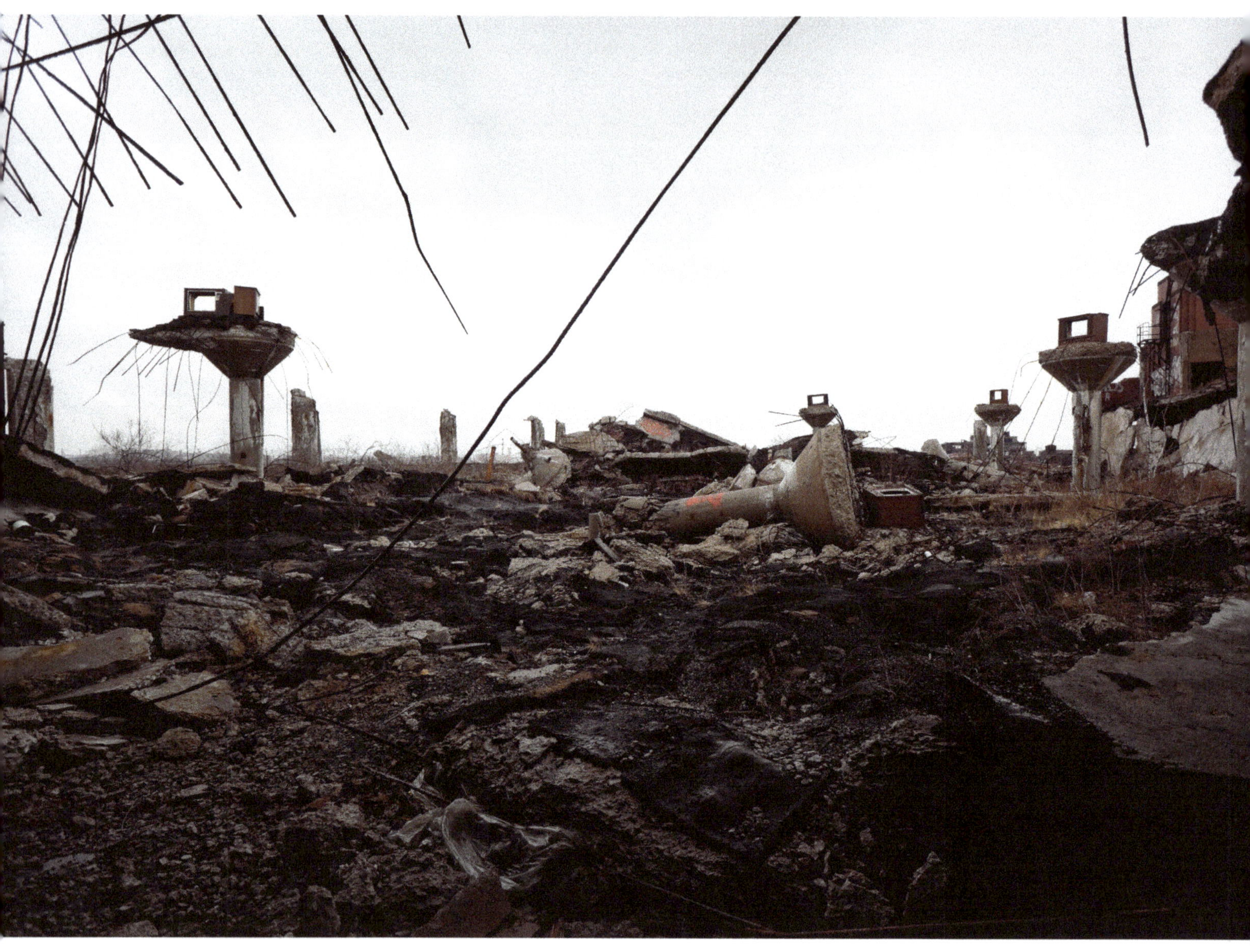

Garden of the Gods, North, Winter, from *Garden of the Gods.* 2009–11. Site-specific installation / photographic documentation. Image courtesy of the artist and Susanne Hilberry Gallery.

is an interesting comparison to his breakout 2001 collaboration *Relics*. The Mercury of the astrologically charged title refers to both the ubiquitous historical object at the center of the show and the mythical winged messenger. Salt reflects the ambiguous nature of permanence and transience; it is a fundamental of taxidermy but an active agent of corrosion. If there is one obvious difference with the 2001 work, beyond Hocking's more exacting command of his central themes, it is his increasingly confident grasp of a sense of theater—or as some might say, of showmanship.

STEVE PANTON, JANUARY 2015

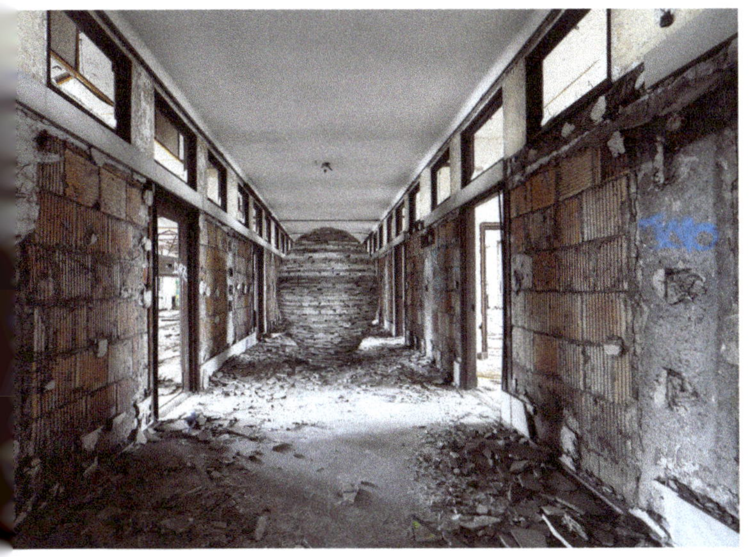

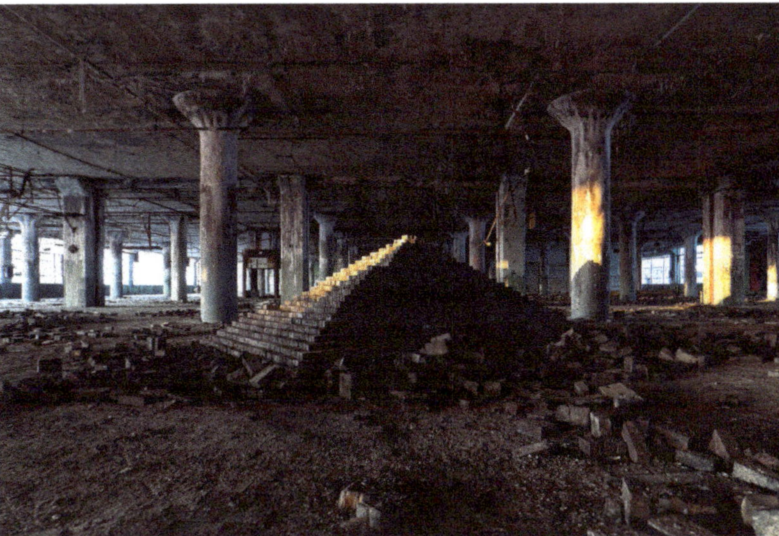

(*Top, left*) *The Egg and MCTS #4718*, from *The Egg and Michigan Central Station*. 2007–13. Site-specific installation using discarded marble fragments found on-site / photographic documentation. Image courtesy of the artist and Susanne Hilberry Gallery.

(*Top, right*) *Ziggurat (Dusk, Midbuild)*, from *Ziggurat and Fisher Body 21*. 2007–9. Site-specific installation using wooden floor blocks found on-site / photographic documentation. Image courtesy of the artist and Susanne Hilberry Gallery.

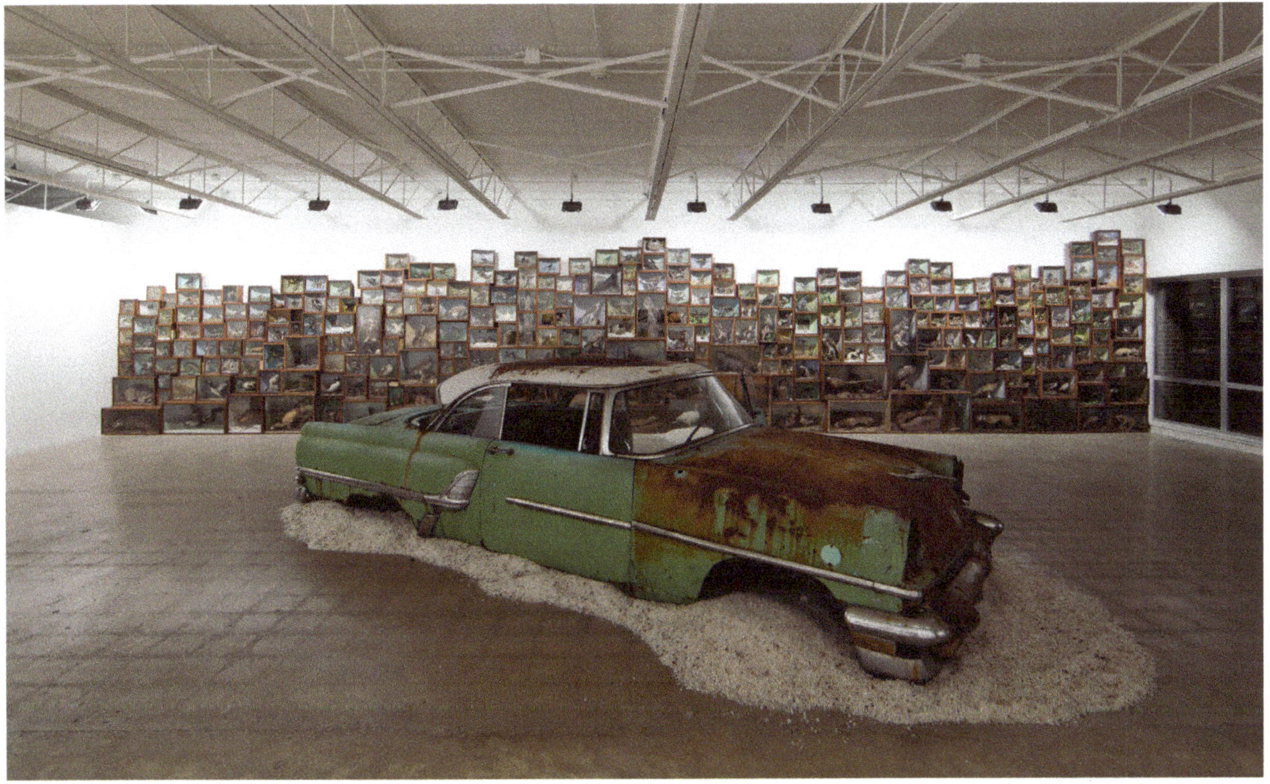

Mercury Retrograde, installation at Susanne Hilberry Gallery. 2012. Mixed-media installation. Image courtesy of the artist and Susanne Hilberry Gallery.

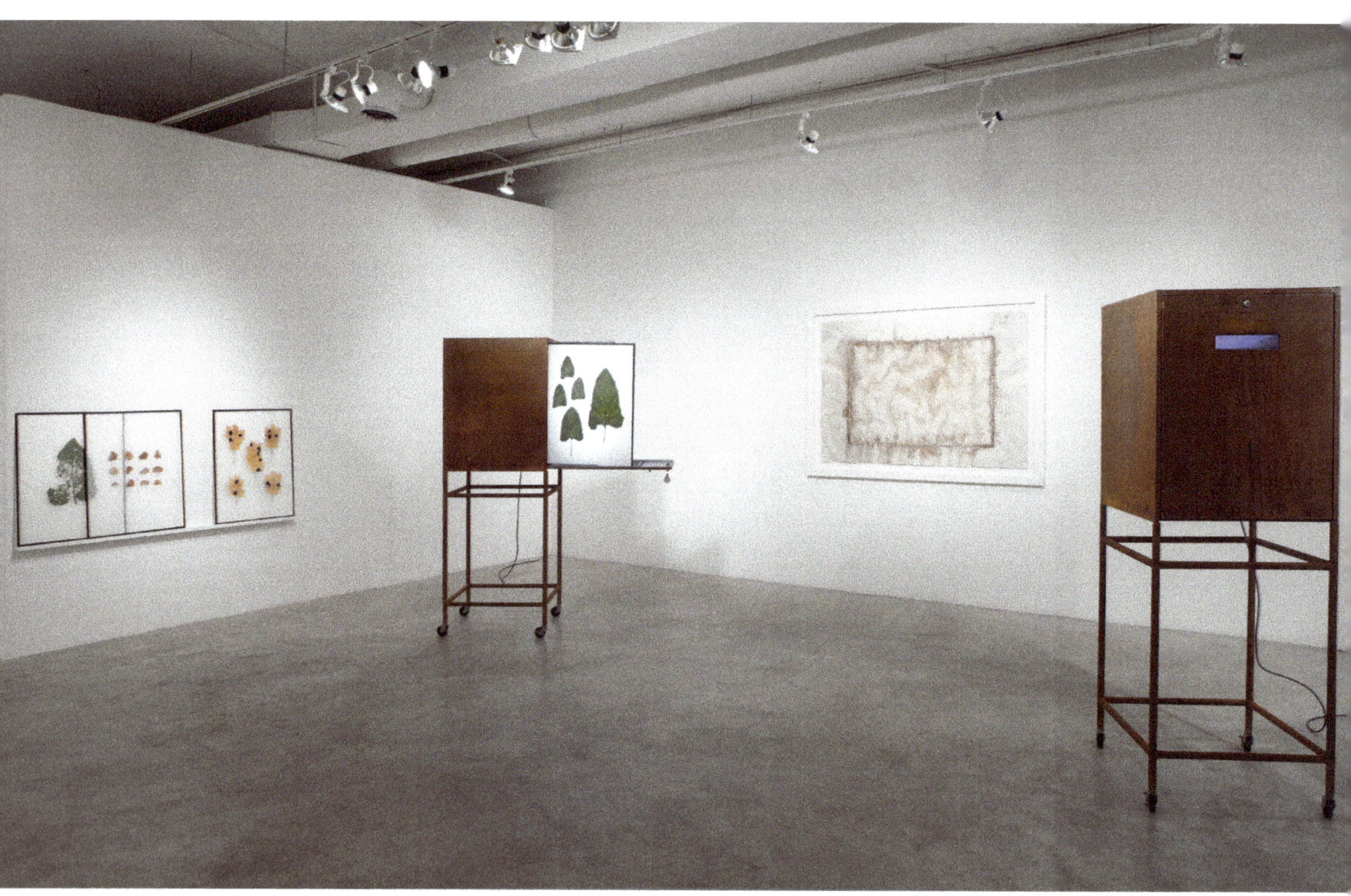

Installation: *Book of Leaves.* 2011. Metal cabinet, pressed leaves, acrylic sheeting. Twenty-one plates, 28 ¾ x 21 ½ in.; cabinet, 70 x 22 x 23 ½ in. Photography by Tim Thayer.

14 // SUSAN GOETHEL CAMPBELL

Born Grand Rapids, Michigan, 1956
BFA, Alma College
MFA, Cranbrook Academy of Art
Lives in Huntington Woods, Michigan

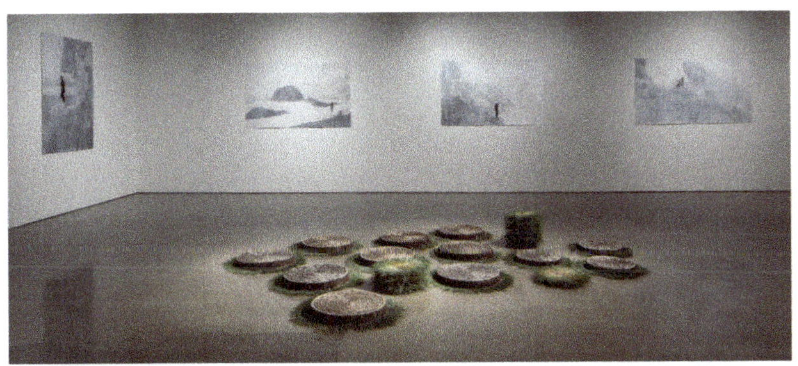

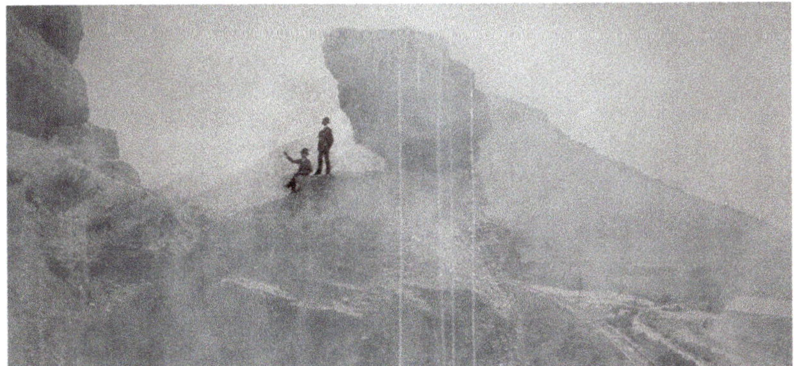

Field Guide was the name of a recent show at Oakland University by Susan Goethel Campbell that included selections from several major bodies of work, spanning an array of media, including video, prints, and sculpture, and more than a decade of artistic efforts. The show's title is fitting in many respects. First, a field guide acts as an index for the natural world, introducing the viewer to flora, fauna, and other recognizable patterns in a specific environment—which is the general subject of Campbell's work. With various "movements" concerning air, pollen, turf, and leaf samples—to name a few—Campbell

(*Top*) Installation view: *Field Guide;* Foreground: *Ground 3;* Background: *Old Stand* series. 2015. Photography by Tim Thayer.

(*Bottom*) *Old Stand #11.* 2015. Gesso, archival digital print, 39 3/4 x 69 in. Photography by Tim Thayer.

Seasonal Print: Winter, no. 1. 2012. Acrylic, paper, 84 x 60 in. Photography by Tim Thayer.

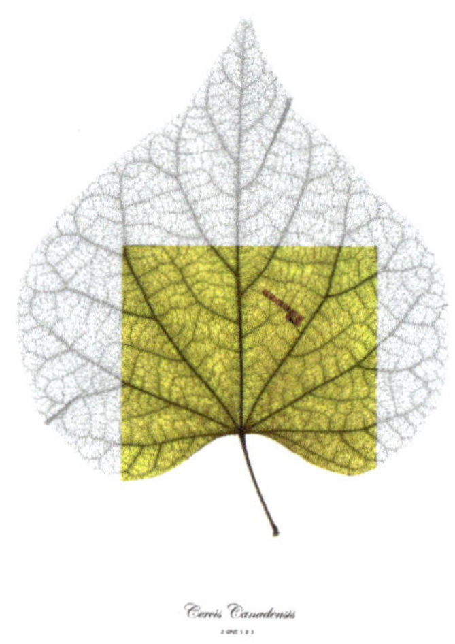

Botanical Prints, Ceris Canadensis (Redbud). 2007. Archival digital print, 48 x 32 in. Photography by Tim Thayer.

meticulously tracks the natural world at work.

Secondly, the field guide suggests navigation of an ecosystem, and there is a distinct consciousness of ecoconnectedness in Campbell's work. Not only does she display an obsessive interest in charting intersections of nature, culture, and technology, such as air pollution, airplane flight paths, and urban patterns of heat and light emissions, her various arcs tend to layer easily upon each other to form a total picture of an environment—specifically her native Michigan, with a focus on the Detroit metro area, where she has lived and worked for decades. Indeed, it might be argued that Campbell's versatility with medium is a tool that enables her to approach the

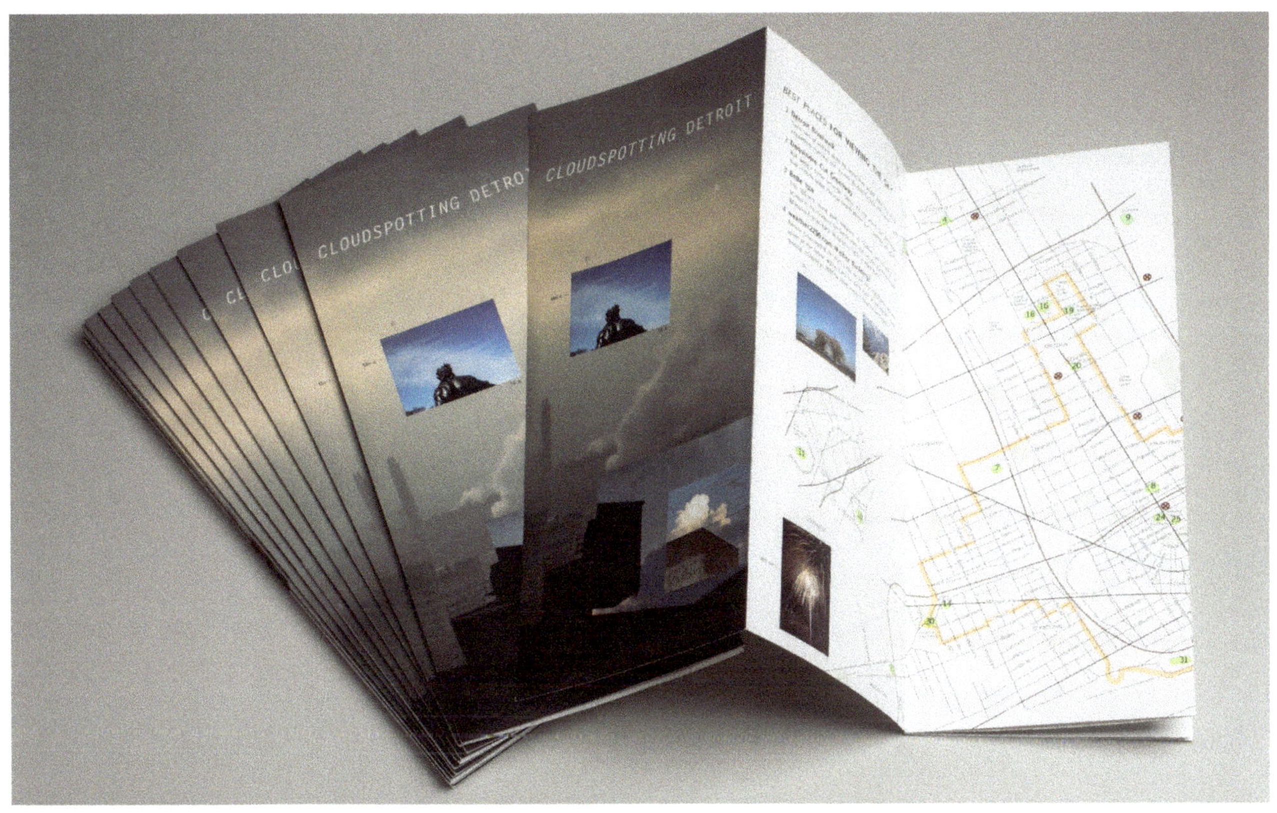

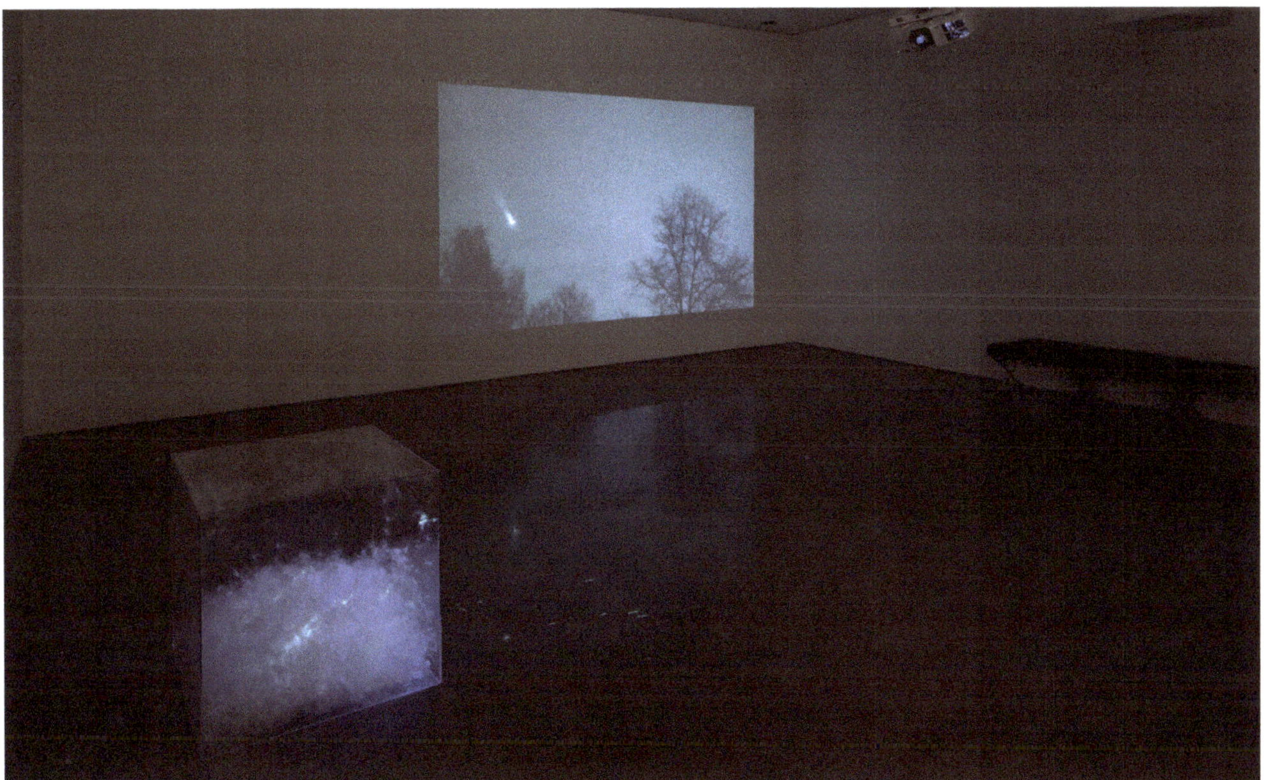

(*Top*) *Cloudspotting Detroit.* 2010. Brochure, 9 x 27 in. (open). Photography by Tim Thayer.
(*Bottom*) Installation: *Big Sky Theory* (wall) / *Flights East with Milkweed* (floor). 2011/2015. HD video / Milkweed, acrylic box, HD video. Photography by Tim Thayer.

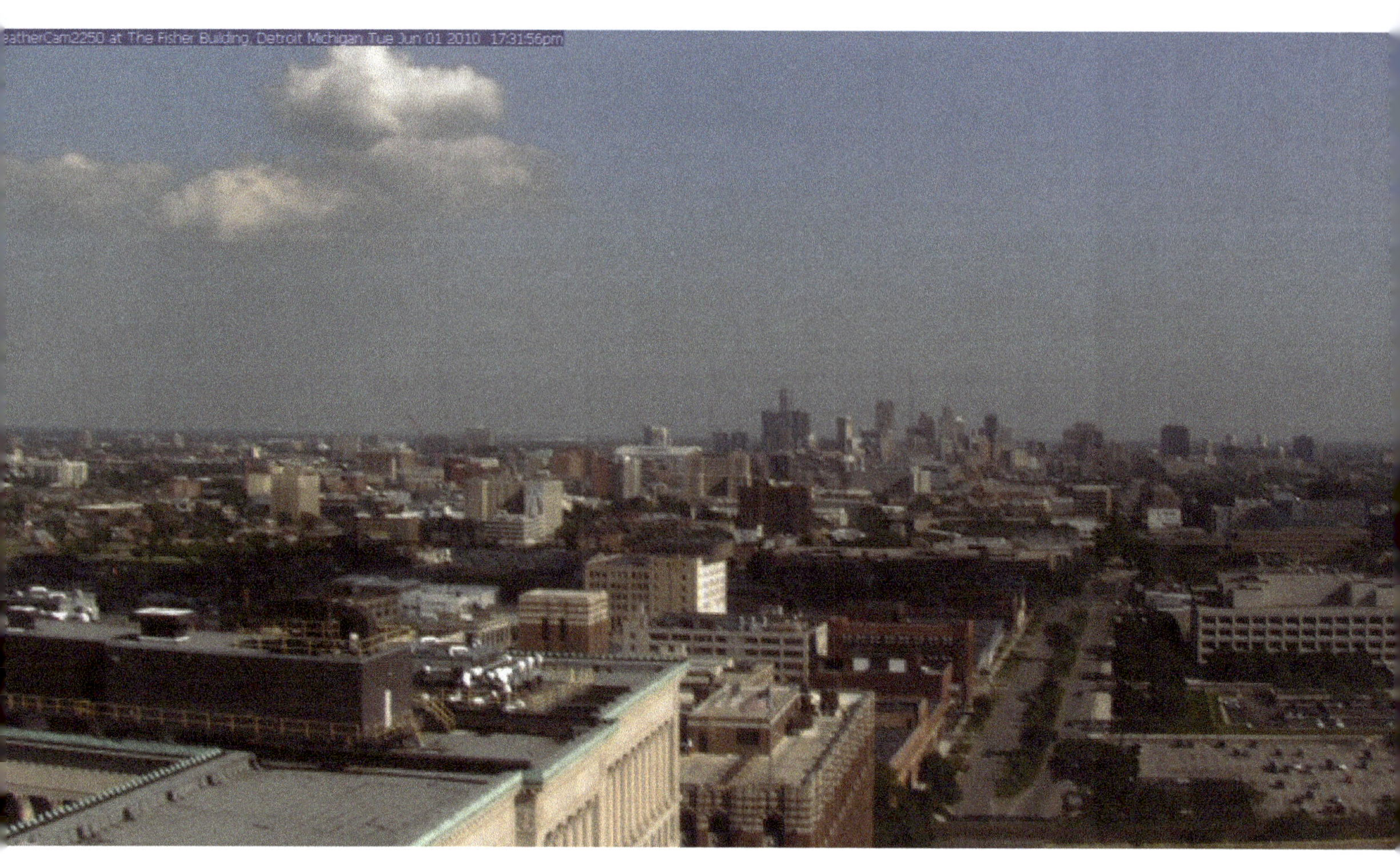

(This and facing page) Detroit Weather: 365 Days. 2011. HD video, three hours.

formulation of her environment from many different directions.

Exploration is itself the subject of the newest works in *Field Guide*, or, at least, explorers, with the 2015 ***Old Stand*** series (which evolved out of an earlier series, begun in 2007). Black-and-white gesso-faded portraits feature turn-of-the-century gentleman explorers posing with Victorian aplomb against the vistas of their travels—the field guide being, of course, the indispensable tool of the intrepid explorer, utilized in the specific identification of established elements of environments. Campbell readily draws upon natural objects as touchstones of her practice, building long-standing relationships with specific patterns of wood grain, or dropping ink-dipped Christmas trees from a ladder to form a graphic base for ***Seasonal Print: Winter, no. 1*** (2012), for example. So too, the field guide mirrors Campbell's pure and obvious love of taxonomy, with 2011's ***Book of Leaves***—sheets and sheets of specimen-mounted leaf collections iterated as stand-alone pieces, following ***Botanical Prints***, a 2007 series that equates the layout of their vasculature with principles of urban planning. "Maple leaves are very much how an engineer would plan a city," Campbell can assure us with confidence, having collaborated with urban planners from University of Michigan on the project.

Indeed, far from the lone-wolf image of the solitary explorer, Campbell's projects contain increasingly social aspects: distributing air filters for people to place experimentally in areas

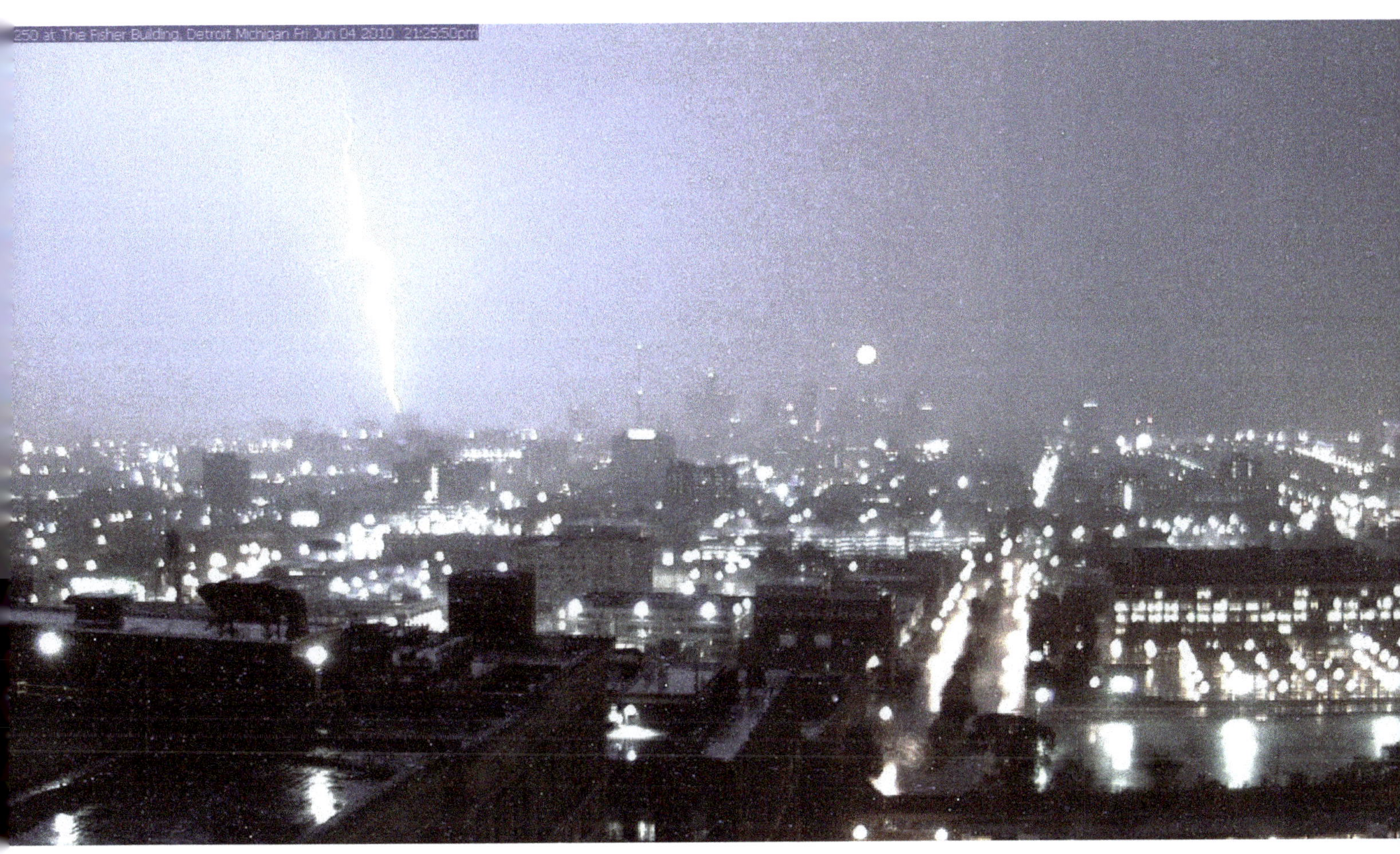

they believe to be dense with air pollution; creating ***Cloudspotting Detroit*** (2010), a guide for Detroit tourists (she accompanied its launch with guided bike tours) that designates the best cloud-watching places in the city, as well as cheekily referencing the steam clouds that emit from the pavement and various "savory clouds" created by barbeque pits. As with many of her projects, Campbell took to the field for hands-on exploration of the source, arranging a tour at Detroit's Water and Sewage Department to track the provenance of the ubiquitous steam clouds. She obsessively filmed the flight patterns of airplanes above her house for the ***Big Sky Theory*** video project (2011).

The final aspect of Campbell's very open-ended observations of her natural and artificial environment: her work serves as a set of guidelines for navigation of our world but imposes little restraint or direction on the viewer in terms of their conclusions. Even in work such as ***Detroit Weather: 365 Days*** (2011), a series of time-lapse footage of Detroit's weather patterns in three directions from a camera placed at the top of the Fisher Building, though inadvertently revealing the impact of industrial emissions on the natural clouds, Campbell refrains from overtly political gestures, instead opting, in field-guide fashion, to generally delineate the parameters of the known, making it all the more clear for viewers to recognize a new connection when it is encountered.

SARAH ROSE SHARP, MARCH 2015

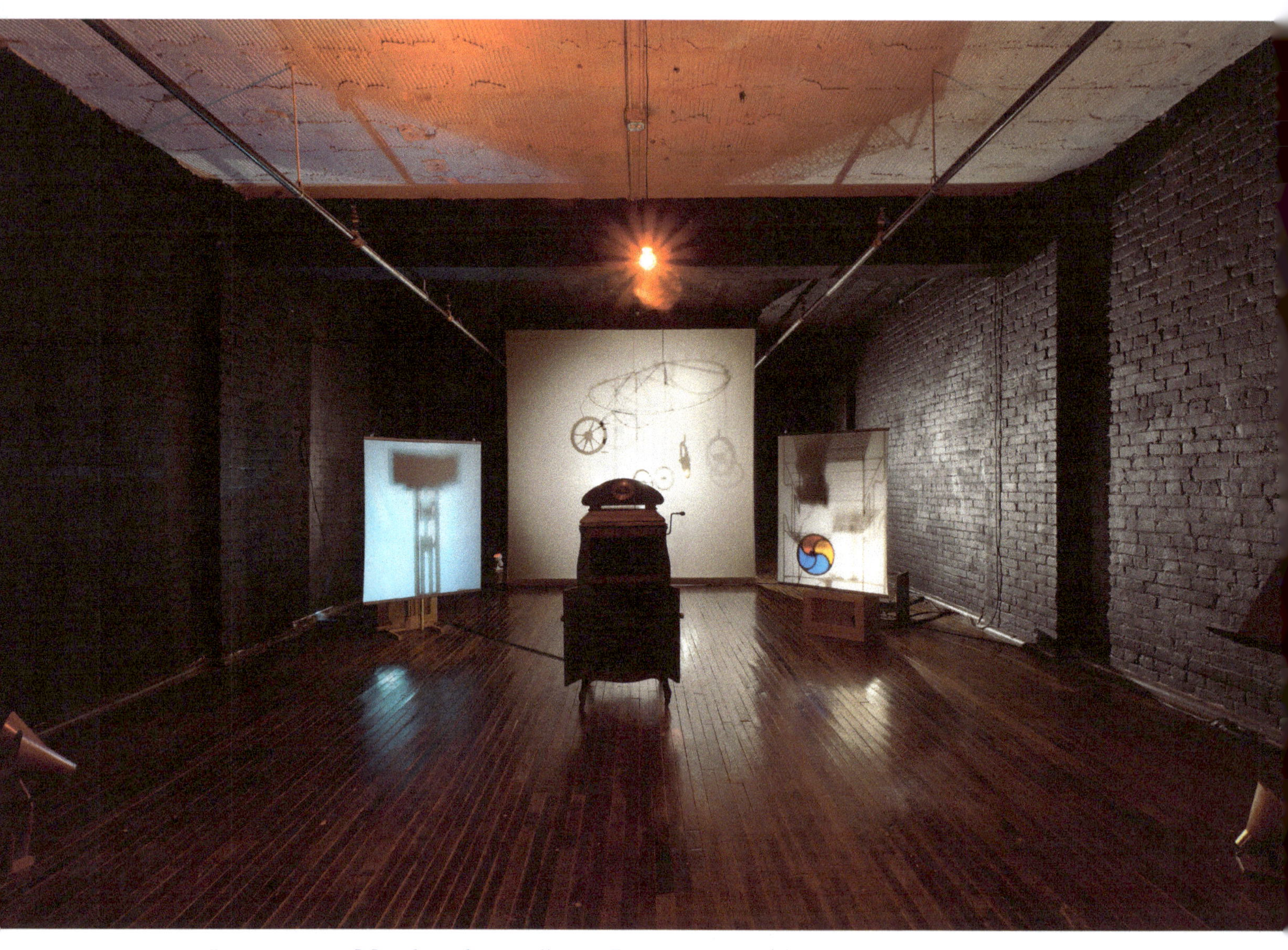

1913 Revisited. 2013. Mixed-media installation. Photography by Tom Little. Image courtesy of the Mattress Factory, Pittsburgh, PA.

15 // FRANK PAHL

Born Trenton, Michigan, 1958
BA, Wayne State University
MFA, University of Michigan
Lives in Wyandotte, Michigan

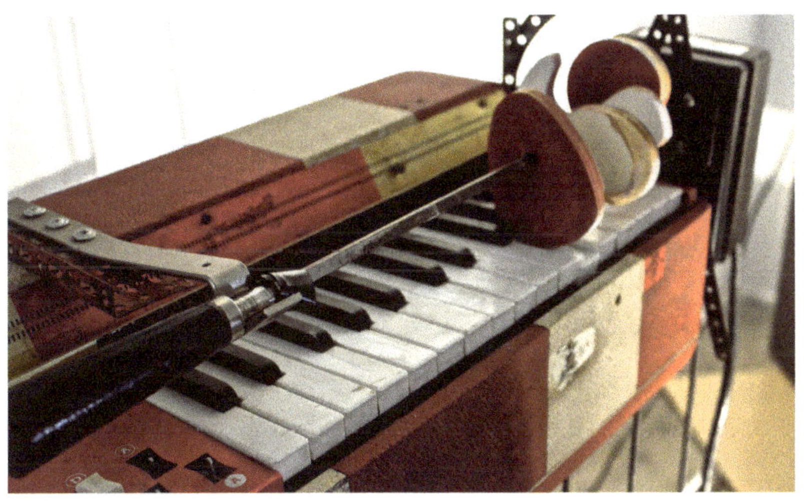

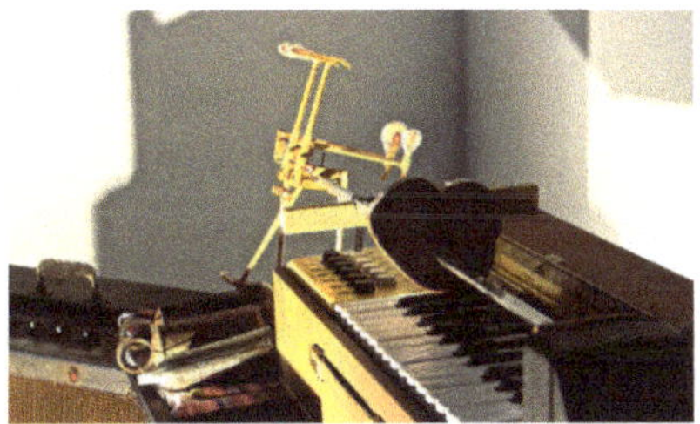

Automatic instruments. 1996 onward.

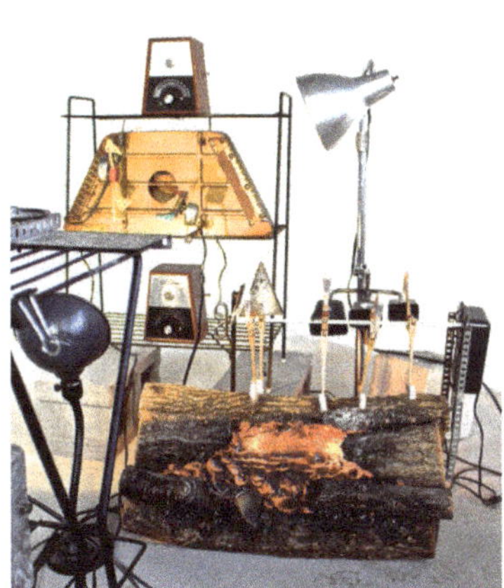

As we enter the age of "the Internet of things," with its universal connectivity and planned obsolescence, what should we make of an artist like Frank Pahl, who uses almost theatrically nonstandard ways to connect discarded objects into sound-making mechanisms? Is it a philosophical statement, or a practical strategy to achieve a certain sound? Pahl will say that "the proof is in the pudding," meaning that the eventual sound has to be just right, but there's clearly also more than a hint of subversive intent in the way he goes about it. In the end, it may be enough just to know that he is that rare artist who can juggle objects, media, and concepts, and in keeping all the balls in the air at the same time, create a singular experience that exceeds the sum of the parts.

Since the midnineties Pahl has been creating ***automatic***

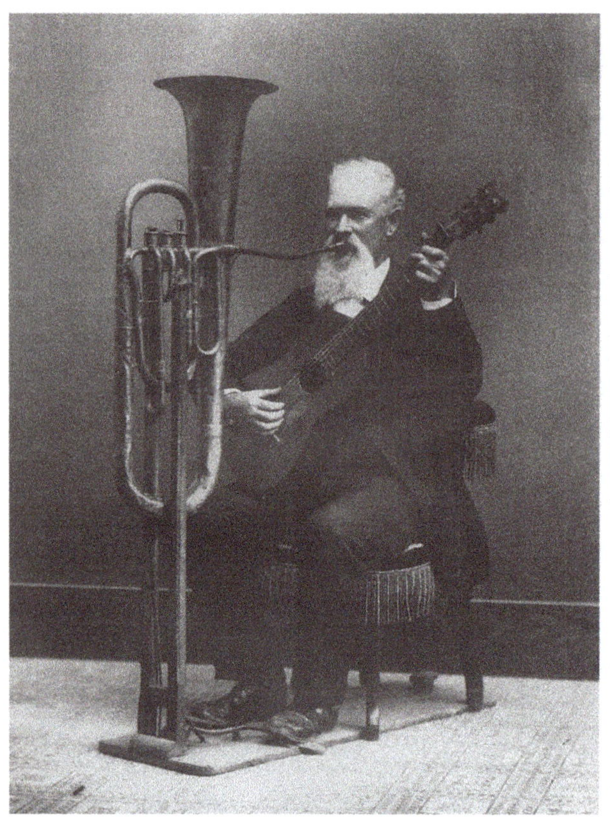

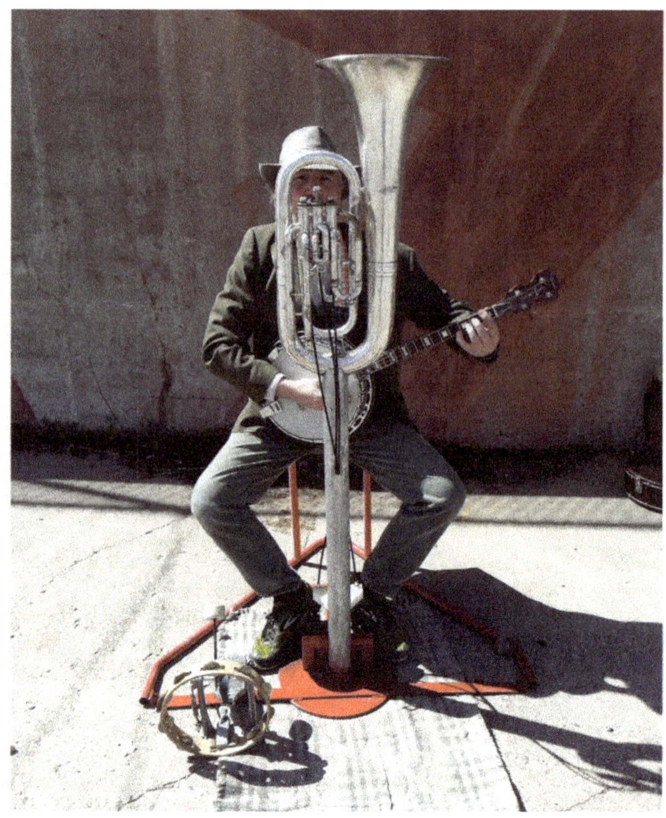

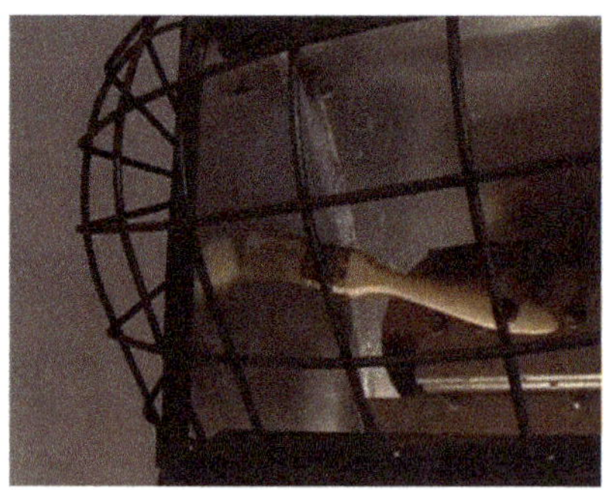

(*Top*) *"The Johnson."* 2013. Original (*left*); re-creation in collaboration with Tim Holmes (*right*). Photography by Tim Holmes
(*Left*) *Homage to Painting.* 2006. Mixed-media. Photography by Terri Sarris.

instruments. To visit his studio is to enter a world where salvaged rotisserie-grill motors turn cams that in turn play vintage air organs, and strikers that play various bells and chimes. Valve amplifiers warm up and turn on. Natural and electric light casts shadows through moving parts. The haunting melody could well be the theme from *Midnight Cowboy*, composed by one of Pahl's heroes, John Barry—an appropriate reference since Pahl has composed over one hundred scores for theater, dance, and short films.

Up to this point, Pahl was best known as a musician and composer, albeit a highly idiosyncratic one. Some key influences in the transition to his later "automatons" were his exploration of traditional one-man-band configurations (for example, his 2013 re-creation, with collaborator Tim Holmes, of late nineteenth-century configuration *"The Johnson"*) and meeting automatic instrument makers Pierre Bastien and Trimpin. Joining the dots, he realized he could create a "one-man band without limits." The fortuitous start of an MFA

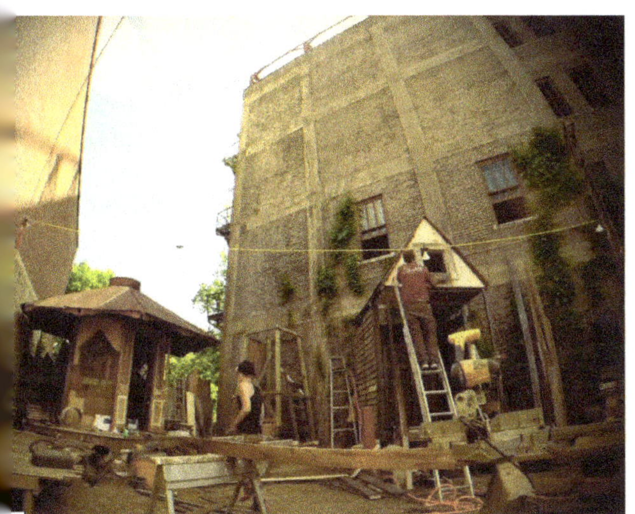
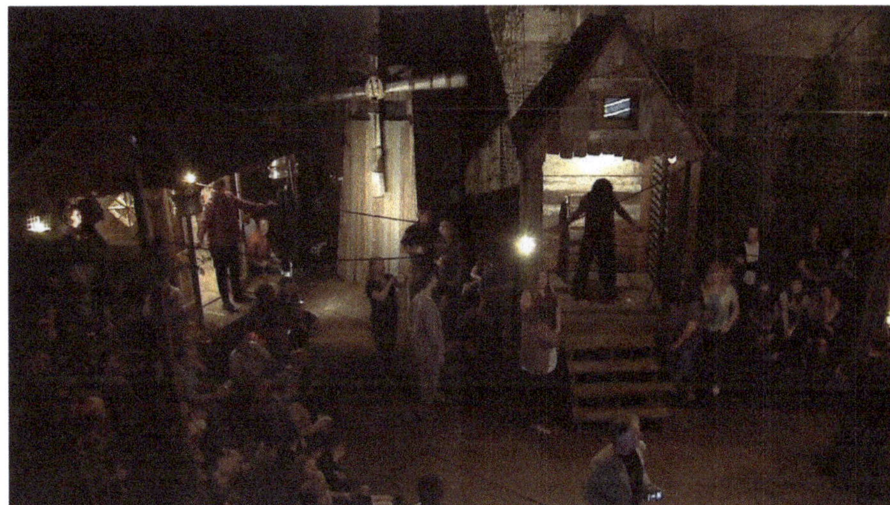

Calantheon Canyons. 2014. Construction (*left*); performance (*right*). Photography by Scott Crain.

allowed him space to experiment, and the rest was history.

Pahl has often used the comparison between Trimpin's daunting technical genius and Bastien's somewhat looser approach to explain his own work. Clearly he gravitates more to Bastien, saying "his music is not *precise*, precise," meaning that like Pahl, Bastien builds from unlikely components but ultimately achieves *exactly* the effect he is after—by embracing imprecision. Pahl has also spoken of Detroit's culture of "the economy of means," or working with what you can find for (almost) free. There is a fine example of this in Terri Sarris's film on Pahl, *Buzzards Steal Your Picnic*, in which Pahl is shown working through the problems of building the small sculptural sound piece ***Homage to Painting*** (2006) from various castoffs. The "painting" of the title refers to the use of a garage-sale paintbrush to create the sound element of the piece, and the filmmaker cleverly uses Pahl's delight in the tiny amount he spends on materials (in comparison to the eventual sale price) as a way to reflect Pahl's obvious pleasure in subversively inserting his downriver blue-collar ethos into the rarefied world of the art gallery.

For someone who often professes a lack of motivation, Pahl has worked on some remarkably ambitious projects. ***Calantheon Canyons*** (2014) was a large-scale installation and musical performance created during an Airlift New Orleans residency in Shreveport, Louisiana. Over a period of one month, Pahl codirected the construction and arranged the climactic musical performance. The resulting video (which can be found online) captures some of the magic of what was clearly a very special event. ***1913 Revisited*** (2013), constructed for a Detroit-themed show at Pittsburgh's Mattress Factory, is based around three seminal events from that year: the global synchronization of time, the premiere of Stravinsky's *The Rite of Spring*, and Henry Ford's introduction of the moving assembly line. Based on Pahl's trademark kinetic sculptures and drone-producing automatons, it is visually sparser but conceptually richer than earlier pieces, perhaps pointing to yet more layers in his future work.

STEVE PANTON, MARCH 2015

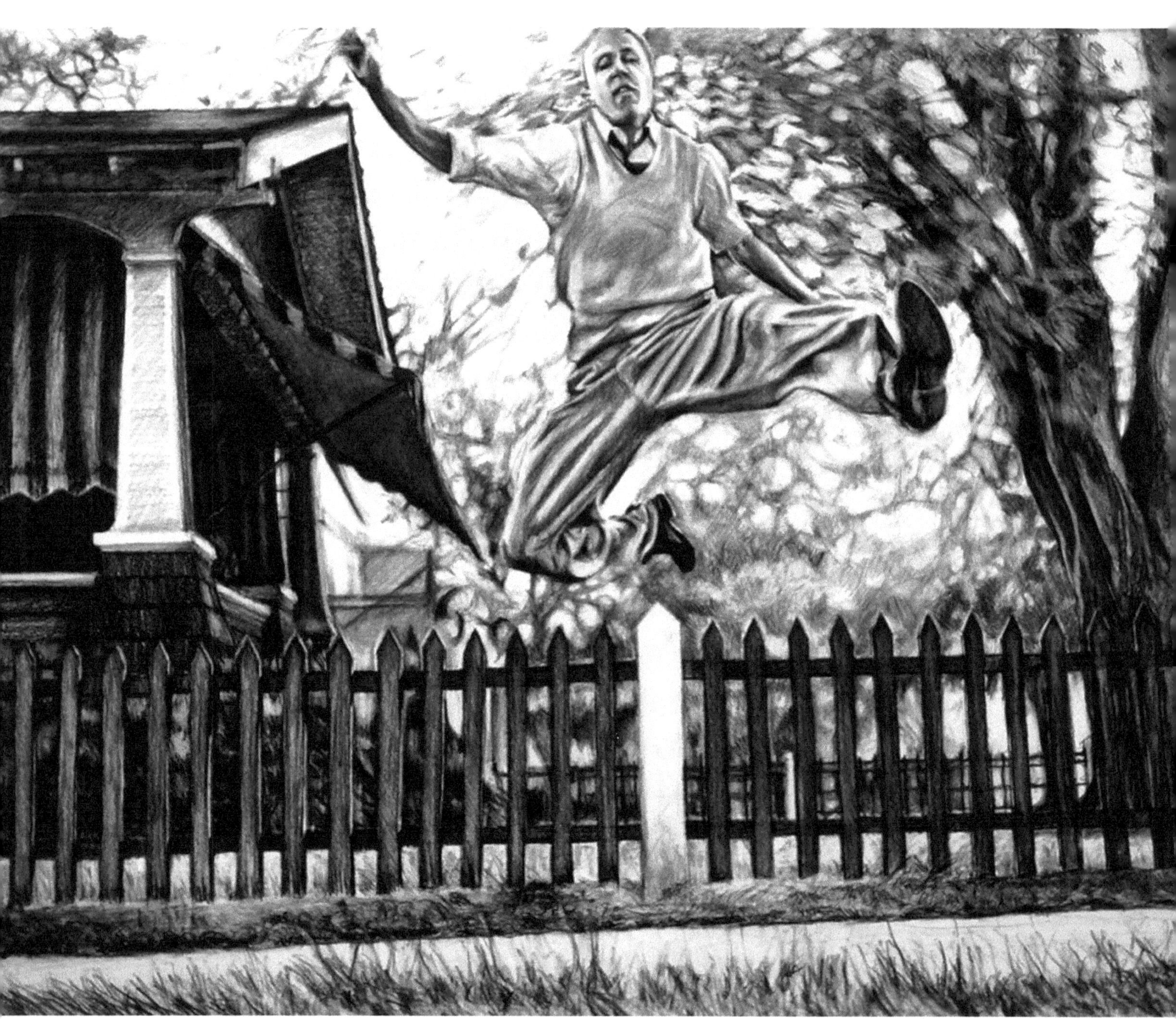

Leaping Man. 2013. Charcoal on paper, 22 x 30 in.

16 // ANDREW KRIEGER

Born Detroit, 1967
Lives in Grosse Pointe Farms, Michigan

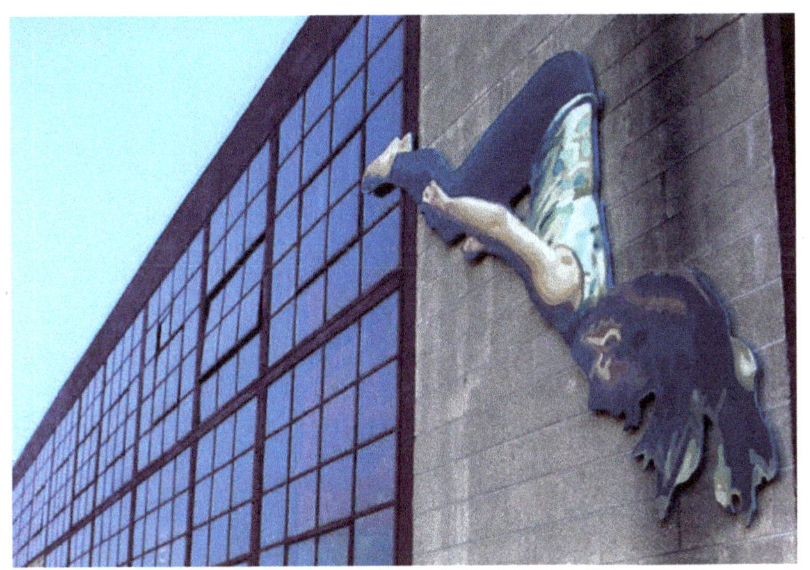

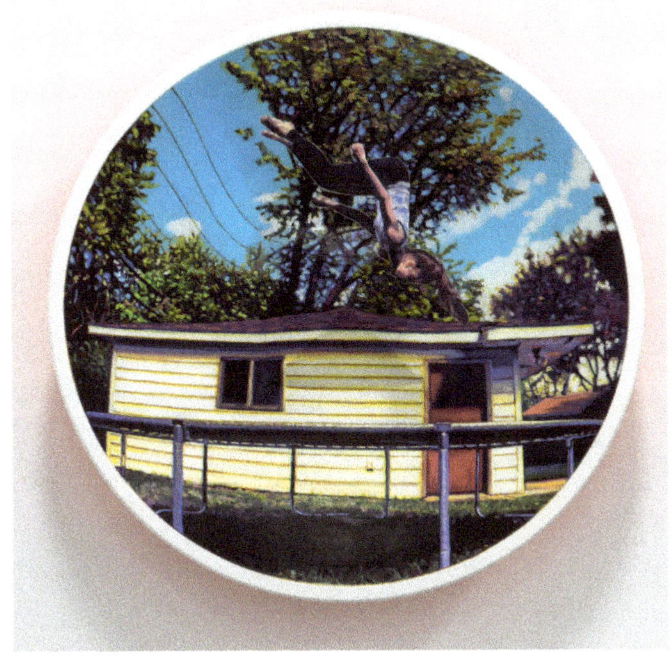

Nostalgia is a loaded term, often associated with a sense of whitewashed reminiscence and a safe contemplation of a past effectively stripped of any alienating realities. But in the work of painter and sculptor Andy Krieger, nostalgia is a tool which leverages a personal well-spring of emotion that translates from artist to work and transmits back to the viewer, creating an enchanting body of work that evokes a sense of connection and half memory of events outside individual experience, a kind of collective ur-history. Much like the films of Richard Linklater, Krieger is a master at the transformation of the personal to the universal.

(*Top*) *Ava.* 2014. Oil on wood, 42 x 144 in. Photography by Sarah Rose Sharp

(*Bottom*) *Still Point of a Turning Universe.* 2014. Oil on wood, 30 x 30 x 8 in.

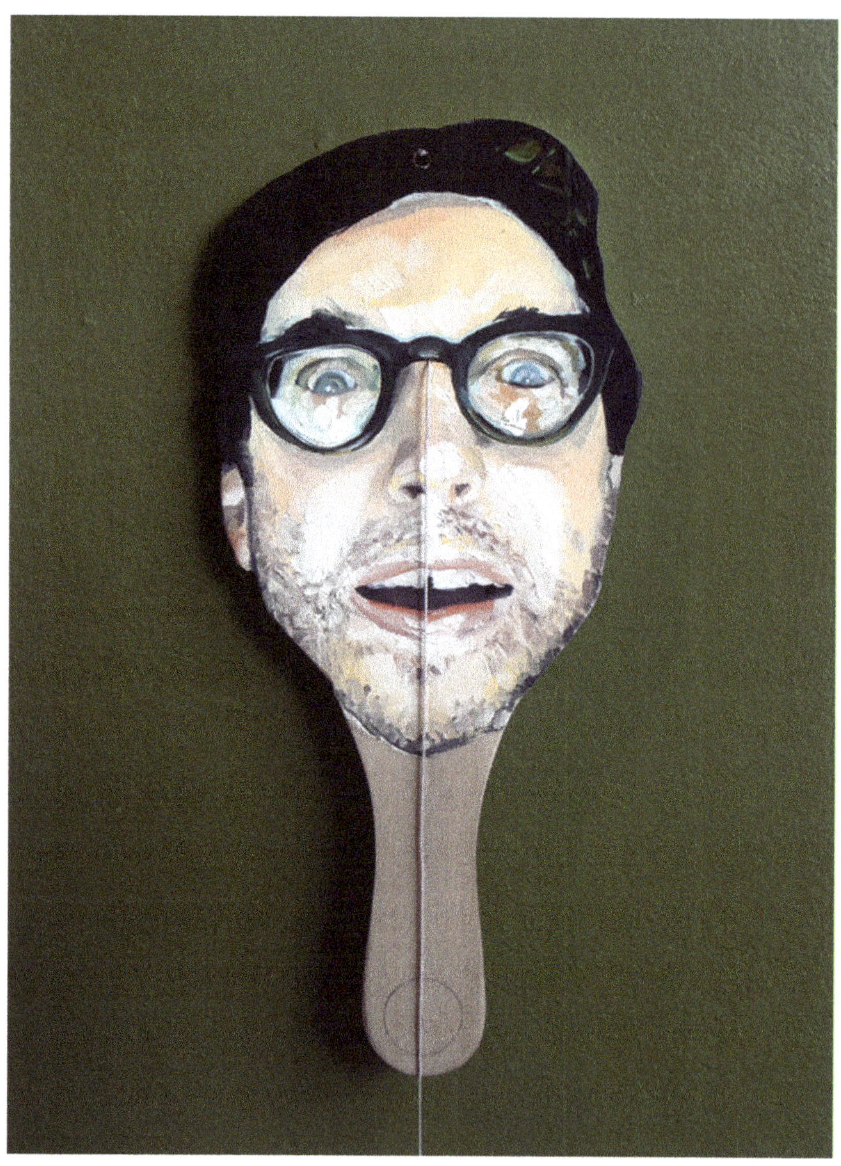

Paddle Ball Portrait: Steve. 2012. Oil, wood, rubber string, ball, 15 x 6 in.

Krieger acknowledges this mechanism of nostalgia as part of his own process of connecting to his art-making—a relationship that became estranged during art school. "They taught me how to think critically," Krieger says, "and then I left." Following that exodus, Krieger defaulted to a carpentry and art-fabrication career that, while ostensibly off the track of his personal vision, unexpectedly provided and honed the skills that have made his return to art so unique and powerful. For Krieger will not be confined to two dimensions, creating instead sculptural paintings that play tricks of perspective and feature subjects leaping, literally, off the surface plane.

These figures are, in many cases, surrogates of some kind, place-holding for characters in Krieger's memory that will be deployed as many times as needed to satisfy his vision. Krieger says of the subject rendered in the charcoal drawing ***Leaping Man*** (2013), for example, "He looks a lot like [but is not] my father," and he's had a dimensional painting of the same subject as a work in progress for some time now. ***Ava*** (2014), which depicts a friend's child tumbling midair on an outdoor trampoline—and was iterated in massive scale for the *Big Paintings at the Factory* group show in the summer of 2014—doubles as an encapsulation of Krieger's childhood ambition of being able to execute a backflip. Much like a writer of comic books, Krieger employs characters in the pursuit of achievements that have eluded him in the plane of reality.

In fact, comic culture is a clear influence, both in the overall playfulness of Krieger's

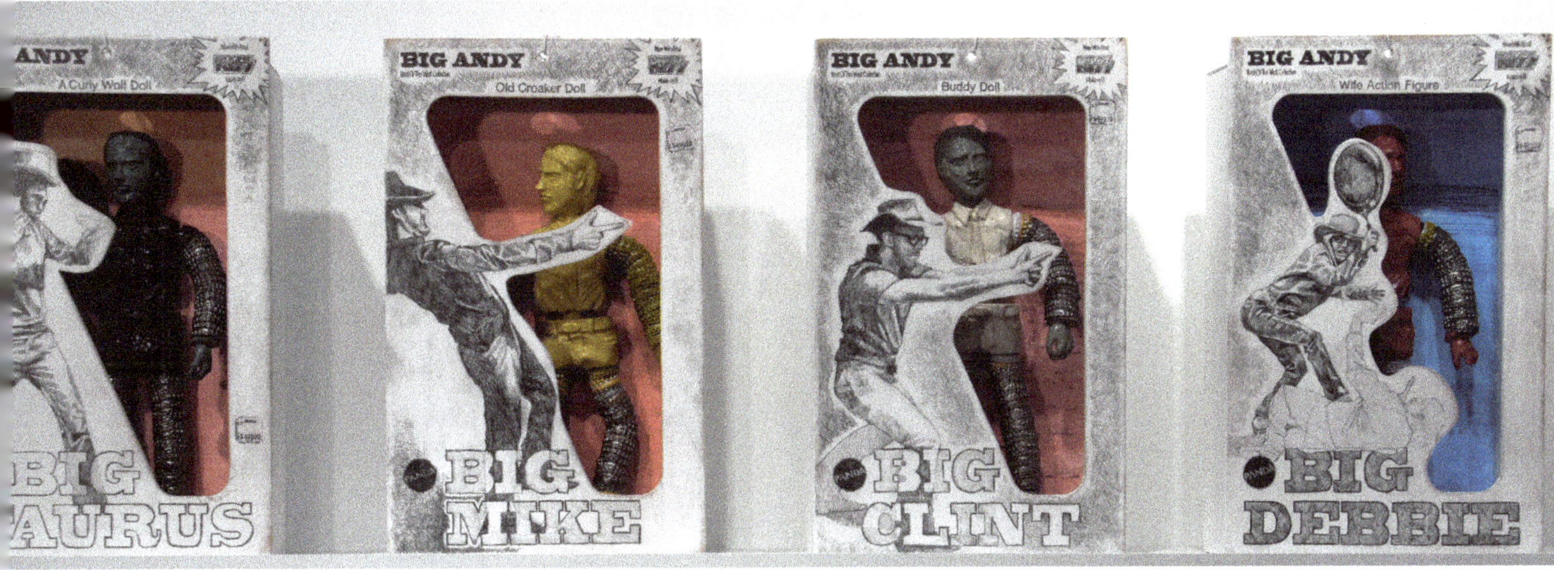

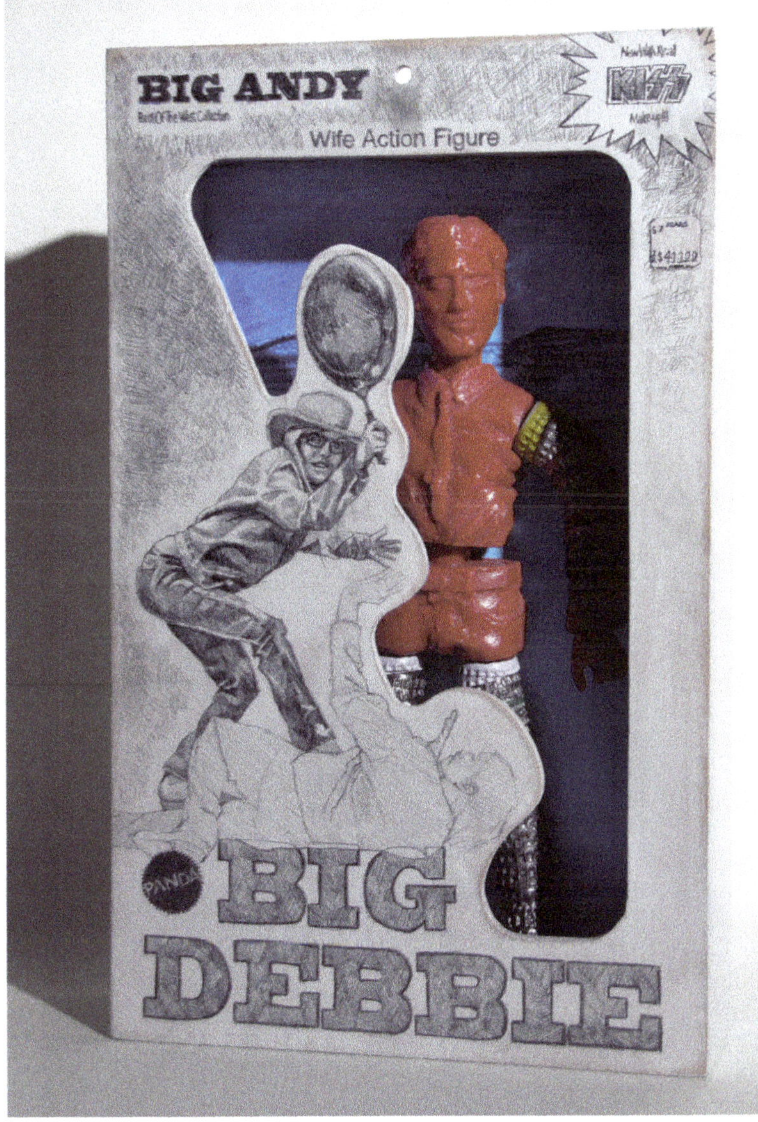

(Top) Big Andy Action Figures. 2012. Bottle caps, molded plastic, wood, pencil, 18 x 11 x 4 in.

(Left) Big Debbie. 2012. Bottle caps, molded plastic, wood, pencil, 18 x 11 x 4 in.

body of work and in specific series, such as his 2012 ***Big Andy Action Figures***—bottle-cap "action figures" influenced by folk art and the Johnny West action figures made by Marx Toys in the late 1960s. These depict important characters, such as wife (***Big Debbie***) and buddy (***Big Clint***). If there exists a layer of abstraction to some of his subjects, there is no doubt that Krieger's work is deeply personal, and some of his most heartfelt pieces are those depicting his closest family, including his wife and two sons. ***Executive Briefcase: Pride and Joy Edition*** (2012) is a two-sided construction, an exquisitely rendered wooden facsimile of an executive briefcase that features portraits of Krieger's sons, Ian and Karl, on each side. The iconic struggle of work-life balance is encapsulated perfectly—family as motivation for a time-consuming day job portrayed on the very device that requires the briefcase holder to be absent from their company (not the type of job that Krieger holds, in reality). And far from a rarified art object, Krieger says he would be happy to see someone carry this briefcase to work; in fact, a number of his pieces seem to dare the viewer to engage them in a process that would be ultimately destructive to the artwork, for example, his ***Paddle Ball Portraits.***

One gets the sense that given unlimited means, Krieger would be producing fully animated works, striving for ever-greater involvement with the audience—and in fact he cites the immersive tableaux of Disney World rides, such as The Haunted Mansion, as examples of what paintings and

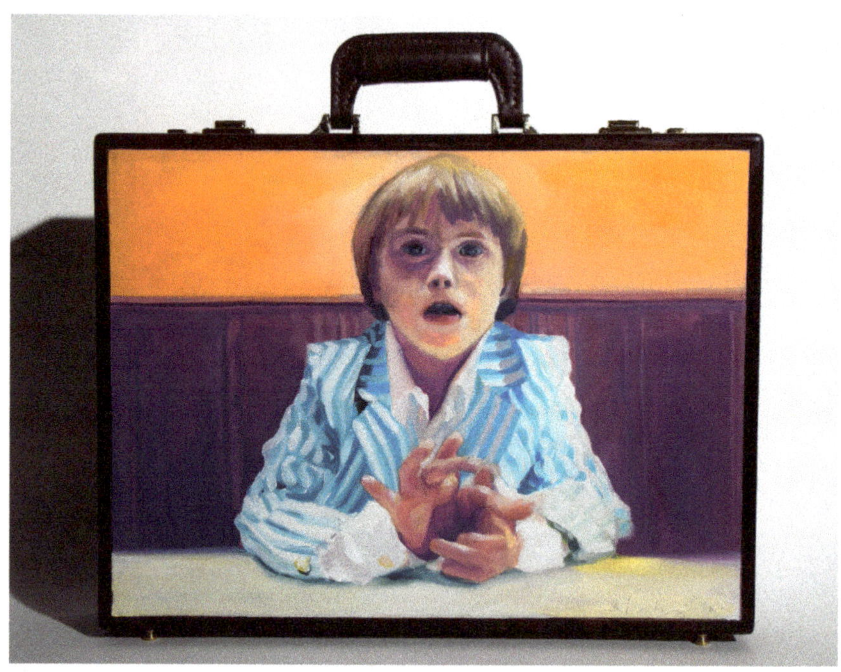

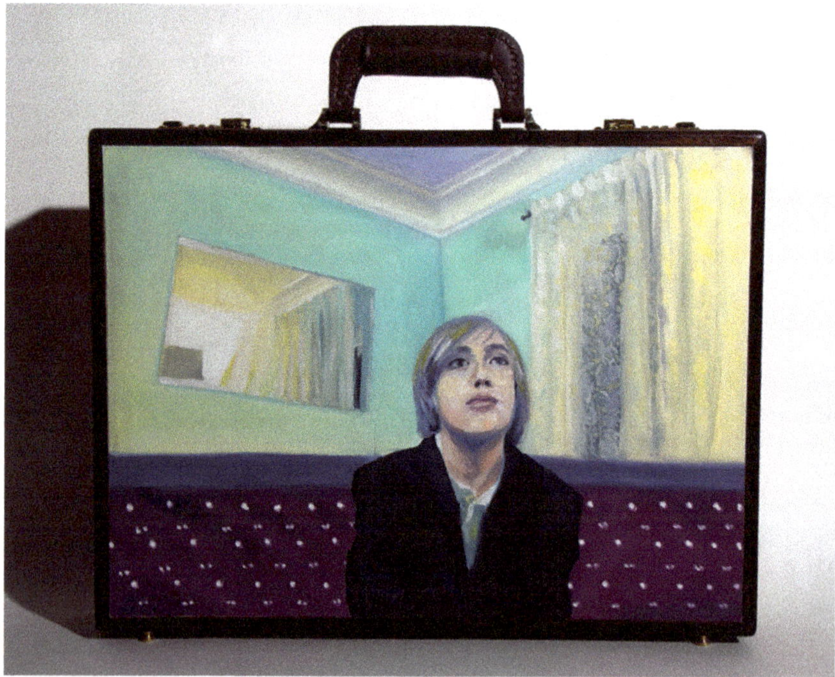

Executive Briefcase: Pride and Joy Edition. 2012. Oil, wood, leather, 18 x 19 x 4 in.

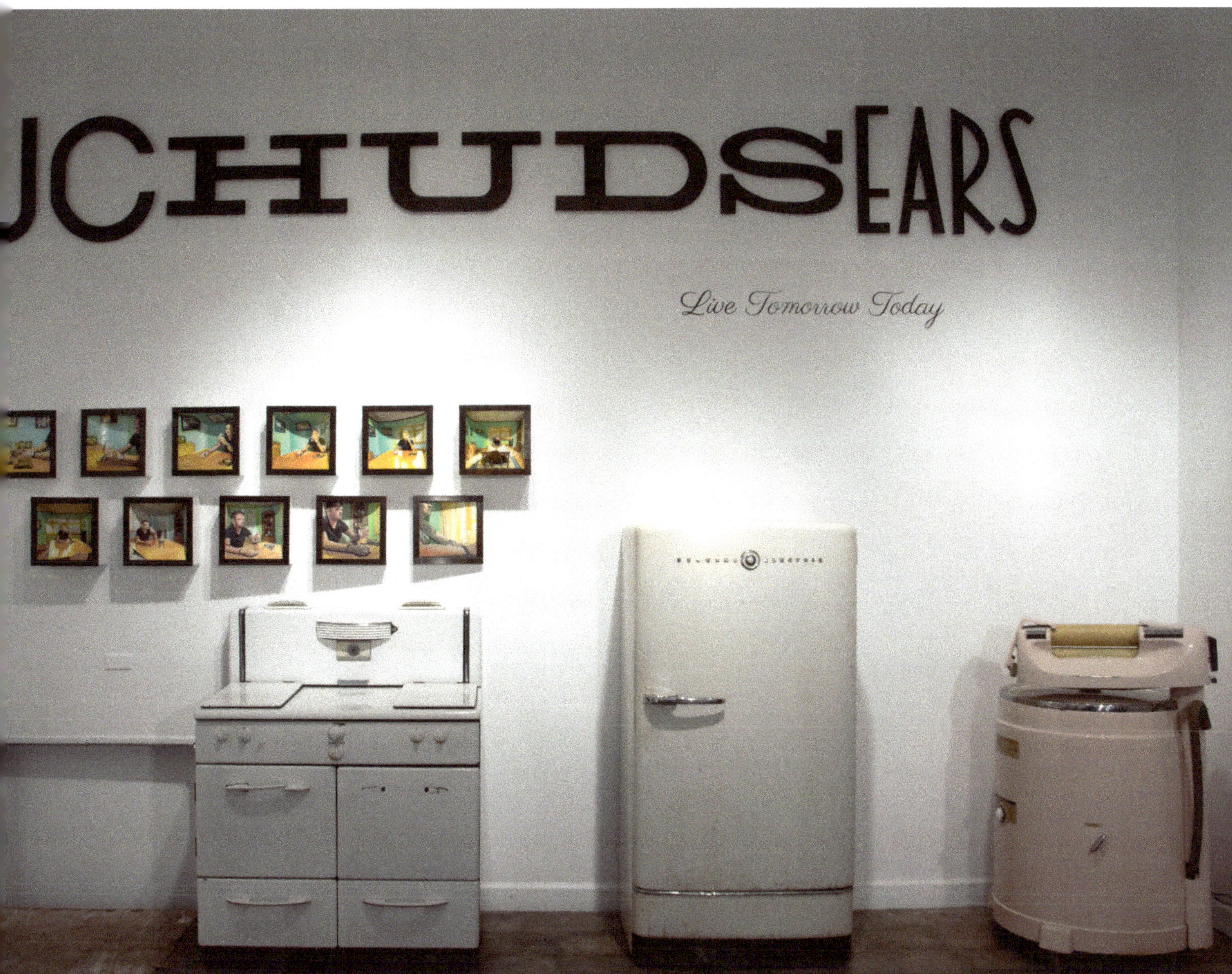

Installation view: *J. C. Hudsears.* 2012.

installation art could be. His 2012 installation ***J. C. Hudsears*** is an attempt to construct a kind of art-rendered department store of yesteryear, and featured numerous points of interaction with its viewers.

Ultimately, Krieger defies constraints of time, dimension, art-viewer relationships, and even the basic sanctity of his finished products, valuing above all the process by which he arrives at a given point in time. With results so compelling, there is a strong case for following Krieger on whatever journey he may next endeavor to take.

SARAH ROSE SHARP, MARCH 2015

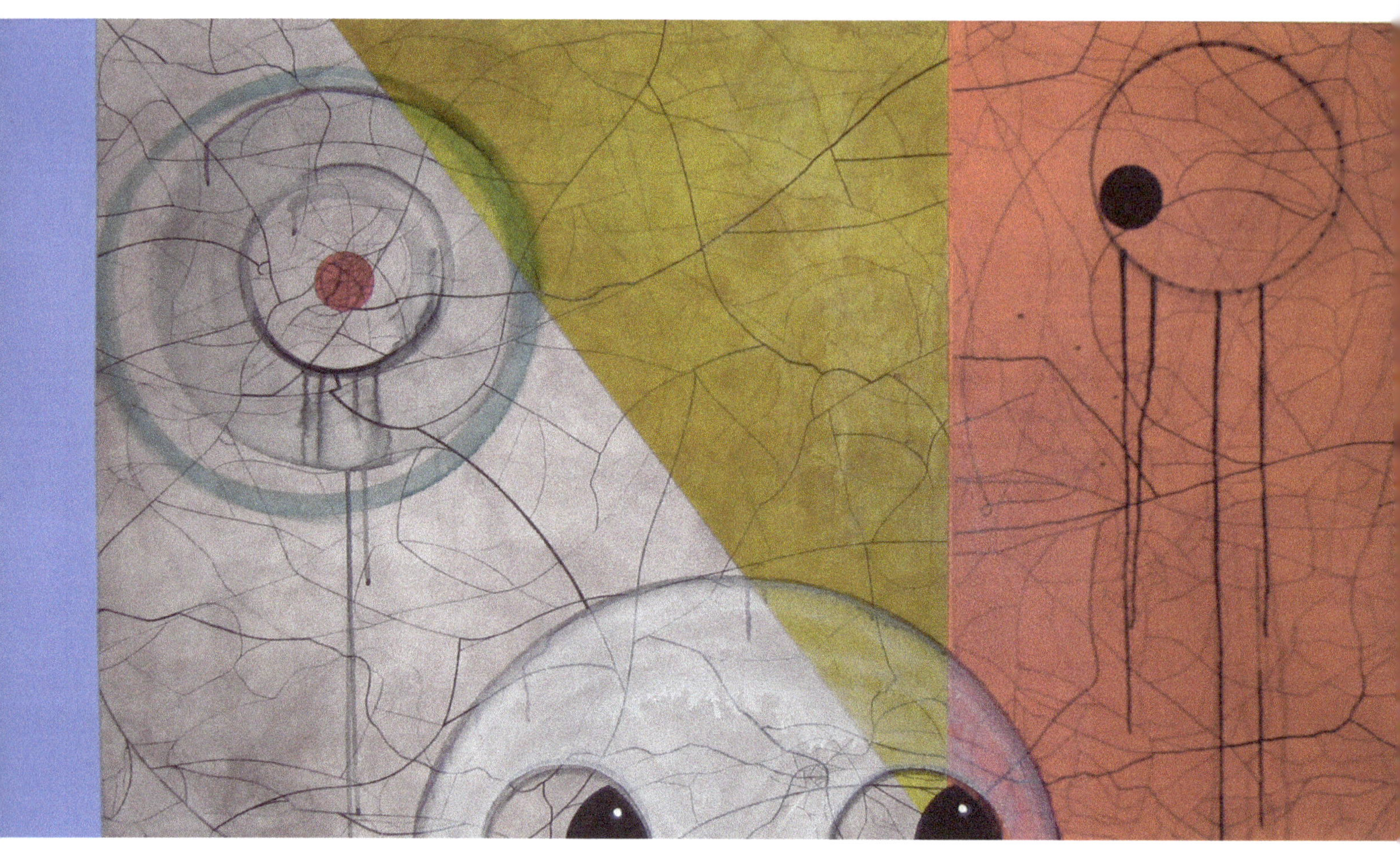

Aspetto. 2008–10. Acrylic, Polyflax, 29 x 54 in.

17 // MEGAN PARRY

Born Hornell, New York, 1944
Lives in Detroit and Alfred, New York

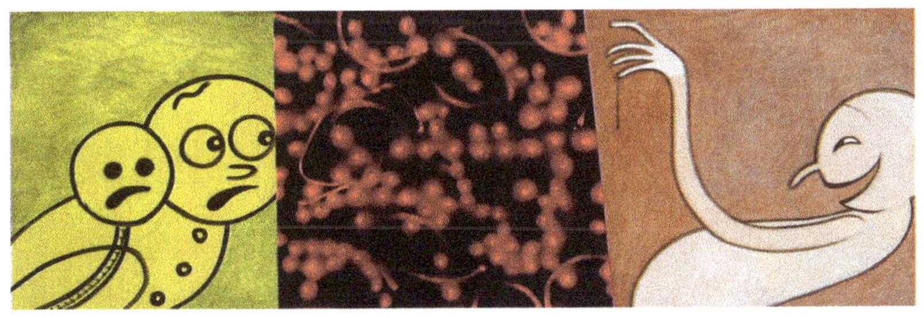

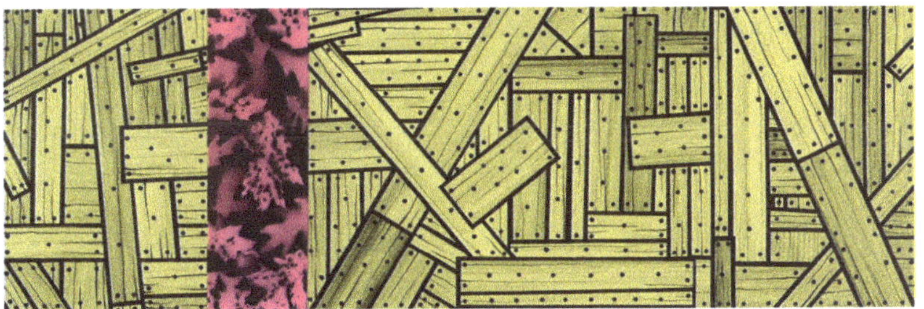

(*Top*) *09.01 B.* 2009. Acrylic, spray enamel, Yarka linen, 16 x 48 in.
(*Bottom*) *0809.00 B.* 2009. Acrylic, spray enamel, Yarka linen, 21 x 63 in.

The paintings of Megan Parry are obsessed with looking. In her wry and varied visual universe, cartoonish, bald-headed figures peer at the viewer, at one another, or at obscure objects of interest that only they can see. Huge, lidless eyeballs (intimations of vast, inscrutable beings that the canvas cannot contain) hover in close-up and stare with a deranged intensity (as in ***Aspetto***, 2008–2010), or else a kind of cosmic serenity. When Parry paints houses, their windows are often eyes: personifying, face-making. Even her multitudinous coffins and "***enclosures***," isolated details of an architecture of confinement, have eyes, have windows—or if they don't, they insistently don't, inviting the viewer to wonder what is being kept in (or out) behind their solid walls.

Inside/outside; looking, watching; windows; the

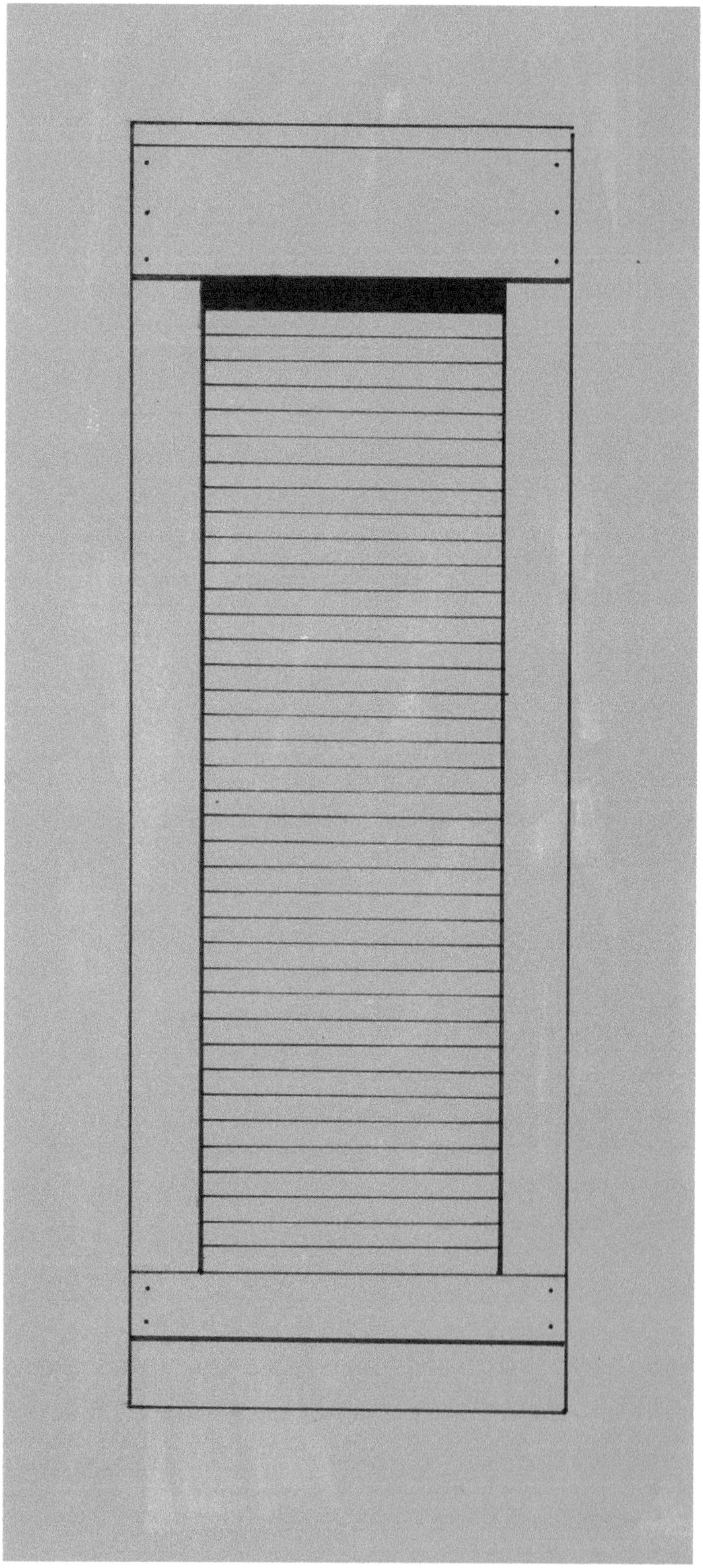

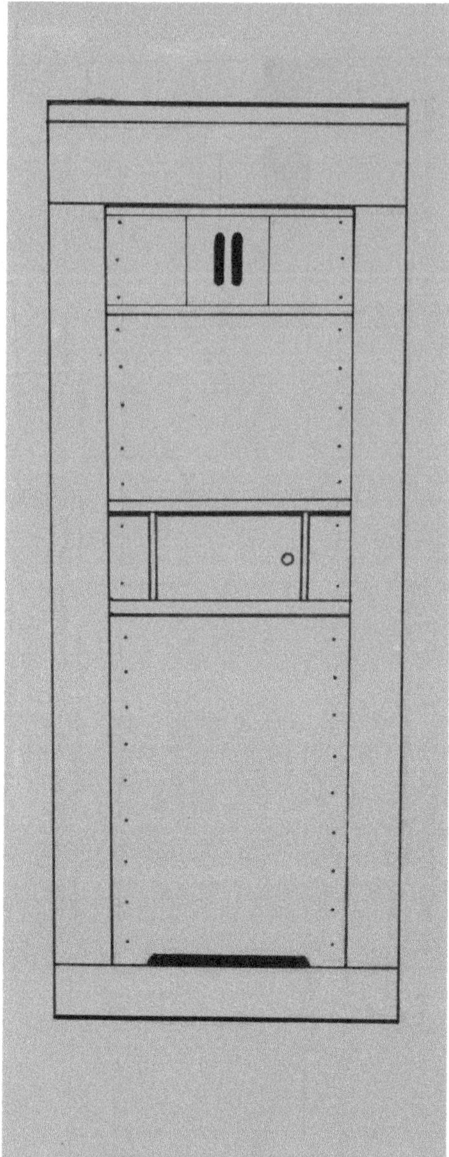

(*Left*) *0931*. 2012. Acrylic, ink, paper, 16 x 12 in.

(*Right*) *0933*. 2012. Acrylic, ink, paper, 16 x 12 in.

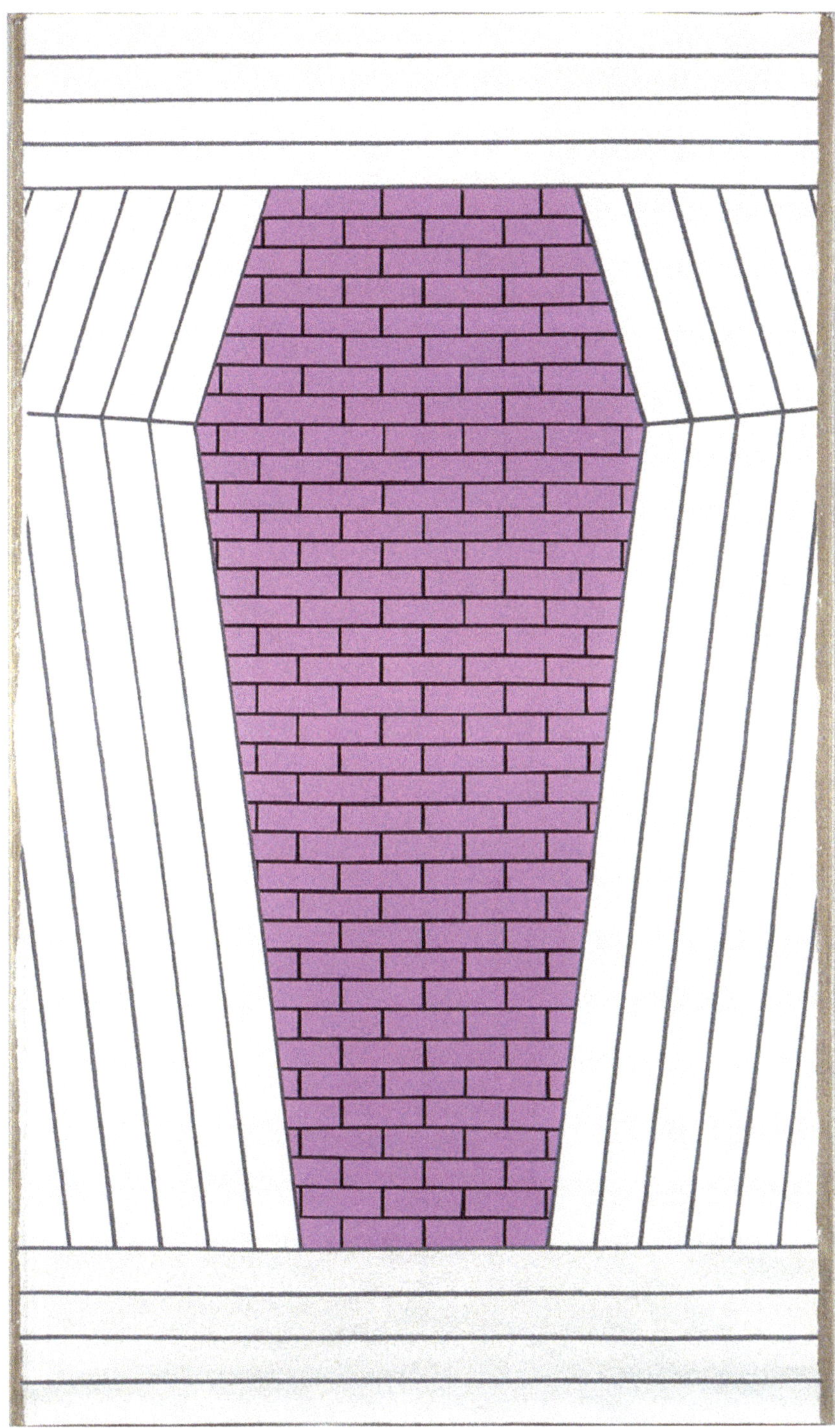

Purple Coffin. 1986. Oil, linen, 54 x 80 in.

architecture of the domestic: Parry has used the master bedroom of her Lafayette Park town house as her Detroit studio for more than twenty years, and it is tempting to associate her work with that singular neighborhood of glass houses and voyeurs. Tempting, too, to see her oscillation between limpid, rectilinear precision, on one hand, and subtle, organic texturing and layering, on the other, as a reflection of that same duality in Lafayette Park's minimalist buildings and abundant landscape. But the analogy only goes so far. Other than, perhaps, "painter" and "postmodern," any attempt to draw a box around Parry, who grew up in Philadelphia and who has lived and worked in Colorado, New York, England, and France, is futile. Her work is too expansive, too multivalent. What to make, for instance, of its humor, whimsy, and menace? Of its deep connection to comics and film? Of her enthusiasm for atypical canvas shapes, collage-like collisions of texture and image, and for filigree, astronomy, and careful, painterly imitation of that cracking, veining tendency of antique

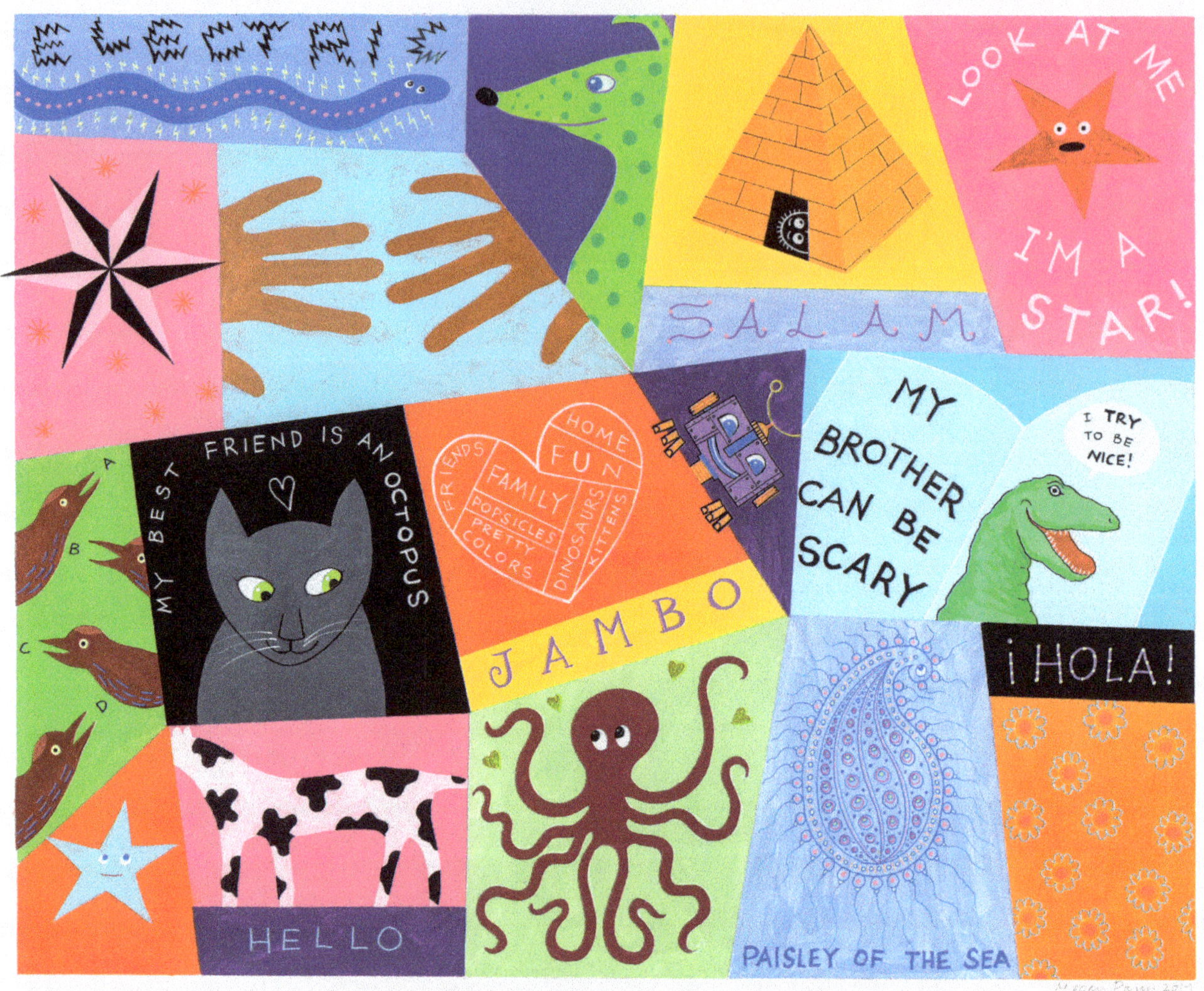

#15. 2014. Acrylic, ink, polypropylene paper, 27 x 33 in.

glaze known as "crazing" (which looks, she notes with interest, conspicuously like a road map when seen up close)?

For much of her career, Parry was active as an architectural stencil artist and muralist, and her commercial work can be seen in Detroit in various wards of three hospitals: Children's, Henry Ford, and Receiving. Her works for young people, including nineteen large paintings made in 2014 for the examining rooms at Children's, brim with an ecumenical assortment of warm cartoon imagery and text, providing their viewers with, as the artist aptly puts it, "a wide range of entertainments (see, for example, ***#15***)."

Parry's natural tendency is, emphatically, toward diversity, and that inclination is nowhere more evident than in her ongoing ***coffin series***. In 2010, she returned to an image from ***Purple Coffin***, a 1986 painting of a precise arrangement of purple brick in the shape of a hexagon/coffin, its contours echoed by pulsating, concentric lines. Since then, she has made more than one hundred related works, usually small, on paper, and consisting of three

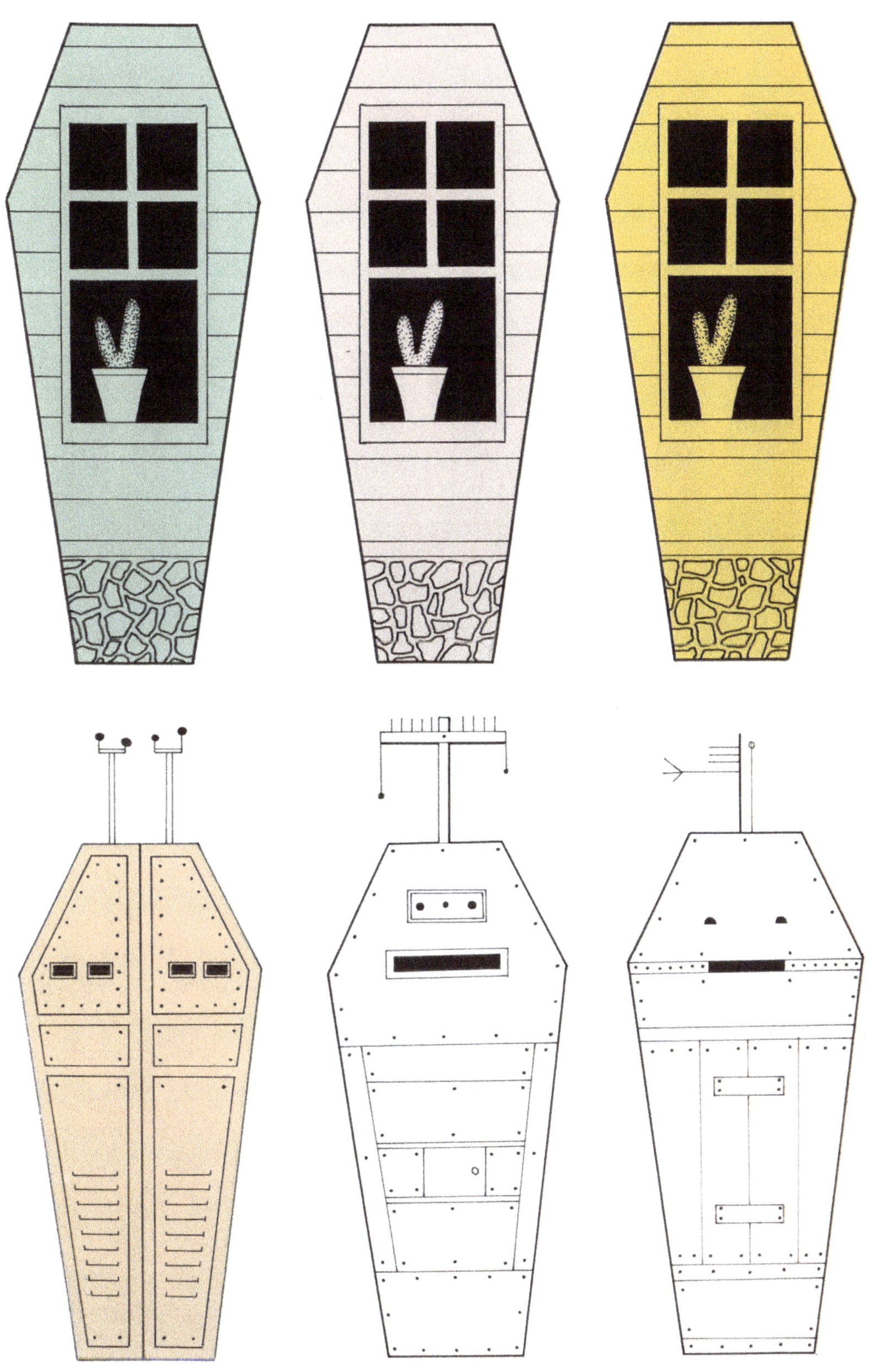

(*Top*) *0662.* 2012. Acrylic, ink, paper, 9 x 12 ½ in.
(*Bottom*) *0671.* 2012. Acrylic, ink, paper, 9 x 12 ½ in.

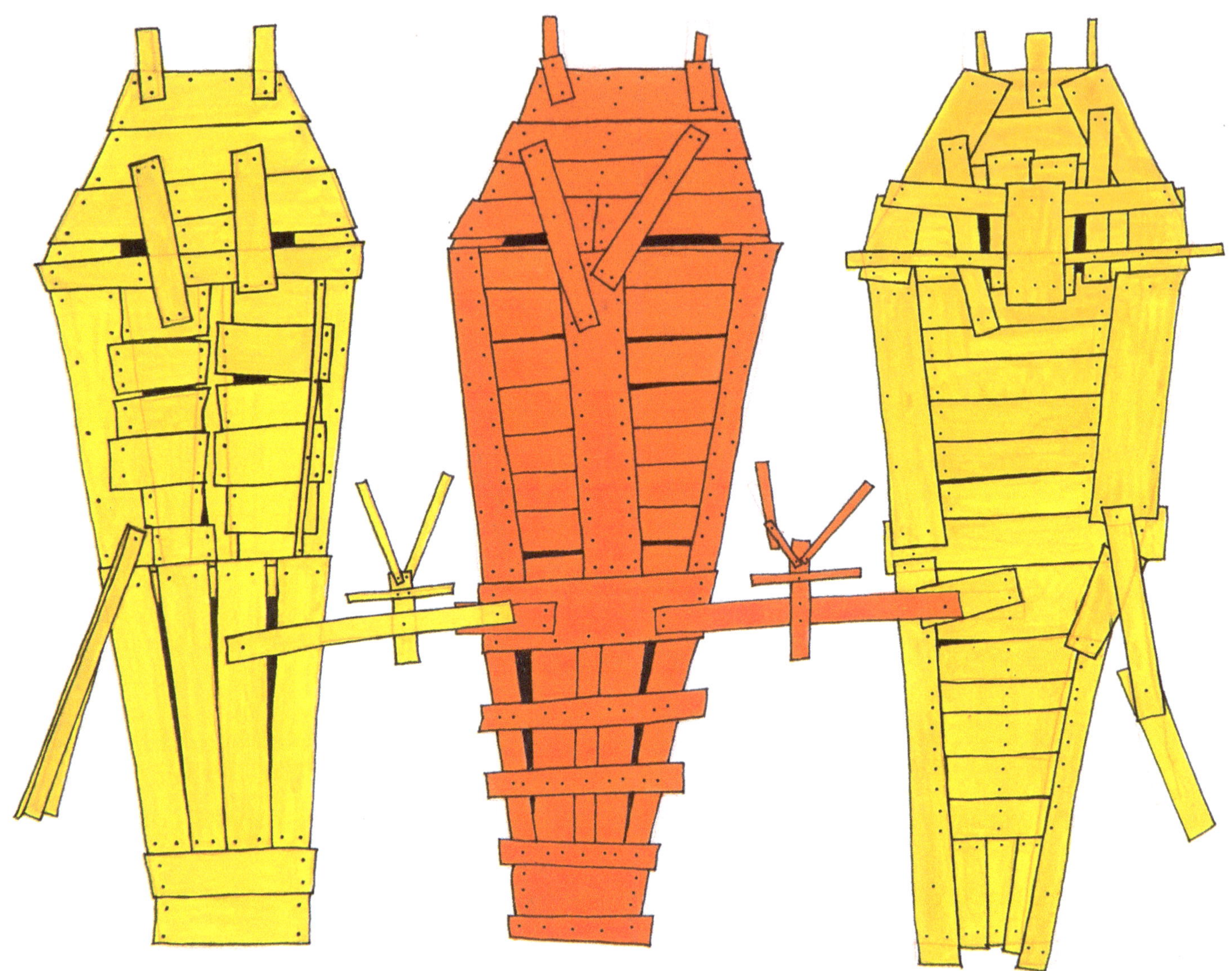

0702. 2011. Watercolor, ink, paper, 9 x 12 ½ in.

corresponding casket shapes that float together in negative space. This project began, she says, as a spoof: "a catalog for potential purchasers" that "wandered off into . . . unexpected byways." In these pieces, which mark a significant reduction and standardization of her otherwise capacious and nuanced sense of space, many of Parry's disparate visual languages are unified, encyclopedically, and the full force of her fertile imagination is on display. These are coffins as houses, prisons, figures, and faces; as compadres, robots, and star fields; as piles of stone and abstract shapes—coffins as miniature canvases. If they are about death, they are about

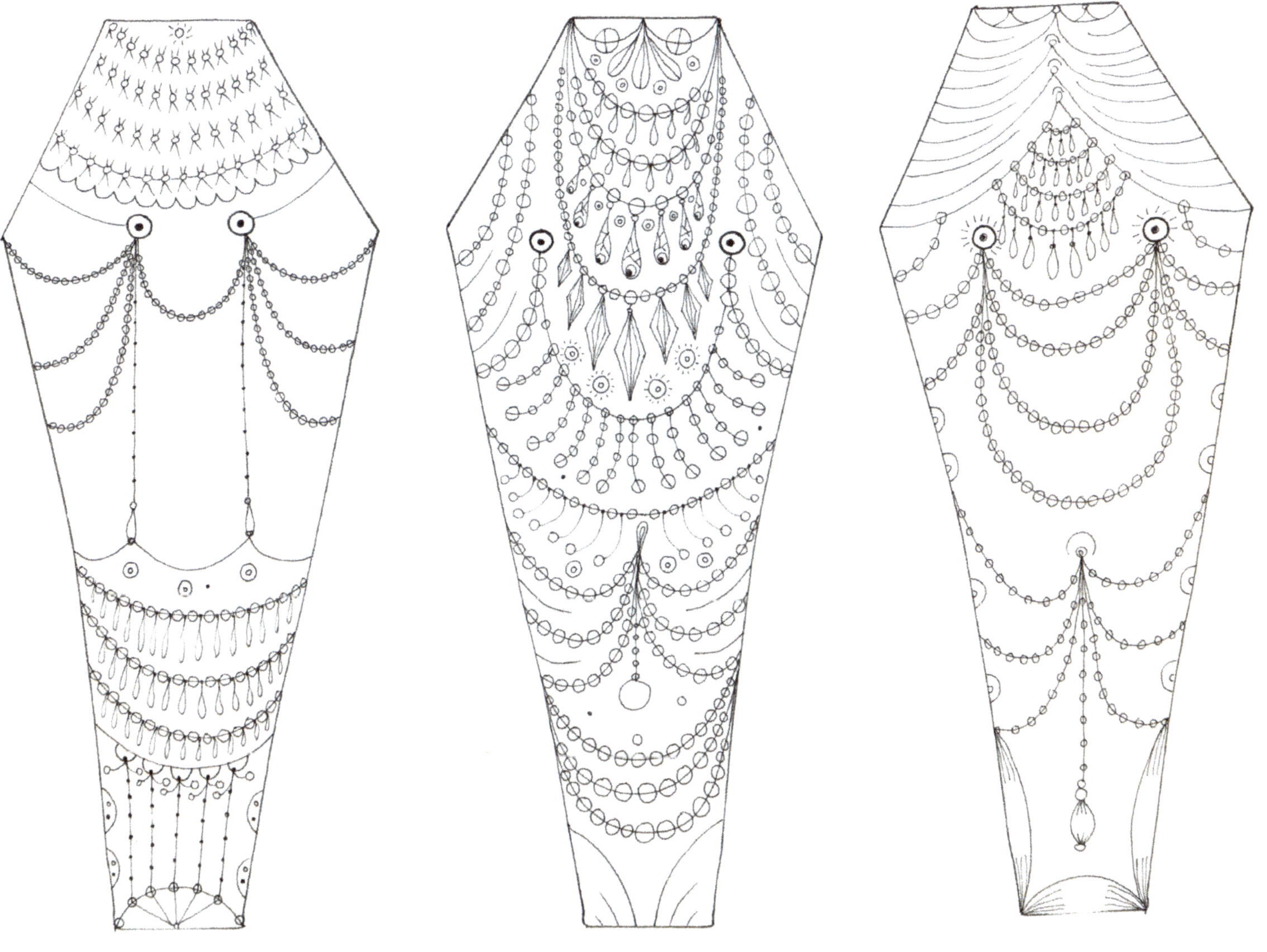

0771. 2012. Ink, paper, 9 x 12 ½ in.

death as both tragedy and
comedy. As creative opportunity.
As a field of infinite variety.

MATTHEW PIPER, MARCH 2015

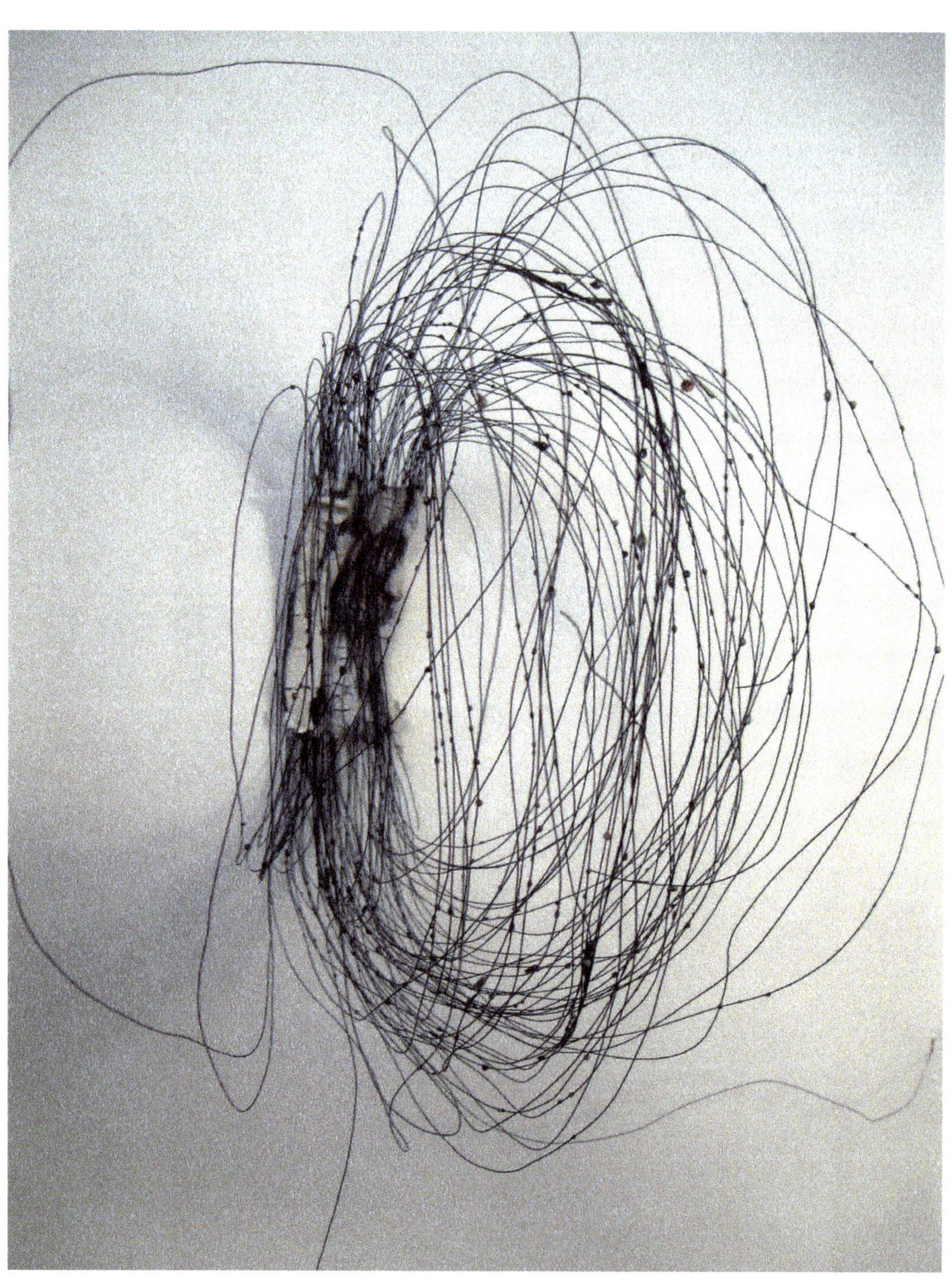

#1. 2013. Salt-fired porcelain, wire, 11 x 3 ½ x 9 in.

18 // ELIZABETH YOUNGBLOOD

Born Detroit, 1952
BFA, University of Michigan
MFA, Cranbrook Academy of Art
Lives in Detroit

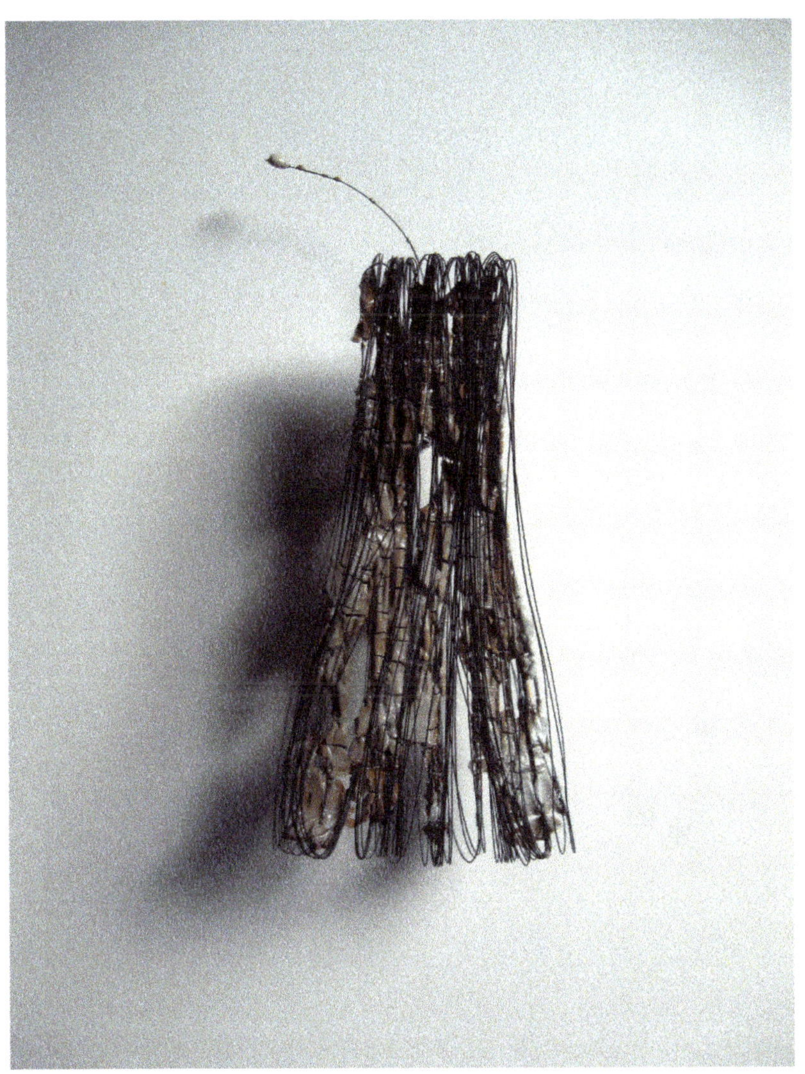

#2. 2013. Salt-fired porcelain, wire, 7 x 4 ½ x 2 ½ in.

Elizabeth Youngblood's work combines great personality and remarkable restraint. Typically starting from a monochrome palette and the repeated graphical element of the line, she has utilized her dexterity with fiber, wire, ceramics, drawing, and paper to quietly produce a visually coherent body of work that has continued to evolve over a period of several decades.

Youngblood's recent show at Detroit's N'Namdi Gallery, which featured wire and porcelain works of breathtaking delicacy (for example, *#1*, *#2*, and *#6*, all 2013), can be seen as the latest iteration of a trajectory that includes fiber pieces (e.g., 1994's ***Black Weaving #1***) and a slowly unfolding long-term series of ink on paper works typified by 1998's ***Untitled (Early Cone)***, 1999's ***Untitled (Cone with Lines)***, 1999's ***Early Meander***,

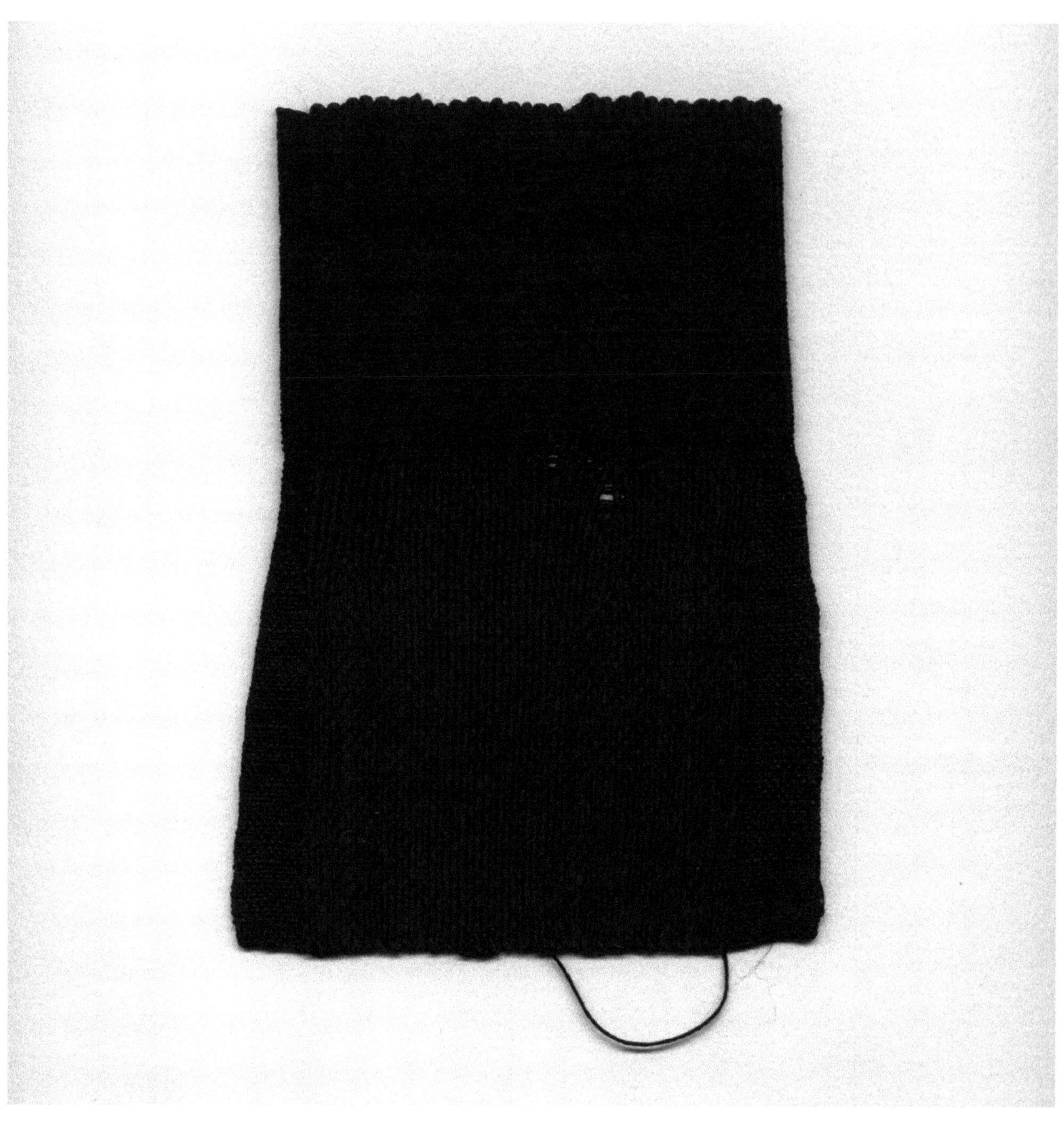

Black Weaving #1. 1994. Rayon, twine, 7 x 4 ½ in.

2005's ***Contemplating Bask***, and 2006's ***Four Holes and a Gash***.

Although Youngblood works with a limited set of elements, her work is far from minimal. A more accurate comparison may be the Korean art movement dansaekhwa (literally "monochrome painting"), which focuses on the meditative aspect of art production through the relationship between materials, material and

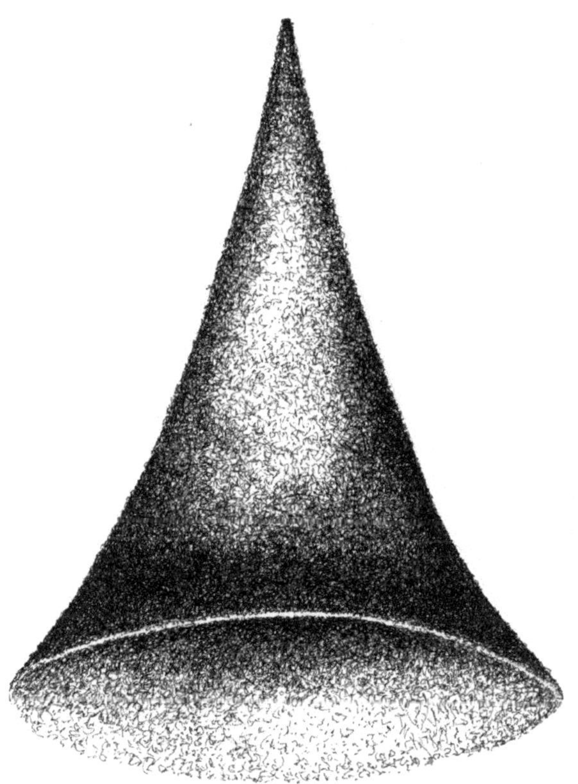

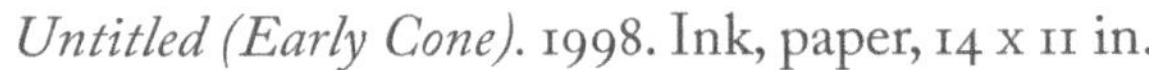

Untitled (Early Cone). 1998. Ink, paper, 14 x 11 in.

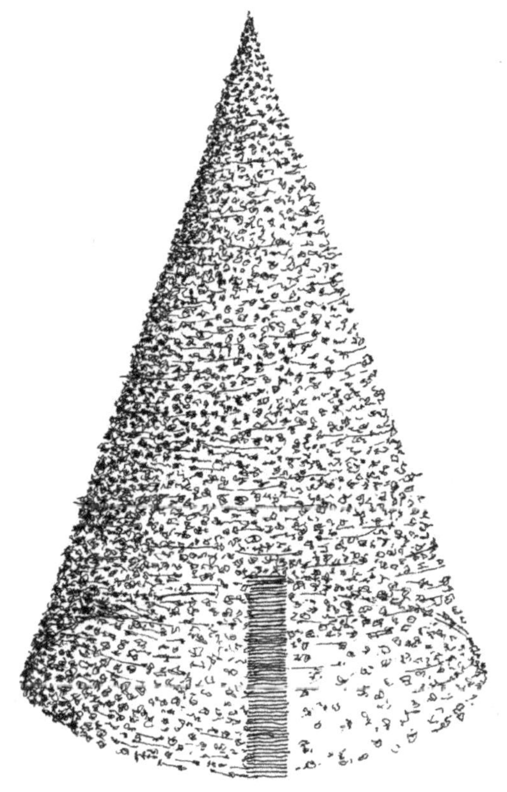

Untitled (Cone with Lines). 1999. Ink, paper, 11 x 14 in.

artist, and artwork and viewer. Interestingly, Youngblood has often commented on art-making as a form of communication, starting with her childhood experience of the intergenerational conversation it animated in her craft-immersed, blue-collar family, and later being present in the dialogue with self, and with audience, that her mature artwork inspired. Equally interestingly, Youngblood's mother had a long-term interest in Asian aesthetics.

Youngblood's heritage of craft has clearly been a formative influence. In 2002 she told writer Glen Mannisto: "My mother made many of our clothes. She was a maker. In fact, I come from a family of makers. My aunts cooked, knitted, crocheted; my uncle Oliver was a craftsman. He taught me how to make things, how to plan and execute a job so it's done right from the beginning. So first, before anything

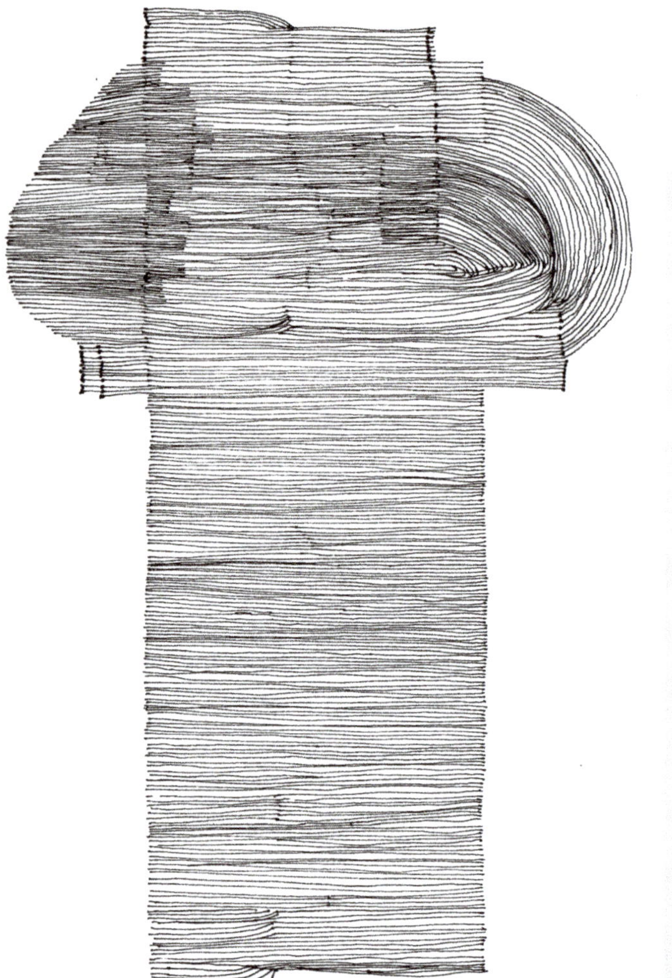

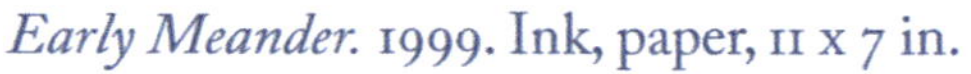

Early Meander. 1999. Ink, paper, 11 x 7 in.

Contemplating Bask. 2005. Ink, paper, 11 x 7 in.

else, I'm concerned with craft." Youngblood still relates to this quote, except she doesn't see craft as her only major concern; rather, she sees it as just one of a network of interrelated and inseparable concerns, including process, materiality, and design, that collectively determine the quality she is seeking in her work. She talks of weaving a basket-like form from wood strips but leaving it unfinished because she could think of no way to secure one of the trailing edges without gluing—which would be a process outside of the craft and material discipline she was invested in. She also talks of the embedded time quality in her work—time spent experimenting with process and material, or meditating on results.

Youngblood also has a serious professional background in graphic design, starting at Cass Tech, where she attended the school's famously rigorous

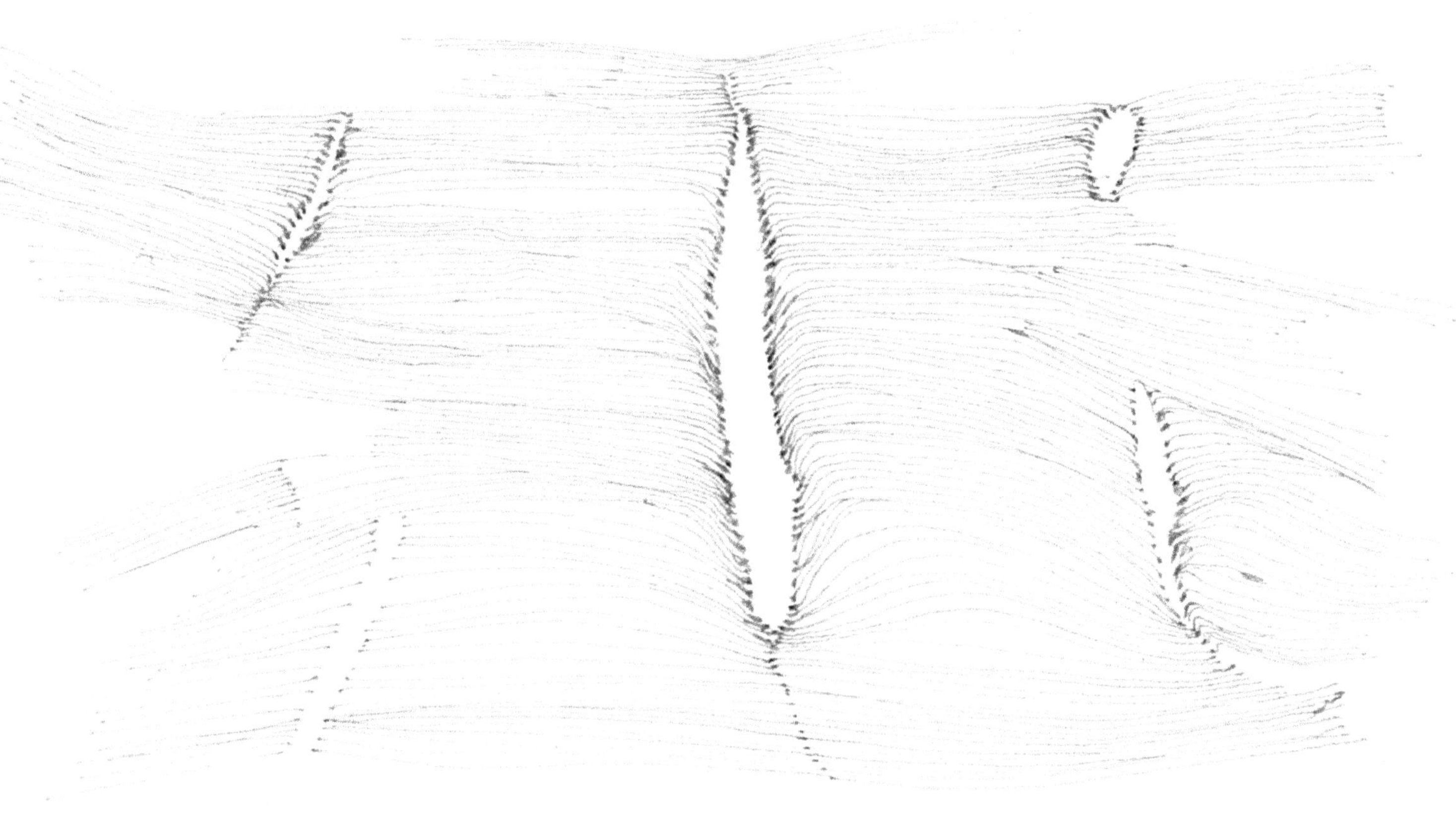

Four Holes and a Gash. 2006. Ink, paper, 7 x 11 in.

commercial art classes. At the University of Michigan, she found the advertising-focused graphic design curriculum uninspiring, instead studying ceramics, but she leveraged the knowledge she had gained at high school to get an on-the-job education working at the university press. In 1974, legendary graphic designer and educator Katherine McCoy suggested that Youngblood come to study with her, and husband Michael, at Cranbrook. McCoy was famous for having a good eye for picking students that would benefit from her unorthodox curriculum. Among the habits that Youngblood learned from McCoy was to constantly question the real meaning of every element in graphic design. She considers that a parallel thought process transferred into her art-making, as exemplified by her constant reexamination of what it means to make a line, and hence the major

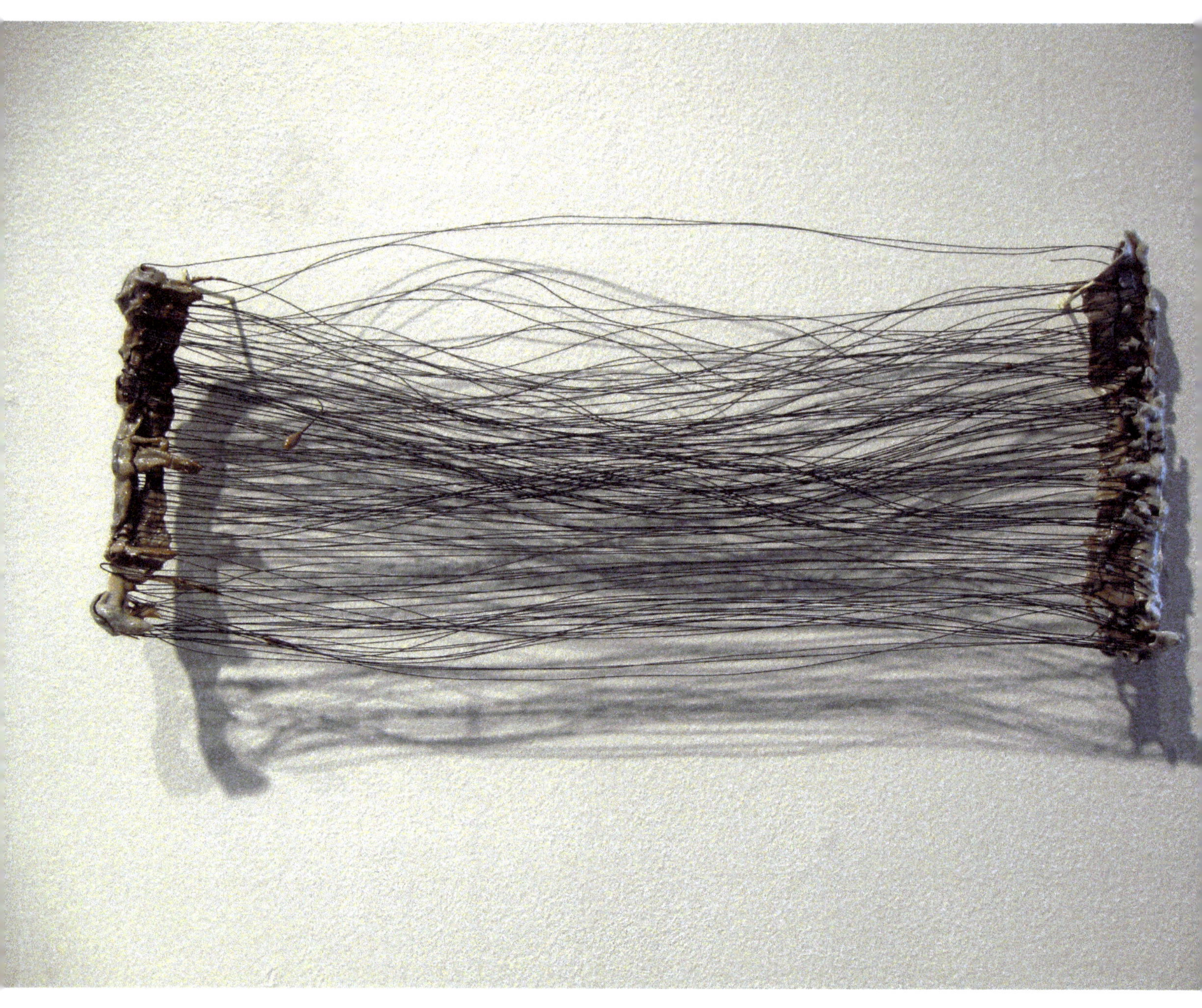

#6. 2013. Salt-fired porcelain, wire, 6 x 14 x 1 in.

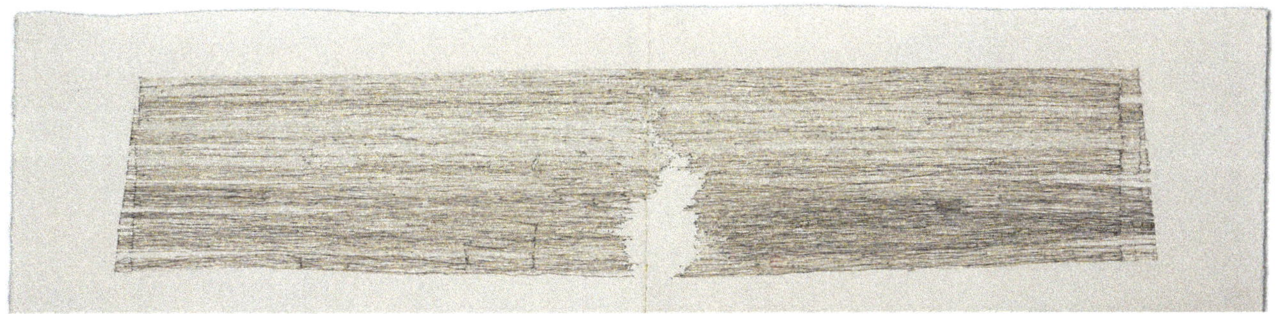

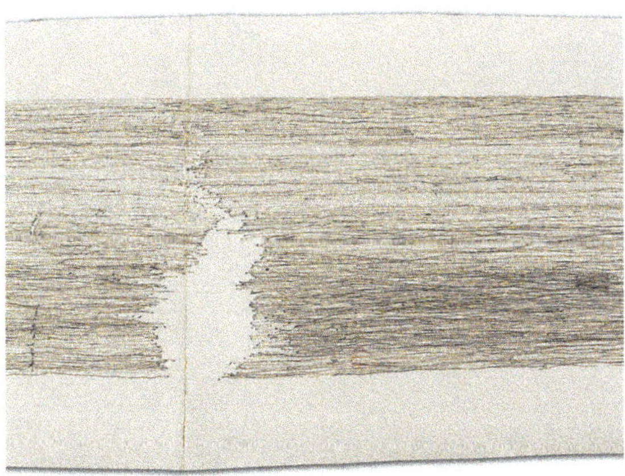

Plinth. 2014. Ink, paper (full piece; detail), 66 x 14 in.

influence of McCoy's teaching on her art is conceptual, not visual.

Youngblood's most recent work has returned to the line with large pieces such as ***Plinth*** (2014), in which the span of the paper is deliberately greater than can be reached in a single gesture of the arm. It is beautiful work, and another incremental step in the experimentation that has characterized her highly considered journey through craft, material, design, process, and artistic integrity.

STEVE PANTON, JANUARY 2015

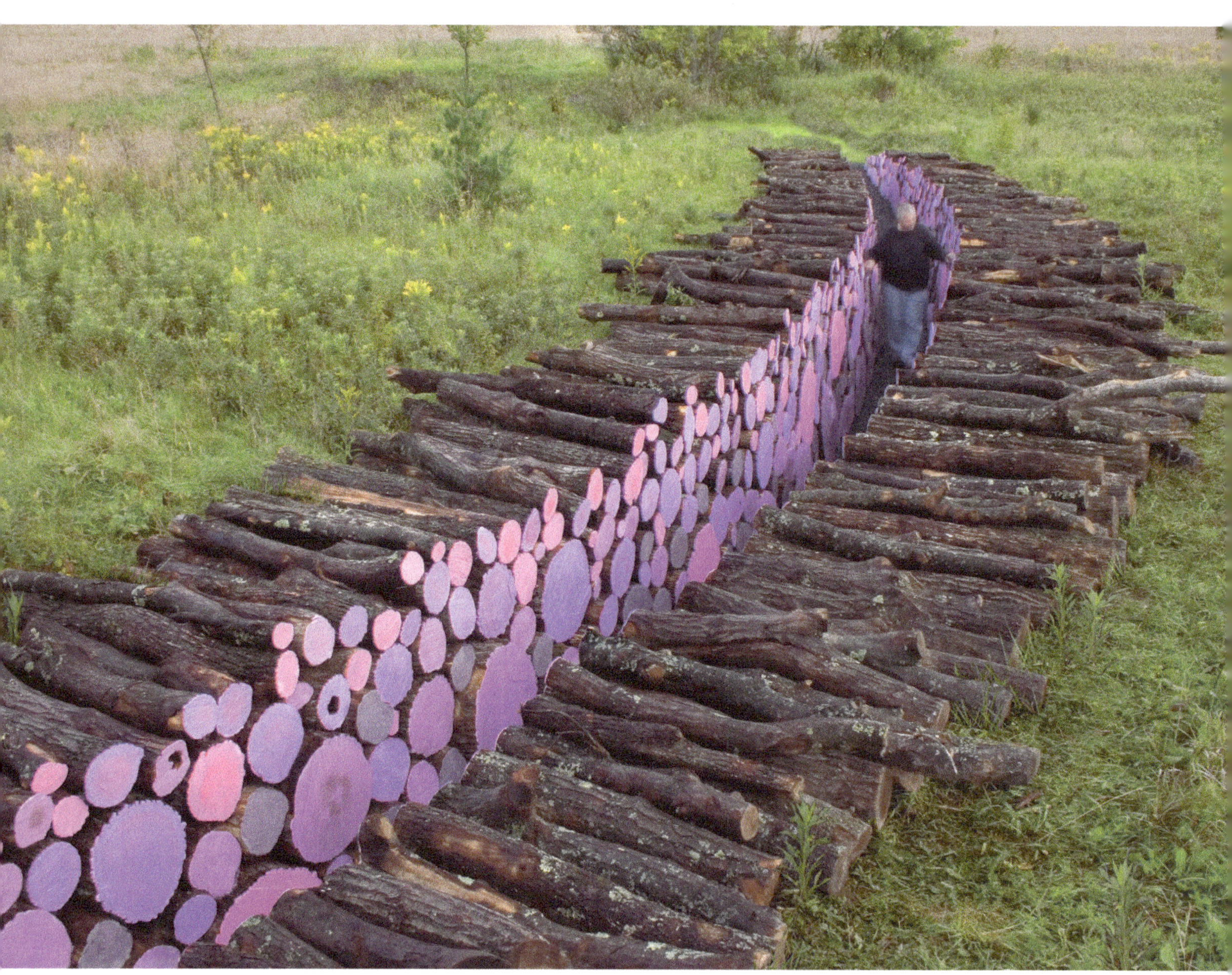

Wake. 2006. Wood, paint, 95 ft.

19 // MICHAEL MCGILLIS

Born Detroit, 1966
BFA, College for Creative Studies
Lives in Royal Oak, Michigan

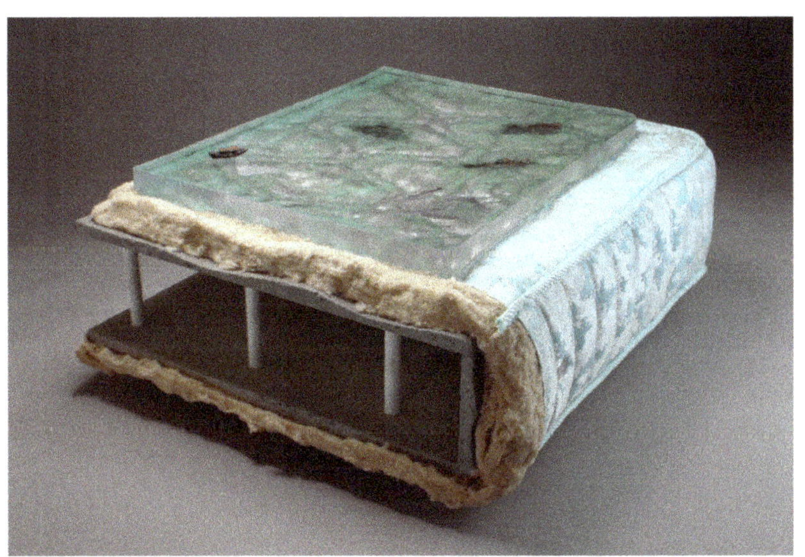

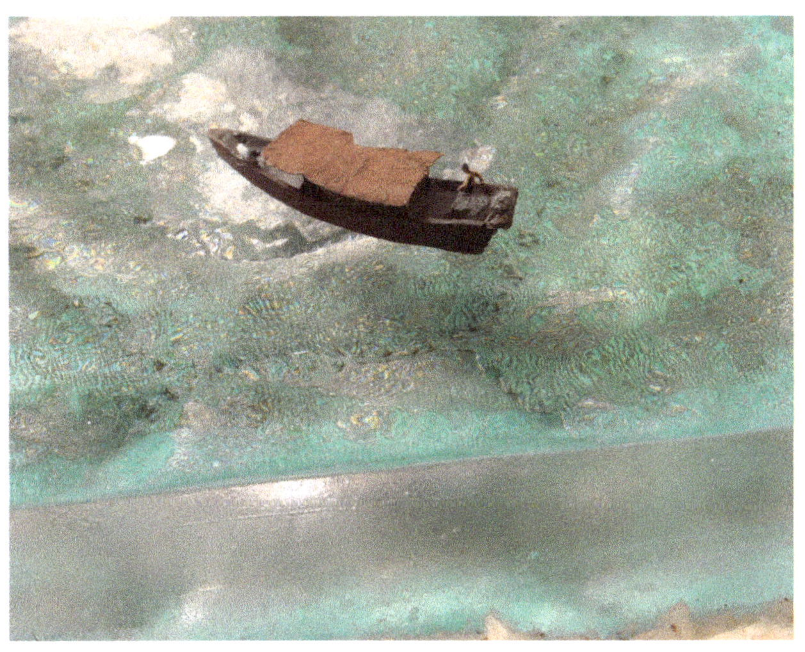

I have suspected for a little while that Michael McGillis is a fulcrum between divergent layers of reality. How else to explain his uncanny ability to peel back the edges of our everyday world, to uncover hidden environments just below the surface? Taken as a whole, McGillis's work could be seen as a kind of sculptural iteration of magical realism, where undefined or fantastic realities cohabitate within the everyday fixtures that are easily taken for granted. Whether outfitting nature with chance art encounters, like ***Wake*** (2006), or constructing immersive gallery installations that synthesize nature in a controlled setting, as with ***Reckoning a Peripheral Wilderness*** (2012), McGillis confesses to an

Blast Fishermen, Semporna, Malaysia. Mattress, polyester resin, mixed-media, 20 x 16 x 9 in.

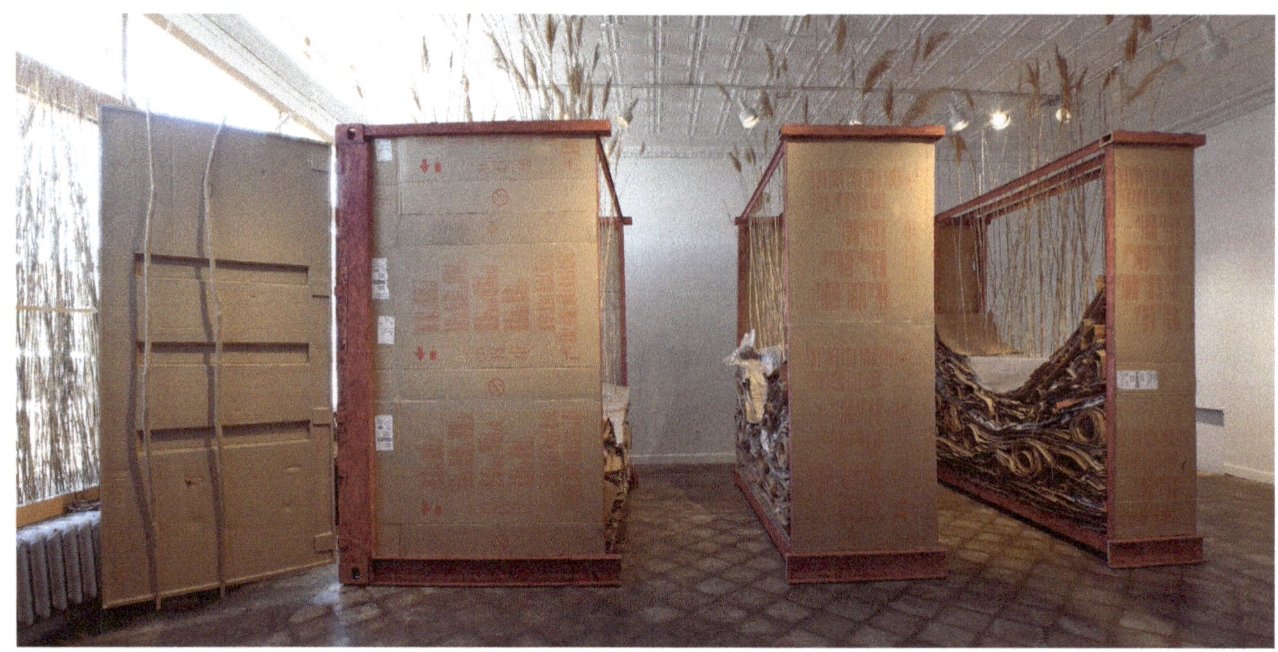

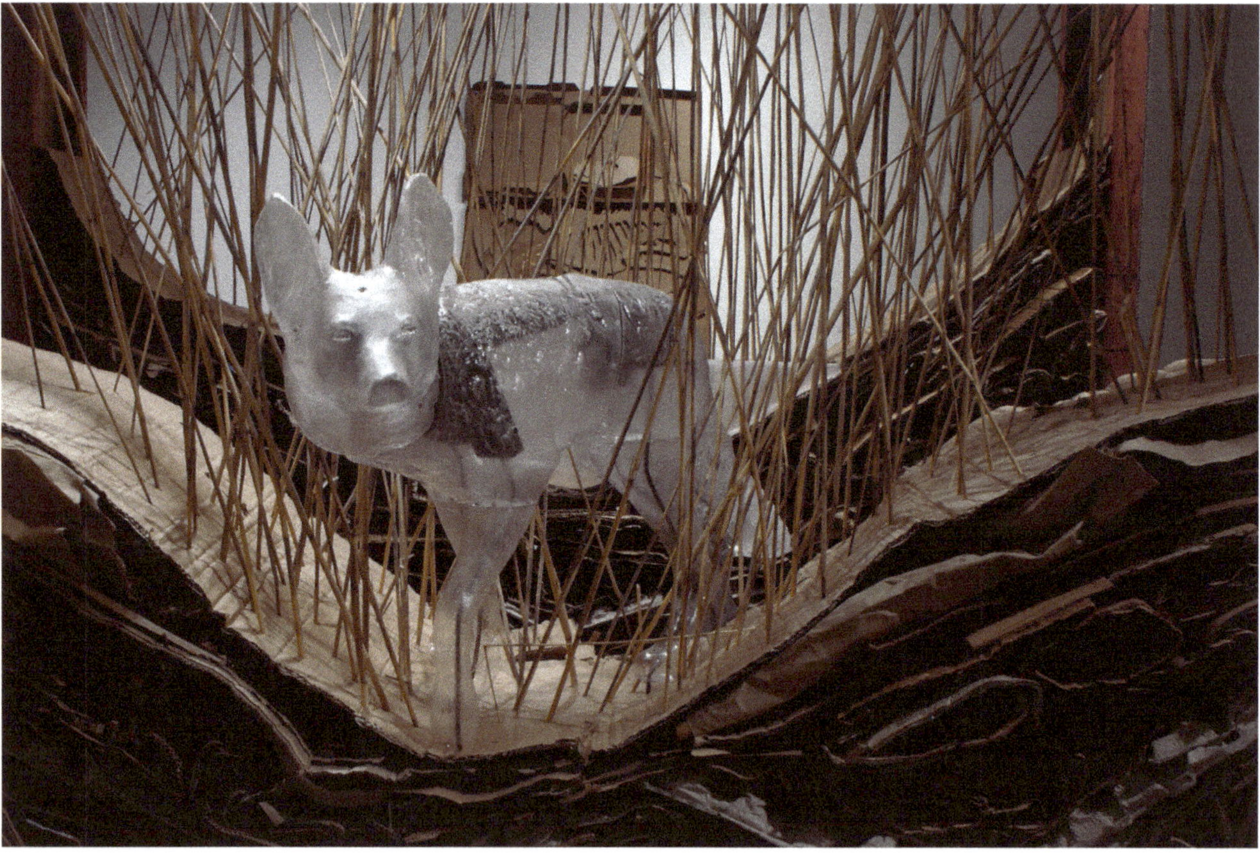

Reckoning a Peripheral Wilderness. 2012. Cardboard, phragmites reeds, plastic, mixed materials.

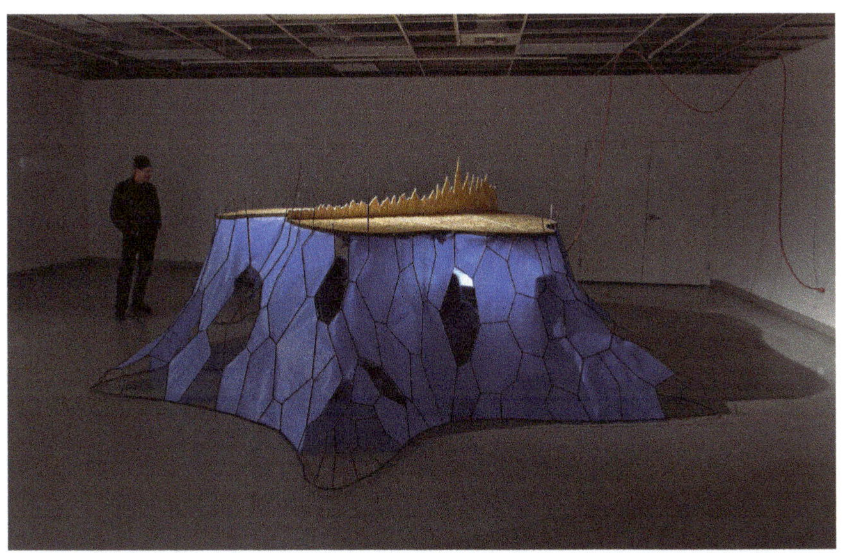

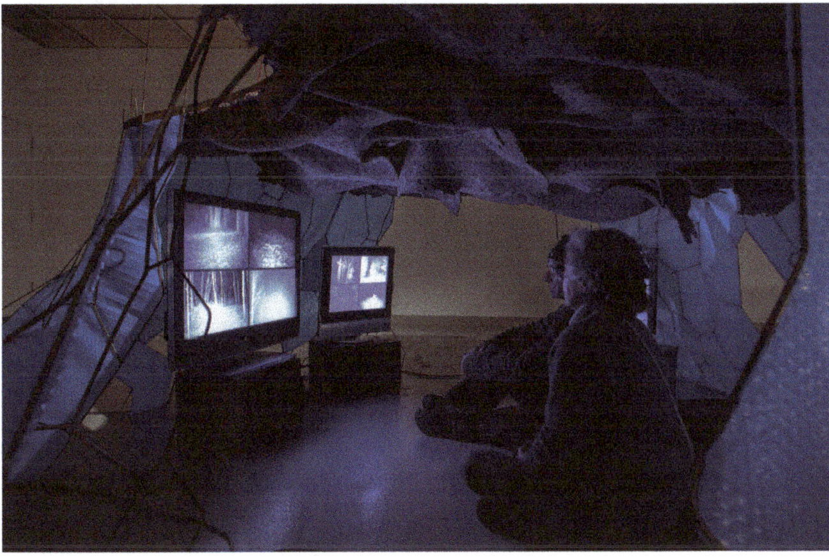

Your Back to the Woods. 2014. Salvaged plastic, steel, wood, video.

"attraction to randomness" that draws him toward found and discarded materials as the foundation for these imagined realities.

These materials—which include phragmites reeds, branches, plastic sheeting, and layers of cardboard in various states of disintegration—help McGillis to do what he terms "collaborating with chance," but he is also quick to acknowledge an element of surrogacy in their use, with materials holding space as proxies for other things, just as his installations carve out microcosmic placeholders within reality. McGillis also enjoys playing with scale, prone to leave the viewer towering above miniature dioramas, such as ***Blast Fishermen, Semporna, Malaysia*** (2003)—with the ocean scaled to approximately half the surface of a discarded mattress—or else reduced to the perspective of a small, root-dwelling mammal housed inside a giant stump, as in ***Your Back to the Woods*** (2014).

But scale is also a mechanism of control, which McGillis wields—consciously or otherwise—to counterbalance the elements of chance that he cultivates. An old fleece jacket may trigger the revelation of a hilly landscape, but then a meticulous diorama

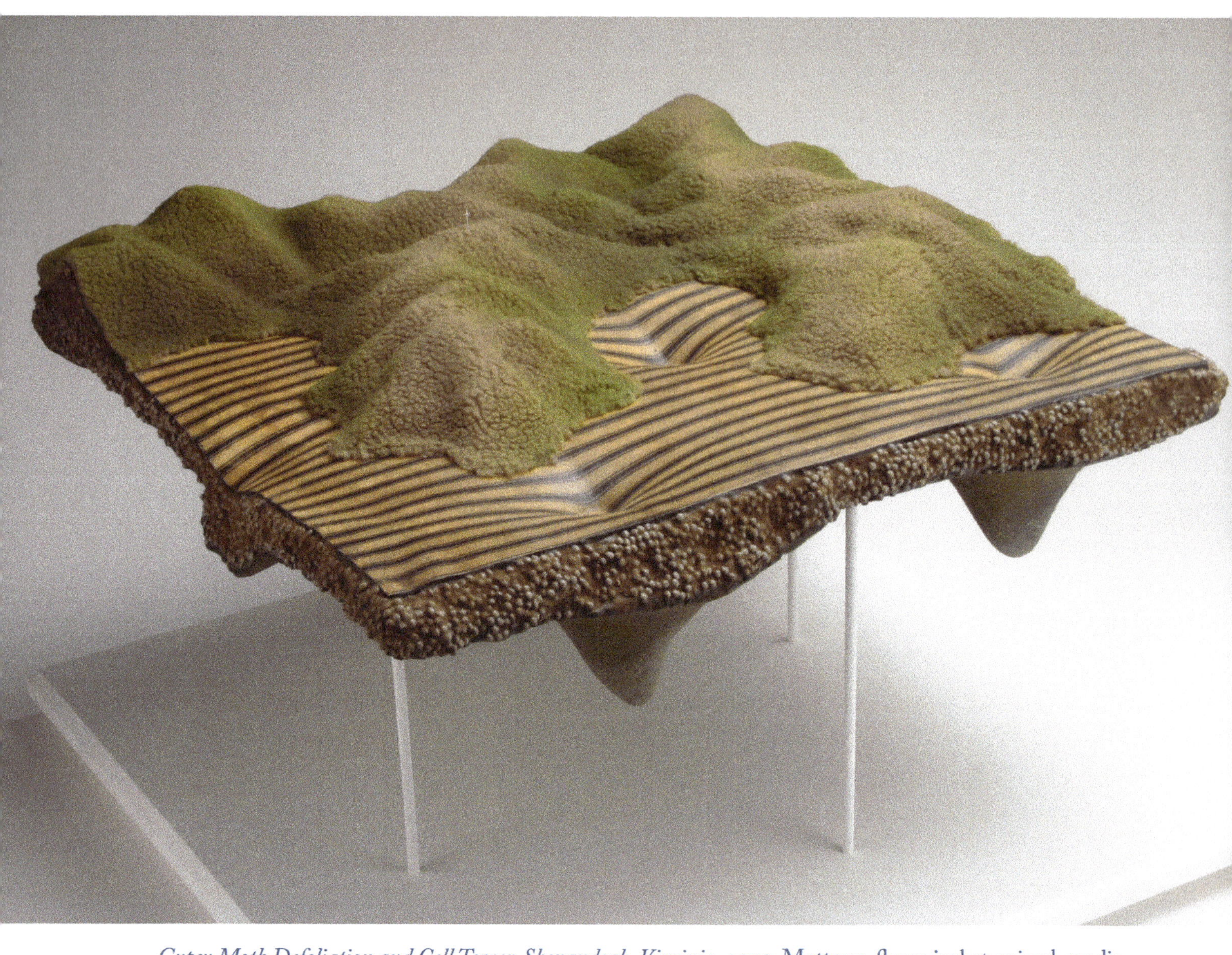

Gypsy Moth Defoliation and Cell Tower, Shenandoah, Virginia. 2003. Mattress, fleece jacket, mixed-media, 24 x 24 x 9 in.

emerges, drawing random inspiration into the tightly rendered formation of ***Gypsy Moth Defoliation and Cell Tower, Shenandoah, Virginia***, part of his 2003 *Micro-Disasters* series. As companion to these mini-environments, McGillis's body of sited works create situational encounters in nature, and these works—positioned to be encountered by chance—regain control through the elements of surprise, immersion, and a kind of involuntary interactivity.

Most recently, McGillis has pushed the frame even wider as he completes the first cycle of a series in Denmark, titled *Sightings and Encounters*, which involves the staging of mysterious events. These events are inspired by the landscapes and locales in and around three small Danish towns in Jutland, on the North Sea, and have drawn locals into the creation of these works with somewhat undefined end points.

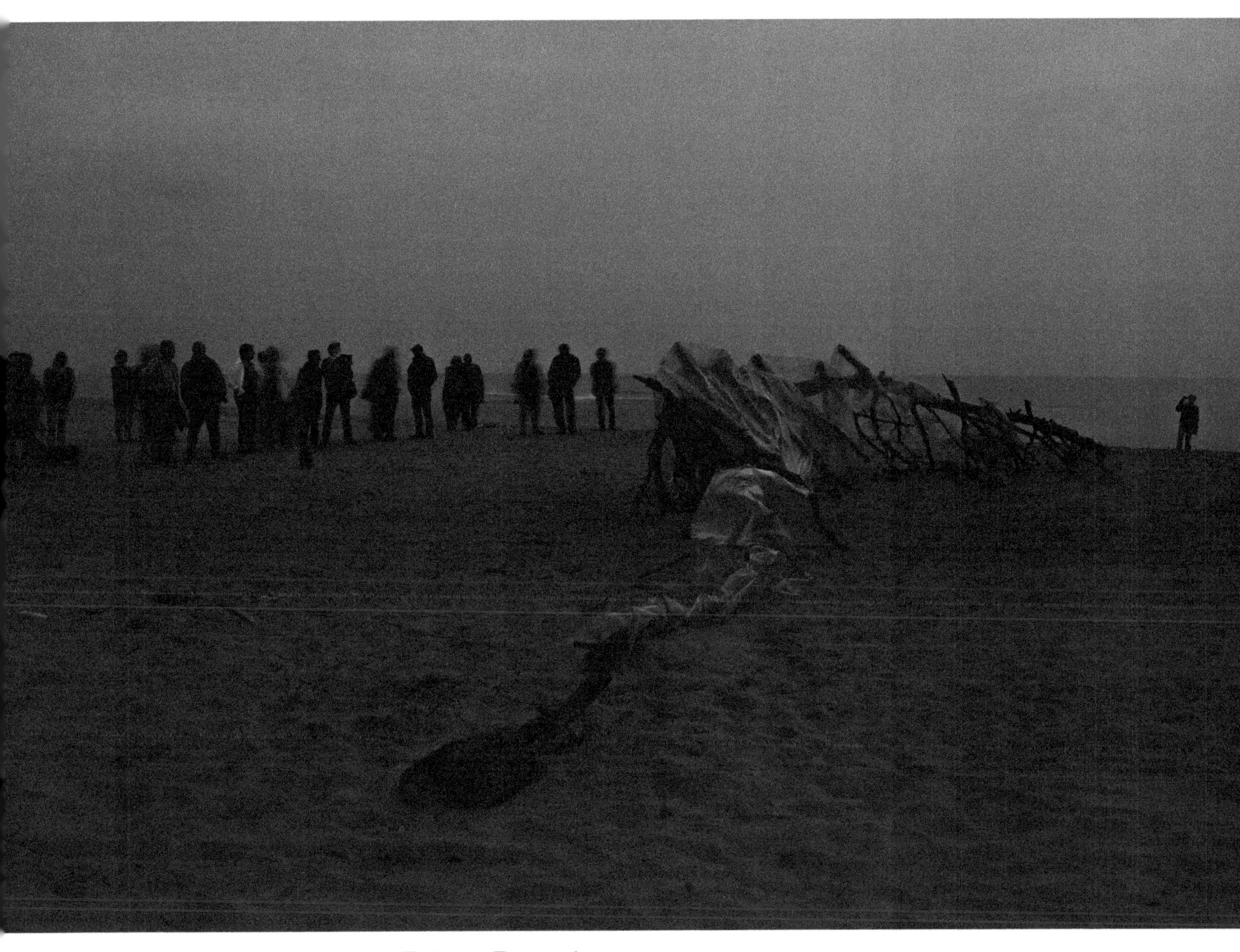

The Beach. 2014. Found materials. Fjaltring, Denmark.

The first starting point (***The Beach***, 2014) is a cold, Scotland-facing shoreline of a land mass called Doggerland, replete with stones and sandy cliffs. Drawing from news accounts about whales having washed up on the beach, but also the prehistory of the place, which was for some reason spared the last ice age, McGillis "started to imagine what this area was like before anyone was there." This line of reasoning evolved to create a "happening" of sorts, which created an opening for the examination or celebration of an occurrence on the beach, a kind of full-sized diorama in collaboration with townspeople. The artistic outcome may be an image, but then, too, it exists in people's memories. "You walk down the beach and you see something on the horizon and you want to examine it," McGillis says. These artifacts and experiences act as pieces of a puzzle

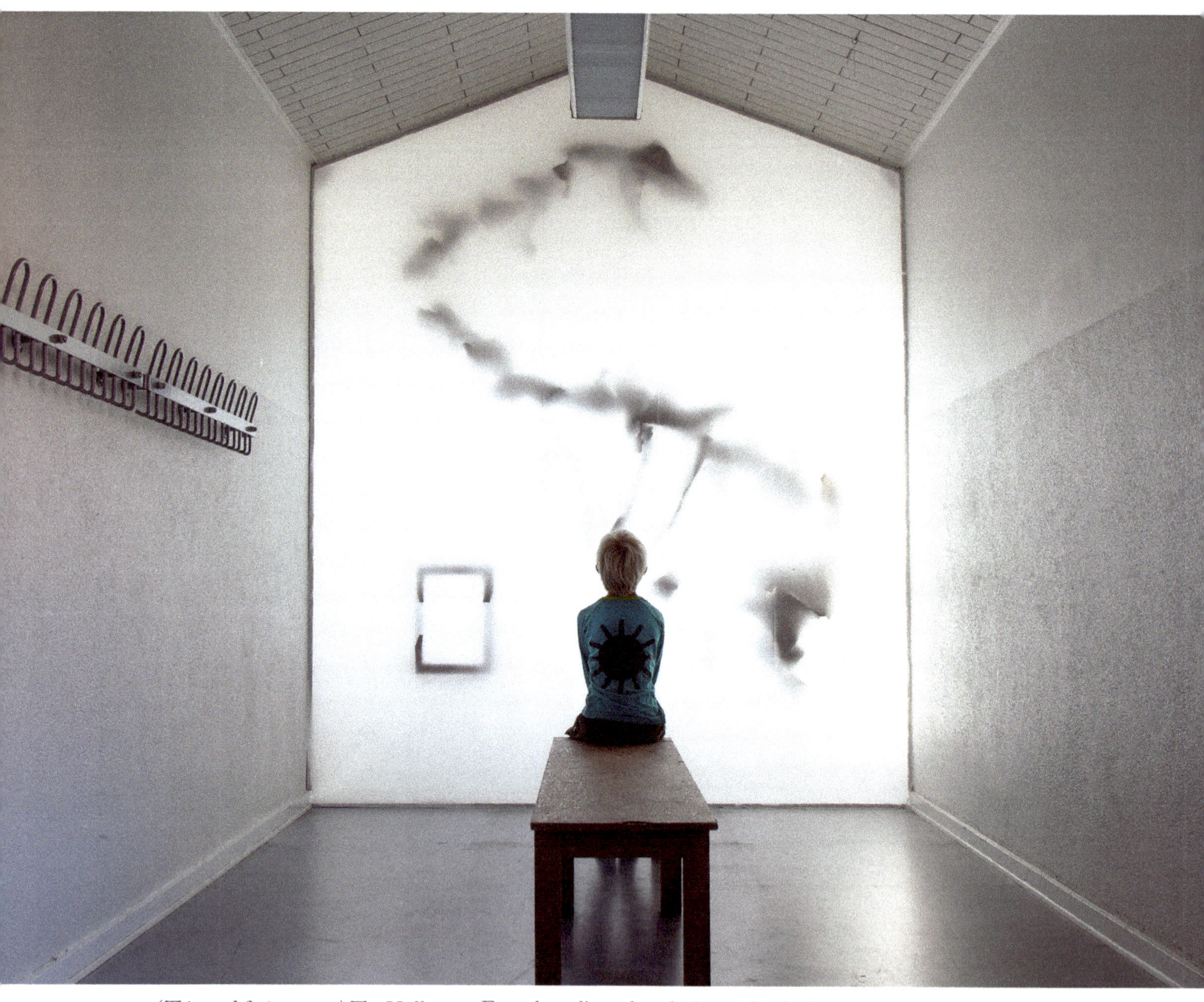

(This and facing page) The Hall. 2014. Found cardboard and plastic. Ryde, Denmark.

coming together in the mind of the viewer. Cut to an interior shot, the hallway of an elementary school in the second town. At the end of the hall, what was once a bright window is now the backlit display of the skeletal remains of . . . something. This second event (***The Hall***, 2014) has a sanctified feel, and remained on display in the school, with little context offered to the children.

This ambiguity seems to be the locus of McGillis's work, a battle between control and

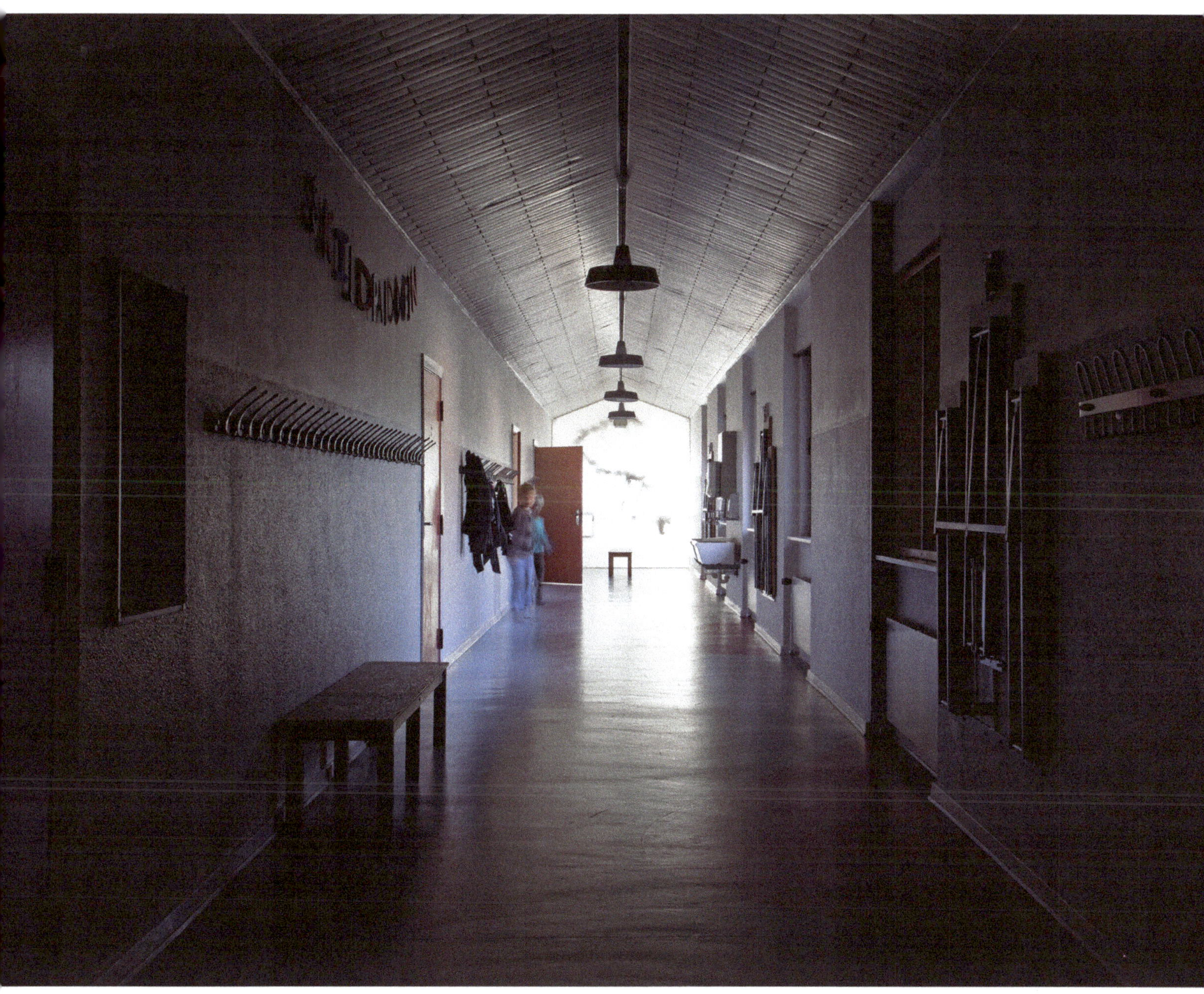

chance, leveraging existing elements as the nucleus for the crystallization of new ideas and structures, ultimately creating things that oscillate between two different states: mythology and science, nature and artifice, life and death, reality and . . . another, deeper reality, one that perhaps cannot be agreed upon universally but invites a universal sort of interest and curiosity.

SARAH ROSE SHARP, APRIL 2015

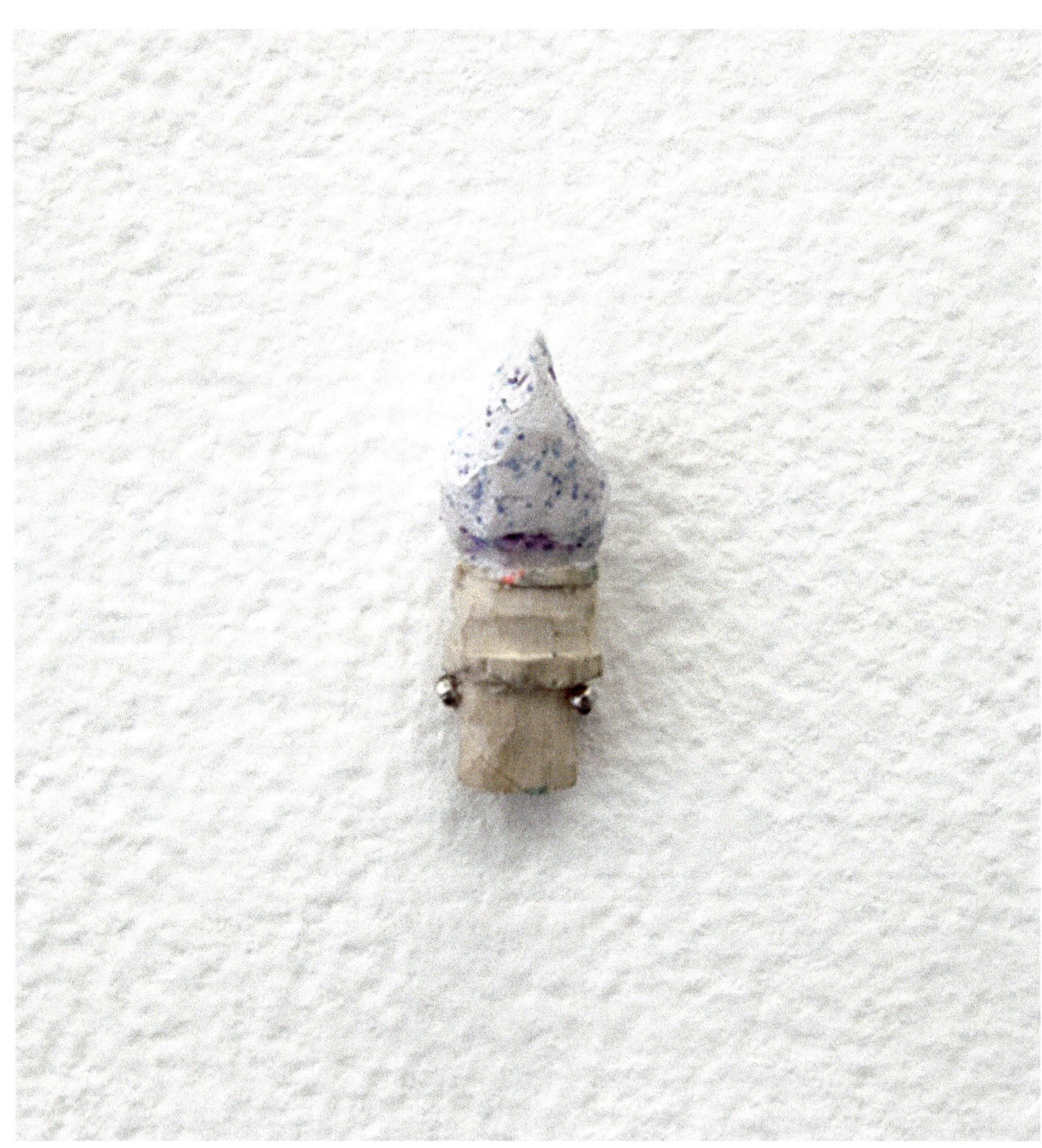

Ice Cream Cone. 2013. Wood, ink, paint, ½ x ½ x 1 3/8 in. Photography by Marc Tatti.

20 // DYLAN SPAYSKY

Born Waterford, Michigan, 1981
BFA, College for Creative Studies
Lives in Hamtramck, Michigan

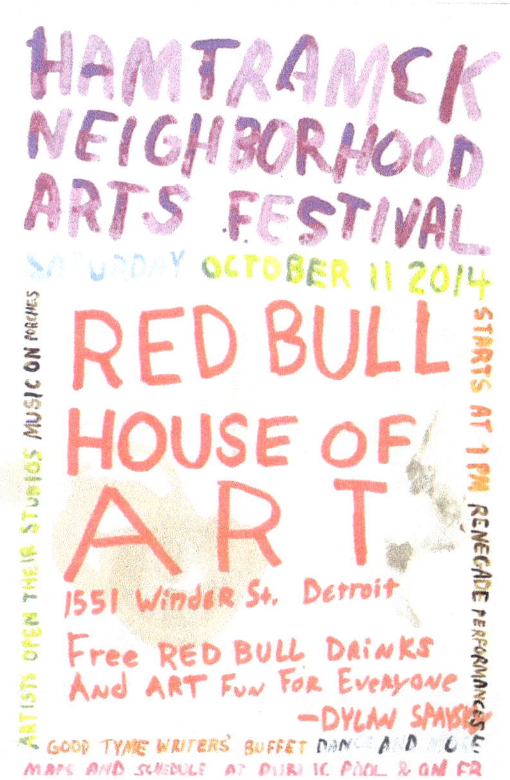

Hamtramck Neighborhood Arts Festival Poster. 2014. Inkjet print, mixed-media, 17 x 12 in.

How do you construct a life in the ex-urban cultural wasteland of Waterford? How do you create meaning from the detritus of America's lowest-common-denominator consumer culture? Two questions that may, or may not, interest the artist Dylan Spaysky. Most likely he would politely decline any such lofty dimensions to his work.

There is a belief that if you want to be heard, you talk with a quiet voice; even so, it takes some sense of purpose to build a solo show at Brooklyn's Cleopatra's Gallery around a series of tiny sculptures whittled from backyard sticks (e.g., ***Ice Cream Cone***, 2013). Spaysky also successfully suggested that a group show at the neurotically image-fixated Center Galleries be given the numbingly anodyne title *Creative Expressions*, and created a poster for the preciously independent ***Hamtramck***

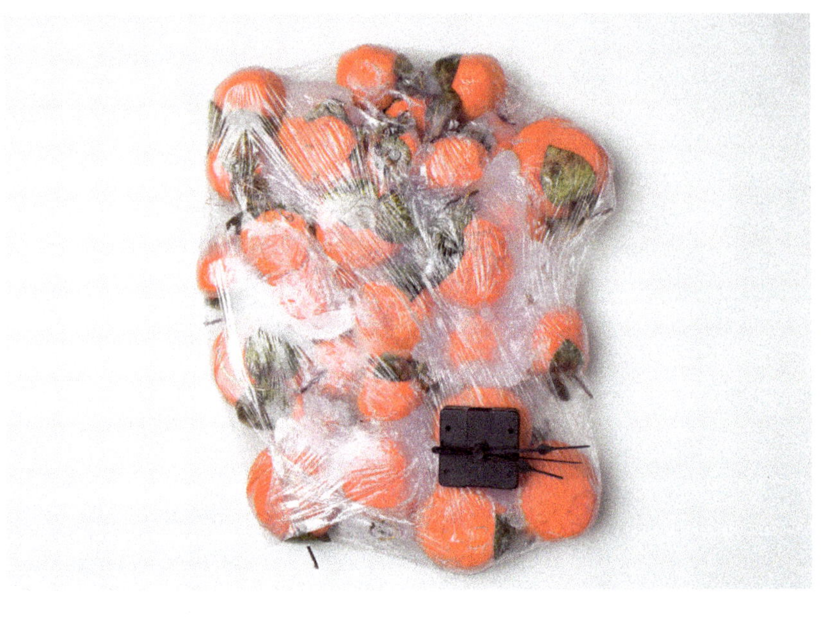

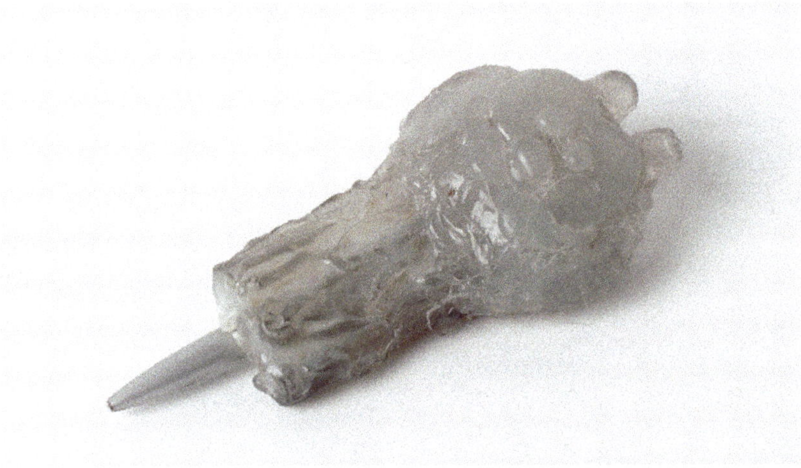

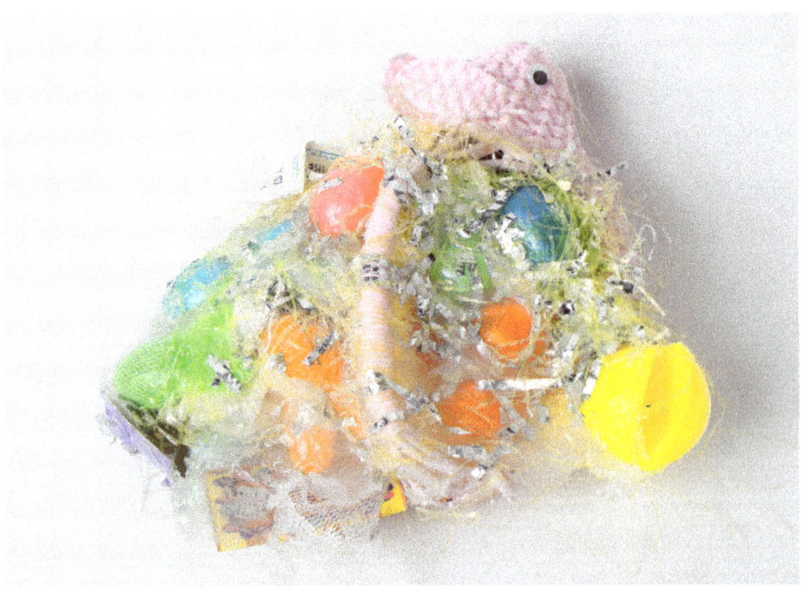

Neighborhood Arts Festival (2014) that features a written homage to the crassly commercial Red Bull House of Art. These deflationary strategies happen too often to be coincidence. In fact Spaysky doesn't believe in coincidence, or chance, but that doesn't stop him embracing processes that produce unexpected imperfections and discarding processes that are too repeatable.

Spaysky is a distinguished graduate of Chido Johnson's "Center for Chido-mensional Studies," and credits the vastly influential sculpture professor with awakening him to the latent meaning of the everyday objects and materials surrounding him. He entered the program seeing art-making as the mastery of conventional craft-based techniques such as painting and sculpture, and left investigating more esoteric

(*Top*) *Apple Clock*. 2015. Fake fruit, plastic, silicone, clock components, 4 x 12 ½ x 15 ½ in. Photography by Joseph Condor.

(*Middle*) *Garfield Pen*. 2008. Hot glue, pen, 6 x 2 ½ x 2 ½ in. Photography by Joseph Condor.

(*Bottom*) *Bunny Wreath*. 2015. Plastic eggs, basket, Easter straw, silicone, 6 x 13 x 14 ½ in. Photography by Joseph Condor.

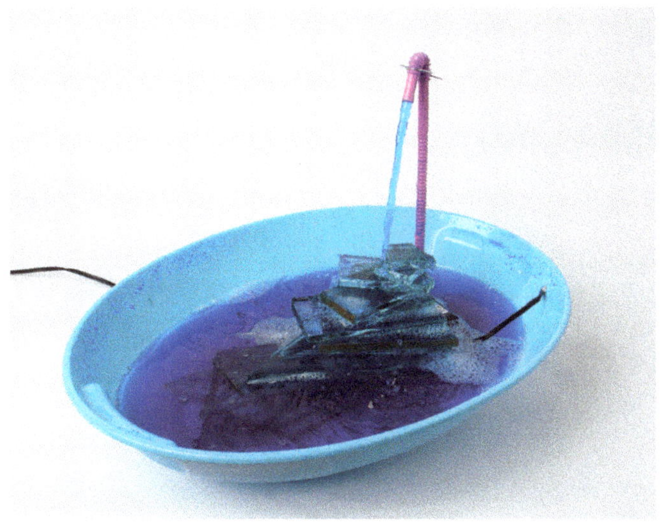

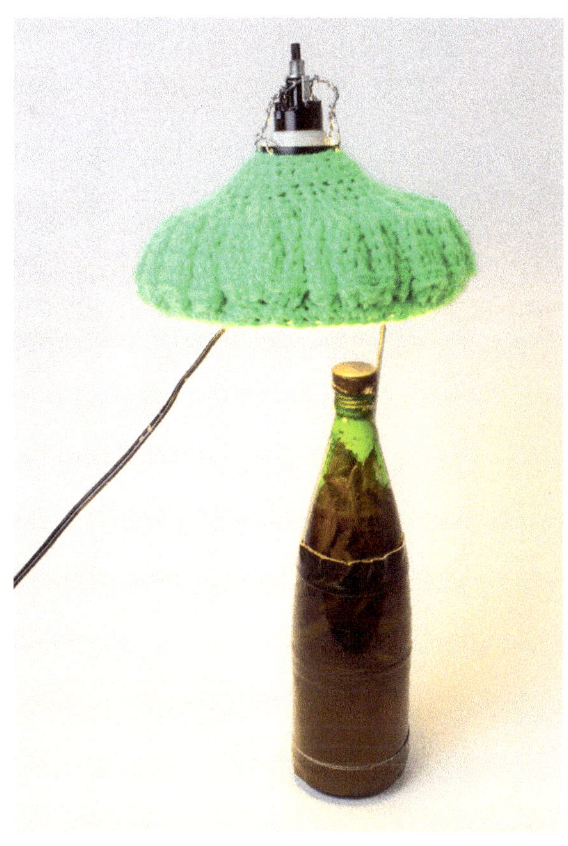

(*Left*) *Blue Fountain.* 2014. Plastic, glass, water, pigment, pump, 19 ½ x 14 x 12 ½ in. Photography by Joseph Condor.

(*Right*) *Crocheted Lamp.* 2014. Glass, wax, tape, candy corn, onions, green beans, vinegar, yarn, lamp components, bulb, 8 ½ x 8 ½ x 8 ½ in. Photography by Joseph Condor.

skills, such as how best to bind discarded fake fruit into a workable media (***Apple Clock***, 2015) or sculpting from hot glue (***Garfield Pen***, 2008). In many cases it would be quicker and easier for him to produce work using his more traditional skills. Johnson describes Spaysky's approach as learning how to do things, and then learning how to hide his expertise.

Spaysky sources much of his starting material from local thrift stores, both for pragmatic financial reasons and because he is interested in thrift-store merchandise as the local indicator for processes of desire, consumption, commodification, marketing, selection, design, etc. In ***Bunny Wreath*** (2015) he took a mixed bag of Easter ephemera, added silicon to allow it to be deformed, and then flattened the resulting mixture by driving over it. In less skilled hands the work could be seen as an act of violence against the crushingly conventional subject matter. In Spaysky's case, you get the impression he is claiming the right for his own individuality to coexist with it.

Tellingly, Spaysky credits the stereotypical Midwestern boyhood trips to Disney World as positive formative experiences, even going so far as to say he would go back there any time. This situates his work both in popular culture and in a certain open-eyed view of the world. In an insightful essay on a 2015 solo show at New York's CUE Art Foundation, Torey Akers describes Spaysky's work (nonpejoratively) as "boy-art." This seems fitting, despite Spaysky's regular use of traditionally feminine crafts such as embroidery and crochet.

Recently Spaysky has created large bodies of work around common, but offbeat, forms, such as the fountain (e.g., ***Blue Fountain***, 2014), the lamp (e.g., ***Crocheted***

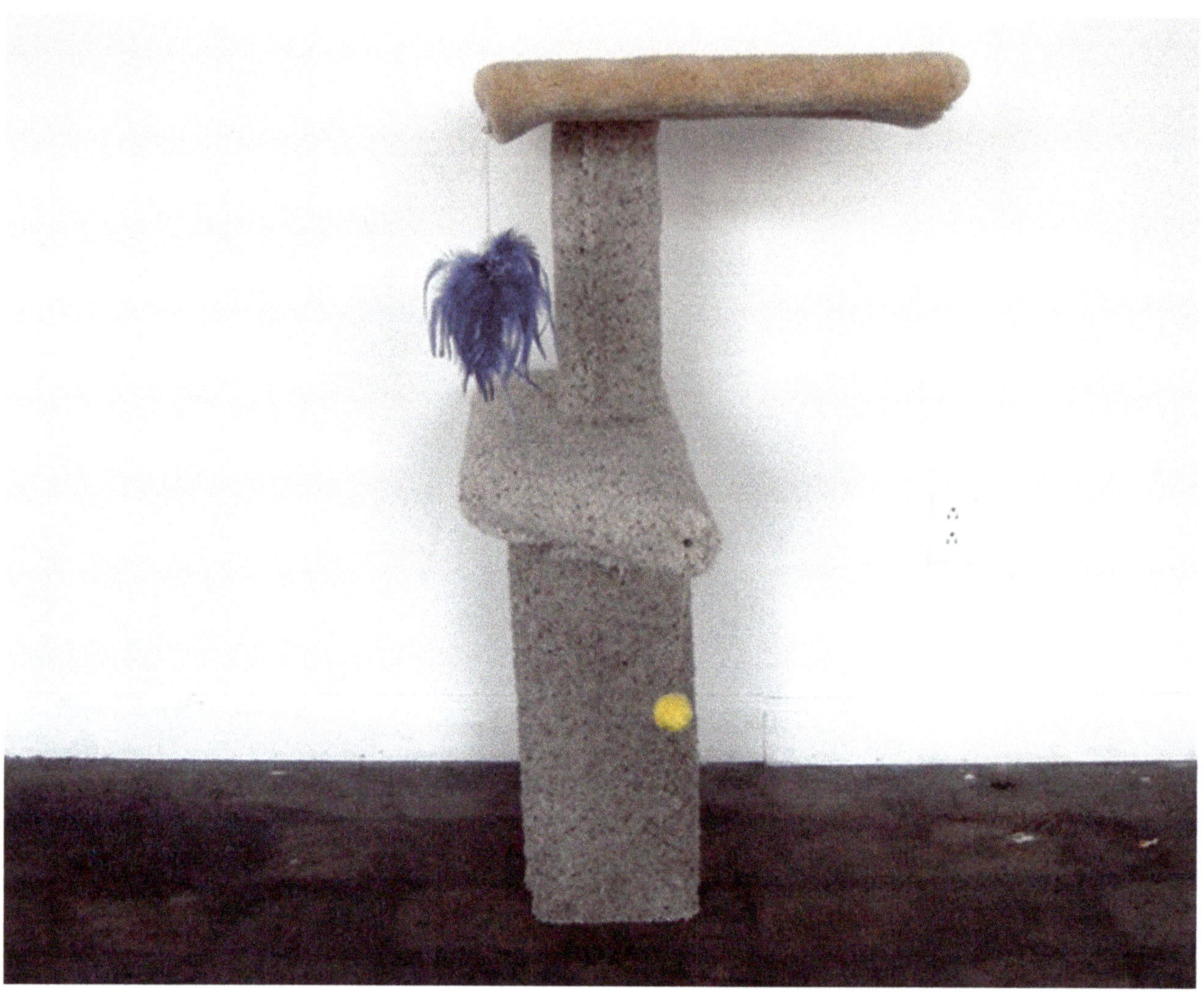

Cat Tower 1. 2013. Carpet, wood, staples, screws, string, plastic beads, feathers, puff ball, 43 x 25 x 32 in. Photography by Joseph Condor.

Lamp, 2014), and, memorably, the cat tower (e.g., ***Cat Tower 1***, 2013). The consumer archetypes they are based on speak to a certain amount of discretionary spending, and, in the case of the lamp and the fountain, some degree of personalization of surroundings. They are representative of easily overlooked objects that over time fill up middle-class homes. Spaysky's adoption of these everyday forms certainly has humor, but it doesn't come across as ironic. Rather, the works appear more as sincere reflections on vernacular creativity and a nonblinkered approach to looking at the world.

Ultimately Spaysky's art, located as it is in his origins in the chronically unfashionable middle-class Midwestern suburbs, tells us that we can choose our home but we can't choose where we're from, that one person's cultural wasteland is another person's culture, and that perhaps the man in the ***Crocheted Mickey Mouse Mask*** knows more than he's letting on.

STEVE PANTON, APRIL 2015

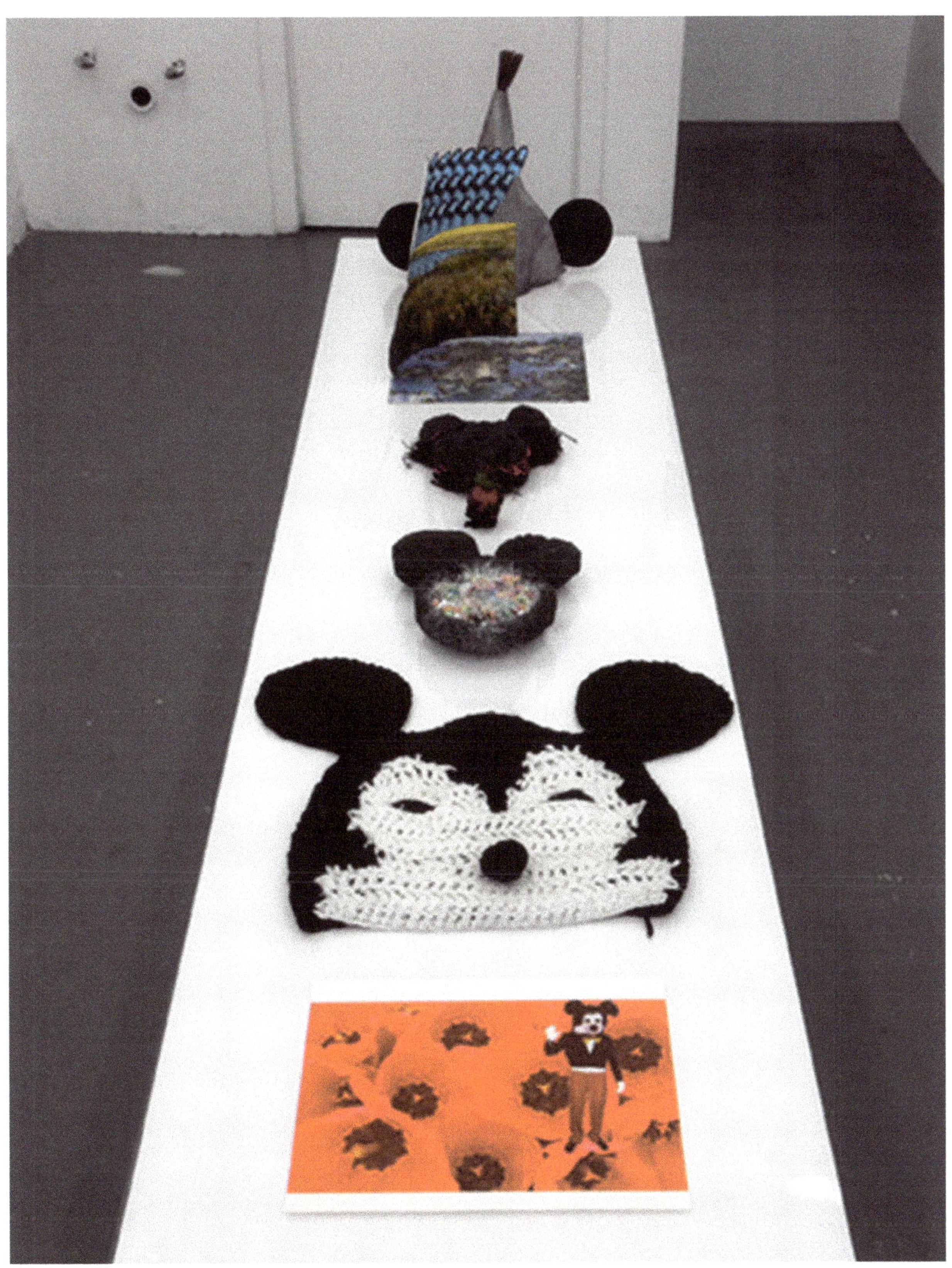

Installation view: *Foot Foot* at Cleopatra's. 2014. Photography by Marc Tatti.

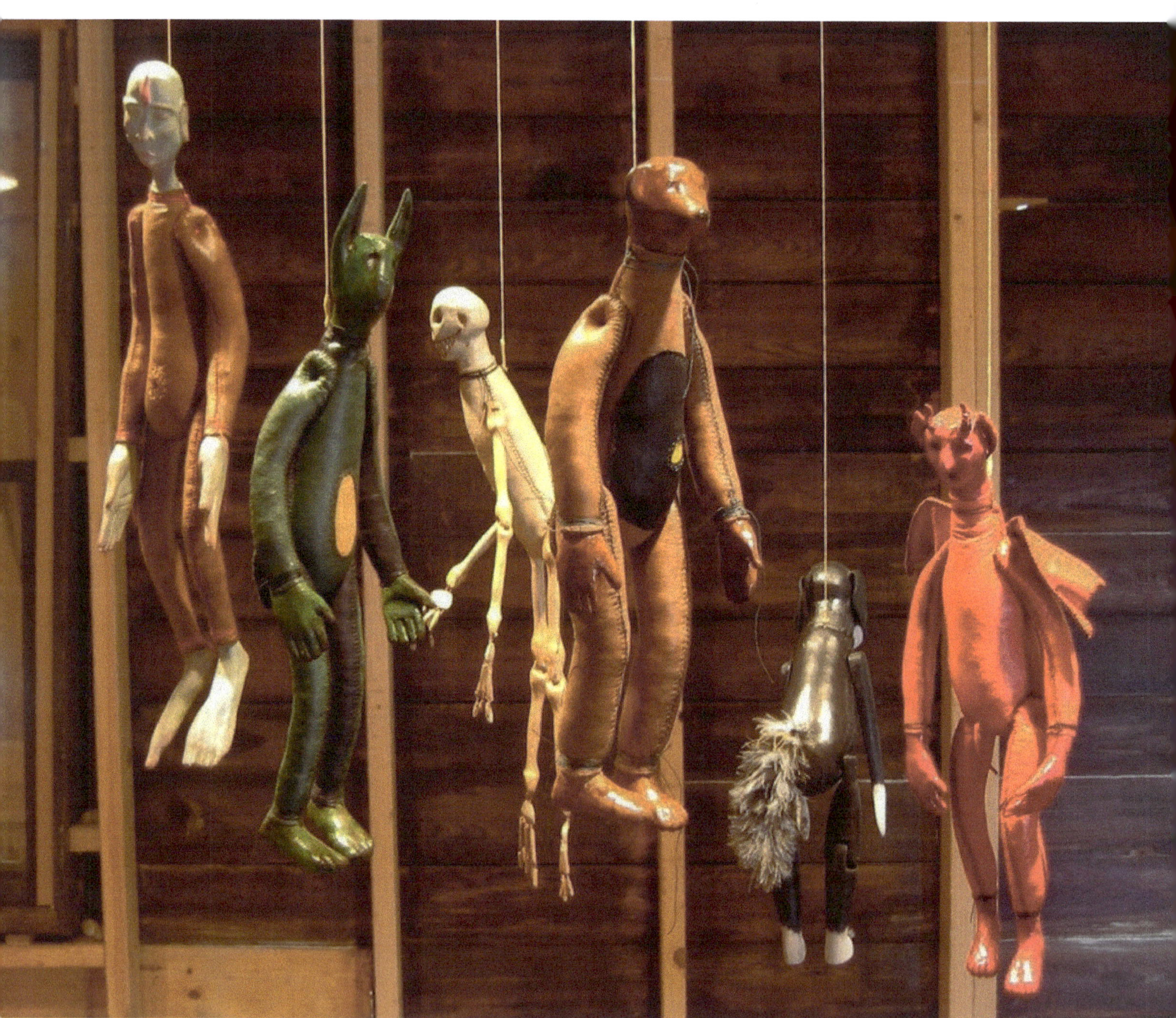

Installation at Alley Culture. 2006. Leather, clay, feather, various dimensions.

21 // MARY FORTUNA

Born Royal Oak, Michigan, 1956
BFA, Wayne State University
Lives in Royal Oak, Michigan

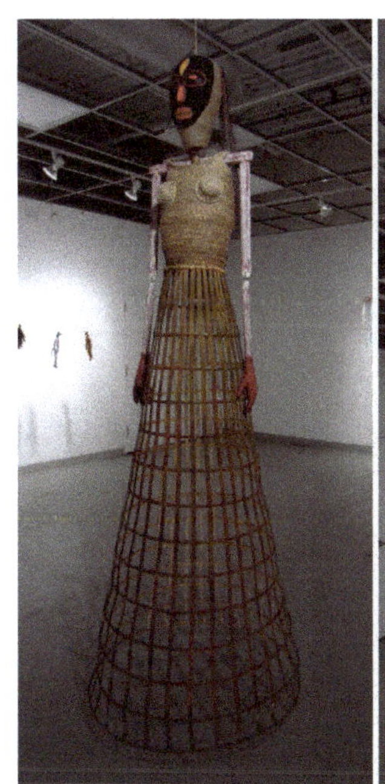

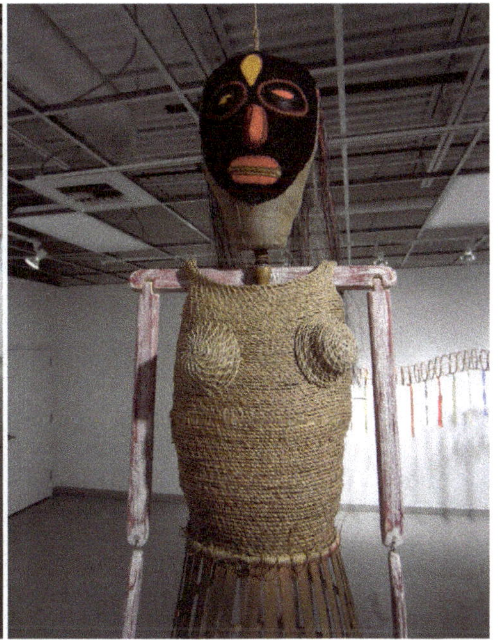

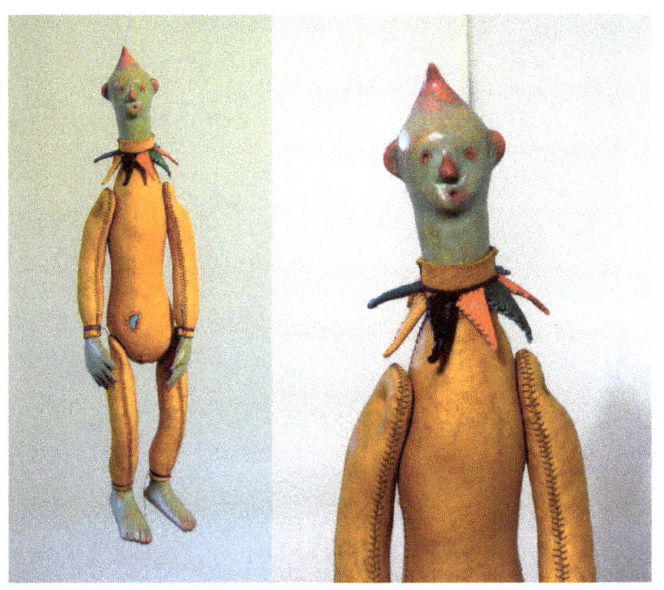

Let's begin with a few words with which Mary Fortuna does not appreciate being associated: multicultural, arts vs. crafts, "women's art," and "art dolls." And a few things she is: generous, frank, inclusive, and deeply intuitive when it comes to locating source material at the very core of human existence. Looking at a single piece produced by this exceptional artist—who has the capacity to draw inspiration from found objects, mythology, religion, folk art, and figurative modeling practices of a great many cultures—it is easy to mistake Fortuna's output as derivative of any number of existing traditions. But her works belong to an overarching whole, and you can no more estimate

(*Top*) *She Towers Above*. 2013. Leather, linen, reed, sea grass, wood, horsehair, 96 x 36 x 24 in.
(*Bottom*) *Pointy Headed Simpleton*. 2010. Leather, clay, 16 in. tall.

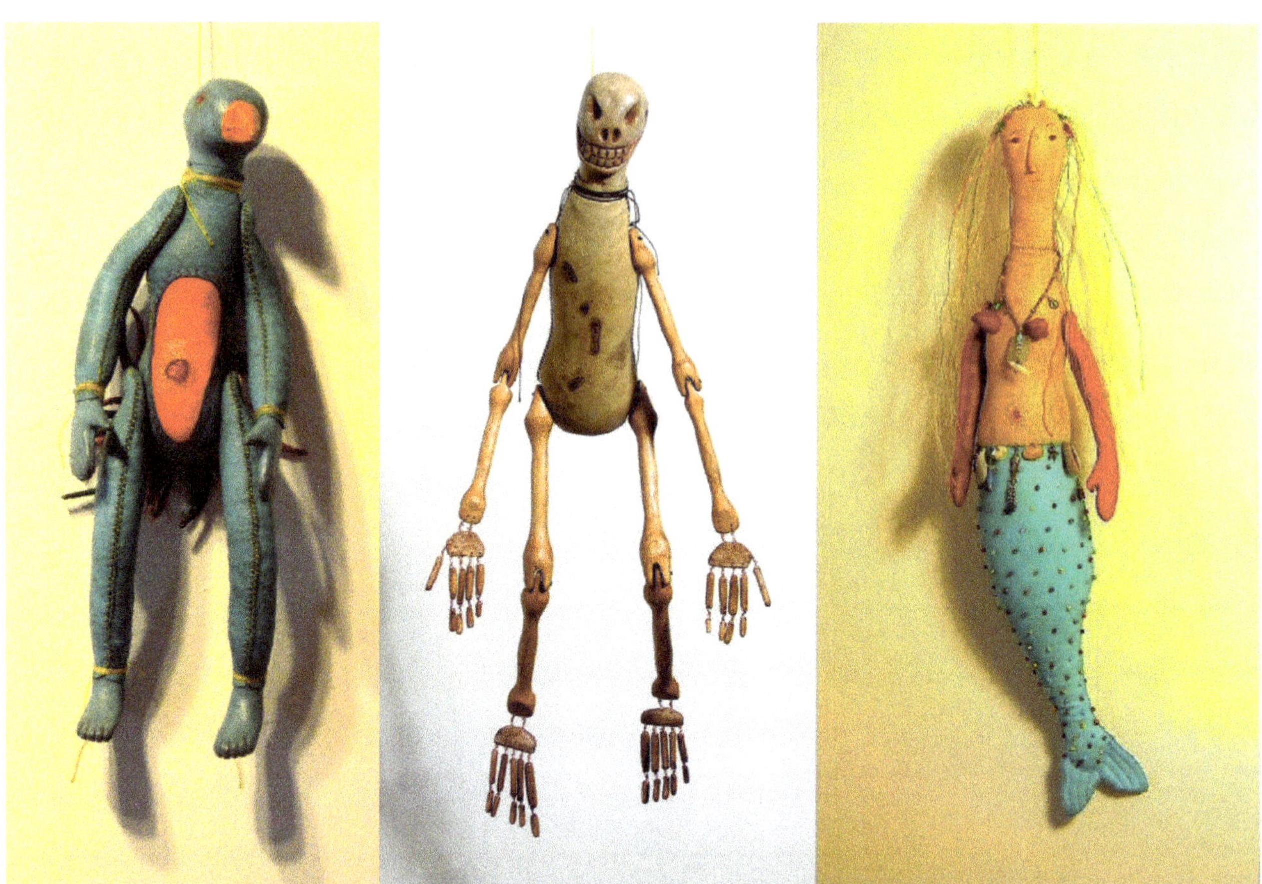

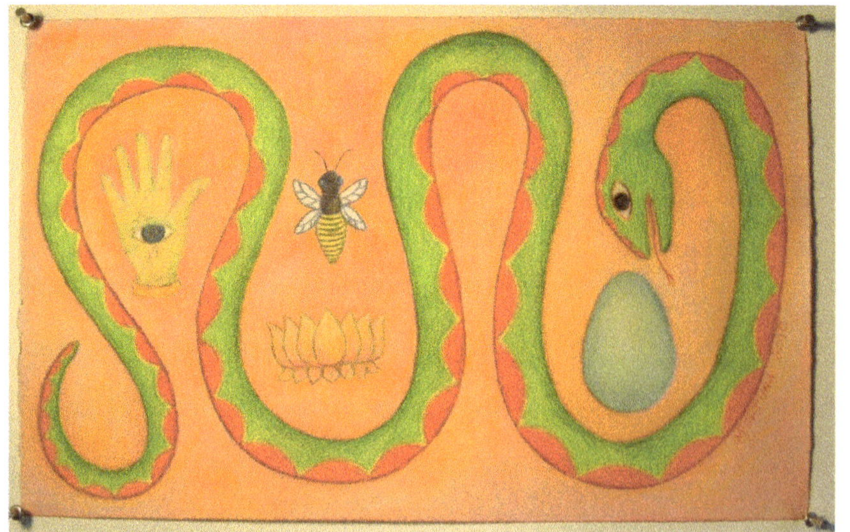

(Top) Bluebird of Happiness, El Muerte, Siren. 2013. Leather, clay, horsehair, beads, various dimensions.

(Bottom) Green Snake with Egg. 2010. Watercolor, Prismacolor, 16 x 20 in.

Fortuna's meaning or aesthetic through a single art object than you can derive a finished picture by looking at a single jigsaw puzzle piece. Hers is a sprawling and detailed personal mythology.

While Fortuna may chafe at certain associations, she is a positive force, constantly broadcasting a deep appreciation for fellow artists, in career moves that have included stints as a curator, and as publisher of *Ground Up* art magazine (1993–96), as well as her constant practice as a social connector. Her process in identifying as an artist didn't unfold until her

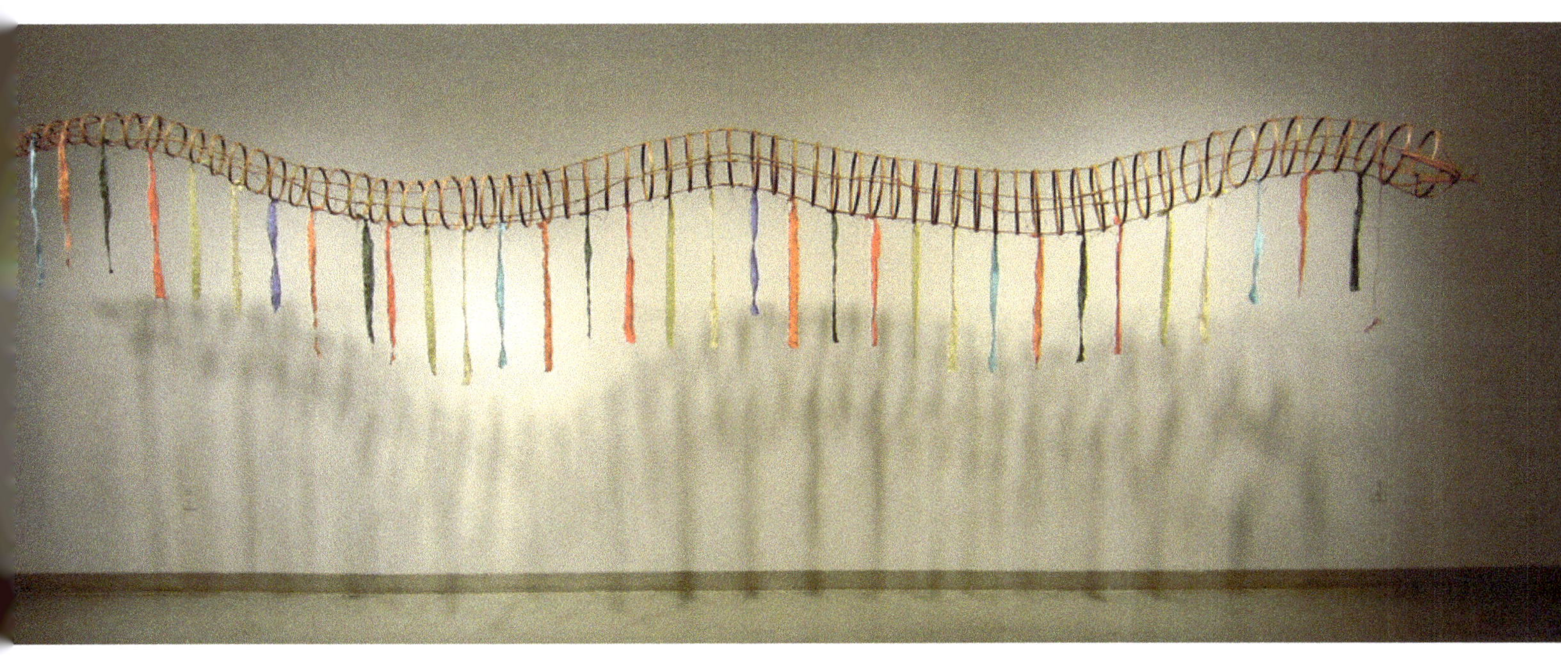

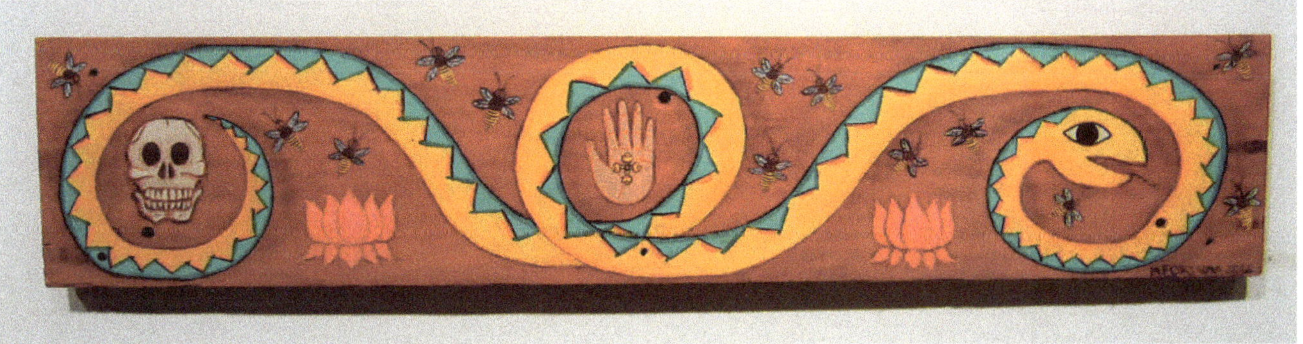

(*Top*) *Big Flying Snake*. 2013. Basket reed, waxed fiber, linen, 20 ft. x 16 in. (*Bottom*) *Yellow Snake with Skull and Bees*. 2012. Acrylic on wood, 8 x 30 in.

midthirties, but her relationship with making began early, and she refers to the influence of her parents on its development. "My mom was smart enough to make materials and tools available, and to let us alone to mess around on our own," Fortuna says. Her father set a strong example, applying the tools of his trade as a film production manager for the Jam Handy Studio in Detroit to a range of creative projects, including the completely original construction of a family tent trailer from plans published in *Popular Mechanics*. Fortuna's output embodies her father's spirit of industriousness and creative generalism—with many of her works executed at the very same dining-room table where she ate dinner or worked on projects as a child—but it also echoes the cinematic process of character design in its truest sense. She is perhaps best known for her iconic dolls: articulated figures, pieced and hand-stitched from leather and found materials, each emanating a sense of personality as determined and palpable as that of their maker, with attitudes ranging from oddball to vaguely sinister. Each bears a name, such as ***Pointy Headed Simpleton***, ***El Muerte***, ***Bluebird of Happiness***, or ***Siren*** (all 2013).

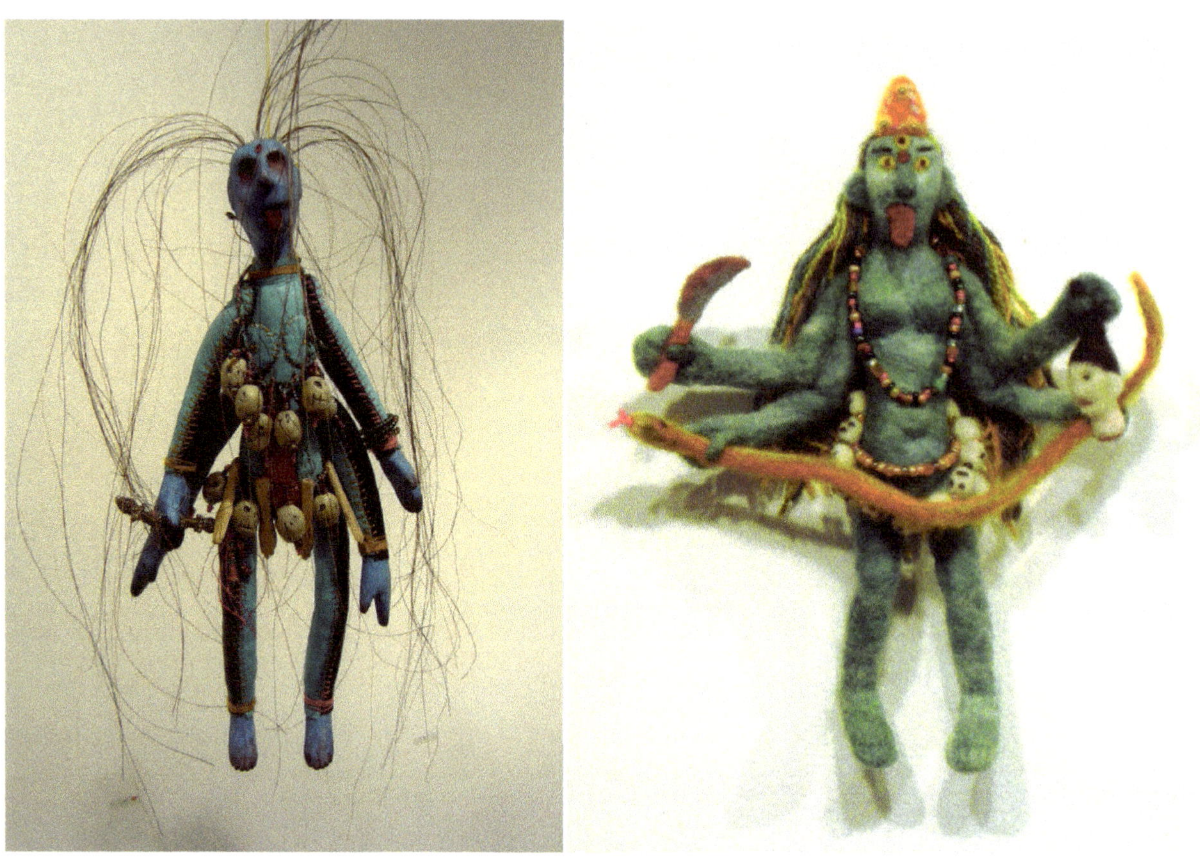

Blue Kali / Kali. 2010/2008. Leather, clay, horsehair, beads, 9 in. tall / Needle-felted wool, beads, 8 in. tall.

She Towers Above was a 2013 solo show at the Birmingham-Bloomfield Art Center—which borrows its title from a song by Alejandro Escovedo, lyrical references being another of Fortuna's common practices—and offered a rich opportunity to examine the broader constellations of her work. Taken en masse, her recurring motifs emerge clearly. Snakes are one of her most fundamental building blocks, appearing in ***drawn and painted works*** as well as three-dimensional hanging sculptures, like ***Big Flying Snake*** (2013), and her works are replete with bees, lotus flowers, sacred hearts, and third eyes. "There have been many occasions where I needed to summon the fierce energy of the ***Hindu goddess Kali***," says Fortuna, but more often her figures reference an ambiguous blend of cultural signifiers. All the world is fodder for Fortuna's interests, the collective mythic-mass of human imagination and faith acting as source material to be processed through the filter of her personal creative process. Beeswax models with generic names like ***Raven Woman*** (2012) sit alongside ***Chick-a-Boom*** and ***Serpent Sisters*** (both 2010)—freak-show attractions, built around salvaged doll parts. Individually, the pieces are strange and enchanting, but taken collectively, they reveal Fortuna's practice as a builder of worlds, with an ecosystem of oddities springing from her fingers. The "she" towering above might be a reference to the ***oversize hanging puppet***

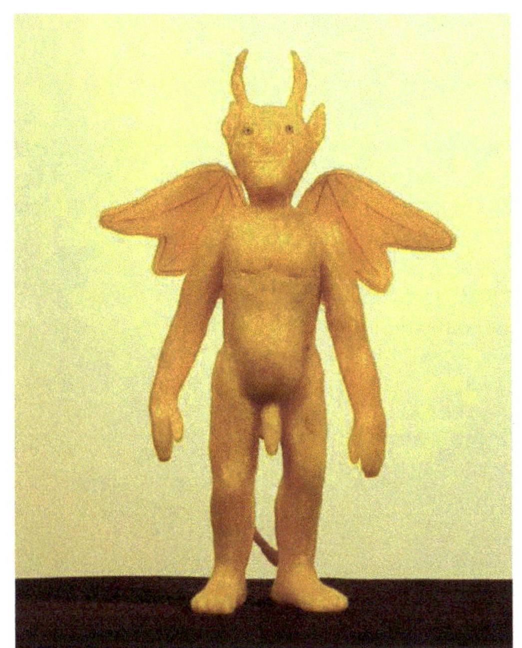
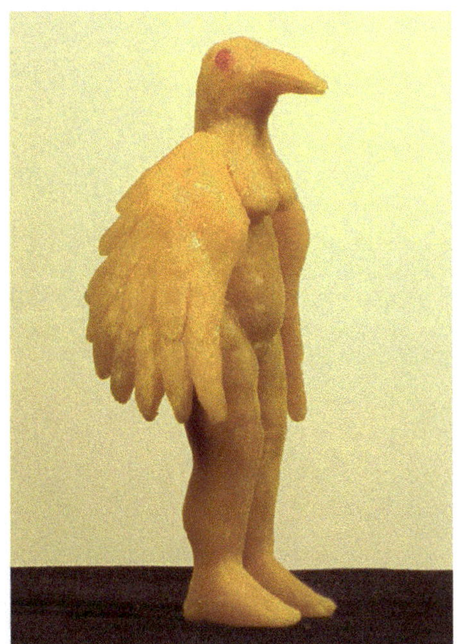
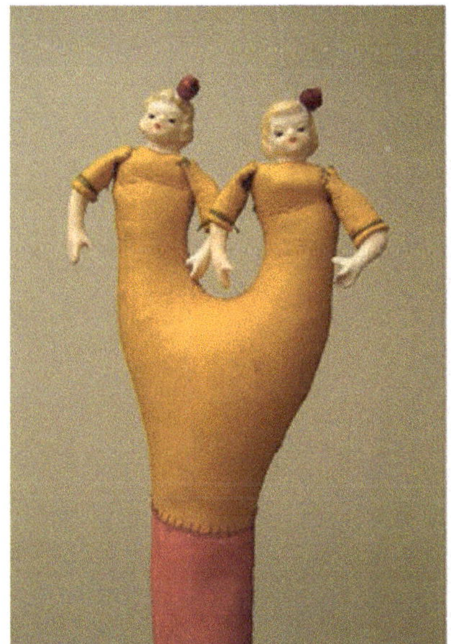
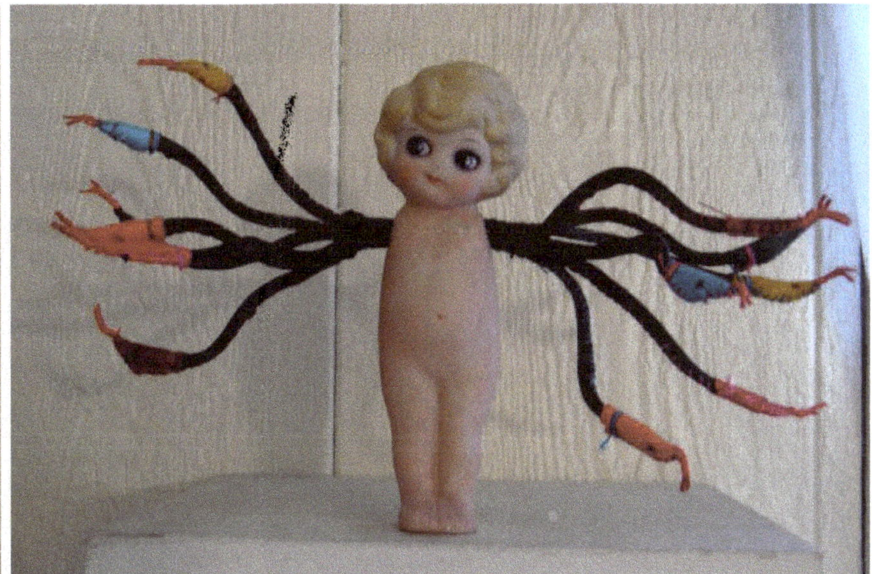

(*Top*) *Beezlebub / Raven Woman.* 2012. Beeswax, beads, copper wire / Beeswax, beads; each 6 in. tall.
(*Bottom*) *Serpent Sisters / Chick-a-Boom.* 2010. Mixed-media, 30 x 6 in. / 6 x 7 in.

and pièce de résistance of the show, or perhaps an oblique reference to Fortuna's relationship as creator to these forms.

One gets the unshakable sense that these are not dolls, waiting for someone to come home and impose narratives on their hollow existence, but active agents in a world that exists whether we are there to observe it or not. In the grand tradition of artists like J. R. R. Tolkien and Tim Burton, Mary Fortuna spins out a mythic existence so clearly realized, it becomes difficult to decide if it is truly her creation or a reality that has always existed.

SARAH ROSE SHARP, MAY 2015

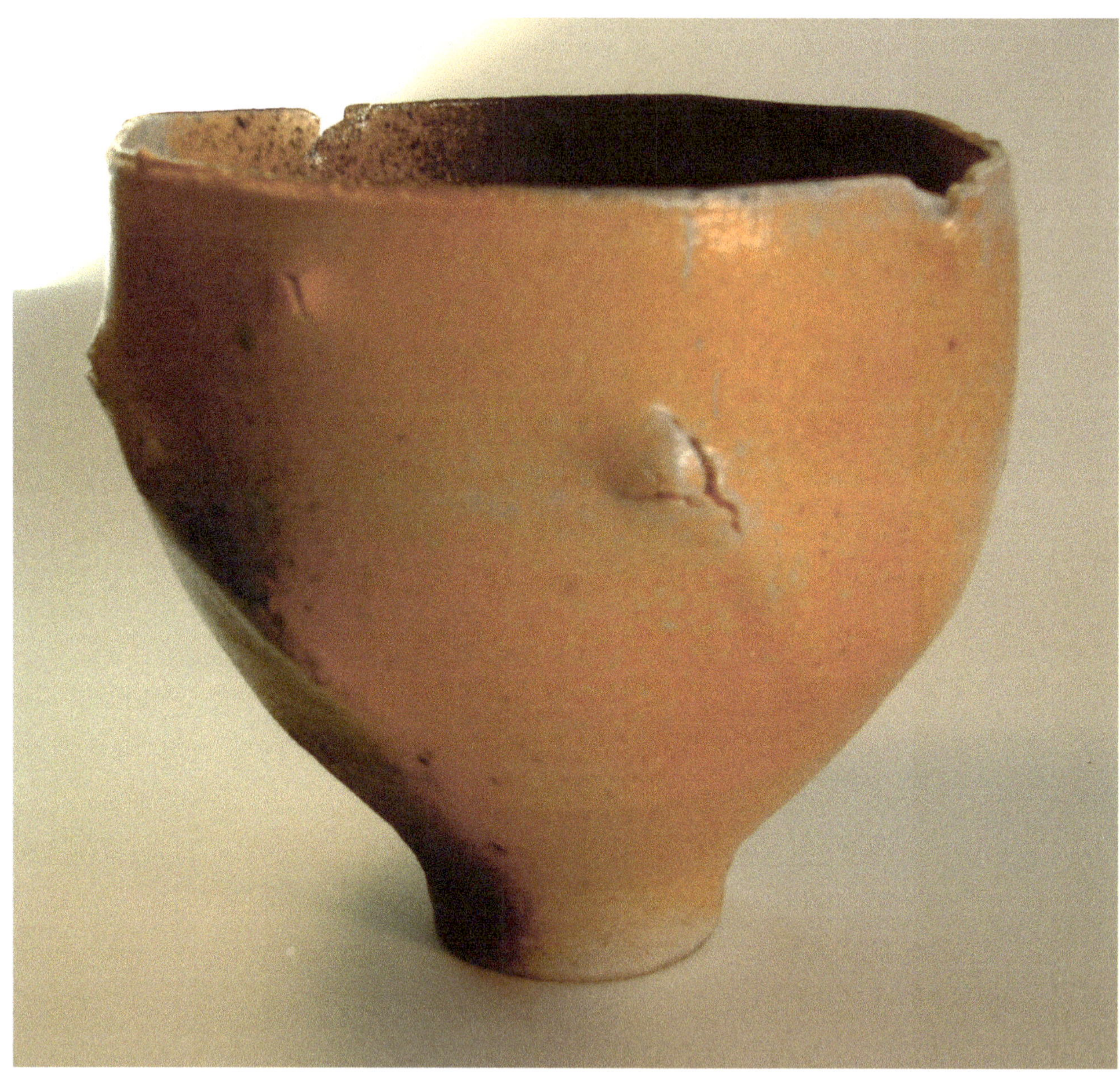

Orange / Black Bowl. 1999. Porcelain, 8 x 9 in. diameter.

22 // MARIE WOO

Born Seattle, Washington, 1928
BA, University of Washington, Seattle
MFA, Cranbrook Academy of Art
Lives in West Bloomfield, Michigan

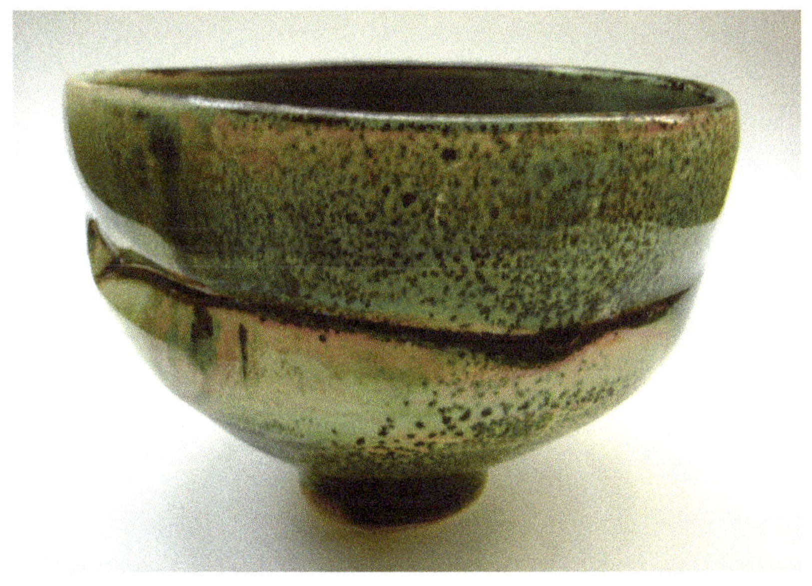

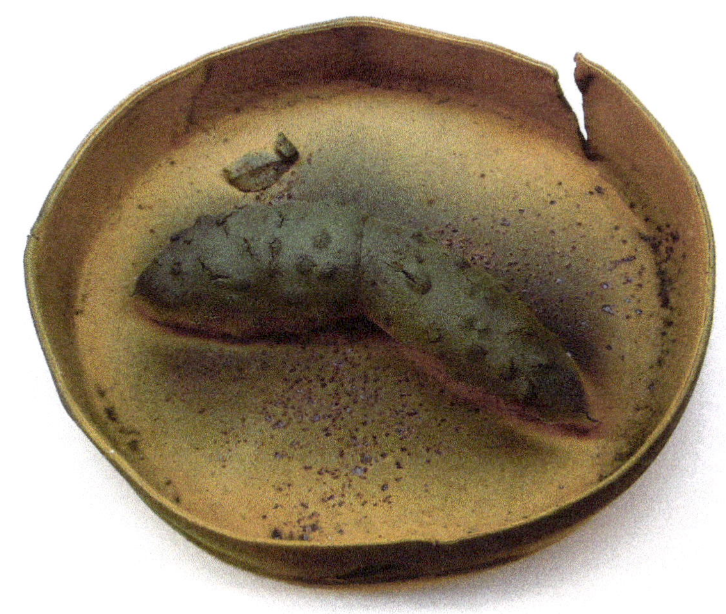

Among the multiple roles Marie Woo has essayed in the course of her career—ceramist, curator, researcher, Asian clay historian, alchemist of glazes, conceptual photographer—one of the most vital was her involvement in the genesis of Clay Ten. "Founded as a group effort by an animated conversation in a crowded school van [on its way] to an out-of-town ceramic conference," Clay Ten functioned not unlike a contemporary pop-up gallery, presenting annual exhibits of ten area potters, including, in addition to Woo, Shirley White Black, Susan Crowell, Kathy Dambach, Rafael Duran, Jim Leacock, Tom Phardel, John Stephenson, Susanne Stephenson, and Georgette Zirbes. Each

(*Top*) *Green Bowl.* 1996. Porcelain, 5 x 7 in. diameter.
(*Bottom*) *Wall Piece.* 2001. Stoneware, 6 x 23 in. diameter.

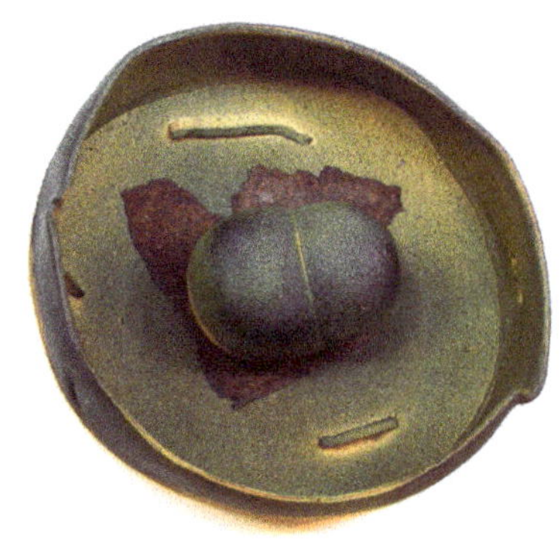

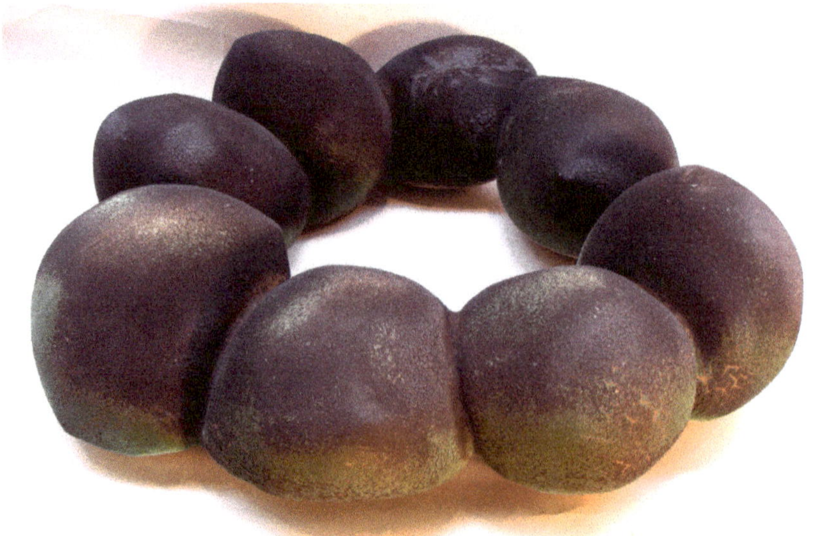

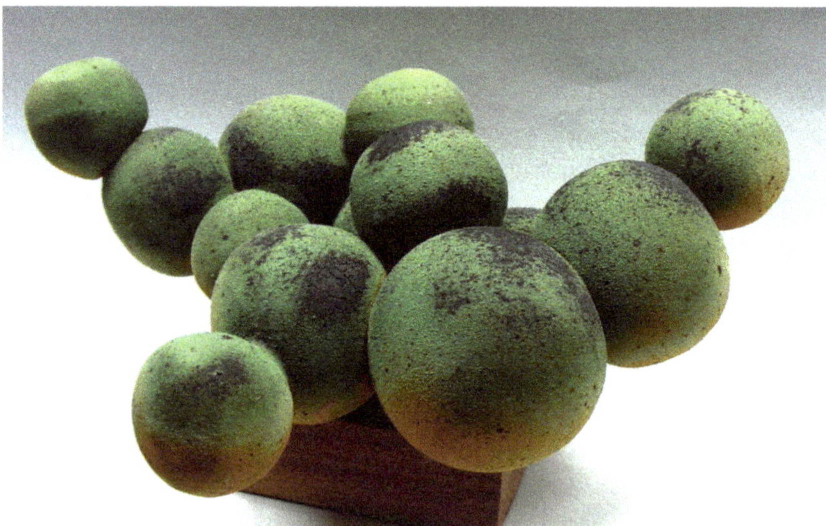

(Top, left) Wall Piece. 2004. Stoneware, metal, 4 x 17 in. diameter.

(Top, right) Winter/Black. 2012. Stoneware, 7 x 24 in. diameter.

(Bottom, right) Spring/Green. 2007. Stoneware, 11 x 17 x 12 in.

year, between 1981 and 1993, in a different location, from Chicago to Detroit, they assembled and staffed a month-long display. Eight years later, in 2001, they regrouped and joined forces once more at the River Gallery in Chelsea, Michigan. As Susan Crowell explained, "In the 1980s there wasn't the interest in clay as there is today. It was difficult to find gallery space because the feelings then were more focused on painting and sculpture."

From the outset, on her own or with Clay Ten, Woo has exhibited her expressive, disfigured vessels, among them bottle, bowl, and platter forms replete with punctures, holes, splits, tears, or slits in both body and edge that annul their utility. These judiciously flawed shapes with protruding ribs or ridges, hollows, or puckers that further animate the form are often glazed with lustrous oranges (perhaps offset by a wispy cloud of charcoal), waves of apple green (dappled with darker speckles), or chaste white. (Her eponymous "Woo Yellow" glaze is famous in the ceramic community.)

Orange / Black Bowl (1999) and ***Green Bowl*** (1996) stand out as particularly felicitous examples of Woo's process. One "sees" or imagines how perfectly functional they would be if not rendered useless by the deformations that, paradoxically, enhance an appreciation of the comely contours rising from narrow base to capacious opening. Albeit aerated here and there, her shapely bowls silently and serenely withstand the disturbances to their forms. Woo's wall-mounted plates arrest attention as well, through their irregular,

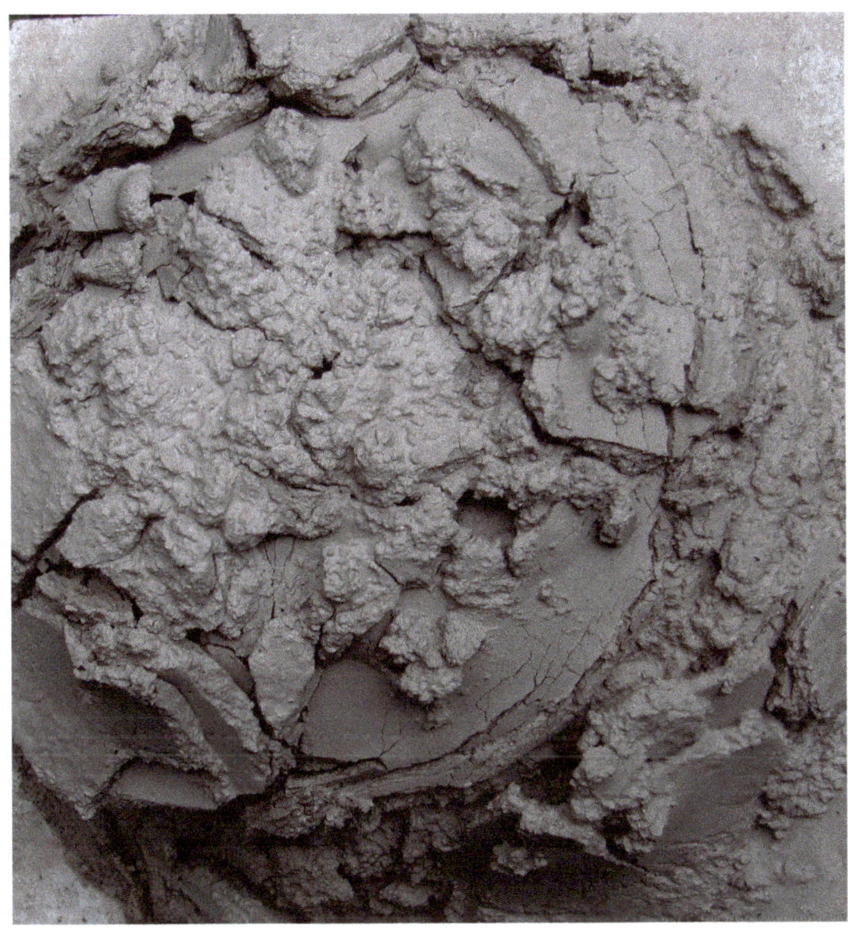

Unfired Stack. 2014–15. Stoneware exposed to nature, 9 x 12 in. diameter.

misshapen contours, torn, split edges, and the evocative, mysterious entities they enclose—from elongated organic elements, as in ***Wall Piece*** (2001), to the bulbous ovoid, poised on a metal fragment, presumably in the midst of mitosis, in ***Wall Piece*** (2004).

Freed from the hospitable embrace of these circular fields, the swelling, expanding forms assert their independence and metamorphose into fully three-dimensional clusters that take on a life of their own. In earthy hues, as in ***Winter/Black*** (2012), they form rings for companionship or protection, while in verdant green tones—see ***Spring/Green*** (2007)—they cantilever in multiple directions like madly replicating orbs.

Woo, in her curatorial guise, has also came to the fore recently. Beginning in 1998, she embarked on a multiyear research and travel project to explore, exhibit, and preserve the wares of Chinese folk potters before their practice became extinct in a rapidly industrializing China. The fruit of her and cocurators Susanne and John Stephenson's efforts is featured in the traveling show *International Chinese Folk Pottery Exhibition*, which debuted at the University of Michigan Museum of Art in 2013. This exemplary display, representing thirty of the one hundred plus examples culled during several field trips to China, attests to Woo's commitment to bring to light the diversity and rich legacy of a craft on the verge of dying out.

Surprisingly (or not, given Woo's unceasing experimentation in her art), a liberating shift occurred in the artist's practice within the last few years. As she explains, "Recently, my work has come FULL CIRCLE, which is to expose unfired clay forms to the natural elements . . . slowly reclaimed and absorbed back to the earth . . . and becomes FORMLESS, the opposite of the clay forms and ideas frozen by FIRE." This concept, documented photographically in ***Unfired Stack*** (2014–15), illustrates Woo's latest foray in an artistic oeuvre brimming with provocative ideas, processes, and a ceramic language all her own.

DENNIS ALAN NAWROCKI,
MAY 2015

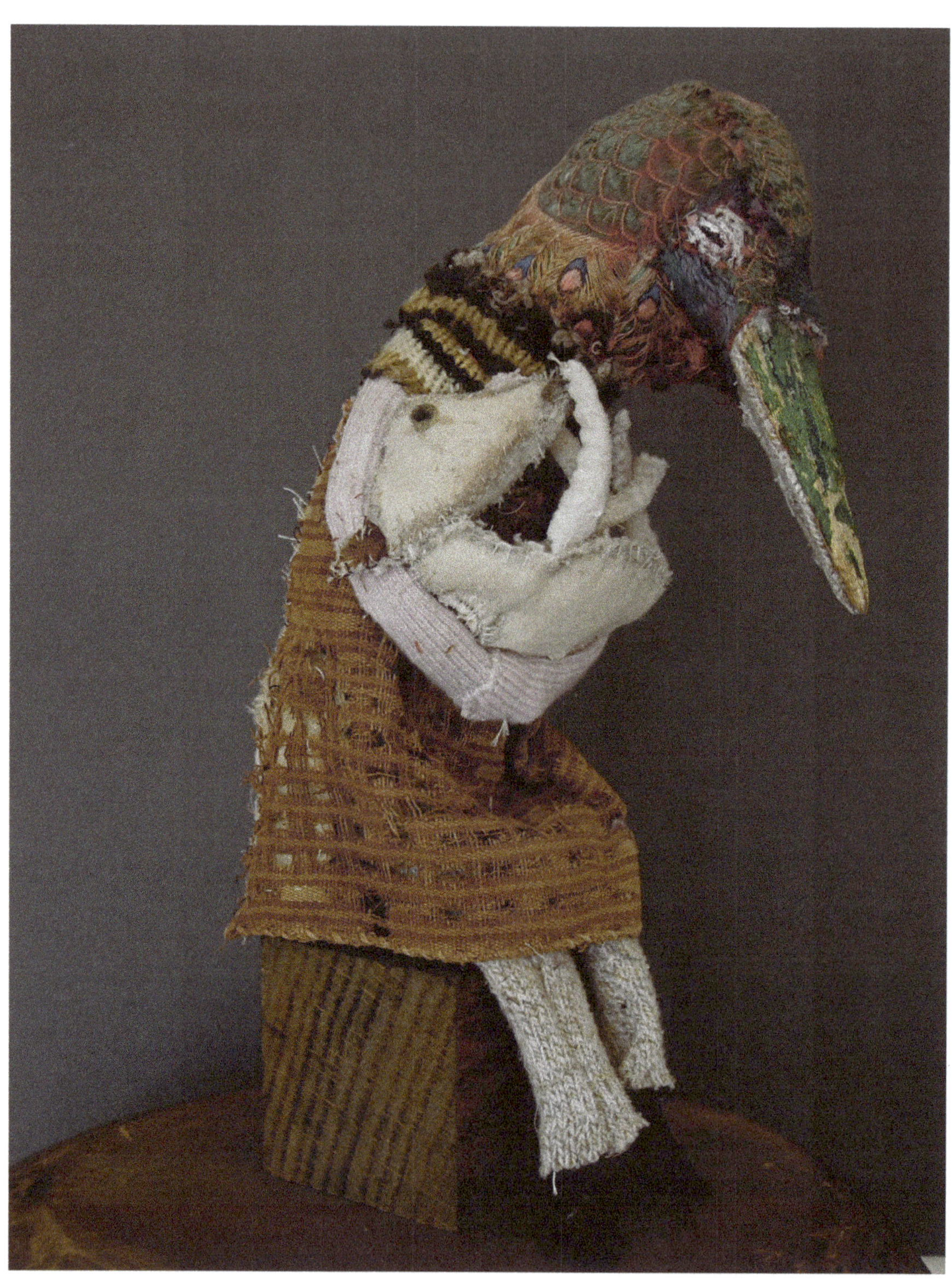

The Surrogate. 2008. Mixed-media, found objects, 12 x 7 x 7 in.

23 // SANDRA CARDEW

Born Detroit, 1947
BFA, MFA, Wayne State University
Lives in Royal Oak, Michigan

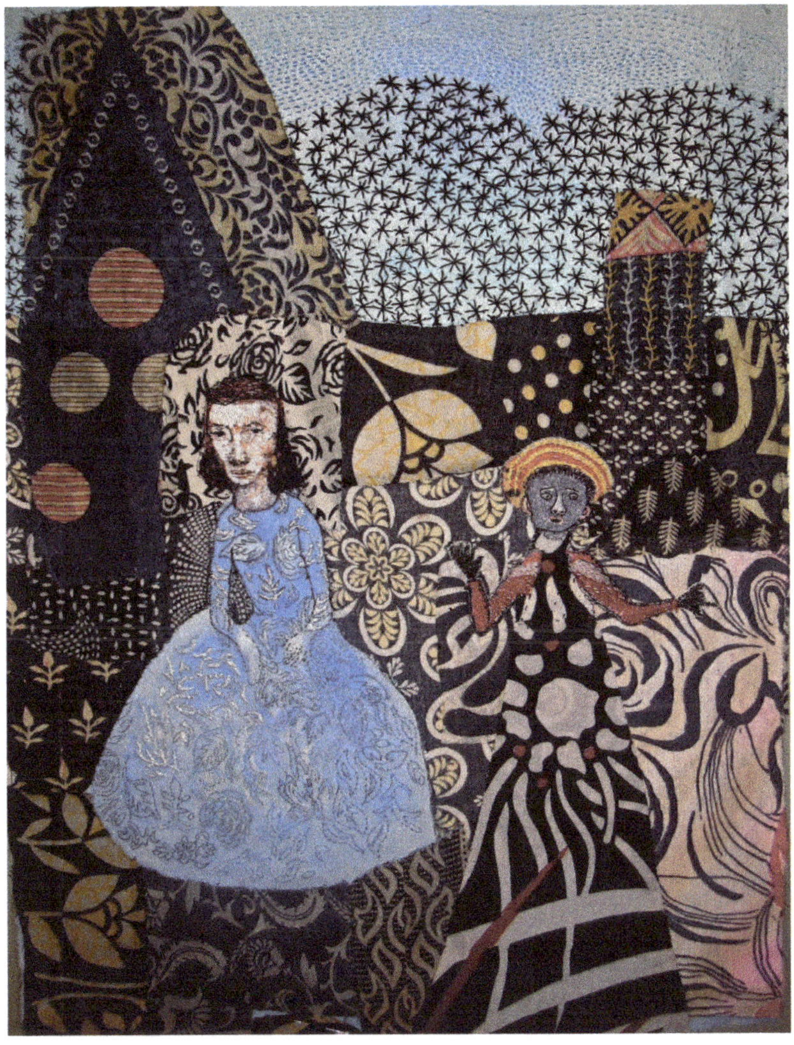

Woman with Spirit Doll. 2015. Mixed-media collage, thread, Kantha cloth, 30 x 24 in.

Sandra Cardew's strange figurative works emerge fully formed from a place that is both totally familiar yet completely unknowable. At their core is a profound command of gesture that is heart-wrenching but impossible to stop looking at. That these gestures emanate from hybrid anthropomorphic figures so otherworldly that even the artist can't explain where they come from, just adds to their disorienting qualities. At times it seems that the only thing stopping the pieces exploding from the power of the contradictory emotions they evoke is the suture-like stitching that literally and metaphorically holds the oddly collaged parts together.

While Cardew's work may be too laden with hidden meanings and possibilities to be reduced to autobiography, it does contain notable autobiographical content. This appears in the obvious

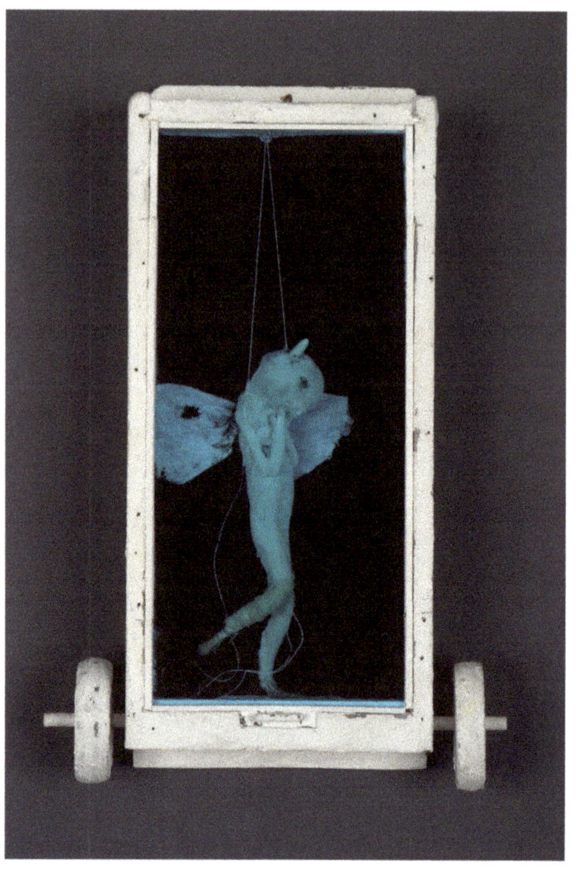

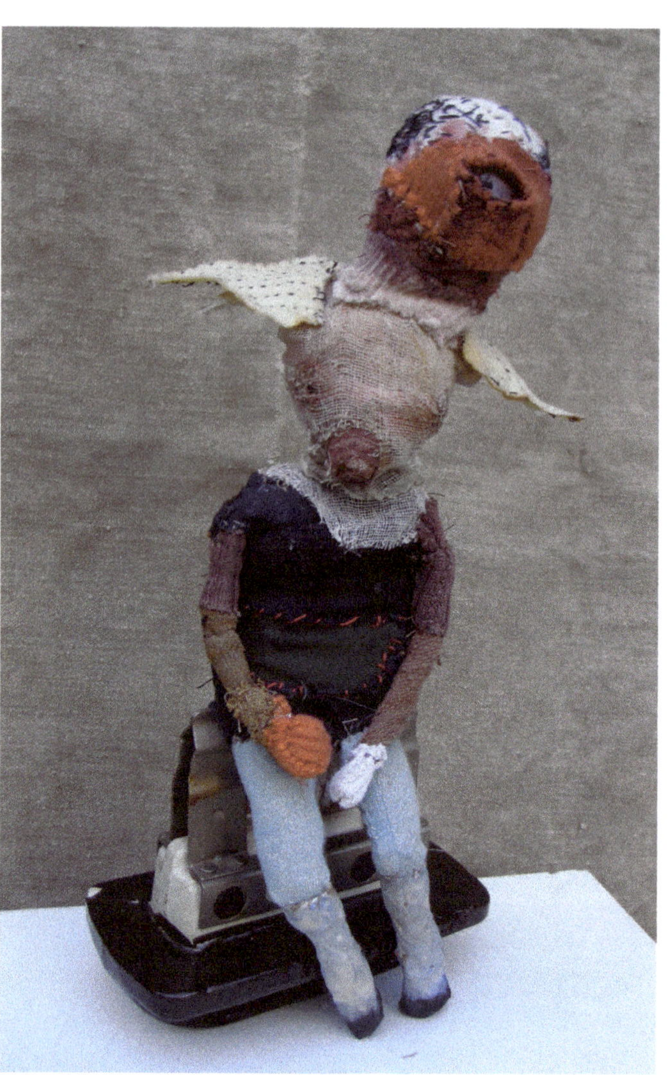

(*Left*) *Ex #14*. 2005. Mixed-media, found objects, 18 x 12 x 4 in.
(*Right*) *Bird Mother #10*. 2012. Mixed-media, found objects, 14 x 7 x 5 in.

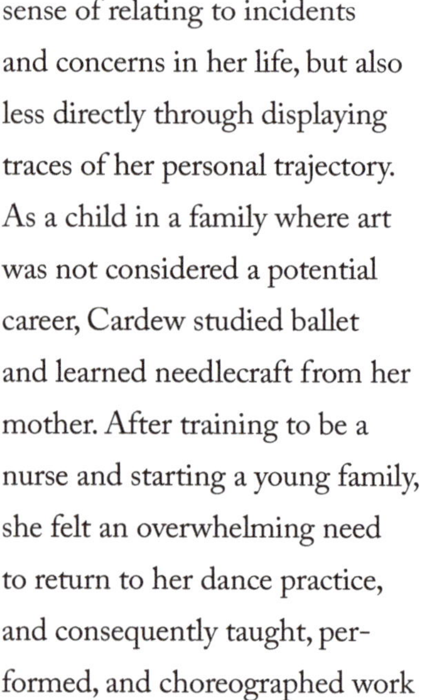

sense of relating to incidents and concerns in her life, but also less directly through displaying traces of her personal trajectory. As a child in a family where art was not considered a potential career, Cardew studied ballet and learned needlecraft from her mother. After training to be a nurse and starting a young family, she felt an overwhelming need to return to her dance practice, and consequently taught, performed, and choreographed work over an intense and exhilarating ten-year period. This passage of her life came to an abrupt and emotionally devastating end due to the onset of chronic fatigue syndrome. Subsequently she directed her creative energies into the less physically demanding world of visual art, pursuing first a late-life BFA and later an MFA. In works such as ***The Surrogate*** (2008), ***Bird Mother #10*** (2012), ***Ex #14*** (2005), ***Star Dancer*** (2010), and ***Rejection*** (2012), it is possible to see recurring themes such as memory, loss, the limits and failure of the body, childhood, the dancer's sense of flight and use of gesture, and the nurse/mother's desire to heal.

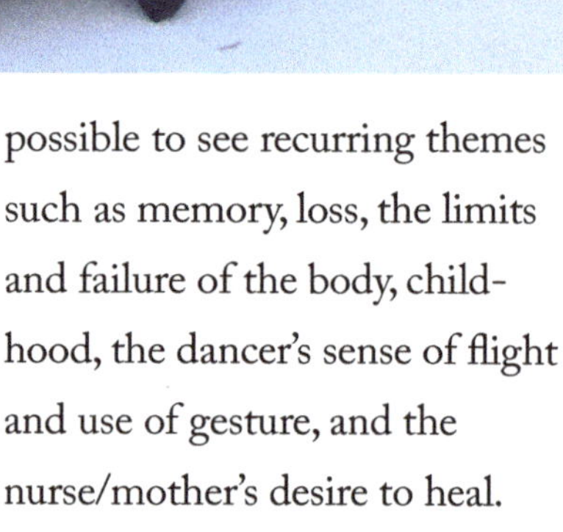

A constant undercurrent in Cardew's work is the human collective unconscious and its interaction with an animist sense of the supernatural. Her personal talisman is the bird, which she features regularly in her work, exploring its vulnerability and

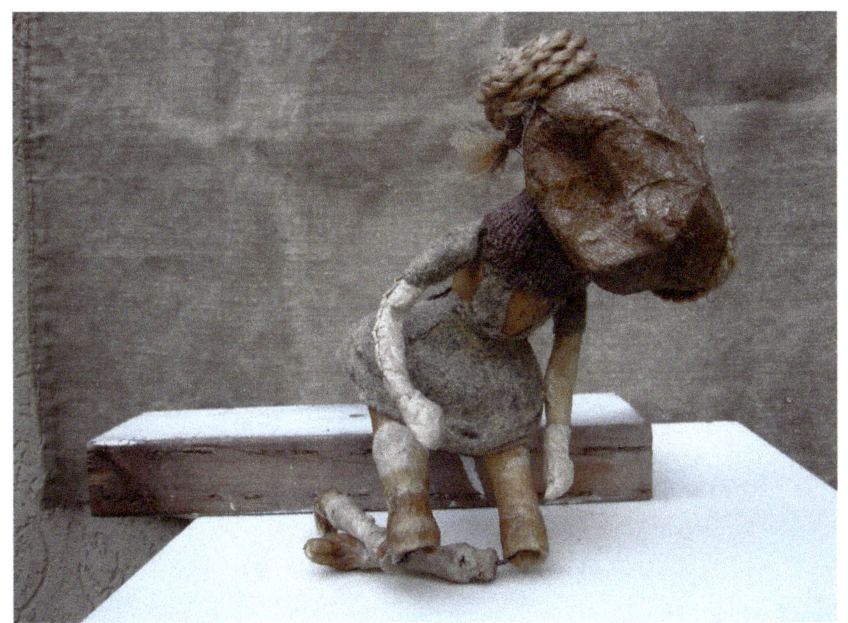

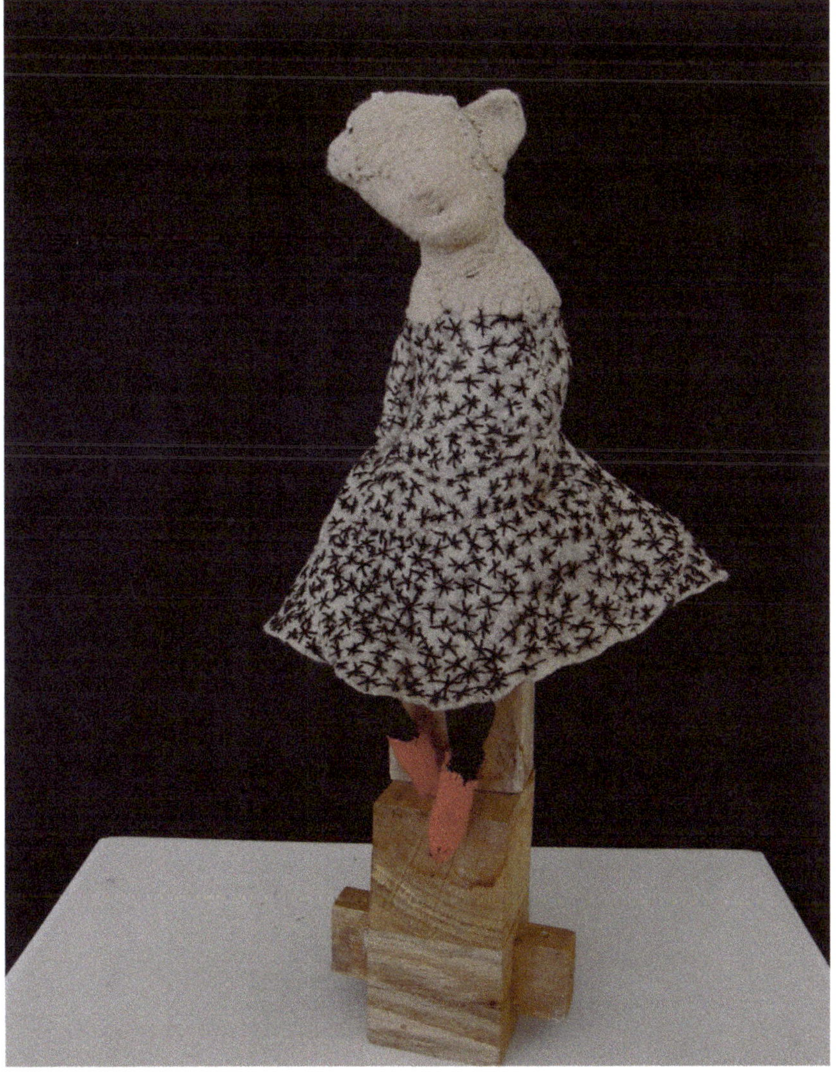

(*Top*) *Rejection*. 2012. Mixed-media, 8 x 6 x 6 in.
(*Bottom*) *Star Dancer.* 2010. Felt, thread, 14 x 8 x 8 in.

suggesting associations between flight and dance. Often the bird is paired with a stronger protective partner, or itself takes on the role of the protector (see, for example, the ***Bird Mother Series***). Other recurring anthropomorphic animal figures are not always so directly recognizable, but often seem to contain elements of the horsc, thc rabbit, and the deer. Cardew stresses that her process is intuitive and spontaneous rather than narrative-driven and conscious, and hence she may know instinctively when a direction feels right or wrong but not know exactly where it is coming from or heading. In this way she leaves room for her own and/or the viewer's unconscious in the work.

More complex, "stage-like" works such as ***Myth of Sisyphus*** (2006) and ***Sanatorium under the Sign of the Hourglass*** (2010) (inspired by painter and writer Bruno Schultz's novel of the same name) show Cardew's background in theater design. As well as allowing the interaction between groups of characters, they

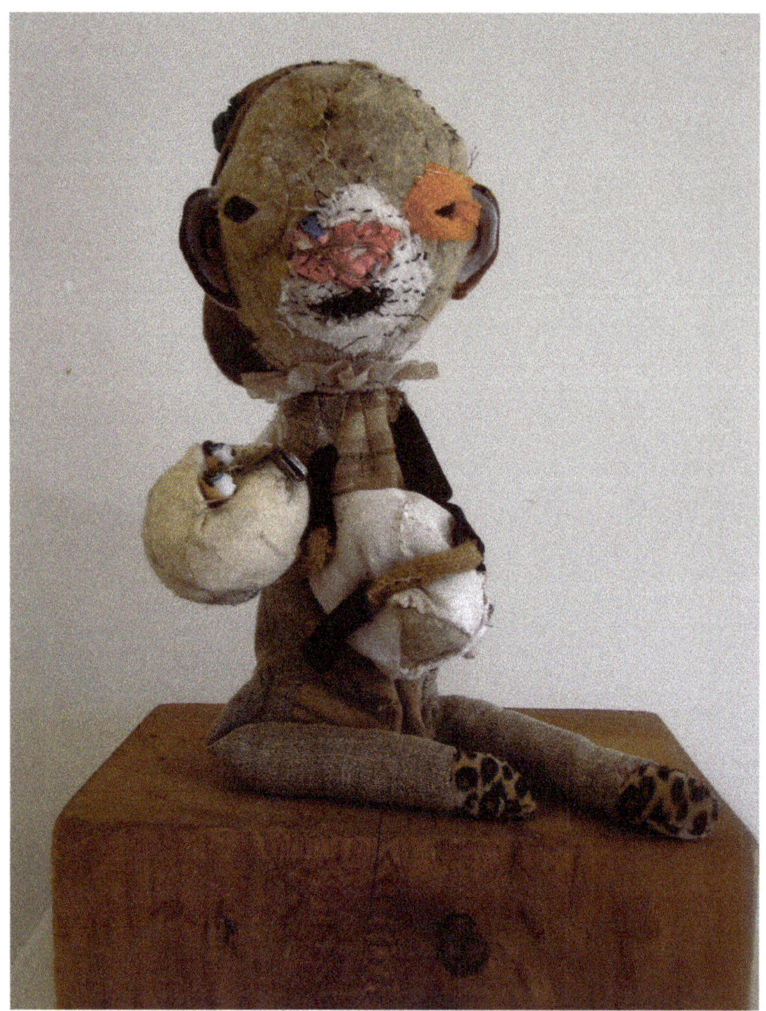

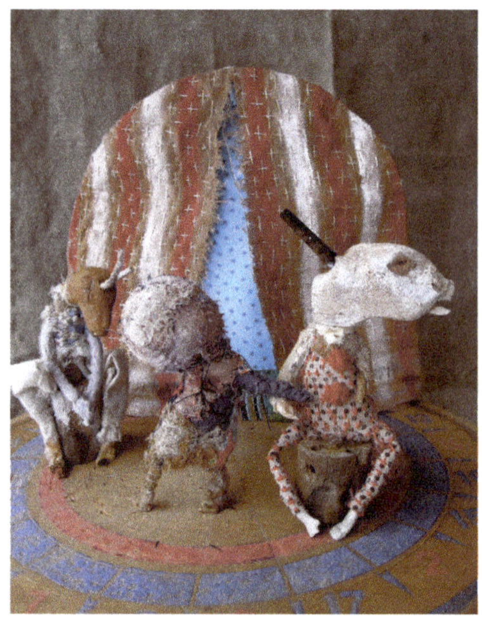

(*Left*) *Bird Mother #11*. 2015. Mixed-media, found objects, 14 x 8 x 8 in.

(*Right*) *Sanatorium under the Sign of the Hourglass*. 2010. Mixed-media, found objects, 15 x 18 x 18 in.

also allow for recurring elements, such as the ladder, the rope, the pulley, and the wheel. There is a palpable sense of both precariousness and inescapability in many of these tableaux, as typified by *No Exit* (2015) (inspired by Jean-Paul Sartre's famous play of that name).

Cardew considers herself a liminal figure, sitting on the boundary between an art world she doesn't feel totally part of and a traditional family life disconnected from the themes of her art practice. Fiber arts such as stitching, sewing, and embroidery perhaps form a bridge between the two. For a long while she felt awkward bringing these domestic aspects of her life into her art, but in recent years she has made them an integral part of her work, using the sewing together of disparate parts as a metaphor for healing, and extending the processes beyond their traditional use. For example, in the recent piece ***Woman with Spirit Doll*** (2015), she uses embroidery (or, strictly speaking, the reverse of the embroidered cloth) to represent faces with an almost paint-like expressiveness. Like much of Cardew's work, it is a piece that both staggers fellow artists and connects powerfully with people who may never have engaged with art on such a meaningful level before.

STEVE PANTON, MAY 2015

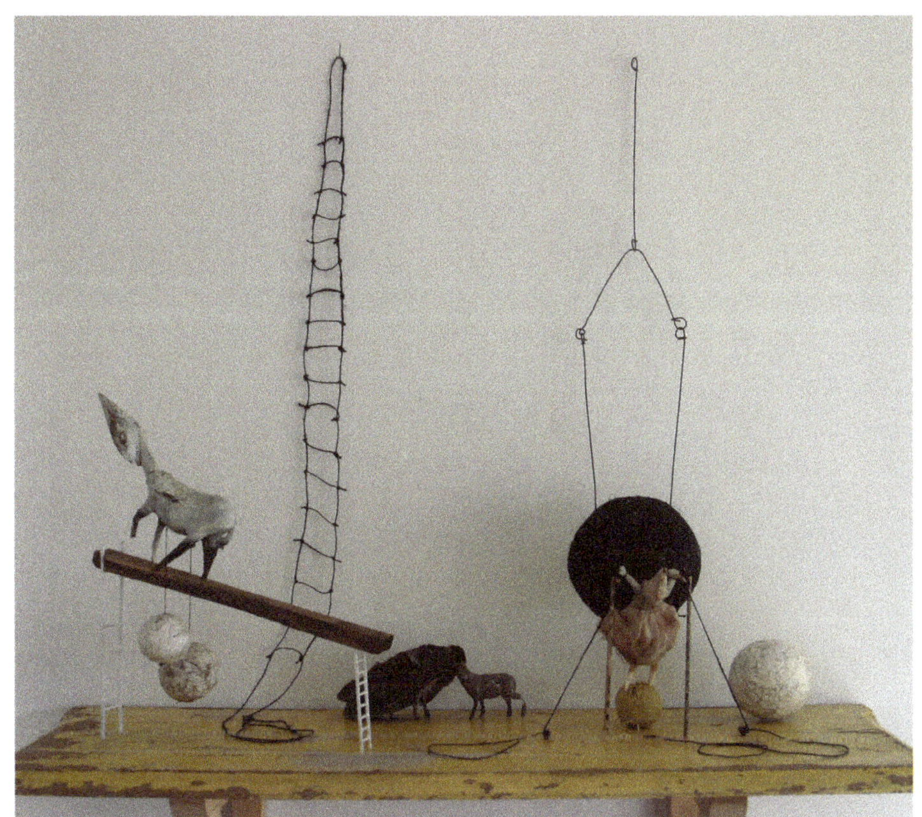

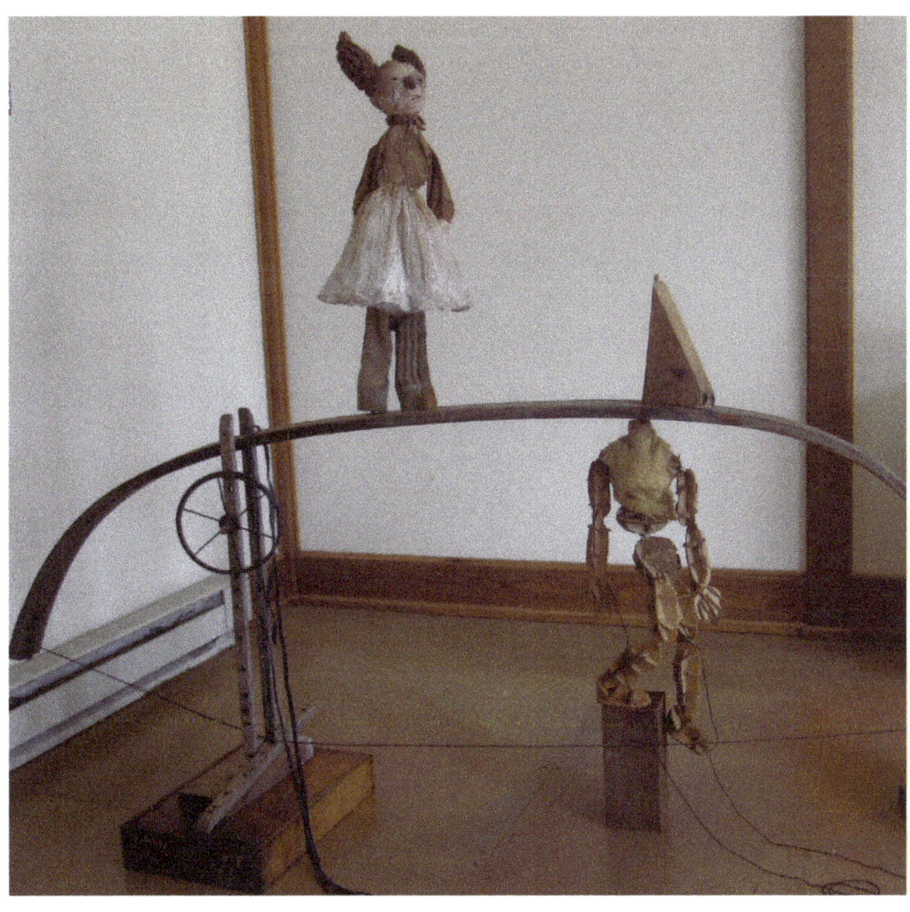

(*Top*) *Myth of Sisyphus.* 2006. Mixed-media, found objects, 30 x 12 x 20 in.

(*Bottom*) *No Exit.* 2015. Mixed-media, found objects, 60 x 50 x 30 in.

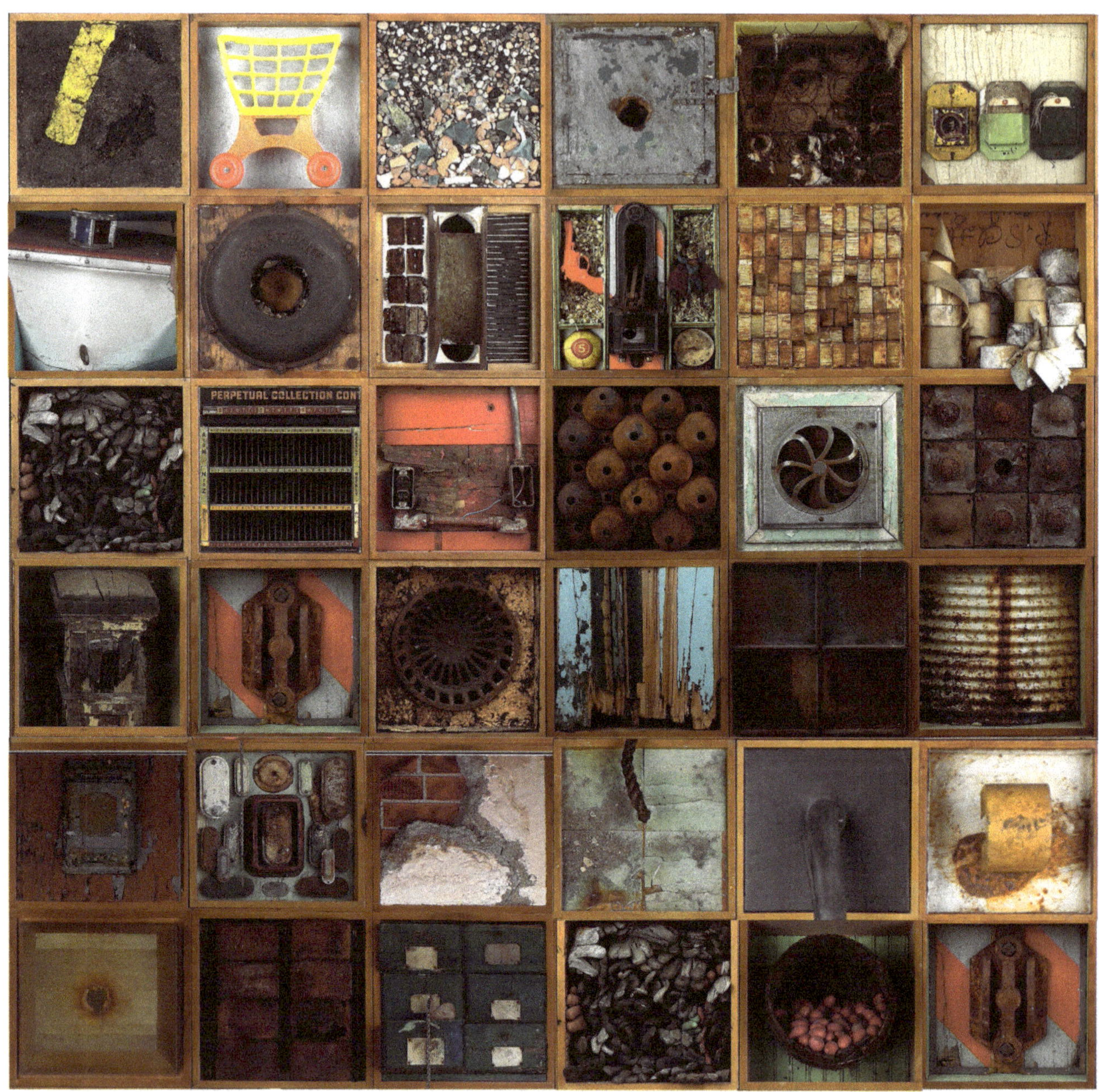

Relics (detail). 2001. Mixed-media installation, size variable.

24 // CLINTON SNIDER

Born Oklahoma City, Oklahoma, 1969
BFA, College for Creative Studies
Lives in Bloomfield Township, Michigan

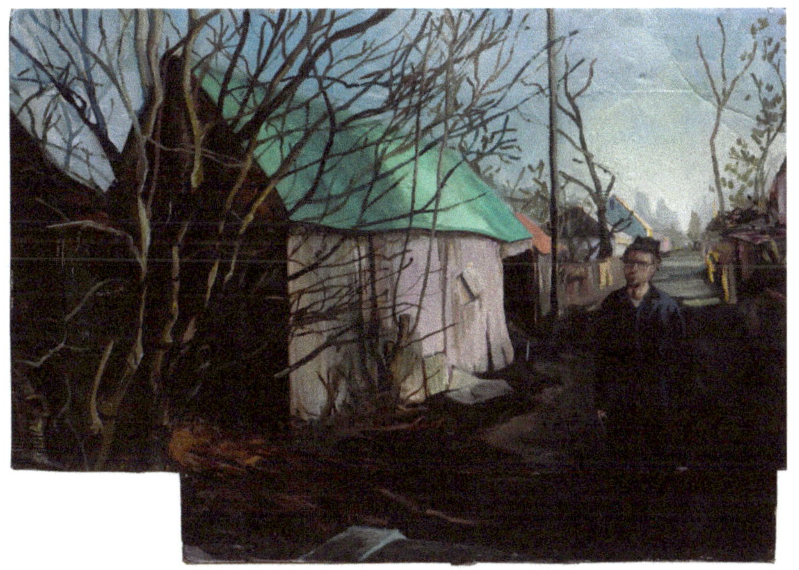

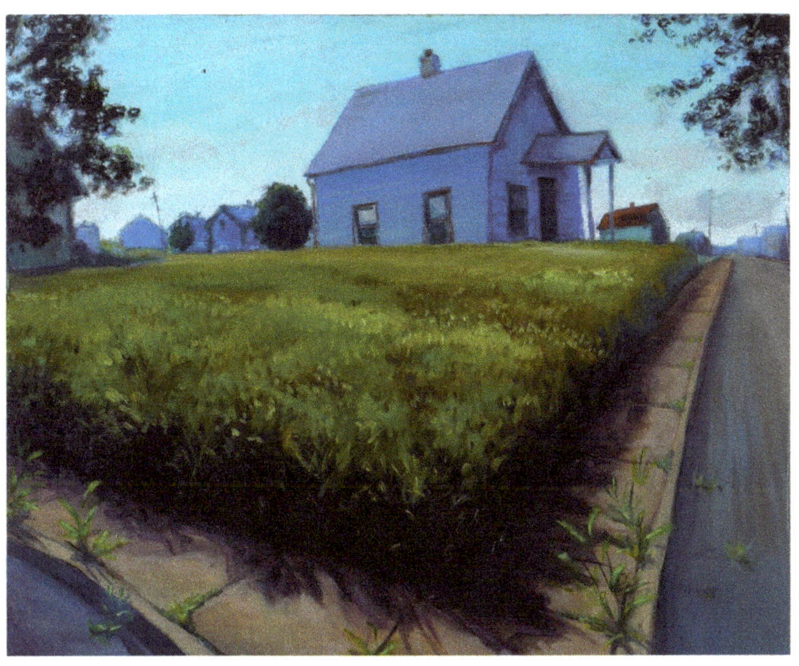

Clinton Snider's beautifully realized paintings examine issues of social and environmental transformation in Southeast Michigan. Often his works talk to their interconnectedness. For example, see 2004's ***Tree and Fence***, which shows an aged, dead, and truncated tree enveloping what appears to be an old fence post. In the far background are more buildings, but between them is an empty space. It is clear that the tree has led a fairly lengthy life, and hence the fence post must also be of some age. The suggestion is that the fence post is the last evidence of a once-populated neighborhood, and that its survival is due to its relationship to the tree. Or alternatively, see 2002's ***Tree of***

(*Top*) *Wanderer in the Alley*. 2008. Oil, cardboard, 42 x 60 in.
(*Bottom*) *Country in the City*. 2004. Oil, wood, 15 x 24 in.

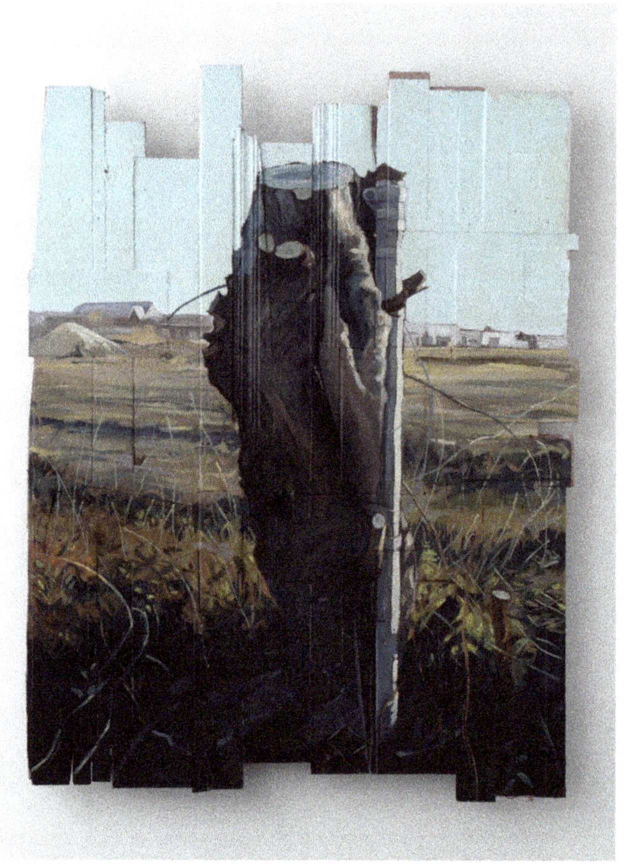

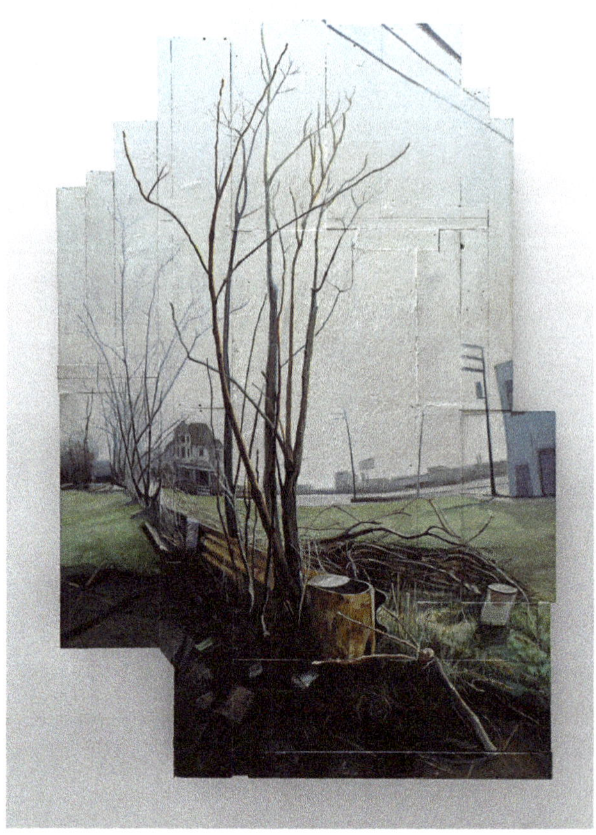

(*Left*) *Tree and Fence.* 2004. Oil, wood, 60 x 40 in. (*Right*) *Tree of Heaven.* 2002. Oil, wood, 96 x 65 in.

Heaven, where the eponymous trees are shown reestablishing themselves in the windbreak resulting from a freeway barrier—their existence dependent on an artifact of human intervention. Clearly Snider is both a formidable painter and a close observer of the city's landscape, alive to indications of the past and of future change. It can also be noted that both of the previously mentioned works are realized on structures of found wood, often sourced close to the location of the painting. By painting on repurposed surfaces, Snider combines the local with broader global concerns of consumerism and recycling.

A pivotal piece in Snider's career was ***Relics***, which he completed with Scott Hocking for a 2001 installation at the Detroit Institute of Arts, and which comprises a large number of identically sized boxes containing assemblages of found objects from around Detroit. The intensity of the experience in creating this work—which totally consumed the artists for a year—and the consequent reflection on this time led Snider to a mindset that allowed the creation of large-scale paintings such as ***Gaia*** (2002). The title refers, of course, to the earth spirit, and the image clearly subverts the typical landscape image of natural beauty but challenges the viewer to see it as anything other than sublime. *Gaia* and *Tree of Heaven* were both shown as part of an expansive solo exhibition in 2003

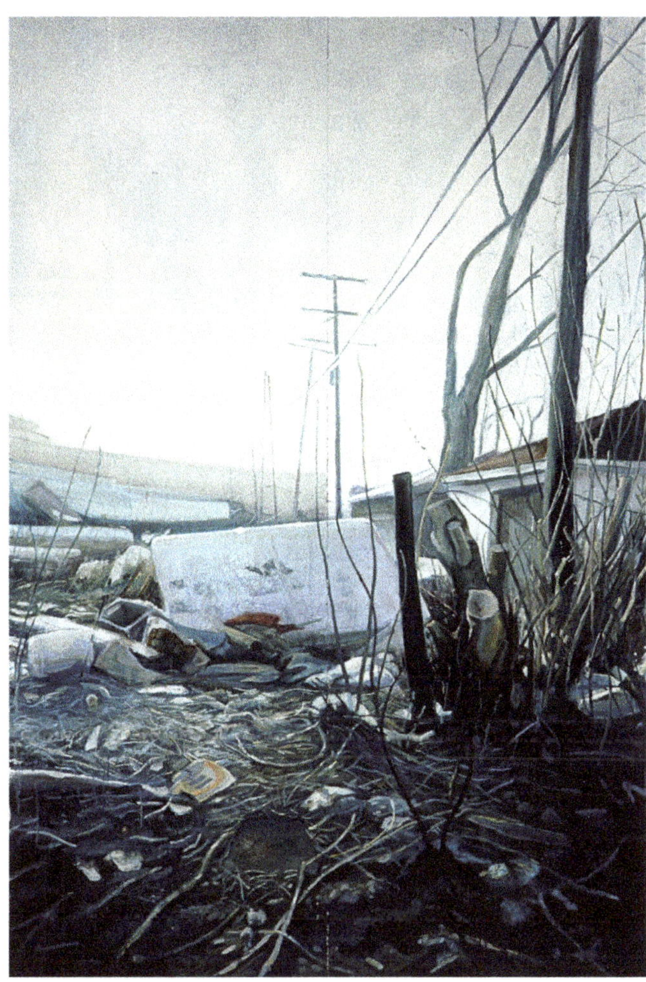

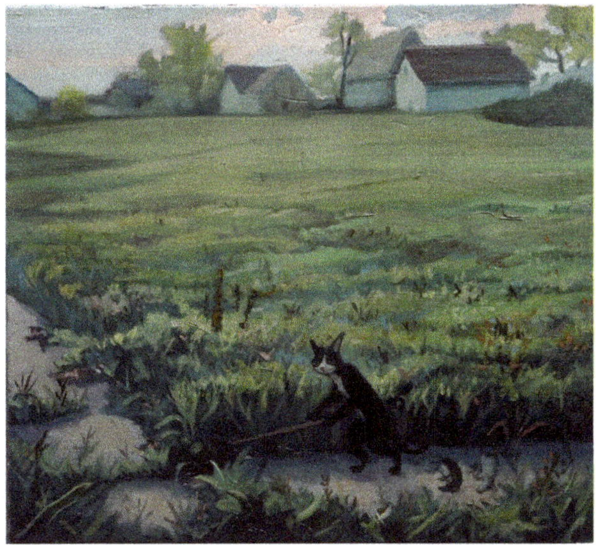

(*Left*) *Gaia*. 2002. Oil, wood, 84 x 56 in.
(*Right*) *The Rat Catcher*. 2012. Oil, wood, 15 x 16 in.

at Detroit's Tangent Gallery, which confirmed Snider's reputation as a major artist in the city.

If the Detroit landscape has been Snider's most obvious subject over the years, it has often been filtered through a distinctive, dreamlike aesthetic. This has manifested itself in various ways, such as the playful curvature of space (see, for example, 2004's ***Country in the City***), eerie lighting conditions that can be difficult to reconcile into either day or night (e.g., 2009's ***The Twilight***), the inclusion of typically expressionless self-portraiture (e.g., 2008's *Wanderer in the Alley*), or the insertion of seemingly feral figures (sometimes the artist's children, such as in 2012's ***Chinese Restaurant***). Works such as *The Twilight*, *Chinese Restaurant*, and 2012's ***The Rat Catcher*** show Snider moving away from the city as a muse and toward more mysterious territory. His latest works include miniature wall-mounted imaginary landscapes, such as the cleverly titled ***Rupture/Rapture*** (2015), which seems to point to an exit from the mortal plane entirely.

Snider describes the process of working through a painting as a meditation on existence. His works often start from a fleeting moment that through some combination of visual or psychological prompts has lodged in his memory. Photographs taken on journeys through the city may act as initiation points for further reflection. He considers a work to be completed to his satisfaction not just when it is resolved

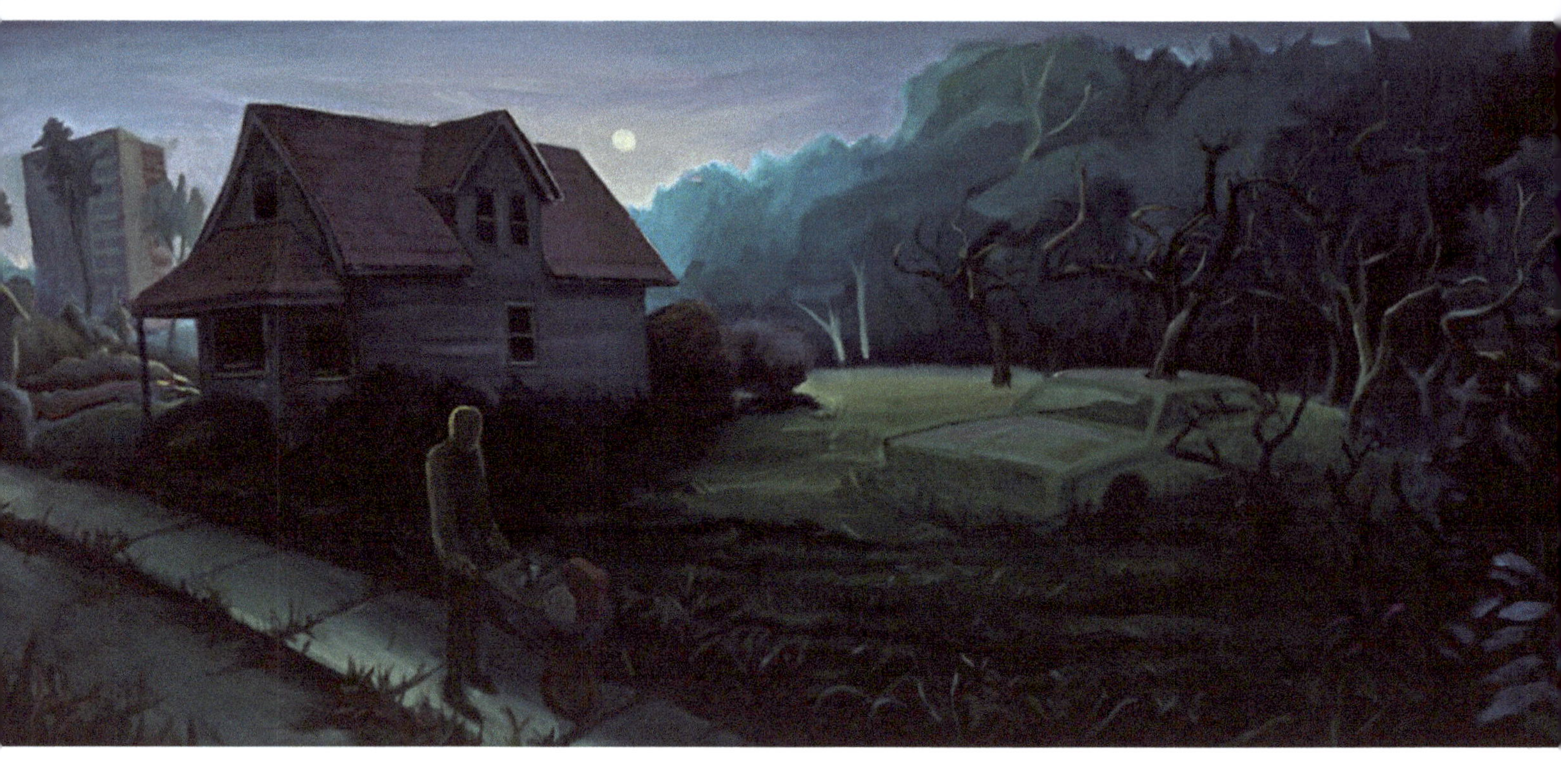

The Twilight. 2009. Oil, canvas, 20 x 45 in.

in a visual sense, but also when he feels that the significance of the moment has been revealed. Until this point he may be repeatedly reworking the image and traversing an internal landscape of experiential, metaphysical, and spiritual concerns. It is a highly intuitive process, the results of which may not be describable in words but which hopefully are embodied in the painting. His benchmarks are works by diverse historical art figures ranging from Van Eyck and Vermeer through to Rothko, which speak to him in a transhistorical, transcultural way of the moment in which they were created. Snider's quest is an exacting one, constantly striving for something just out of reach and simultaneously trying to convey it through his painting. Ultimately his work is about showing the interconnectedness and interdependence of it all—a profound and universal vision.

STEVE PANTON, JUNE 2015

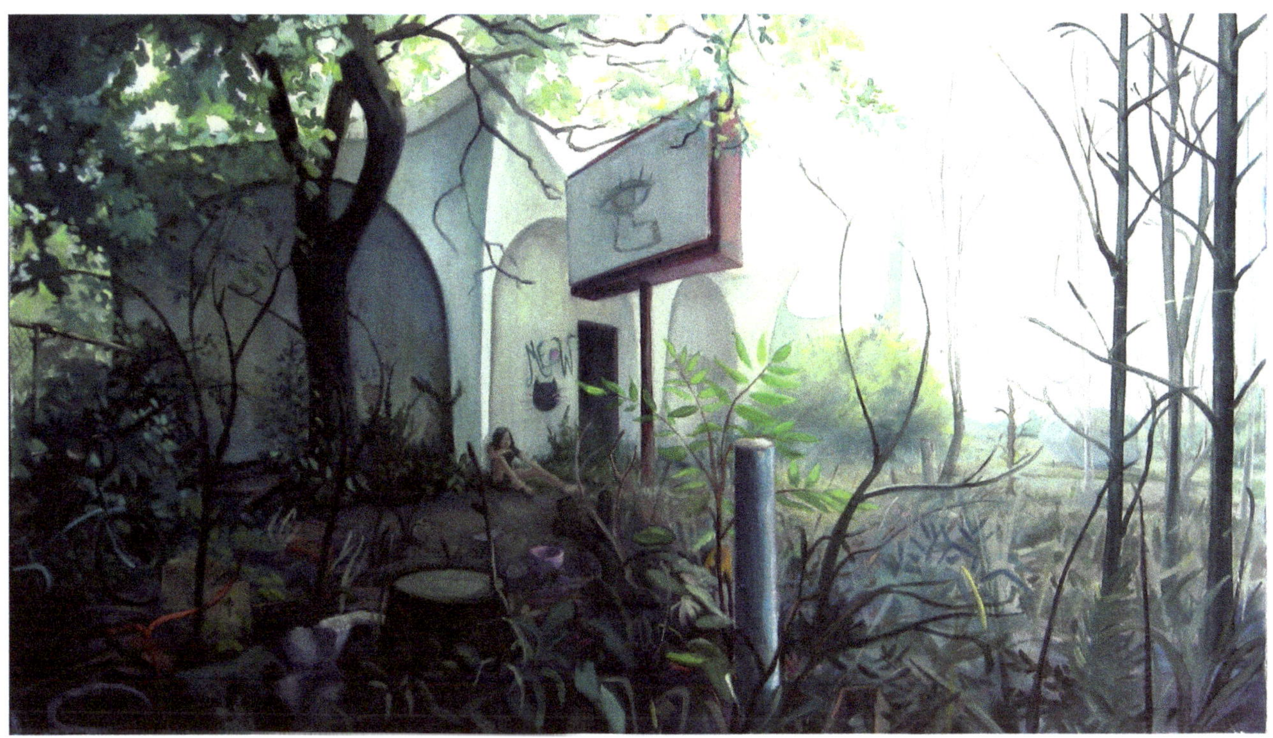

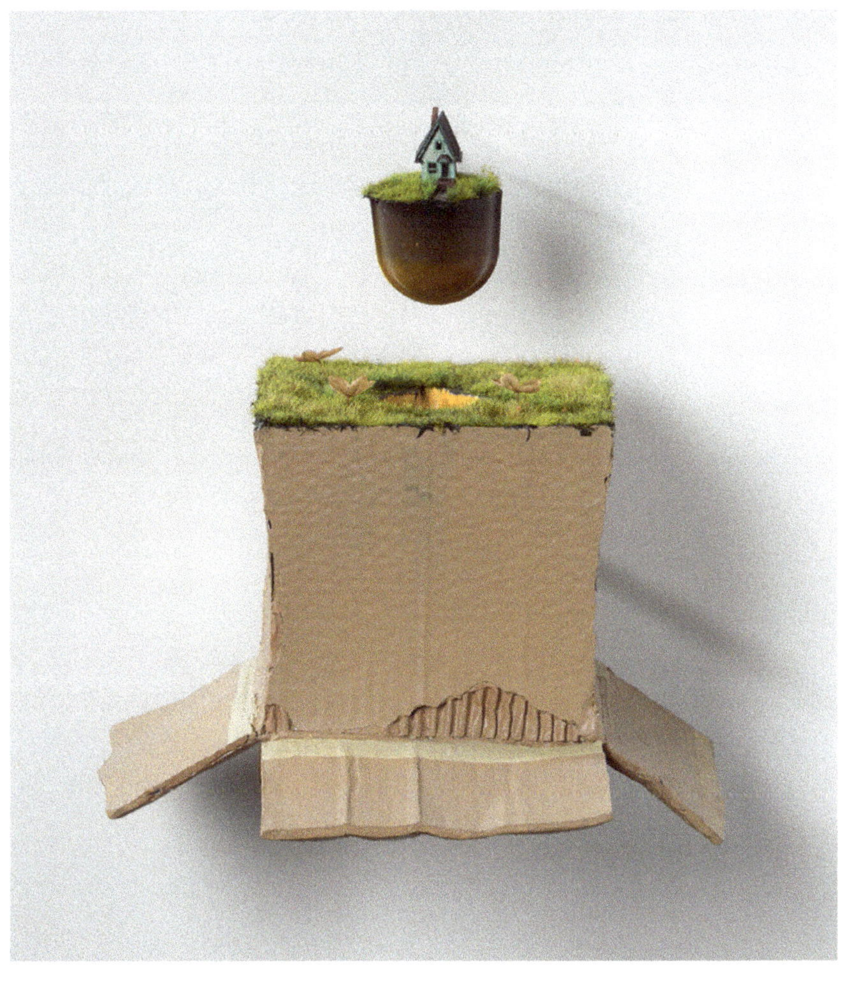

(*Top*) *Chinese Restaurant.* 2012.
Oil, wood, 30 x 48 in.

(*Left*) *Rupture/Rapture.* 2015.
Aqua resin, paint, wooden sticks, 18 x 10 x 10 in.

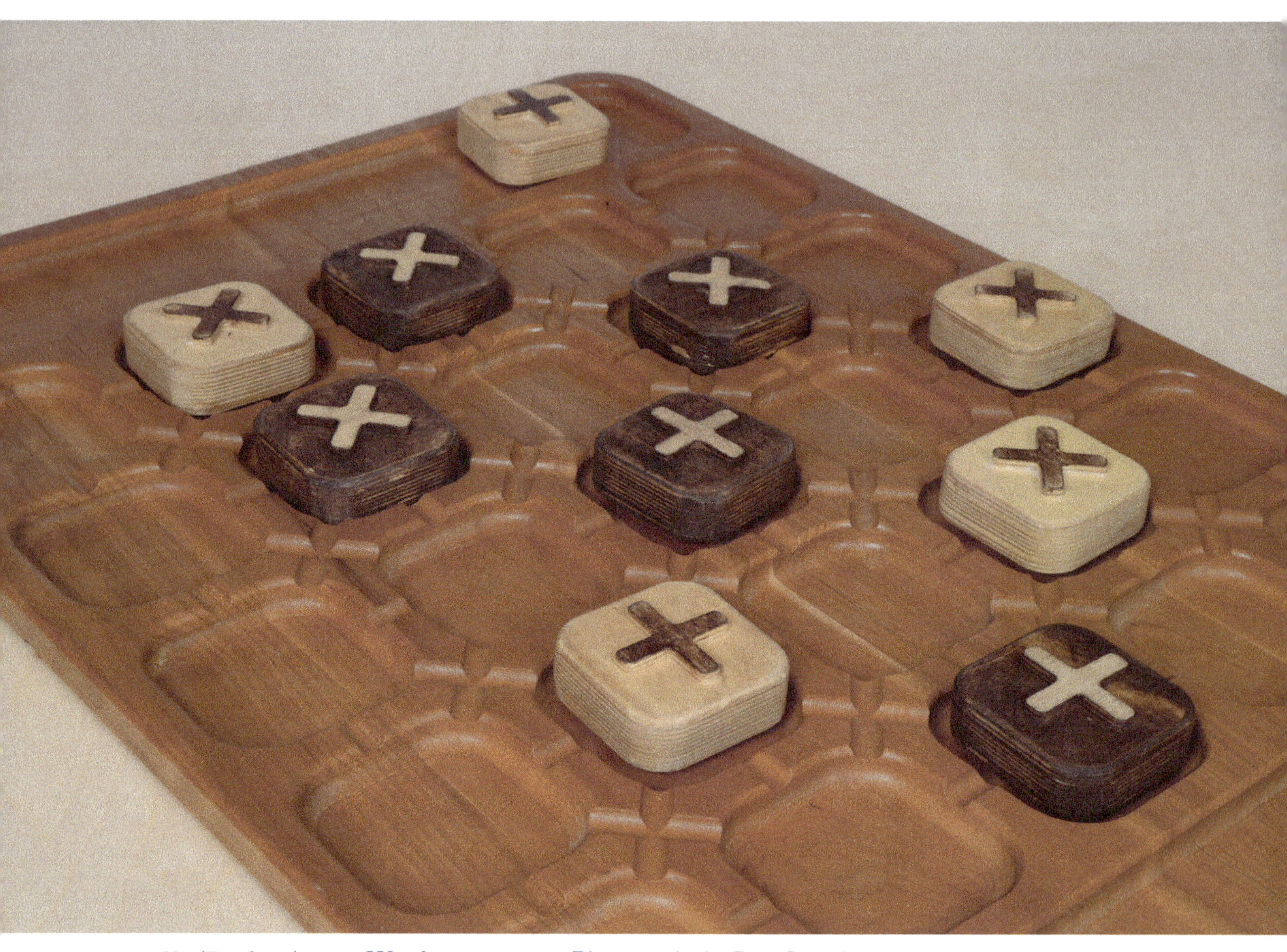

X+ (Ex-Cross). 2006. Wood, 2 x 22 x 30 in. Photography by Riva Sayegh.

25 // ANDY MALONE

Born Detroit, 1972
BA (Architecture), University of Detroit
Lives in Royal Oak, Michigan

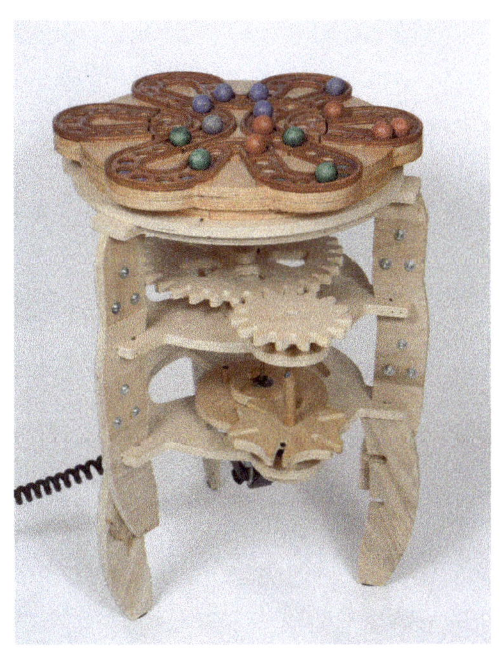

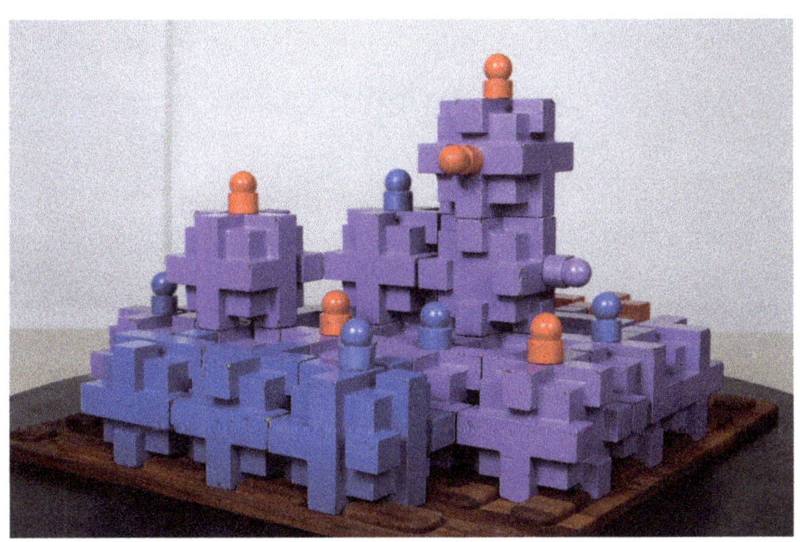

On the game-board shelf in Andy Malone's living room, stuck in between Castle Blast and Where in Space Is Carmen Sandiego?, is a nondescript wooden box containing a game of his own creation, called *X+ (Ex-Cross)* (2006). Players line up two-sided wooden game pieces, each embedded with the eponymous X on one side and + on the other, along the back row of a modified checkerboard. In three-movement turns, players navigate the board, trying to capture each other along diagonals for X and orthogonals for +. Each piece can, at any time in a turn, flip to alter its capacity to move. Malone used this game as an opportunity to discuss with his

(*Top*) *Meander*. 2006. Wood, 33 x 22 in. diameter. Photography by Riva Sayegh.

(*Bottom*) *Nexus Game*. 2008. Wood, magnets, base 32 x 32 in. Photography by Riva Sayegh.

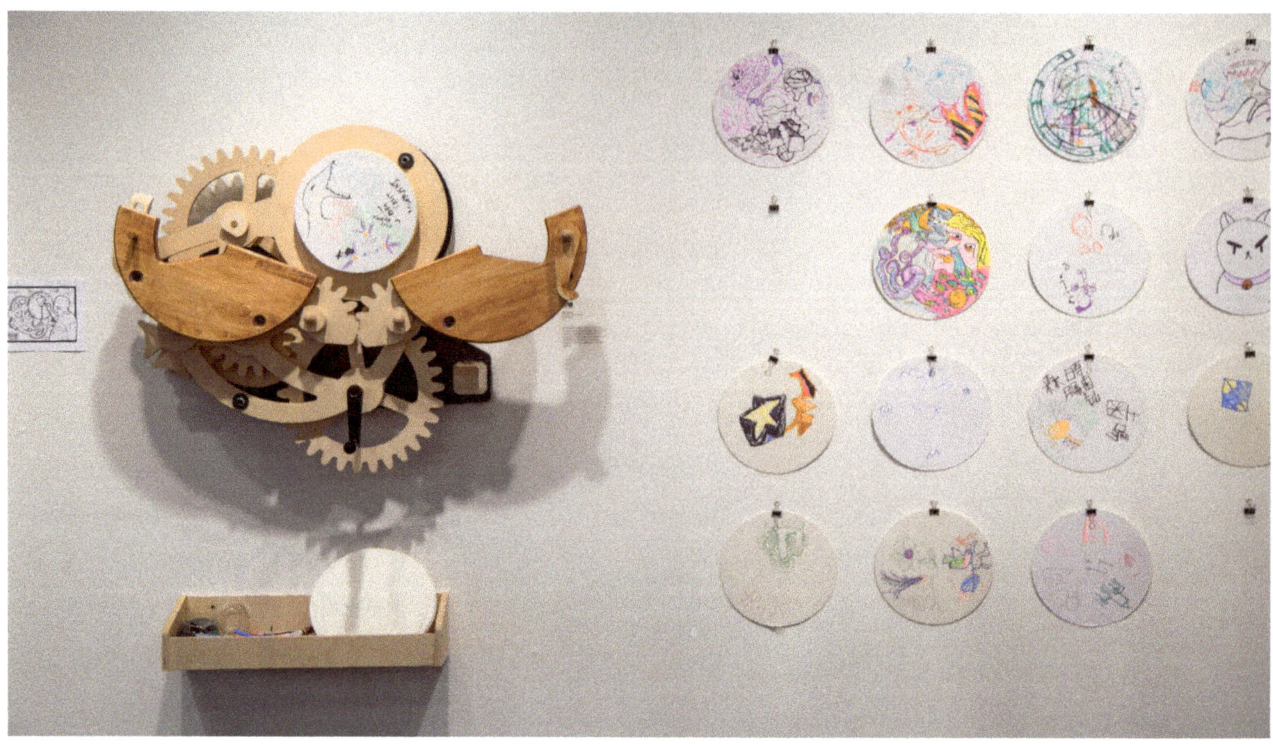

Exquisite Corpse Machine (Prototype 2). 2003. Wooden gears, mixed-media, 27 x 29 x 9 in. Photography by Corrie Baldauf.

daughter, Julia, the opposing philosophies of Dr. Martin Luther King Jr. and those of Malcolm X. As Malone sees it, each of these civil rights leaders was locked into a singular kind of movement, but ultimately an individual has better options when able to think flexibly.

This microcosmic example contains all the hallmarks of Malone's artistic practice: intricately handcrafted woodworks, kinetic movement, analog technologies, didactic games with open-ended outcomes, a thoughtful practice of viewer engagement, and deft sugarcoating to serious subjects. His work is poised between generations, using games and engineering as an outlet for an artistic practice that was both inherited from and inhibited by his father's career as a painter, but also as a tool for communication and learning with his own children. Increasingly, science recognizes the importance of games as a method of developing and reinforcing neural plasticity, and Malone is endlessly engaged in a practice of leveraging their ability to change thinking, in himself and others. His current piece, *Quatern* (working title), acts as an attempt to disrupt Malone's self-reported tendency for "analysis paralysis" by having players take turns simultaneously, the action forced along by a motorized mechanism. It sits on the workbench in his home studio—a garage replete with hanging wooden gears and clockworks stashed in the rafters, salvaged from old projects and recycled into new ones.

Malone's pieces are all meant to be handled and played with—he does not consider his works complete until someone engages with them. Sometimes people play nicely, yielding collaborative results, such as with his ***Exquisite Corpse Machine (Prototype***

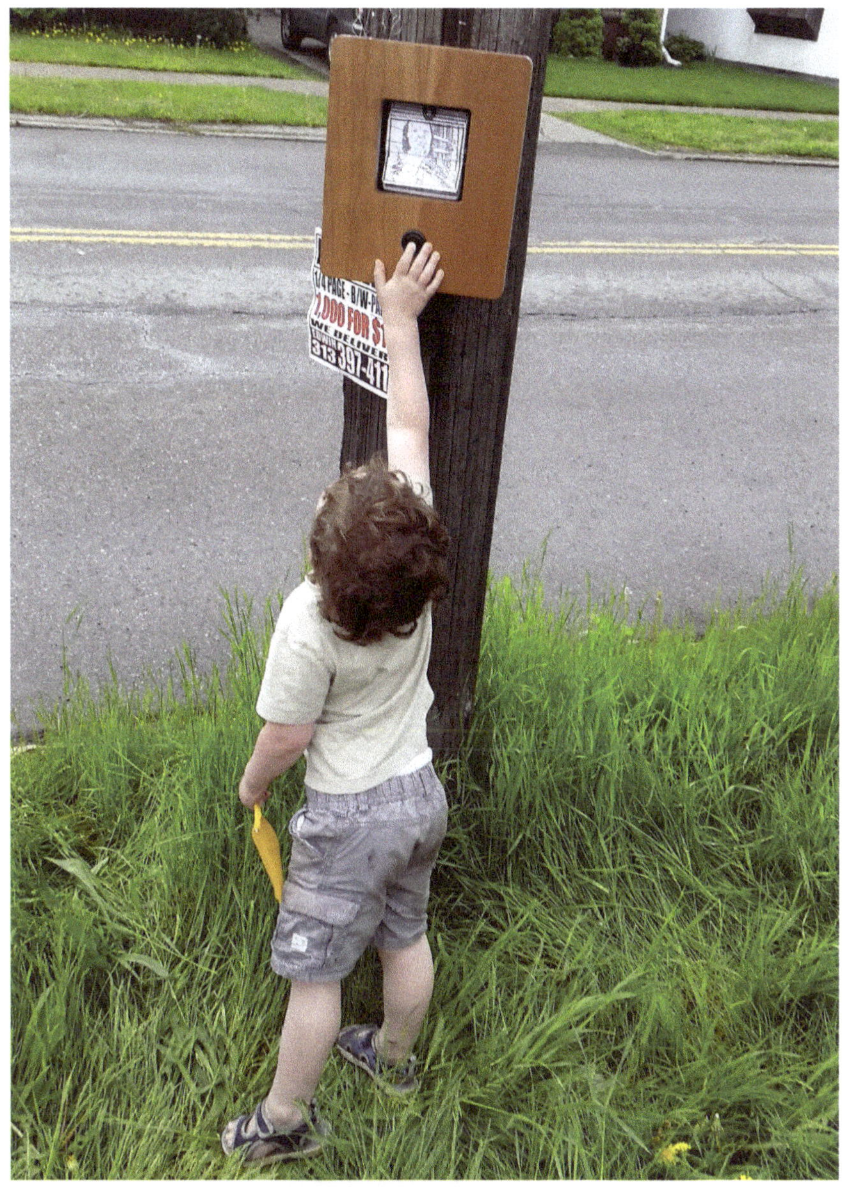

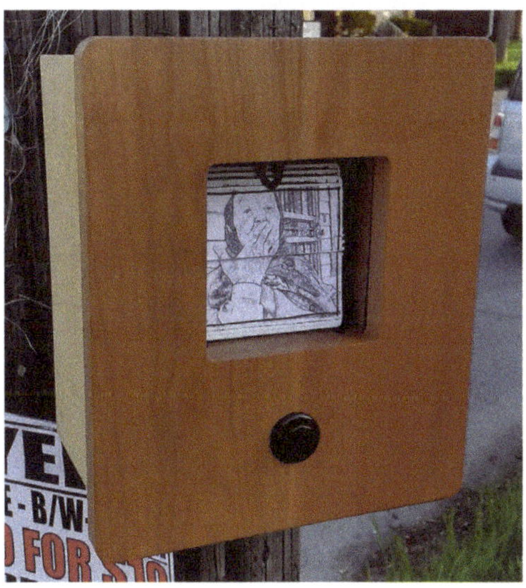

Grandma Loves You, A Mutoscope (prior to being destroyed by vandals). 2015. Wood, index cards, motor, 12 x 10 x 8 in.

2) (2003), which enables viewers to create drawings that overlap with the work of others at the edges. Sometimes, people are not as respectful of Malone's delicate clockworks, but he appears to accept with relatively magnanimity the occasional collateral damage of placing art in the public sphere. When the ***mutoscopes*** created for Hamtramck's Porous Borders Festival were trashed by vandals, he regathered the scattered stop-motion cards to create a new, fever-dream-like narrative. In some regards, Malone sees this "collaboration" as an improvement on his own vision—though it was clearly traumatic for him to see the images of a beloved neighborhood elder named Tekla disrespected.

Reconciling trauma and destruction is a primary function for several of Malone's most powerful works. ***Blight Melody*** (2015) couches the poignancy of vacancy in Malone's childhood Detroit neighborhood in the wistful mechanism of a music box (another lost vestige from a time of analog technologies). When engaged by the viewer, the music box plays a tinkling melody to underscore the realization that the punch holes in the paper, which trigger the notes, represent vacant lots where homes once stood. This innocent trapping makes the dawning reality hit that much harder. Revelations of this nature are unavoidable in the context of ***1967 Detroit Rebellion Chess Set*** (2003–6), a masterwork that took three years to complete. Each of thirty-two standard chess pieces is rendered as a wooden mechanical figurine, representing the pawns and major players in this historic event that has come to exemplify the race and class struggle in Detroit. As with much of Malone's work, the masterful rendering and playful surfaces of this piece often lead a viewer to engage in the game before understanding its didactic content; it is this quality of hidden learning that is his profound gift, even compared to his other obvious gifts of craft, engineering, and cartooning.

Sure, Andy Malone is just playing. But his endgame is devastating.

SARAH ROSE SHARP, JULY 2015

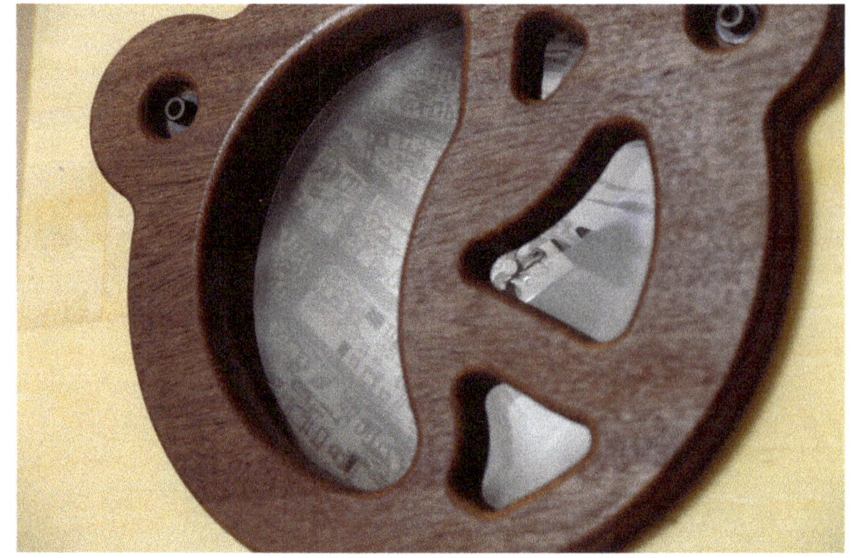

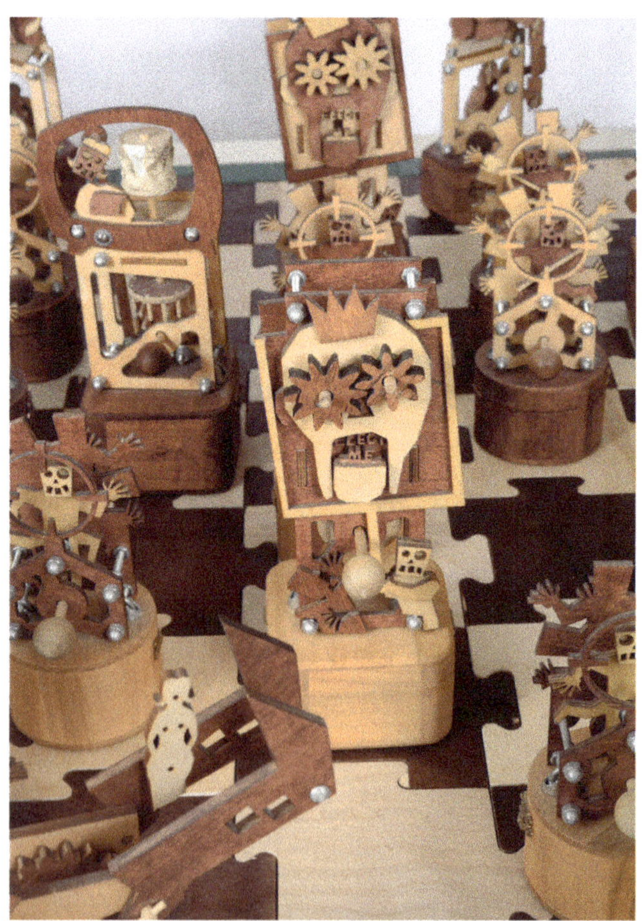

(*Top*) *Blight Melody*. 2015. Salvaged wood, paper, motor, 14 x 27 x 6 in. Photography by Riva Sayegh.

(*Bottom and Facing page*) *1967 Detroit Rebellion Chess Set*. 2003–6. Wood, various hardware, 13 x 60 x 60 in. Photography by Riva Sayegh.

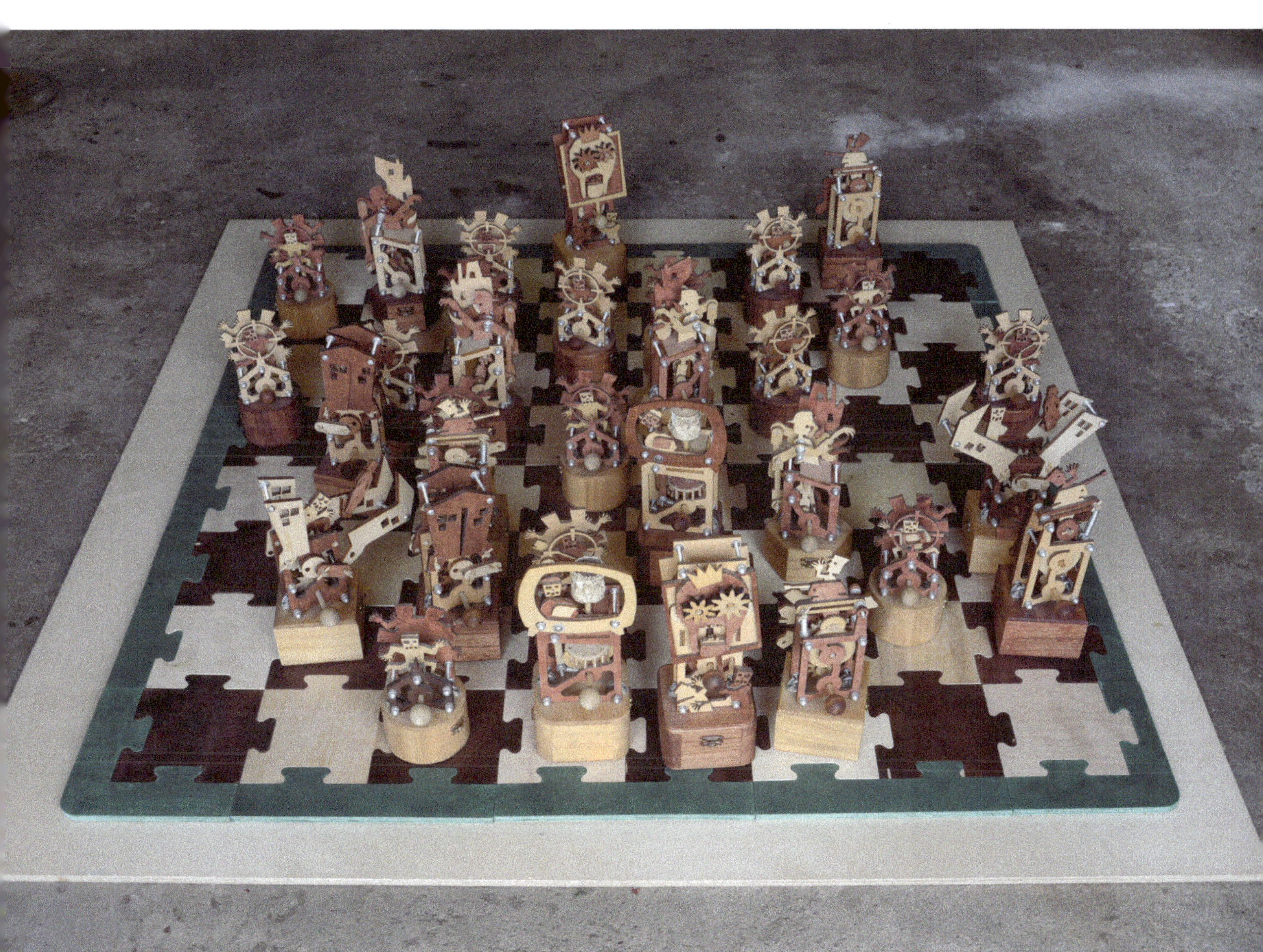

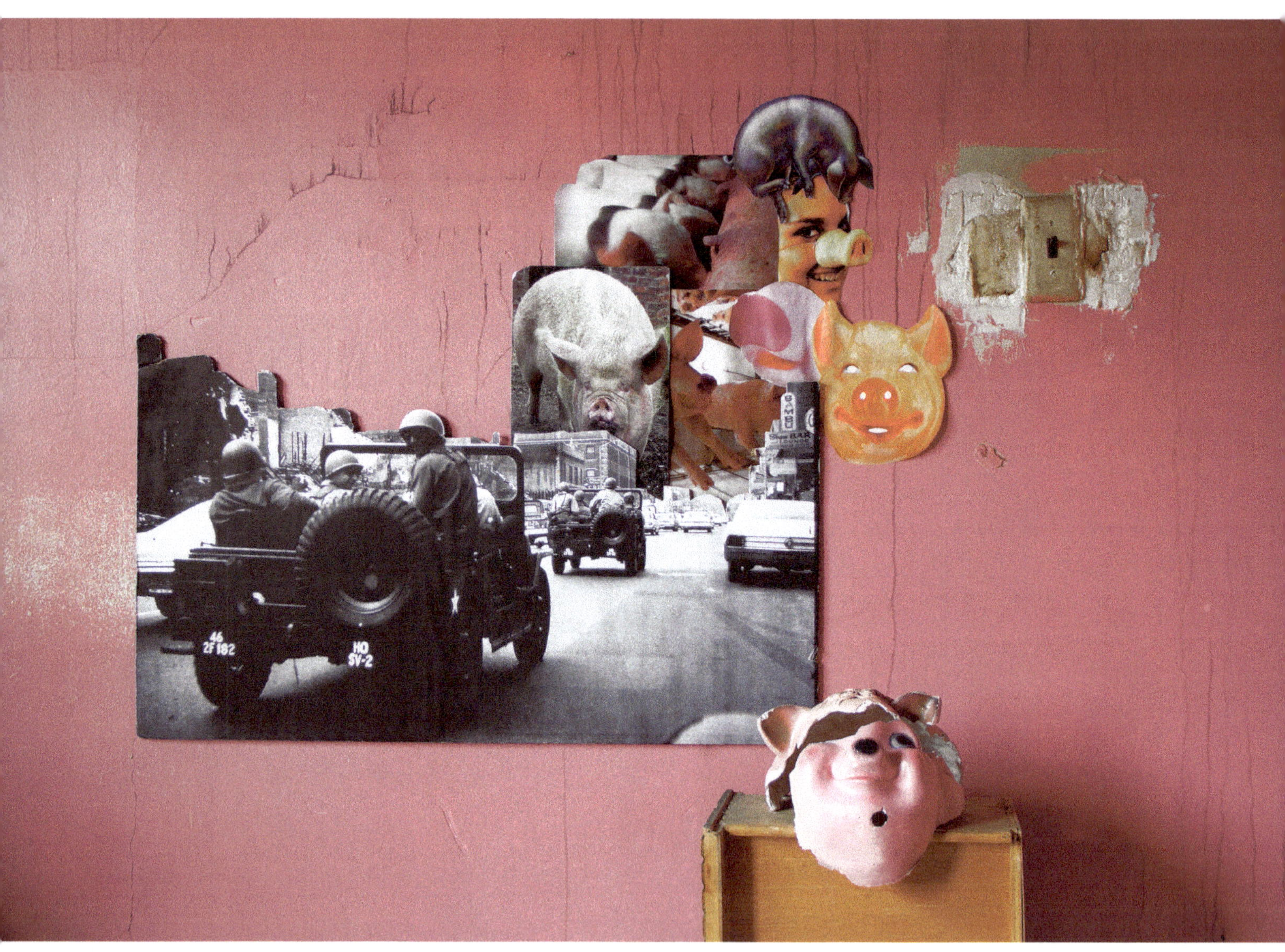

From the series *Black Day in July.* 2013. Archival inkjet print, 20 x 30 in.

26 // SHANNA MEROLA

Born Bridgeport, Connecticut, 1980
BFA, Virginia Commonwealth University
MFA, Cranbrook Academy of Art
Lives in Hamtramck, Michigan

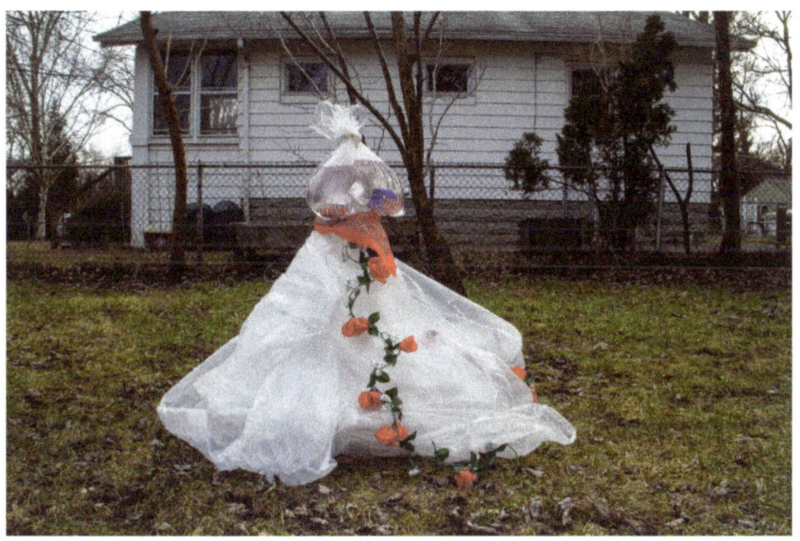

From the series *Another Country*. 2012. Archival inkjet print, 20 x 30 in.

It is a foundational concern of Shanna Merola's that all of her work be firmly embedded in its historical context. Observance and urgent communication of moments of injustice are the center of her personal, professional, and artistic life. In light of this, an overview of her many bodies of work, while intimidating in its breadth, quickly falls into a sensible pattern. There is a vast, triangular power brewing here—of form, composition, and context—that jacks out of every image, a seething social urgency. For example, ***Black Day in July*** (2013) is a series of collages/assemblages that were installed and documented at various sites in Detroit's Twelfth and Clairmount neighborhood, and address the 1967 riots and their aftermath in that community. The sample shown might shock the viewer with its palette (a cluster of lurid

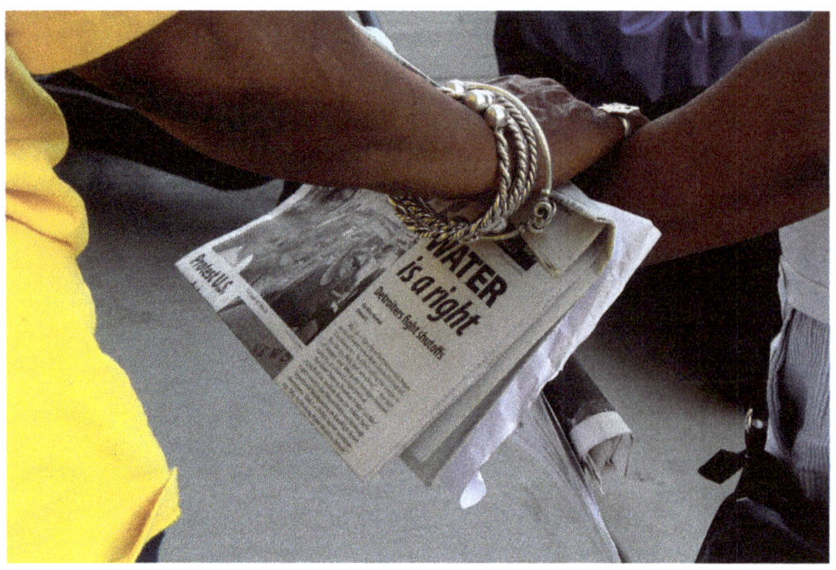

Image from *Freedom Friday Detroit Water Rights Rally*. 2014. Archival inkjet print.

pinks like those of Philip Guston, one of her favorite painters) and its formal cascade of imagery shooting across a pocked, stained pink wall like projectile vomit, and yet it keeps one interested and becomes more subtle and formally fine the longer one looks. The work is baldly political in its use of traditional revolutionary imagery—pig masks and collage looming over documentary-style photographs of soldiers moving in jeeps across a grim landscape. The pig is the totem animal in this piece. Glancing over it, one is interrogated by pig eyes darting out from collage and empty masks. The distinction between the gaze of the pigs and that of the soldiers becomes hazy, though they certainly share the right to look back at the viewer. The assemblage is installed on a wall in an abandoned house next to a gutted light switch in a simple, but potent, second nod to the power of the Pig, be it spirit animal or National Guardsman.

This impression continues as more of Merola's work comes into view. In ***Another Country*** (2012), tacky, sinister still lifes rise out of humble backyards and fetid swamps in the style of homemade memorials and symbolic markers. The triangular, tent-like forms festooned with American flags, shoes, and containers of liquid again evoke Philip Guston, this time in composition and iconography as well as in tone—the low simmer of tension that weaves through both artists' work comes in part, perhaps, from the collapse of values into lurid, parallel bands of color the viewer must sift through. One often encounters this phenomenon in documentary photography, due to the lack of orchestrated composition. Merola creates a similar "real world" effect in her fine art photography by taking the colors we notice and admire in passing and making them central. One feels the earnestness behind it. The concerns Merola chooses to highlight in her work—police brutality, corruption in local government, and, more recently, ***Detroit's rash of water shutoffs***, are those she feels to the depths of her bones. In order to make good, politically and socially engaged work, one's commitment to one's causes can't be light.

Merola walks the walk. Her political drive has led her to participate in, as well as photograph, actions of the Grace Lee Boggs Center and the Detroit Coalition against Police Brutality. Her documentary and studio practice share a focus on images of abuse of power and resources with the aim of ending all such violence, unequivocally—she credits her time with the Boggs Center for instilling that focus.

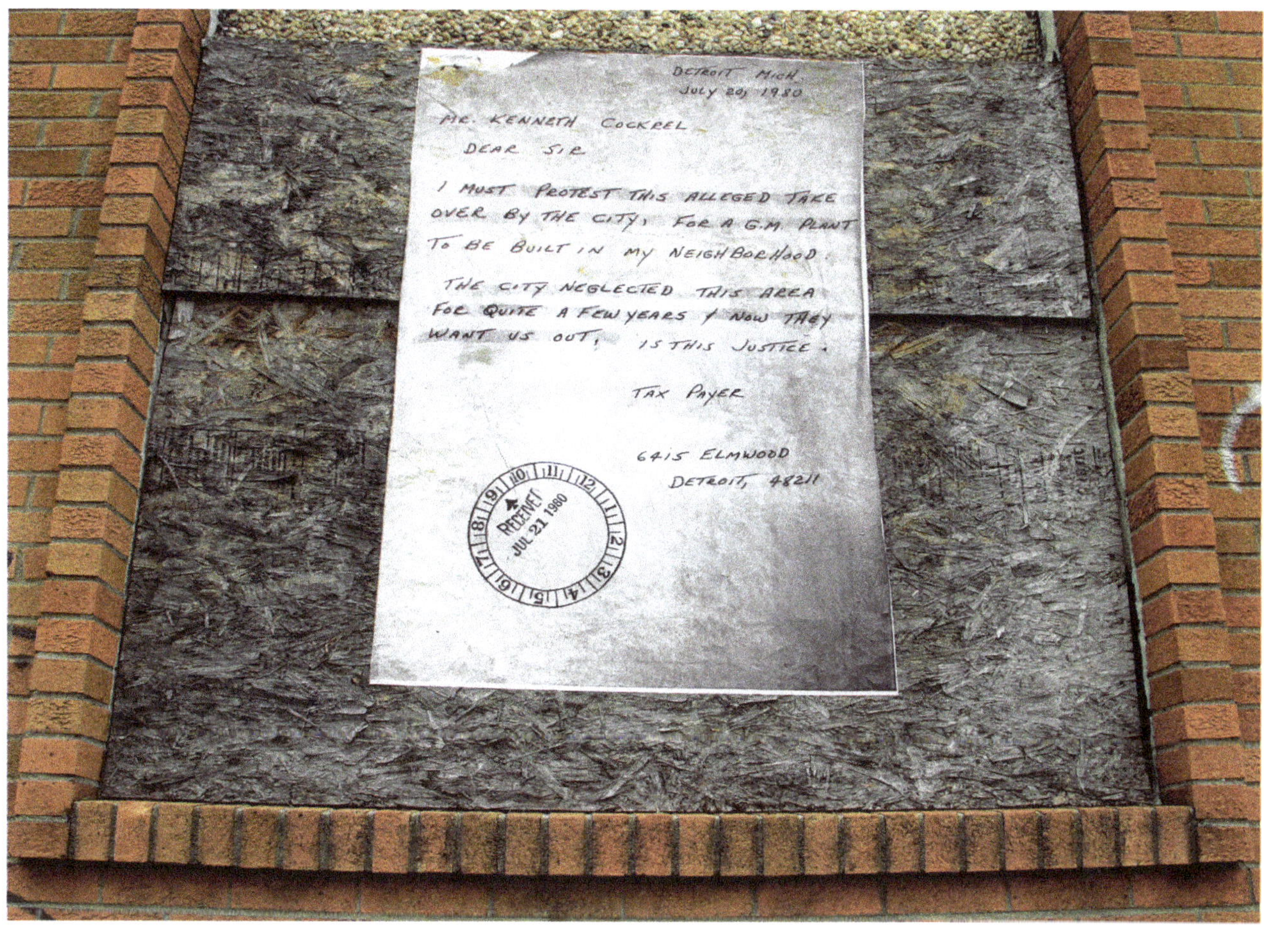

DETROIT MICH.
JULY 20, 1980

MR. KENNETH COCKREL
DEAR SIR

I MUST PROTEST THIS ALLEGED TAKE OVER BY THE CITY, FOR A G.M. PLANT TO BE BUILT IN MY NEIGHBORHOOD.

THE CITY NEGLECTED THIS AREA FOR QUITE A FEW YEARS & NOW THEY WANT US OUT, IS THIS JUSTICE.

TAX PAYER

6415 ELMWOOD
DETROIT, 48211

RECEIVED
JUL 21 1980

From the collaboration *Don't Ignore the Messenger.* 2015. Wheat-pasted archival digital image, 40 x 30 in.

She also works as a legal observer for the National Lawyers Guild, where her job is literally to bear witness to events that have the potential to erupt into brutality between powerful entities and the individuals who confront them. The apparent rapid-fire compositional style in her work masks a canny formal power that whispers of deep loss and humble beauty in a dialogue parallel to its more ascendant political voice.

Her touch courses through the actions of Detroit Homeland Security, a collective consisting of herself, Kate Levy, and Bryce Detroit. The group stages performances and assembles sound pieces as well as dropping guerrilla photographic installations into shuttered public spaces. In the 2015 series ***Don't Ignore the Messenger***, the group wheat-pasted enlarged prints of letters sent from residents along the Hamtramck/Detroit border in 1980 to the facades of structures along that same geographic seam. The letters all come from the Ken Cockrel Jr. Archive at Wayne State University's Law Library and respond in various ways to the announcement of the then-new GM Poletown Plant. Despite their status as almost verbatim found objects, they share a quality with Merola's more orchestrated studio work—a deep sincerity, and a formal beauty that seems to spring from a bare-bones request for a better tomorrow.

CLARA DEGALEN, JULY 2015

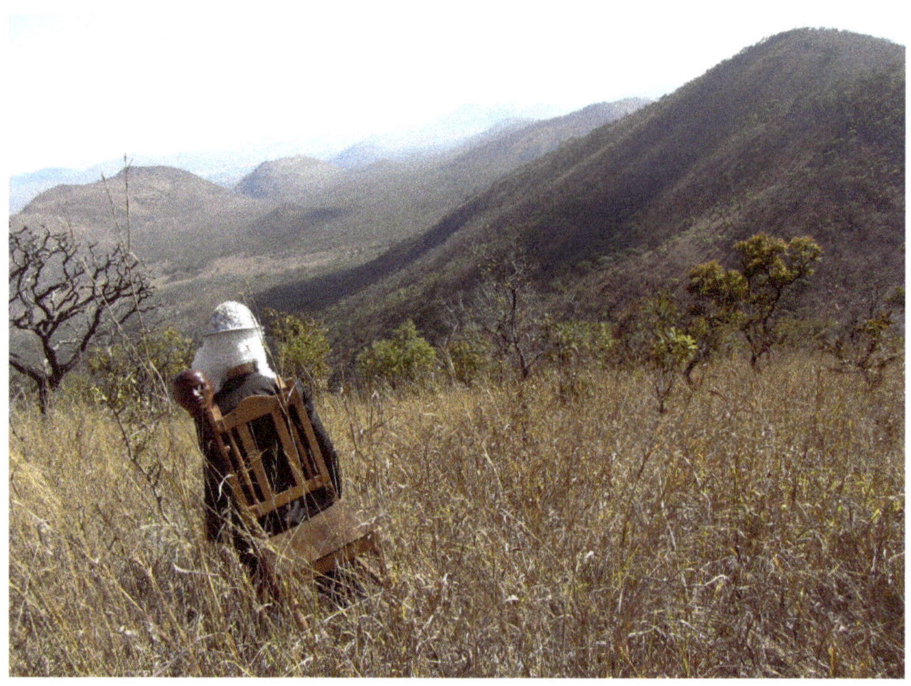

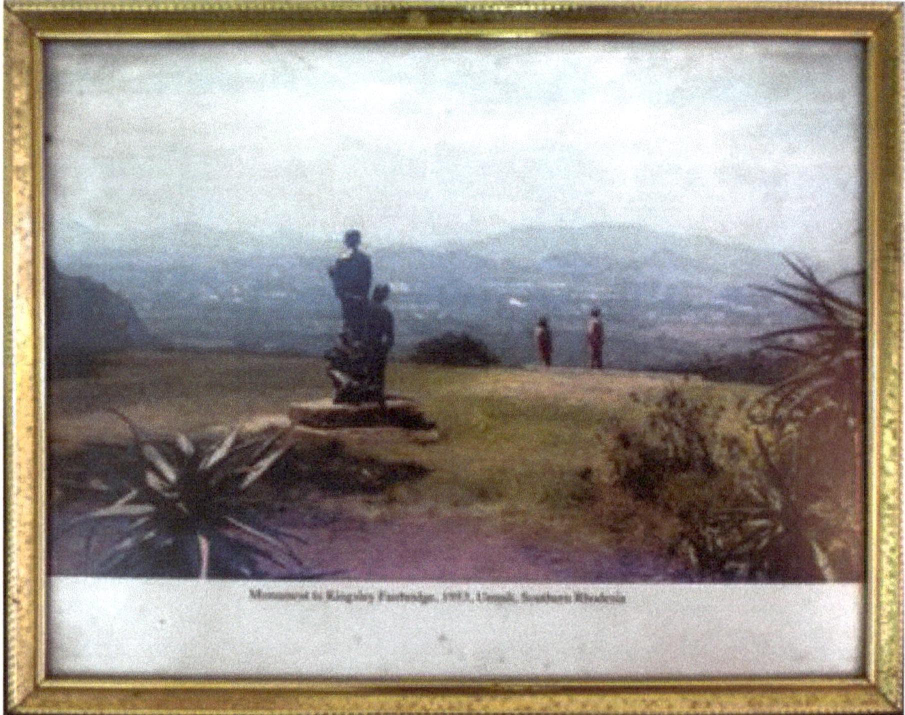

Jack's Vision. 2011. Mixed-media installation.

27 // CHIDO JOHNSON

Born Nyadiri, Zimbabwe, 1969
BFA, University of Georgia
MFA, University of Notre Dame
Lives in Detroit

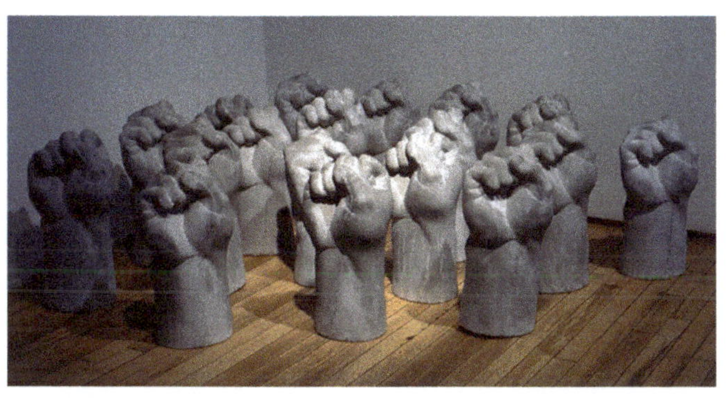

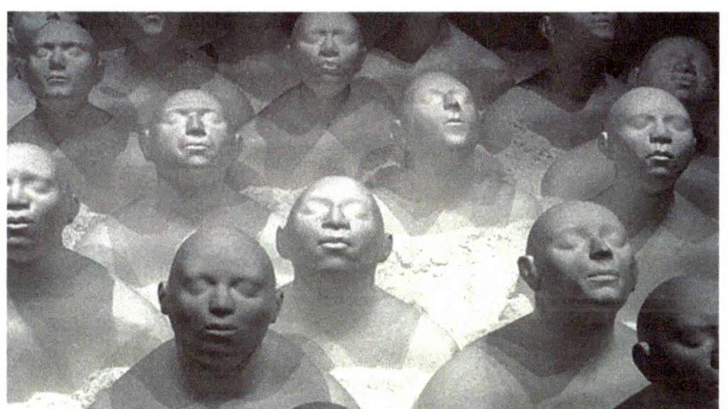

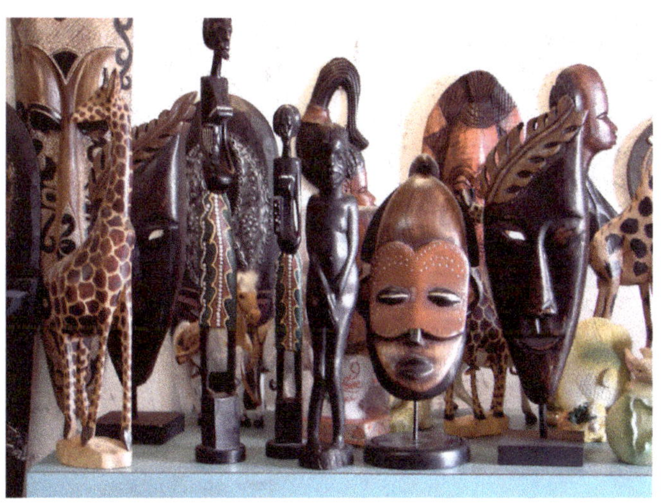

Chido Johnson grew up knowing the meaning of struggle. His Methodist missionary parents were deeply committed to the Zimbabwean independence movement, and one of his early memories is of the family being deported for his father's political cartoons. It was a climate in which education, the church, political struggle, and, to a certain extent, art, were interlinked. Temporarily relocating to neighboring Zambia, the family returned to Zimbabwe after independence, at which point Johnson attended the equivalent of high school—racially the only white boy, but

(*Top*) *Revolutionary Residue.* 2000. Cast cement fists, 18 x 10 x 10 in. each.

(*Middle*) *Square Grid Humility.* 2000. Gessoed ceramic, lime, raised-floor installation, 16 x 16 x 2 ft.

(*Bottom*) *me me me.* 2008. Carved tourist artifact, 9 x 3 x 3 in. (pictured center).

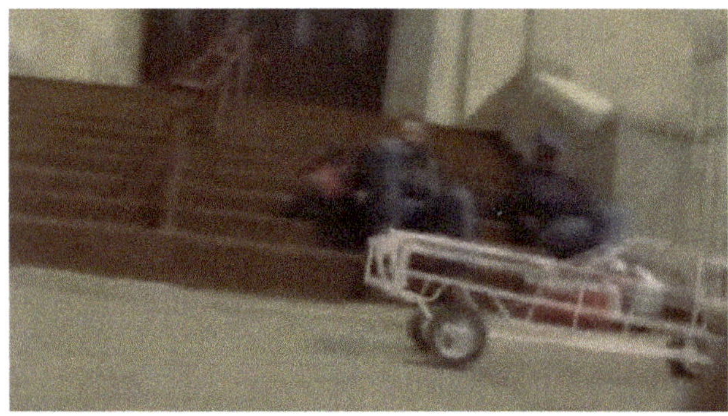
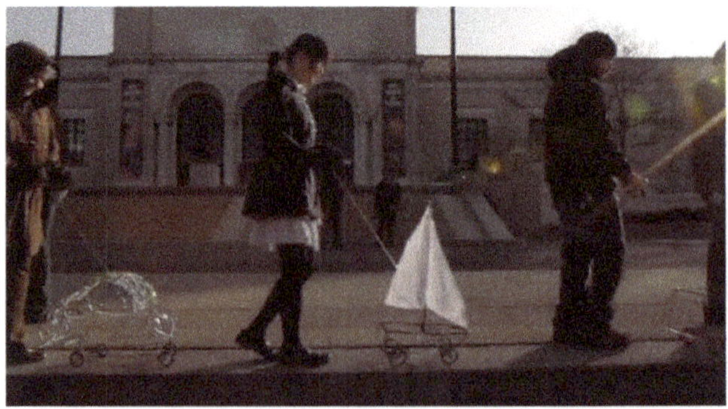
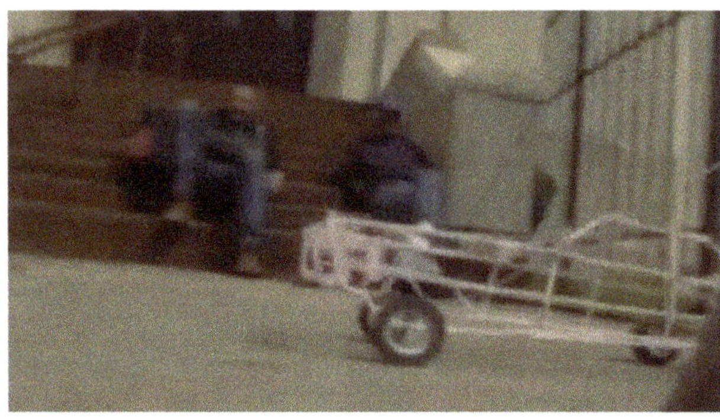
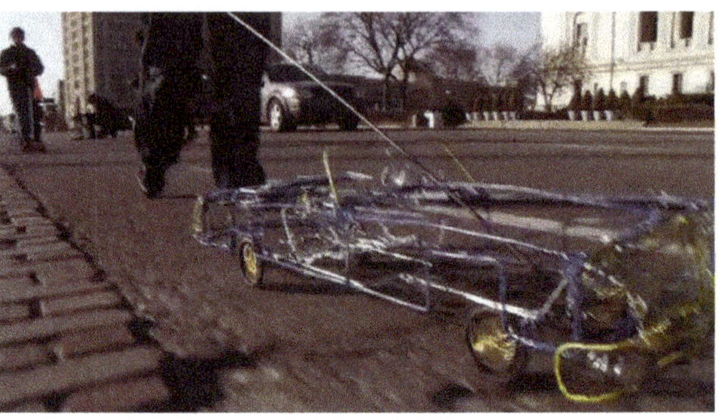

(*Left*) *my pink caddi.* 2009. Video stills from performance. (*Right*) *a dance for Diego/WAWAD.* 2011–present. Video stills from collaborative project.

totally culturally integrated into the politically charged environment of that postcolonial moment.

Relocating to the US in 1987 to continue his education, Johnson struggled with culture shock and eventually returned to Zimbabwe to apprentice with sculptor and stone carver Tapfuma Gutsa. A traditional craft, stone carving was also a major component of Zimbabwe's postindependence cultural renaissance. Gutsa was to become a key mentor, exposing Johnson to seminal anticolonial writers like Frantz Fanon and challenging him on who he was as a person and an artist. In a pivotal early lesson, Johnson presented a meticulously polished carved head, expecting to receive praise; Gutsa responded by asking him, "Who taught you to carve like *that*?"—chastising Johnson for making a work that was technically realized but which didn't have any of his heart in it. When Johnson finally started his university studies in the US, he arrived knowing that he wanted to study stone carving and firmly identifying as a postcolonialist. His studies culminated with works such as his MFA thesis piece, ***Square Grid Humility*** (2000), and the multiple clenched fists of ***Revolutionary Residue*** (2000).

Arriving in Detroit to teach sculpture at CCS, Johnson realized that this was also a city that grew up knowing struggle, but one that only indirectly corresponded to his own experiences. The encounter that typified this awareness was seeing the iconic Joe Louis clenched fist and recognizing the redundancy of exhibiting a *Revolutionary Residue*–type work here. Subsequent pieces like ***me me me*** (2008)—which shows a table-mounted African tourist figure recarved in Johnson's image, and with defensive body

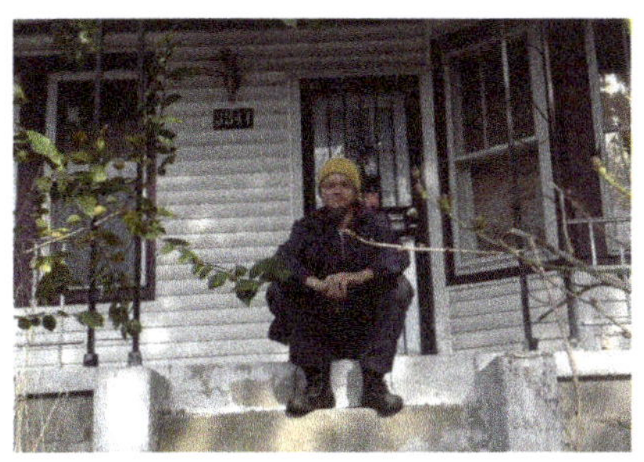

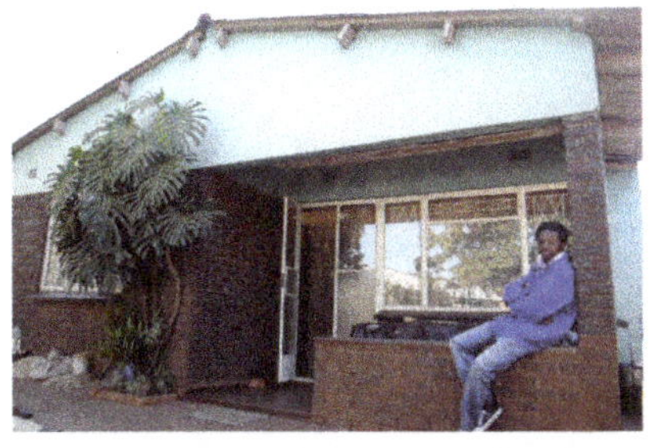

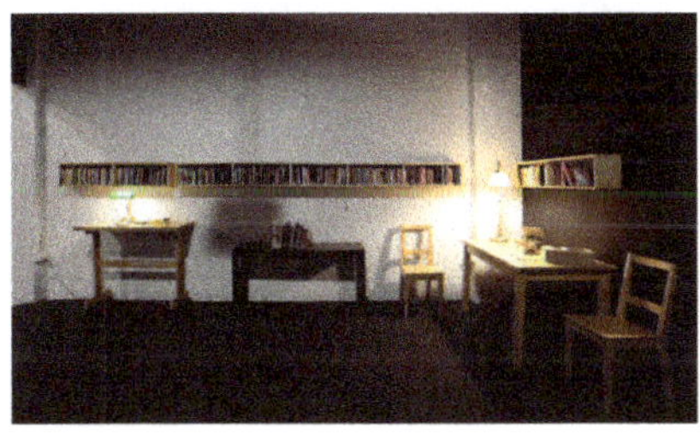

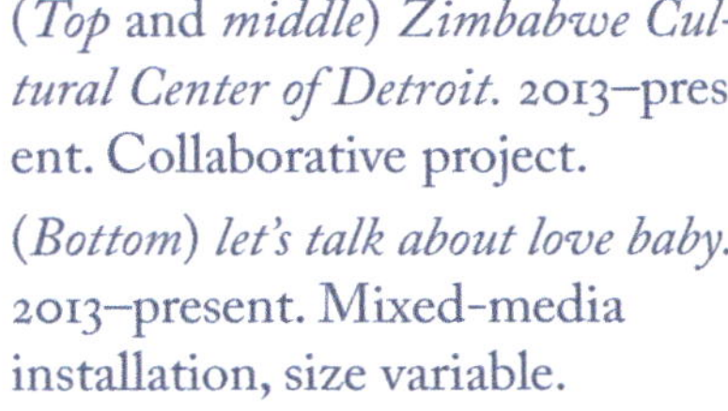

(*Top* and *middle*) *Zimbabwe Cultural Center of Detroit.* 2013–present. Collaborative project.
(*Bottom*) *let's talk about love baby.* 2013–present. Mixed-media installation, size variable.

language—point to a loss of certainty in the African post-colonial identity in which he had earlier considered himself firmly embedded. Gradually, Johnson saw himself as sitting in the "hyphenated area" between African and European American cultures, and he became increasingly comfortable positioning his work to examine this space.

In 2009, Johnson made ***my pink caddi***, a replica 1967 Cadillac fashioned in a similar manner to the wire-car toys that he knew growing up in Zambia and Zimbabwe. A low-grade ground-level video of the car being pushed along Woodward from Jefferson to Eight Mile shows the shivering skeletal car as an almost ghostly presence in the Detroit landscape—a surreal transmission between continents and across time. This project grew into ***WAWAD (Wireworker Autoworkers Association of Detroit)*** (2011–present), a socially based work in which people are invited to become part of *WAWAD* by completing a wire-car and participating in a "cruise." It is a project that works on many levels, but most of all, it is about art's capacity to propagate culture outside of fixed national and racial categories. So far *WAWAD* has several hundred members across several continents. Other projects that fit into Johnson's "hyphenated" world include the ***Zimbabwe Cultural Center of Detroit*** (2013–present), which uses physical spaces in Detroit, Mutare, and Harare to facilitate a virtual community spanning three "cities in crisis," and ***let's talk about love baby*** (2013–present), a growing library of artist-created romance novels that reference a genre of literature common in the Africa of his youth. ***Jack's Vision*** (2011) documents Johnson's climbing of a mountain above his childhood home to the abandoned site of a monument to Kingsley Fairbridge, the European "discoverer" of Mutare, and his "trusted helper" Jack. It is an emotionally and thematically complex work that weaves between Johnson's personal story and broader issues relating to the history of the area, and that, perhaps, still awaits final resolution.

Clearly, Johnson's recent projects have a pedagogic aspect, and one of the constants in his life has been the desire to teach. His achievements as an educator are remarkable, with, for example, former students like Michael E. Smith and Kevin Beasley being represented at the Whitney Biennial in 2012 and 2014 respectively. Tellingly, Johnson keeps his teaching and art practices separate for fear of becoming one of those professors who turns out copies of himself; his greatest pleasure as a teacher is to see his students find *their* identity.

STEVE PANTON, JULY 2015

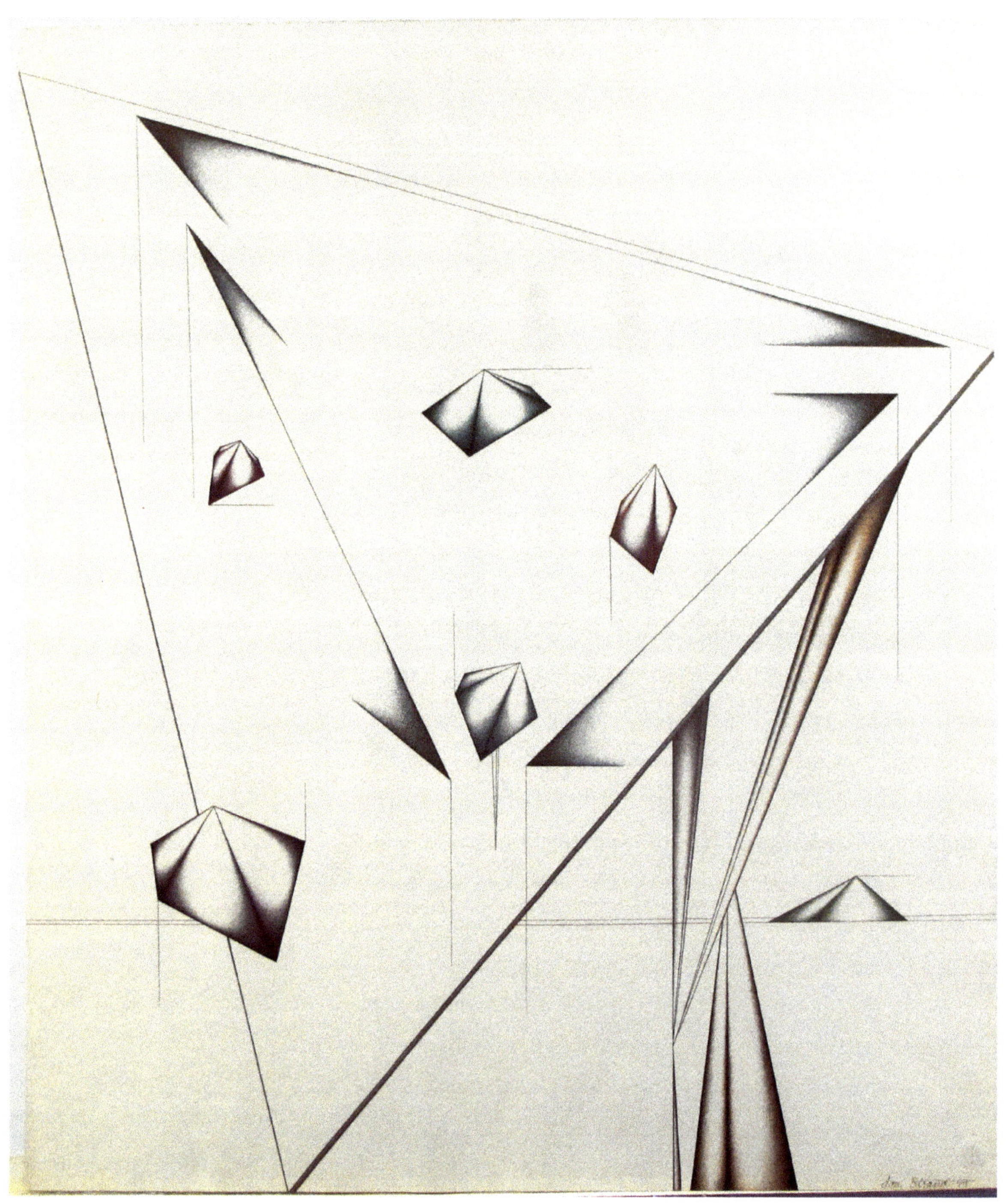

Land of Somer (Chapter Obsolescence). 1979. Ink, paper, 26 ½ x 22 in. Photography by Matthew Piper.

28 // JON STRAND

Born Detroit, 1948
BS (Education), Wayne State University
Lives in Detroit

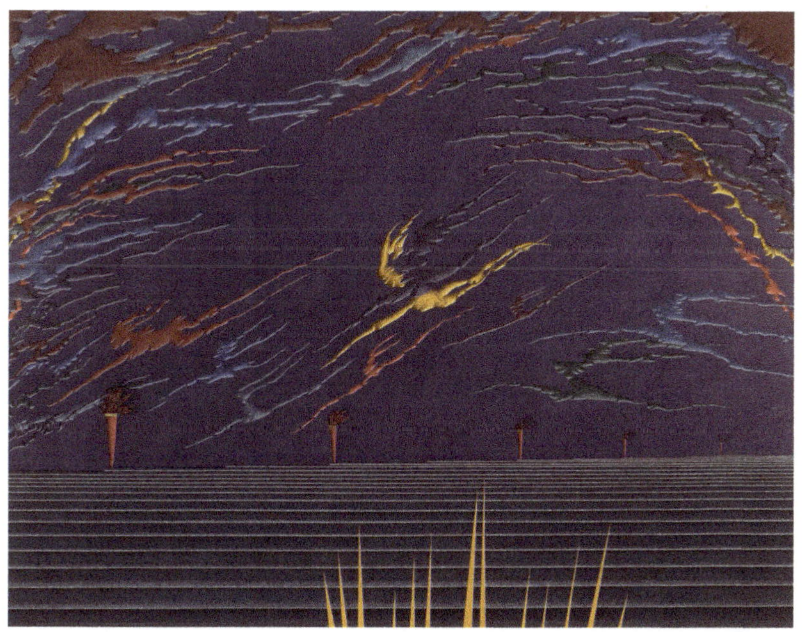

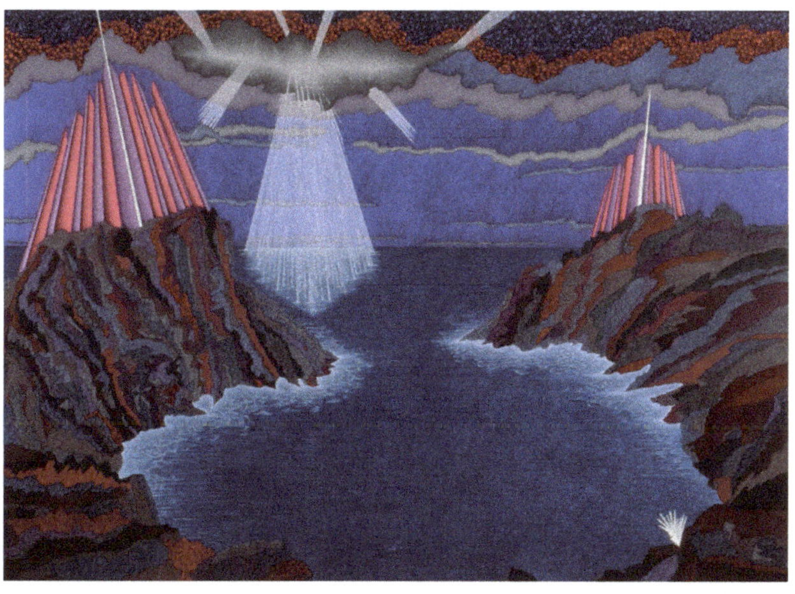

For Jon Strand, making art is a long-distance sport. He is a twenty-first-century pointillist, manifesting his elaborate visions by applying layer after layer of tiny dots to paper with the use of a rapidograph (a technical pen of German manufacture). When he discusses his "ink paintings," Strand provides an offhand but remarkably precise account of how long each takes to create: 1,874 hours for this one, 717 for that. This tendency toward quantification originated in the formative advice of a curator friend: that an artist should effectively communicate the extent of his labor in order to be taken seriously enough to earn a living wage. But an appreciation of Strand's work must go beyond its curious and

(*Top*) *As Above, So Below.* 1990–91. Ink, paper, 42 x 54 in.
(*Bottom*) *Are You Apollo?* 1997–98. Ink, paper, 42 x 56 in.

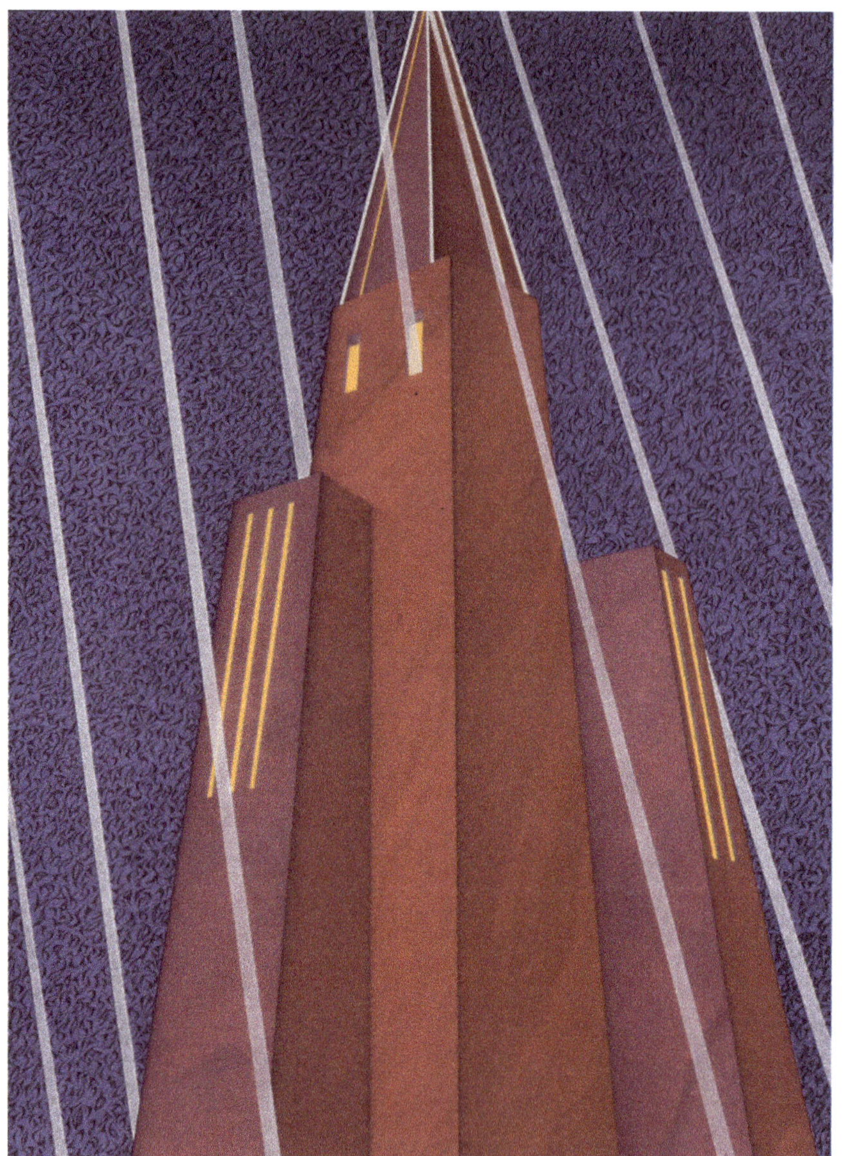

Relying Purely on Courage. 2000–1. Ink, paper, 41 ½ x 21 ½ in.

compelling means of execution, because his art, like other long-distance endeavors, is about much more than endurance and technical accomplishment; it is about transcendence.

In 1984, Strand, a decade and a half into his pointillist practice, inhabited the thirty-third floor of the mostly vacant David Broderick Tower. His home and studio were in a onetime office suite with three sets of French doors and three balconies, from which he overlooked the struggling downtown. A friend's comment about a New York penthouse for sale ("You'd have to have the money of the gods to afford it") got him thinking from his deserted, lofty perch about both ancient mythology and the bald inequities of the day. Thus was born Strand's "alter ego," Jonny Strange, and the body of work that occupied him for twenty-two years. The Jonny Strange series, comprising 106 ink paintings and one animated short film, tells the story of the titular character's journey from our troubled world to Neo-Helicon, home of the nine muses and the god Apollo. Strand describes Jonny's epic quest to find the gods of old as a response to the horrors of the world that they'd abandoned and an appeal to the eternal virtues they represent. The architectural forms that came to dominate the series' striking visual language—pyramids, obelisks, temples, and towers—were inspired by the ancient world, as well as the Art Deco skyscrapers Strand saw every day, but they also grew out of his earlier, abstract work, like ***Land of Somer (Chapter Obsolescence)*** (1979). In his contemporary reimagining of classical myth, the muses appear as billowing, colored clouds (see ***As Above, So Below***, 1990–91), and Apollo takes the form of light, as in ***Relying Purely on Courage*** (2000–1). Jonny, meanwhile, illustrates Strand's puckish delight in mixing the high with the low, appearing in the sublime, saturated landscapes as either a

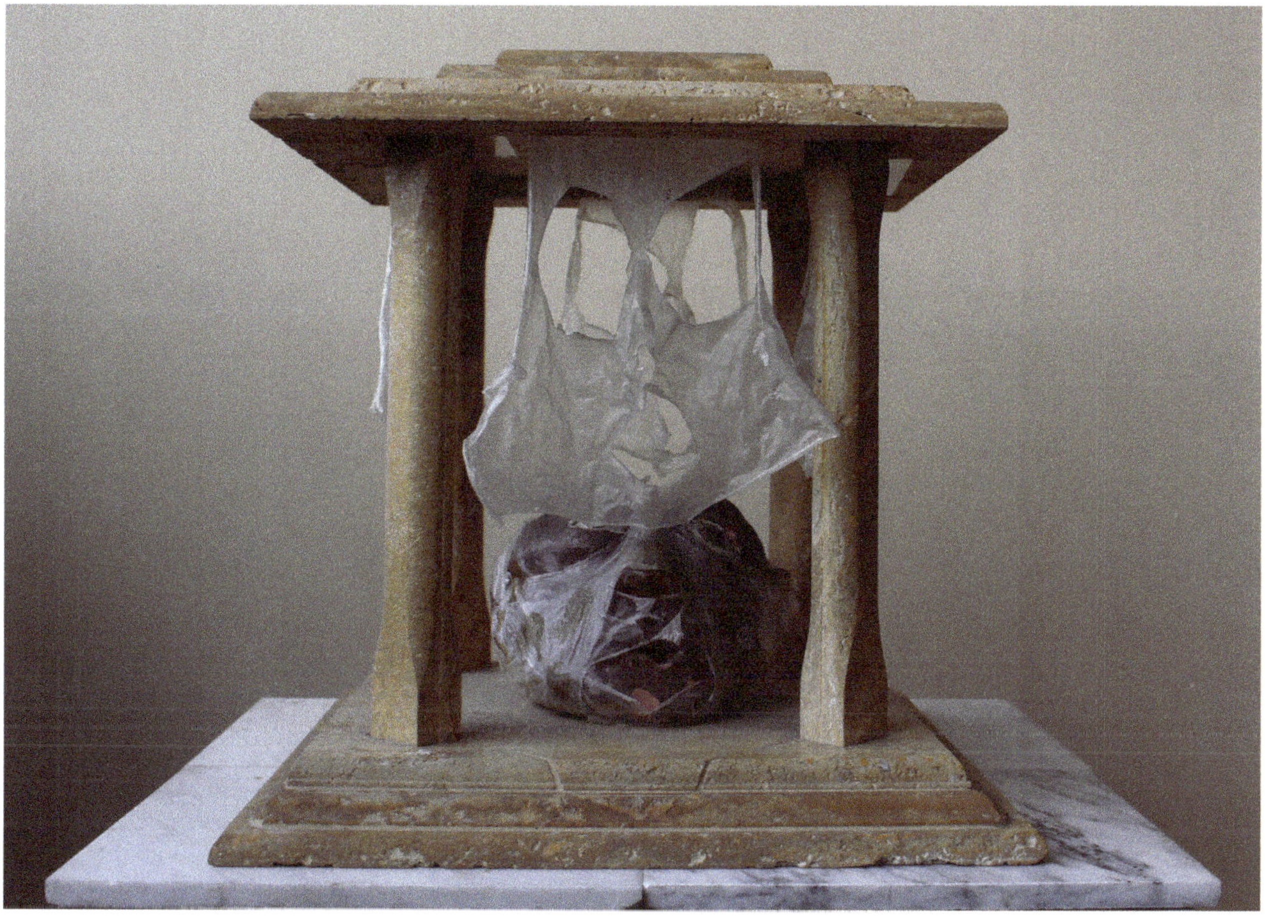

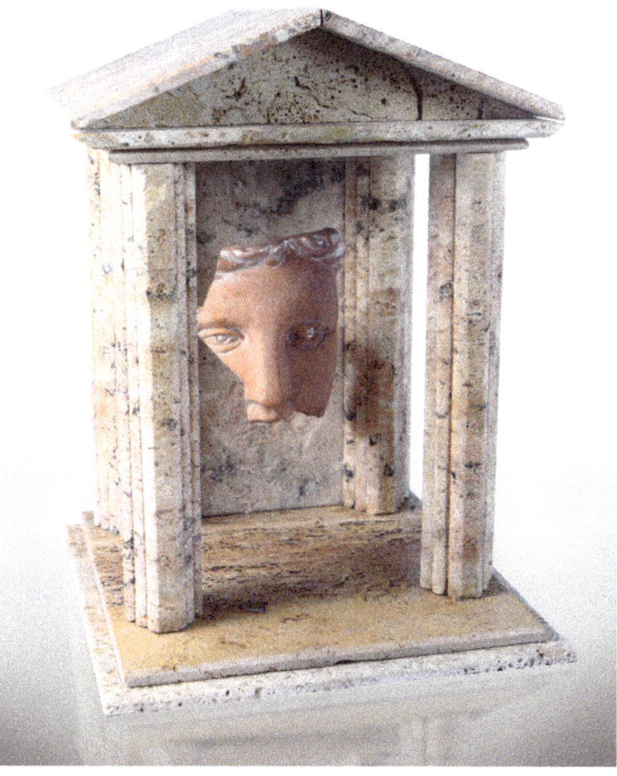

(*Top*) *The Oracle of the Golden Temple.* 2008. Marble, clay, peel-off facial, 15 x 15 x 15 in. Photography by Matthew Piper.

(*Bottom*) *The Oracle of Mysteries.* 2011. Marble, terra-cotta, 16 x 12 x 12 in.

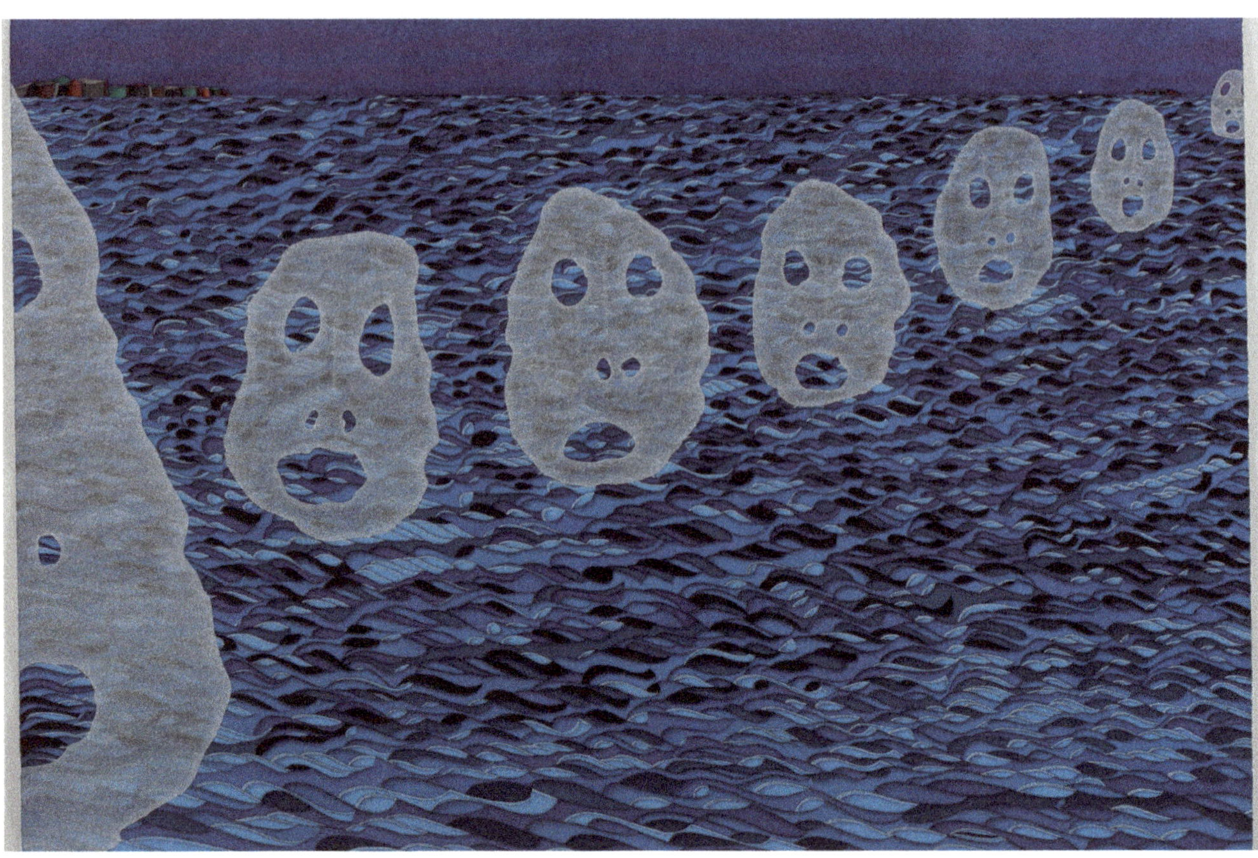

A Chorus of Oracles. 2011–12. Ink, paper, 42 x 58 in.

tiny, spiky-haired cartoon head (as in ***Are You Apollo?***, 1997–98) or else glimpsed in extreme close-up as a fan of radiating blond peaks.

Strand's practice took a notable turn in 1993, when, in response to a friend's death from AIDS, he created an installation of preserved and subtly embellished facial peels (otherwise-ephemeral by-products of his daily skin-care ritual). In 2008, he incorporated several of these haunting, mask-like objects into ***The Oracle of the Golden Temple***, a sculpture that brought into three dimensions his reinvigoration of the ancient world's architectural forms. This piece, which also included a contractor friend's leftover gold marble and a found sculpture of a human head, started out as a kind of joke (an exercise in making art out of "dubious materials") but ended up heralding a new and ongoing body of related sculptural work—see, for example, ***The Oracle of Mysteries*** (2011).

Strand's ink paintings, meanwhile, persist. Representations of his facial peels hover over a teeming sea in 2011–12's ***A Chorus of Oracles***, forming a bridge between his sculptures and his most recent series, ***An Epic of Distance and Time***. In nearly sixty pieces and counting, Strand has filled his paper to its edges with luminous seas populated by robust, undulating waves that appear so tangible, so corporeal, they look as though they've been carved. Neo-Oceanus, perhaps? There's no sign of Jonny Strange or anyone else in this vast, drowned world, where the waves alone remain.

MATTHEW PIPER, AUGUST 2015

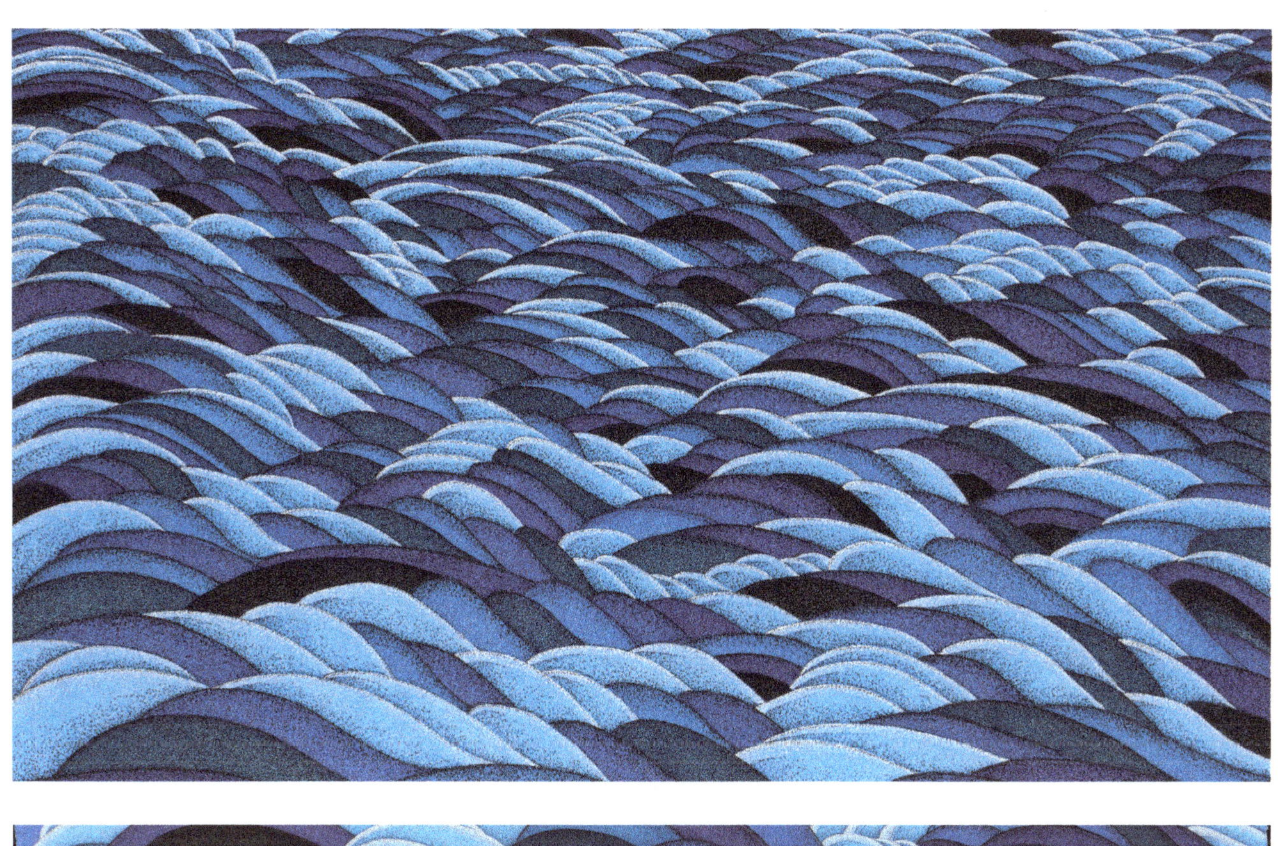

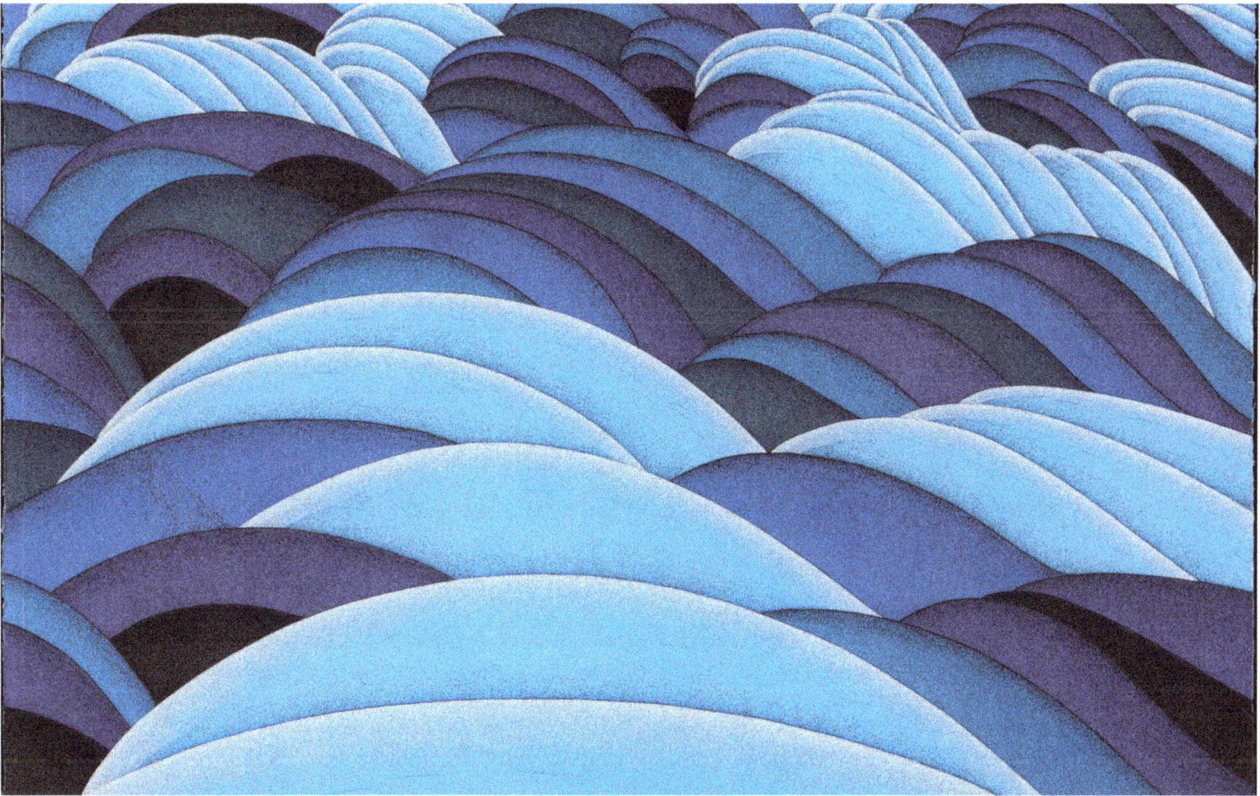

(*Top*) *An Epic of Distance and Time, Part XIII.* 2012. Ink, paper, 15 x 22 in. (*Bottom*) *An Epic of Distance and Time, Part XVIII.* 2013. Ink, paper, 29 ½ x 41 ½ in.

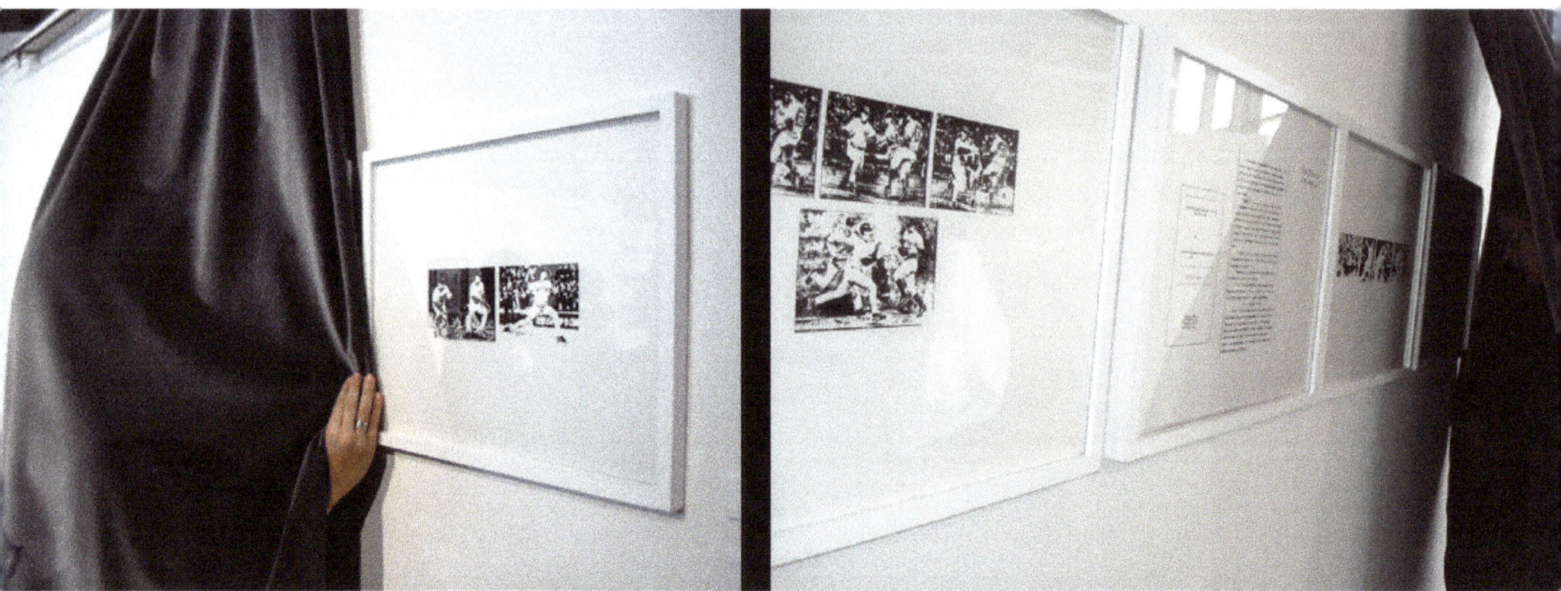

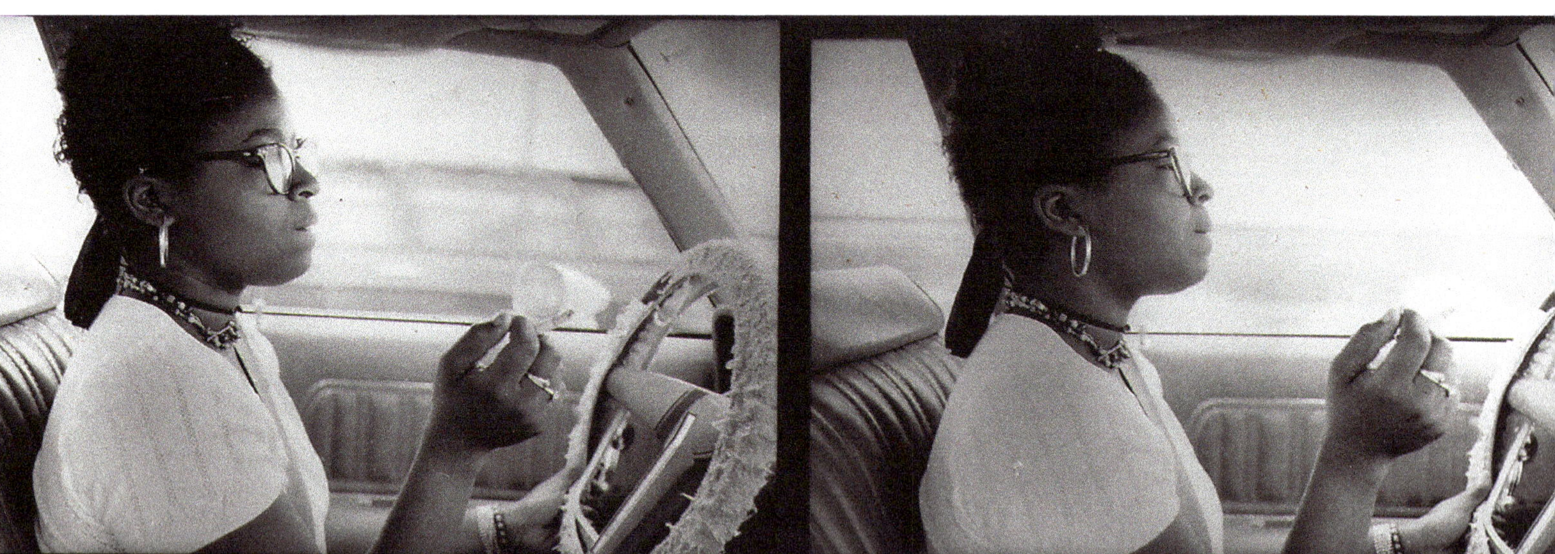

(*Top*) *The Curse of the Bambino.* 2006. Eight glow-in-the-dark screen prints and curtain installation, 15 x 22 in.

(*Bottom*) *Documents of Elapsed Time.* c. 1996–2001. Gelatin silver prints and C-prints, various sizes.

29 // TOBY MILLMAN

Born Chicago, Illinois, 1975
BA, Hampshire College
MFA, University of Michigan
Lives in Hamtramck, Michigan

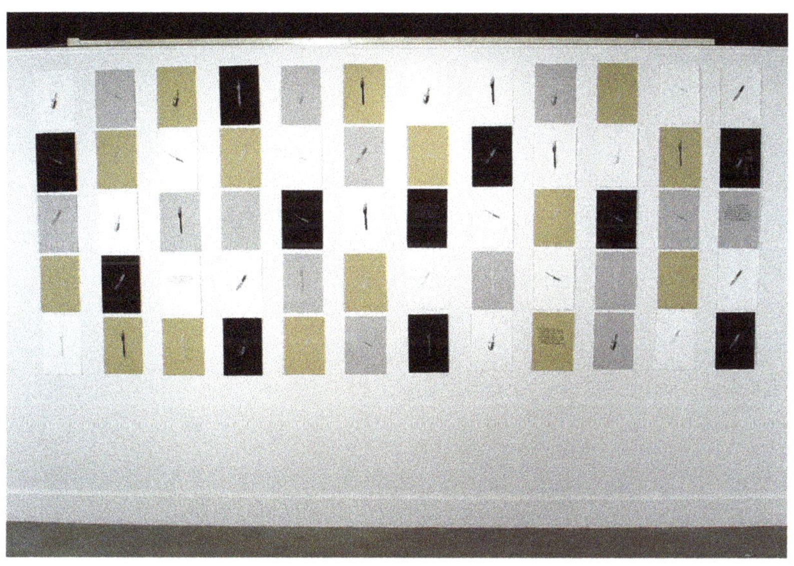

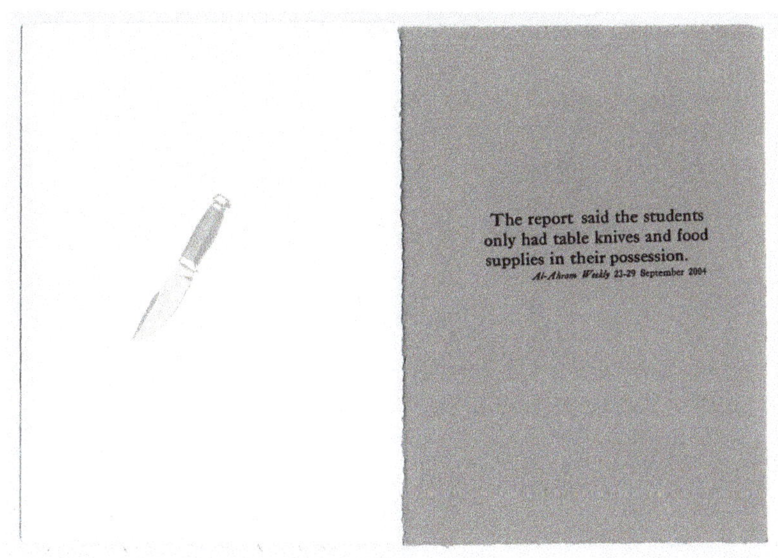

Printmaker Toby Millman is not one to talk unless you are listening. Her presence, like her work, is often quite understated, indicating not a lack of depth but confidence in what you will find when you take the time to notice. One thing you will find is a body of work that interjects quiet reflection into scenes of active conflict—the calm at the eye of the storm—and focuses on populations who experience struggle and social division, both in Michigan and as far afield as Palestine, the central locations for a large cross section of Millman's oeuvre.

The inherent tension in a Jewish artist creating a body of Palestine-based work is not lost on Millman. She has categorically eschewed any obvious

1001 Arabian Knives or The Strange Case of the Six Students (excerpts). 2004. Fifty-six lithographs and four letterpress prints, 11 x 7 ½ in. each.

identification with Israel, despite having Israeli roots and making regular childhood visits to family in Tel Aviv. In work that explores a budding awareness of Israeli/Palestinian relations, Millman began with a neutral perspective, producing ***The Curse of the Bambino*** (2006), which juxtaposes historic documentation of the Israeli/Palestinian conflict (rendered in glow-in-the-dark screen prints visible beneath shrouds at the opening) with those addressing the long-standing rivalry between the Boston Red Sox and the New York Yankees. ***1001 Arabian Knives*** (2004) is a series of lithographs and letterpress prints that assemble and illustrate documentation from a 2004 incident implicating six Egyptian students in an array of intended acts of terror. However, the combined effect of two residencies in East Jerusalem and Ramallah affected the tenor of her work dramatically, and future explorations are increasingly reflective of and sympathetic to a Palestinian perspective. ***Access & Closure: Stories from in and out of an Occupied Palestine*** (2008) is a sixty-four-page letterpress book that collects fragments and significant moments from two lengthy visits to Palestine, paired

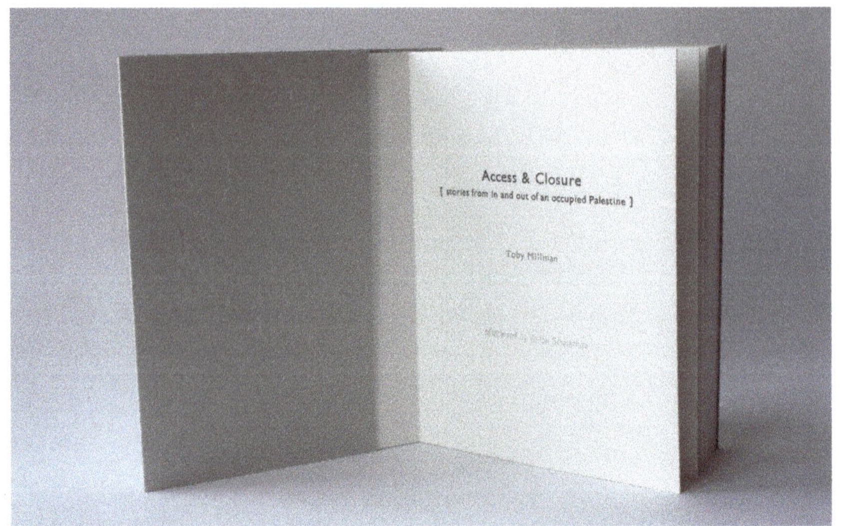

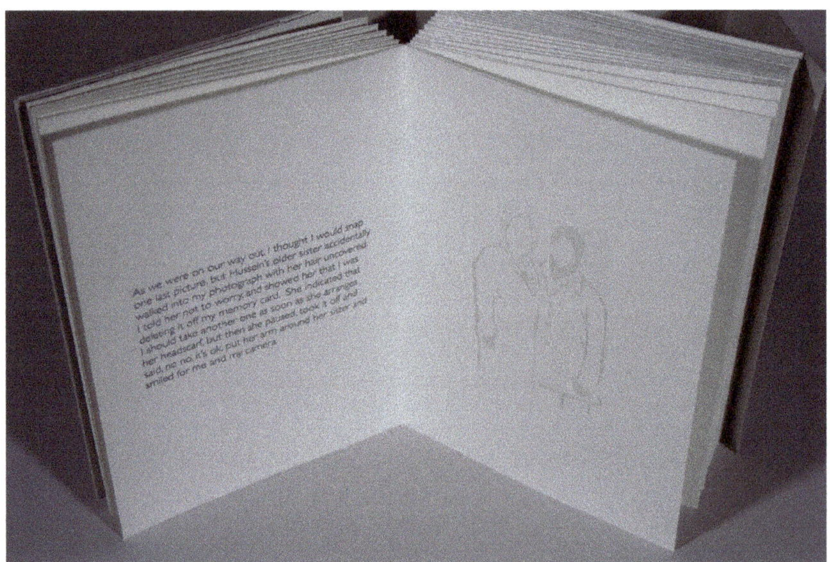

Access & Closure: Stories from in and out of an Occupied Palestine. 2008. Letterpress book, sixty-four pages (edition of fifty).

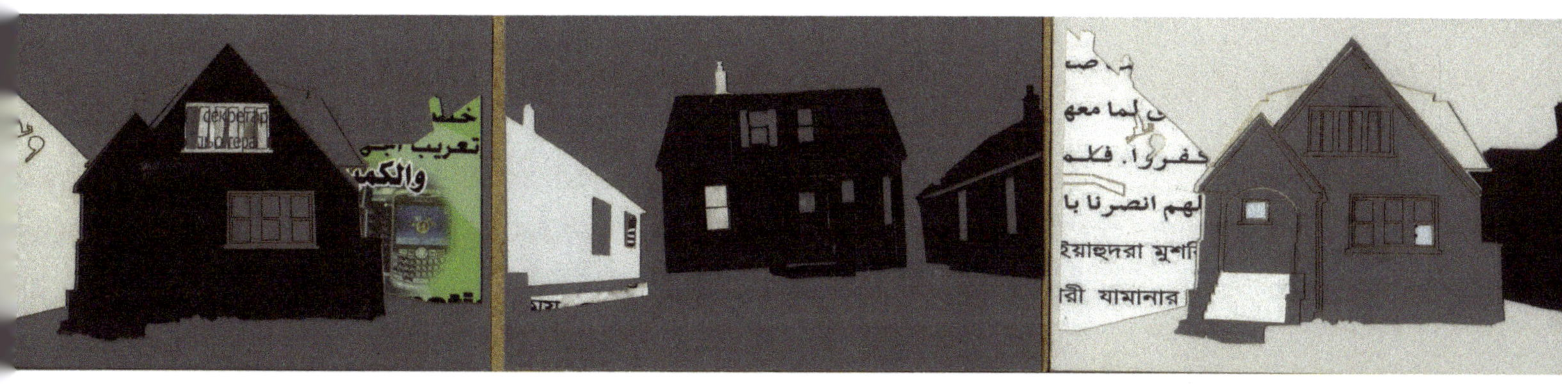

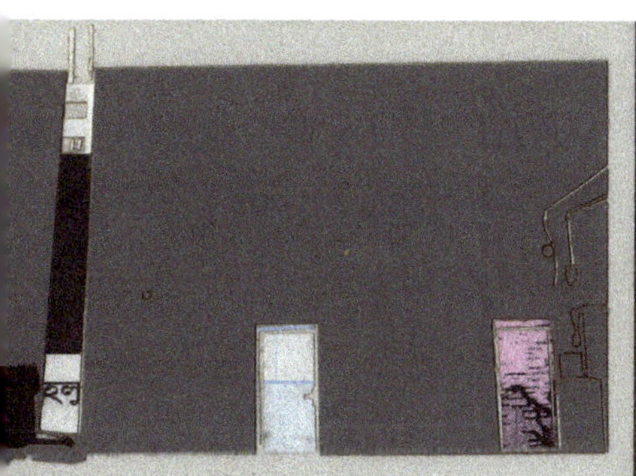

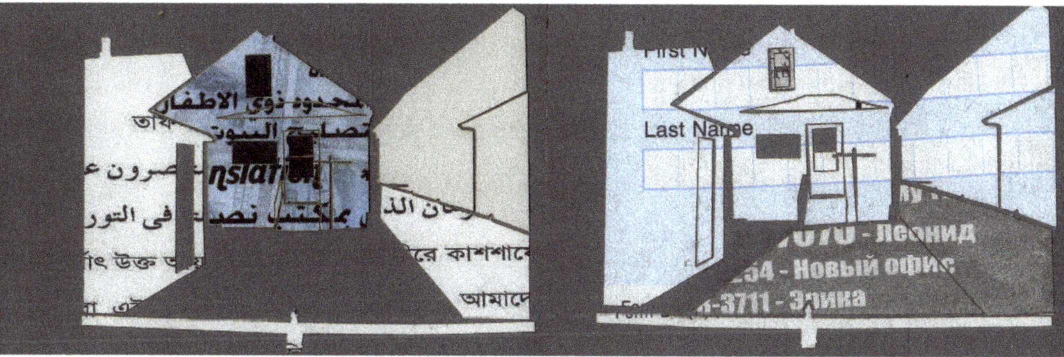

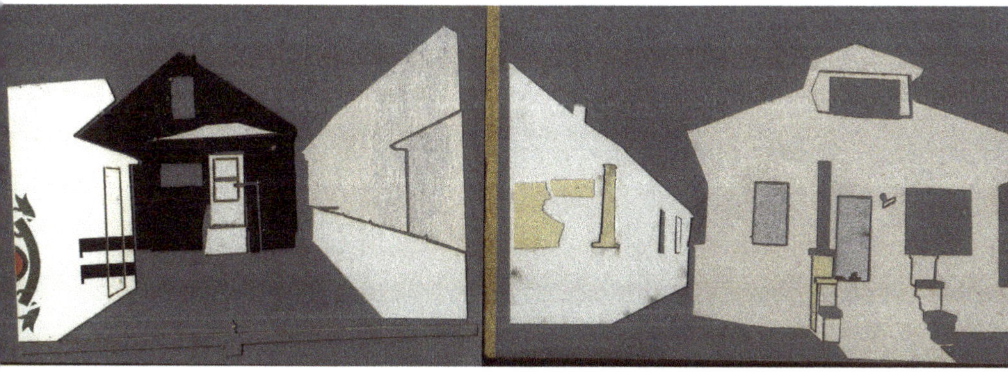

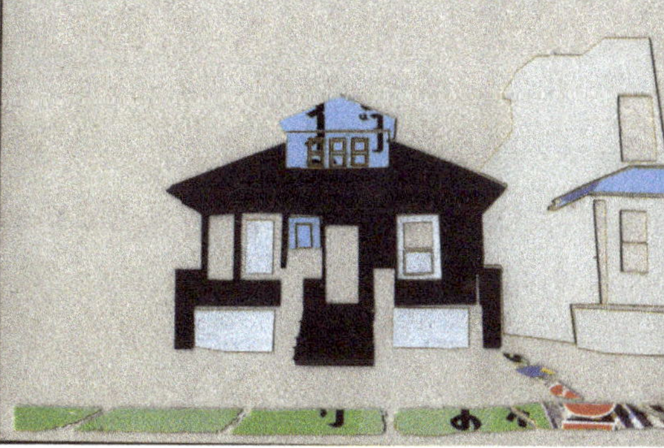

Census 2010: 48212. 2011–13. Wood, laser-cut found paper, 2 ½ x 3 in. each.

with astonishing paper-cut images traced from photographs and maps. The indentation these leave on the page seem to physicalize the deep impression left by these visits, and the text elements accompanying the images take on first-person narration, even in the retelling of the stories of others—Millman has made herself part of the picture.

Maps crop up frequently as a motif in Millman's work and are a convenient form of visual shorthand for her habit of exploring divisions—even those as localized as the border between Detroit and Hamtramck, as with her collage series, ***Census 2010: 48212*** (2011–13), which uses found paper from Hamtramck, laser-cut to form houses. Even in her work ***From Here on Out*** (2012), which ostensibly examines life in Hamtramck, there is an eastward-looking quality, an irresistible draw to tie the current population of Hamtramck back to its largely Yemeni roots. Dealing directly with maps is ***Facts on the Ground*** (2011), which was inspired by a commercially

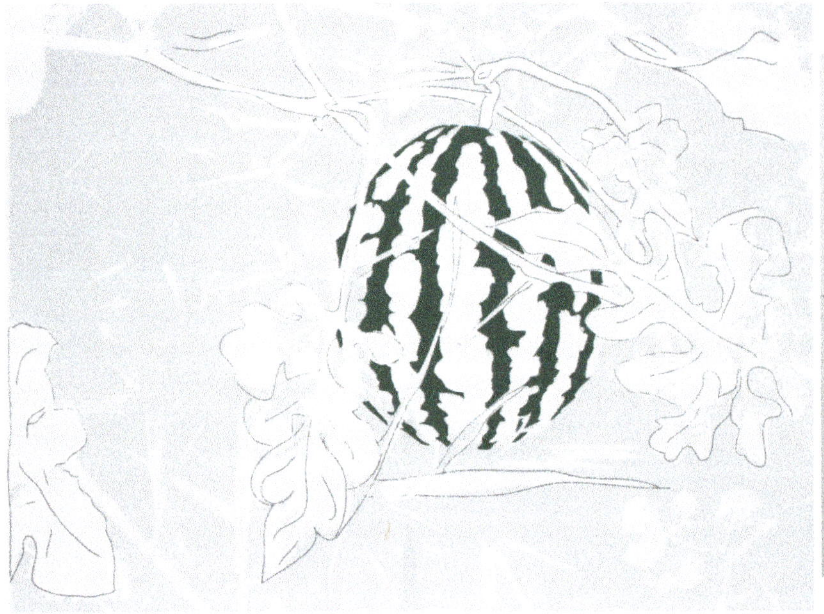

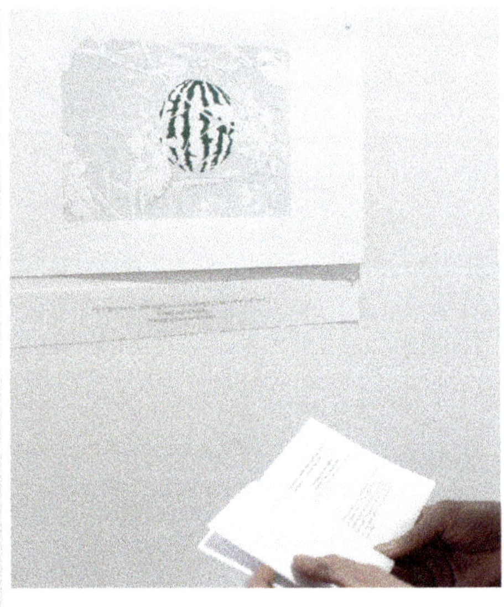

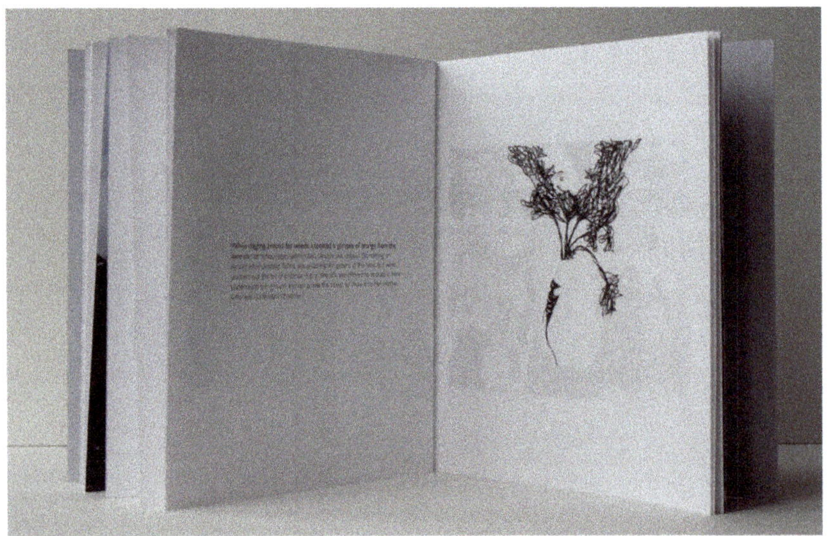

From Here on Out. 2012/2014. Archival inkjet prints, screen prints, photocopied zine; various sizes (2012); digitally printed book, thirty-two pages (edition of fifty, 2014).

available map of Jerusalem that, as Millman discovered, did not acknowledge the Arabic names for streets, even in neighborhoods where the population is predominately Arabic-speaking. The fifty-two-page hardbound book is punctuated by cutout maps; again, the physical implementation of Millman's printmaking speaks to a psychic reality, in this case omission or nullification of a people's signifiers of place.

While Millman's finished pieces are typically prints or collages, photography plays a crucial foundational role in her process; much of her print imagery is traced or otherwise lifted from her own reference photos. Earlier bodies of photographic work indicate this form of image-making was once an end point, but it is now relegated to a primary process. Still, selections from ***Documents of Elapsed Time*** (1996–2001) reveal Millman's consistent interest in the progression of events—and art acts as a mechanism for dealing positively with her own resistance

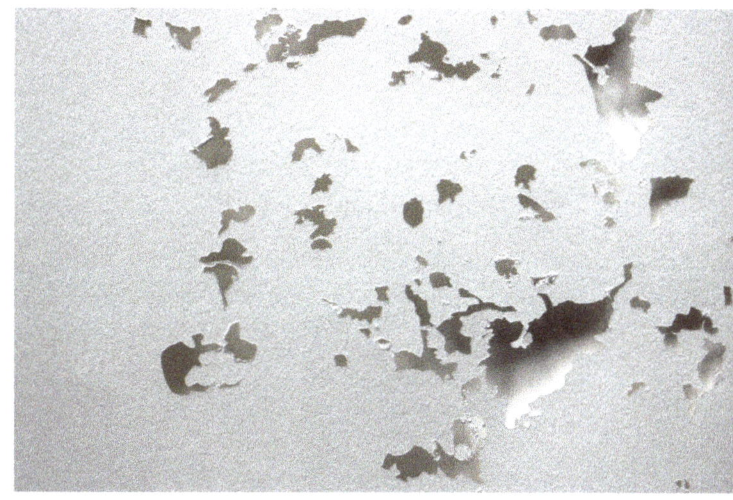

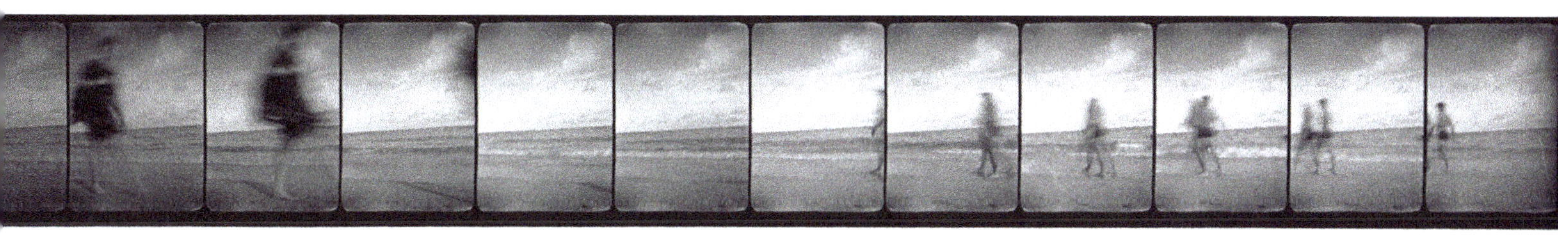

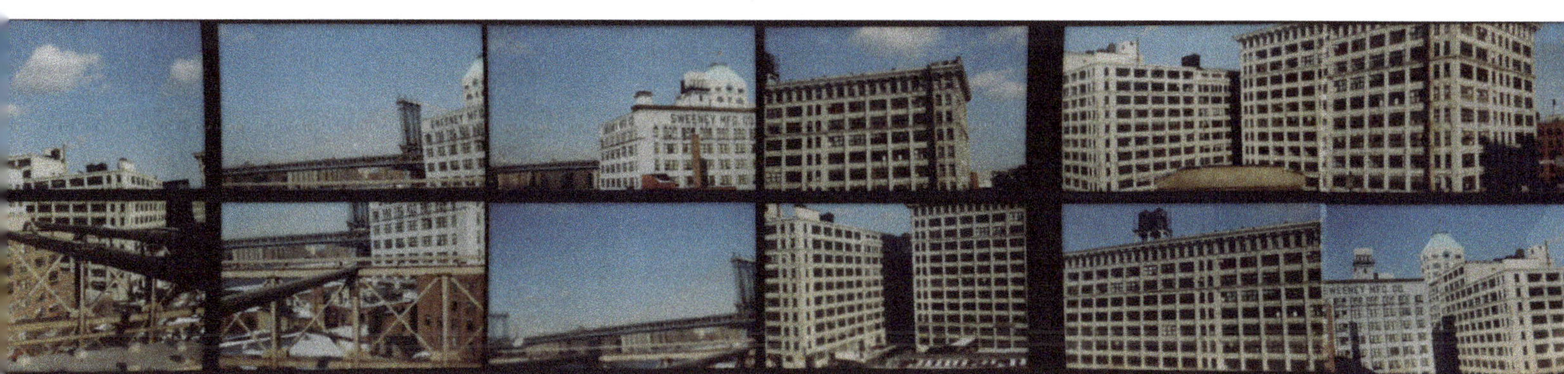

(*Top*) *Facts on the Ground.* 2011. Hardbound book with silkscreen, letterpress, digital cutouts, and inkjet printing, fifty-two pages (edition of fifty). (*Middle and Bottom*) *Documents of Elapsed Time.* c. 1996–2001. Gelatin silver prints and C-prints, various sizes.

to change or the inevitable march of time. Perhaps it is this instinct that draws Millman to focus on blank spaces and interstitial moments—her latest body of work is comprised of minimalist cityscapes, taken out of time and rendered in washes of ink that nearly fade from the page. Much like the abandoned storefronts and empty marquee signs that populate Millman's newest work, she is advertising nothing; her messages, and indeed the images themselves, are only detectable through dedicated and careful consideration. Toby Millman is not going to shout at you, and she doesn't need to; the power of her work is enough to make you lean in, even when she lowers her voice.

SARAH ROSE SHARP,
AUGUST 2015

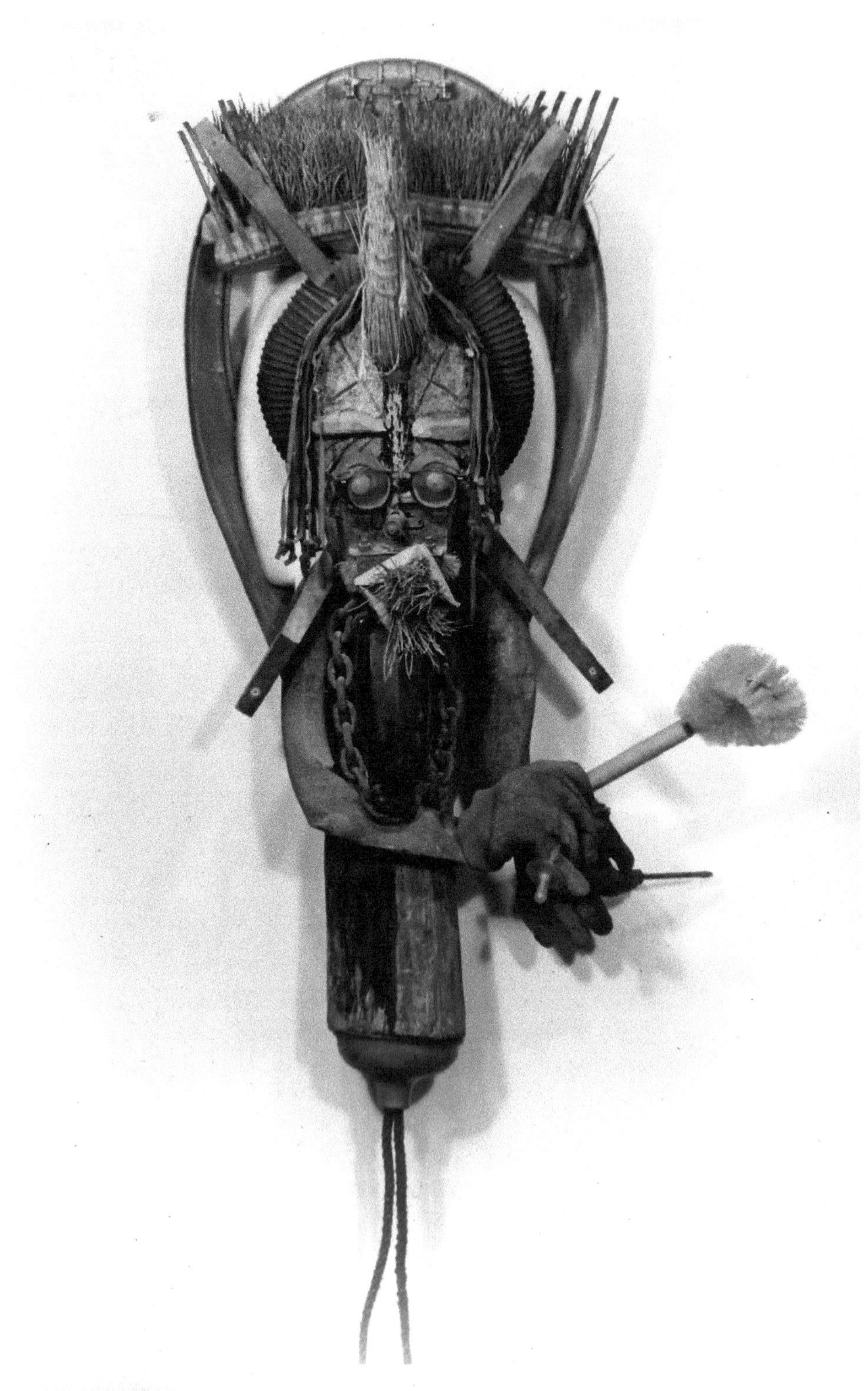

The Taskmaster. 1980. Mixed-media assemblage, 45 x 30 x 18 in.

30 // MATT CORBIN

Born Pittsburgh, Pennsylvania, 1945
Studies in Industrial Design,
College for Creative Studies
Lives in Detroit

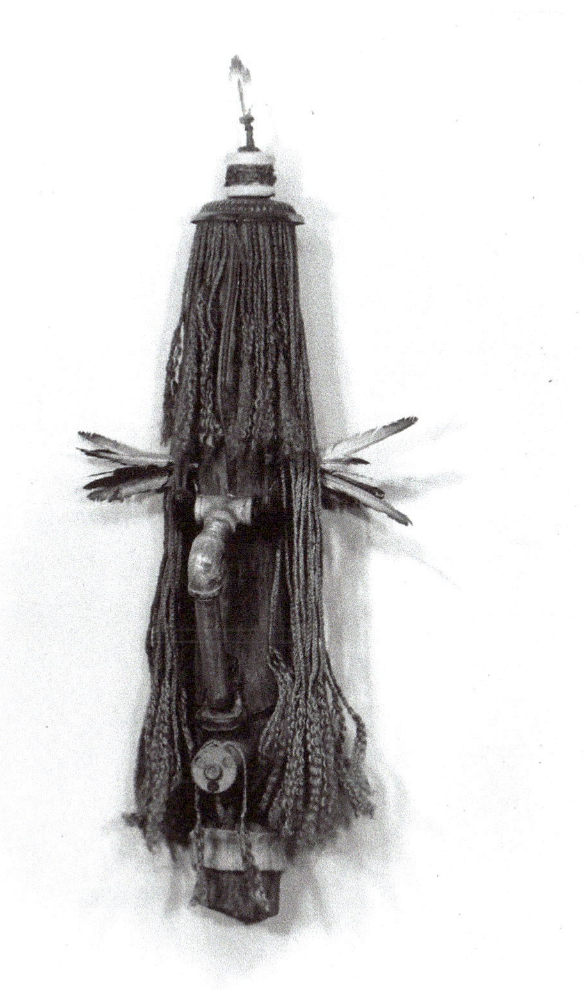

Bird Brain. 1979. Mixed-media assemblage, 32 x 12 x 10 in.

What does Matt Corbin's performance piece ***GYMSHOELIFE-STYLE*** (2001–8), in which he periodically wore size-twenty-two gym shoes to the high-school class he taught, have in common with the found-object assemblages he has been making for nearly four decades? Actually more than you might think. For a start, they both emerge from a philosophy of first understanding, and then working with, what's already there. In the case of the performance piece, Corbin builds from the footwear fixation of his students to make a gently humorous point about the absurdity of consumer society and how to subvert this to carry your own message. With his found-object sculptures he examines, then recycles, the detritus of a disposable culture to construct works that he hopes may outlive all of us. With Corbin, clearly it is pointless

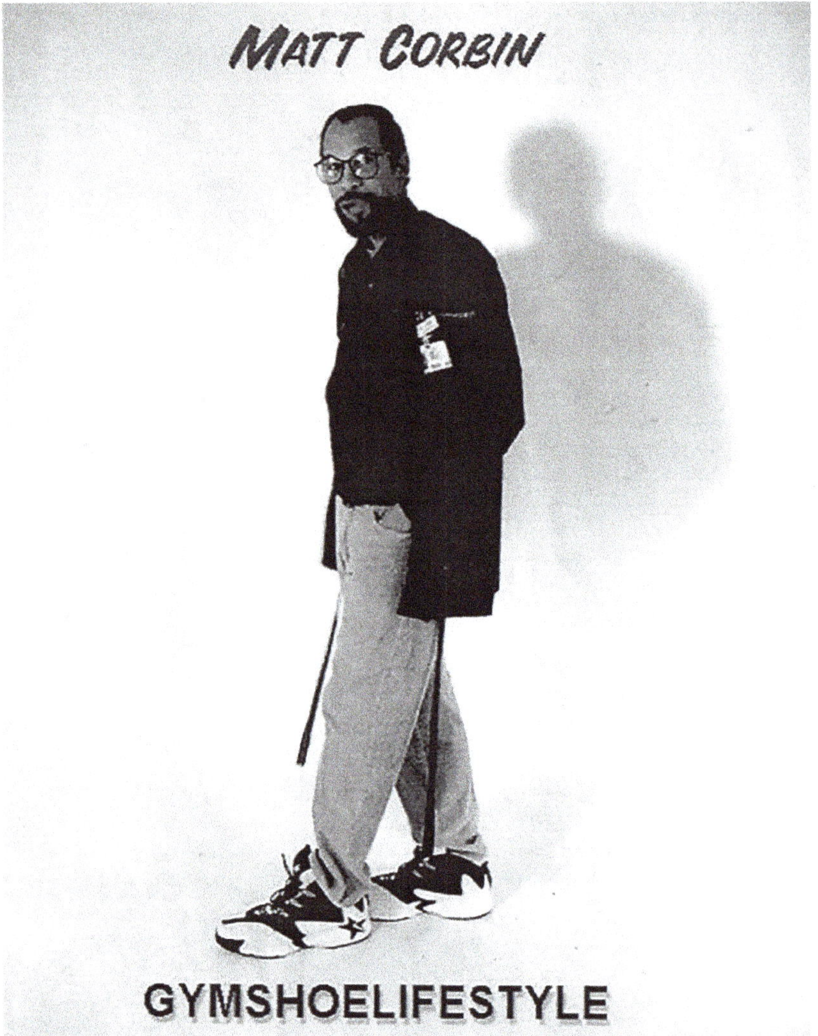

GYMSHOELIFESTYLE. 2001–8. Performance documentation.

to try to separate his life, his educational mission, and his art.

Corbin's trajectory into art education was circuitous. His father, a Tuskegee Airman, instilled a lifelong interest in drawing, transportation, and exploiting the learning potential of every situation. After graduating from Cass Tech, Corbin studied industrial design at CCS, but he sensed that the racial climate of the late 1960s, and his disdain for convention, would make the car industry a difficult work environment. Instead he took a job creating window displays for Hudson's department store, a position that provided him with freedom, resources, and the endless new challenges he desired. Later he worked at the Children's Museum, creating exhibits, displays, and lesson plans. This led to an offer to teach art in Detroit Public Schools and eventually the dream job of teaching twice-daily open-ended studio classes in commercial art to creatively gifted kids from throughout the city.

While studying design at CCS, Corbin was also paying close attention to the contemporary artists in the DIA's collection. Louise Nevelson's large monochrome sculptural wall piece *Homage to the World*, with its use of everyday found objects within a consciously designed modular structure, was particularly influential. In the 1970s Corbin started work on his own series of found-object assemblages. This led to the solo show *Afro-Urban Fetishes* at Detroit's Museum of African American History in 1979, in which Corbin convinced the museum director to cover the gallery floor with sand, and subsequent shows at George N'Namdi's early gallery space in Detroit's Whitney Building. Representative pieces from this era, such as ***The Taskmaster*** (1980) and ***Bird Brain*** (1979), show wall-mounted sculptures that reference African masks, popular culture, and autobiographical elements. *The Taskmaster* is based on Corbin's steelworker grandfather, but the eponymous figure's aura of formidable creative energy and

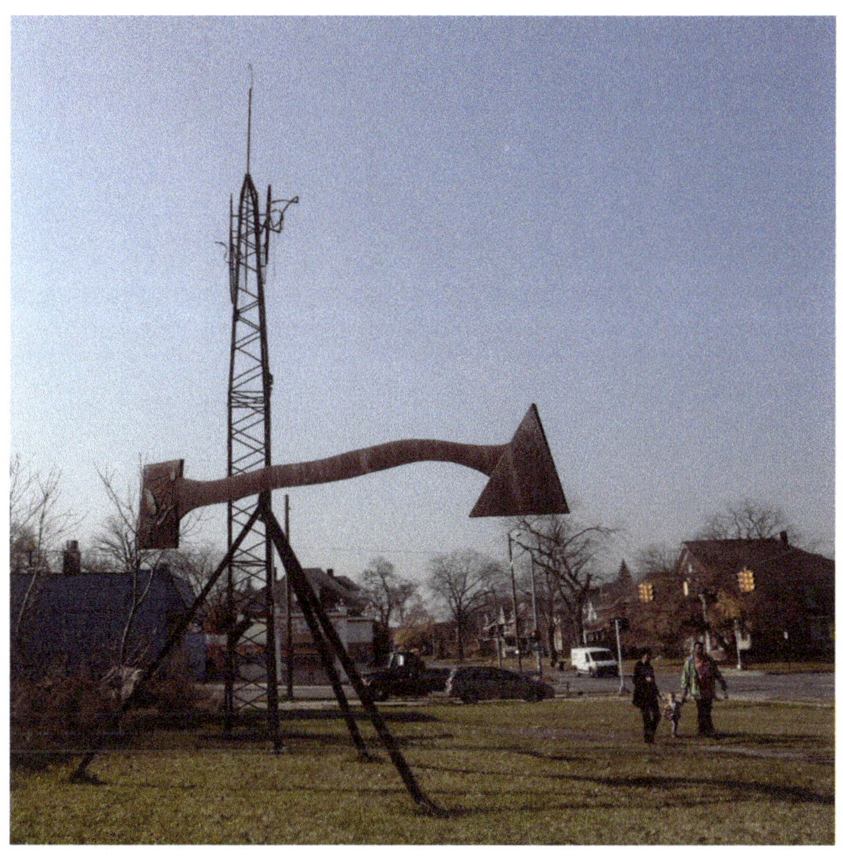

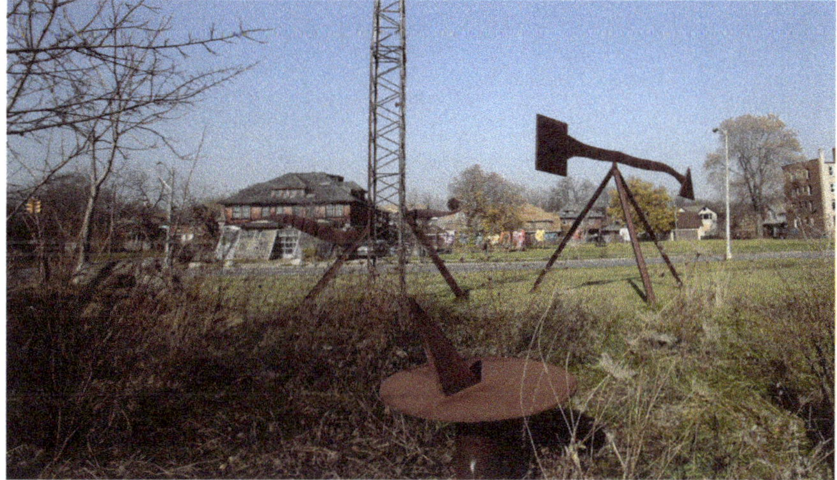

Geome Tree (created in collaboration with Richard Bennett). 1987. Metal sculpture, 30 ft. high (approx.) at largest point. In lower image note (i) the sundial, visible front center, (ii) *Mir* and *Spectra-Gate* across street. Photography by Rebecca Cook.

thoughtful attention to matters at hand might just as well refer to the artist himself. *David's Rising*, from 1988, is a large work that was constructed as a meditation on mortality and a tribute to Corbin's brother-in-law. It is a transitional piece in which Corbin started to investigate the greater flexibility of displaying his work on floor-mounted frames.

Corbin's magnum opus is the collection of large-scale art projects he has been building around his home at Clairmount and Woodward. On the south side of Clairmount stand the imposing obelisk-, pyramid-, and sundial-inspired forms of the thirty-foot-tall metal sculpture ***Geome Tree***. The 1987 work was a collaboration with fellow artist Richard Bennett, whose earlier visit to Egypt provided the inspiration for much of the piece's content. It was commissioned under the remarkable condition that it had to be finished within two weeks. Across the street is ***Spectra-Gate*** (2012–present), a growing collection of floor-mounted monochrome sculptural reliefs. The "Gate" in the title is a nod to Christo and Jeanne-Claude's expansive site-specific work in New York City's Central Park, but Corbin's work situates it firmly in a Detroit ethos of design, manufacturing, and the use of material at hand.

If *Geome Tree* and *Spectra-Gate* are the public part of Corbin's project, its hidden beating heart is *Mir*, the house/artwork he has been modifying since the late 1960s. The name refers to the former Russian space station, which famously survived, and continued to evolve, despite the cataclysmic breakup of the Soviet Union. In Corbin's usage it implies a psychological and physical environment that's connected to the world but equally out there in orbit—a space where anything is possible, but only with the resources that come from within.

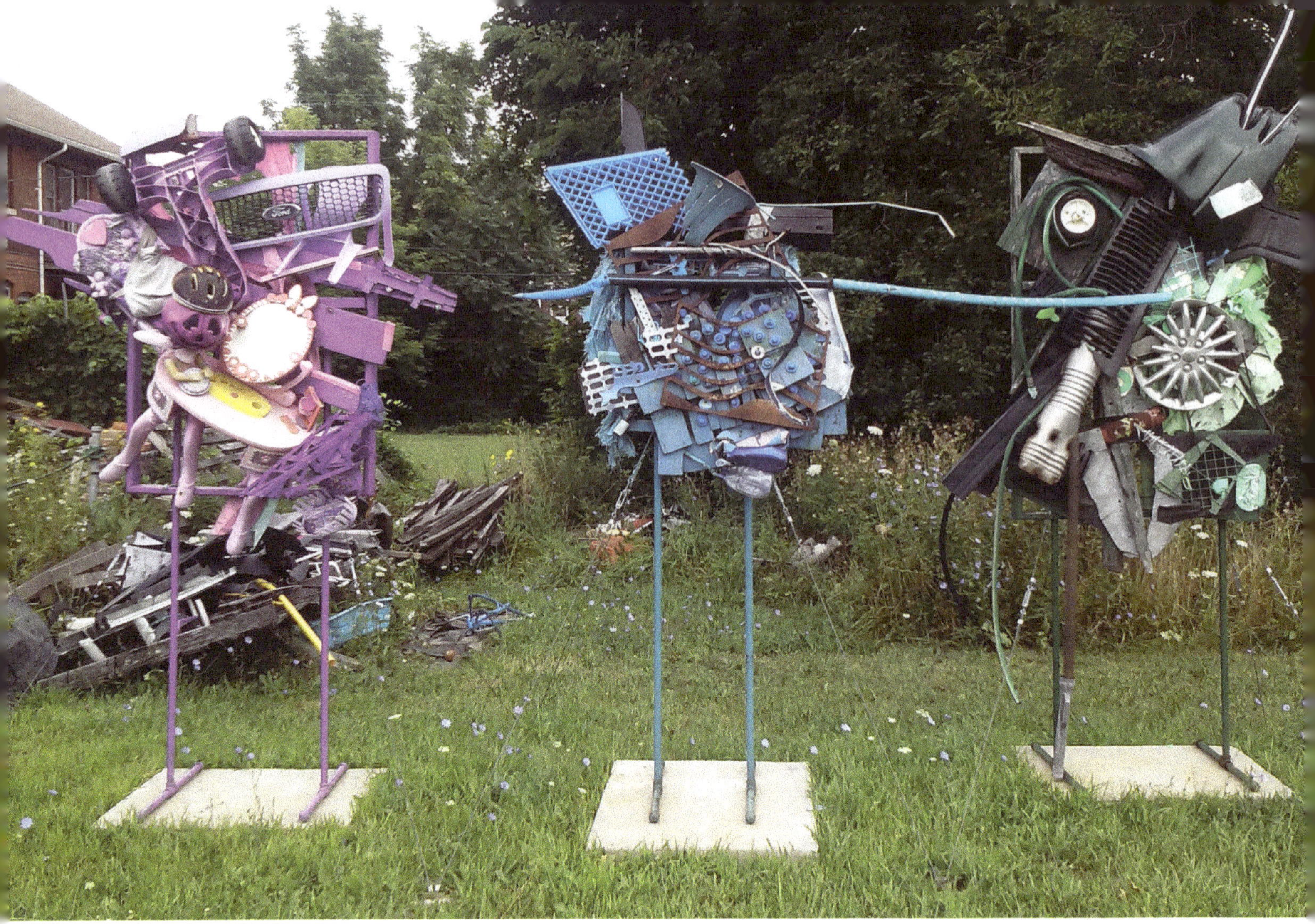

STEVE PANTON, AUGUST 2015

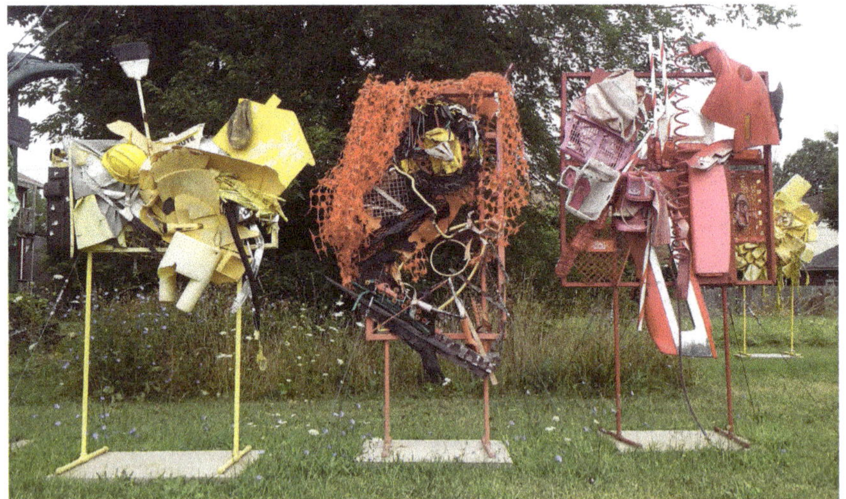

Spectra-Gate (details). 2012–present. Mixed-media assemblages, various sizes. Photography by Rebecca Cook.

www.ingramcontent.com/pod-product-compliance
Lightning Source LLC
LaVergne TN
LVHW070408060826
844660LV00040B/1444

* 9 7 8 0 8 1 4 3 4 2 2 7 5 *